A HAPPY WORLDLY ABODE

CHRIST CHURCH CATHEDRAL 1839/1964

BY MARGUERITE JOHNSTON

Book Credits

Art Director and Designer: Jim Culberson
Illustrator: Fred DuBose
Publishing Coordinator: Charles Thobae
Published by: Cathedral Press, 1964.
Printed by: Gulf Printing Company, Houston.
© 1964 by Marguerite Johnston

Dedicated To

Charles Wynn Barnes

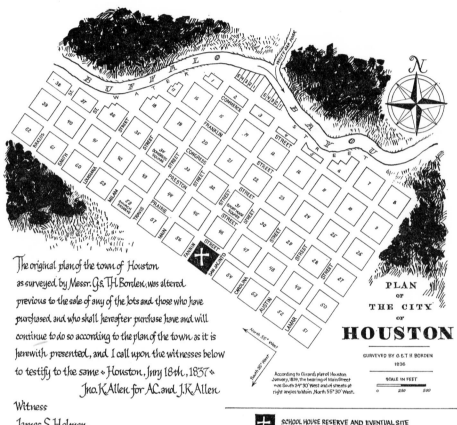

The original plan of the town of Houston as surveyed by Messr. G & T.H. Borden, was altered previous to the sale of any of the lots and those who have purchased and who shall hereafter purchase have and will continue to do so according to the plan of the town as it is herewith presented, and I call upon the witnesses below to testify to the same ❧ Houston, Jury 18th, 1837 ❧

Jno. K Allen for A.C. and J.K. Allen

Witness
James S. Holman
Thos. J. Gazley

PLAN
OF
THE CITY
OF
HOUSTON

SURVEYED BY G & T H BORDEN
1836

SCALE IN FEET

0   250   500

According to Girard's plat of Houston January, 1839, the bearing of Main Street was South 34° 30' West and of streets at right angles to Main , North 55° 30' West.

North 55° West

South 55° West

✠ SCHOOL HOUSE RESERVE AND EVENTUAL SITE OF CHRIST CHURCH CATHEDRAL

TABLE OF CONTENTS

Clerical ventures and worldly adventures in a new capital, new republic, and new state. 1837-1845.

The first brick church, the ladies sewing circle, and gentlemen's disagreement. 1845-1855.

Slow growth of the second church through epidemic, war, and diversities of opinion. 1856-1885.

The good old days of church picnics and Easter Sunday parades to controversy and depression. 1885-1933.

Fire, the consecration of bishops, and the making of a cathedral. 1934-1964.

History in pictures. 1839-1964

Foreword

This book was planned as a part of the celebration of the 125th Anniversary of the founding of this historic church. We were fortunate to persuade Marguerite Johnston to undertake the task of writing this history. She has worked arduously and fruitfully despite many obstacles. In this history she has demonstrated the rare talent to make the long-since dead live for us again and to bring the past into our present. She has presented a panoramic view both of the growth of Christ Church and of the City of Houston which it has served. She has traced the lineage and described milestones in the careers of families that made both Christ Church and Houston. Personalities which hitherto were known merely in local legend, incidents which otherwise would have been forgotten, are here preserved and charmingly described.

It is not easy for most of us to realize as we go about our everyday tasks that history is in the making. The development of an institution, like the development of a person, takes places so gradually that the changes come to be a matter of course and their extent and their significance almost escape notice. In this history the author enables us to pause and look back over a span of years upon Christ Church, Houston, and Texas. She pictures many families whose lives are interwoven with each other and with the history of church, city, and state. She restores in imagination things as they were in contrast with things as they are. She shows the progress that has been made and the contribution of those who have had most to do with that progress. By her aid, we can review the century and a quarter of the life of Christ Church and pay tribute to those who, during that time, have guided its destinies and molded its character.

The history of Christ Church is a long story, beginning when Texas was a Republic, and continuing to the wide expansion of the present time in the space age. This volume testifies to the spiritual vigor of countless souls who have borne witness to our faith during a century and a quarter of life of Christ Church in Houston and in Texas. It attests the determination of churchmen in each succeeding generation and bids us remember with thanksgiving those who labored so devoutly to give us Christ Church Cathedral. It challenges us to build on the foundations laid by our predecessors to the glory of the Great God Triune and the inspiration of man.

J. Milton Richardson
Dean, Christ Church Cathedral

Houston, Texas, April 15, 1964

1 Clerical ventures and worldly adventures in
a new capital, new republic, and new state. 1837-1845.

Chapter 1

Urbane Beginning

Christ Church, founded March 16, 1839, is Houston's oldest church.

It was founded when Houston was scarcely two years old, and in a year when the Episcopal Church had only begun to recover from the destructive forces of the American Revolution. Its founders were men who were trying to build a new republic, a new city and a new church simultaneously, and who had to put the demands of the republic ahead of the needs of either city or church.

Houston had been a precocious child since its birth.

Before it was a year old it had one theater, before it was three it had two. *School for Scandal* and other plays were put on.

The proverbial American pioneers moving westward were sturdy men and women in homespun, driving wagons or prairie schooners which held all their worldly goods, prepared to clear and till land to make their fortune.

The proverbial American city was one which began with a trading post or water hole and gradually grew to hamlet to village to town.

Houston was—from the beginning—different.

It was born a city before John K. Allen cut the first coffee bean weeds with his bowie knife to make a muddy path up the bayou, and it attracted city people from the first—traveled, enterprising, sometimes unprincipled, often well educated and cultured people.

That in 1837 it was still a settlement of tents and log cabins did not alter the fact that in character of population, Houston was a city—a city undergoing its first building boom. Augustus C. and John K. Allen had always envisioned it so.

They had at first hoped to buy in the Harrisburg area, but soon became interested in the region at the junction of the Buffalo and White Oaks Bayous. There were few families settled anywhere in the vicinity.

The land Augustus Allen thought most suitable had belonged to John Austin, who had died in a cholera epidemic in 1833. Austin had been granted the land by the Mexican government. The Allens gained title by purchase, part from William T. Austin who was acting agent for John's father, and part from Mrs. T. F. L. Parrott of Brazoria, Austin's widow who had since married Doctor Parrott.

With clear title, they were ready to do business.

The *Telegraph and Texas Register* and several newspapers in the United States carried the Allens' advertisement:

"The town of Houston, situated at the head of navigation, on the west bank of Buffalo Bayou, is now for the first time brought to public notice because until now, the proprietors were not ready to offer it to the public, with the advantages of capital and investment. By reference to the map, it will be seen that the trade of San Jacinto, Spring Creek, New Kentucky and the Brazos, above and below Fort Bend, must necessarily come to this place, and will at this time warrant the employment of at least ONE MILLION DOLLARS of capital, and when the rich lands of this country shall be settled, a trade will flow to it, making it, beyond all doubt, the great interior commercial emporium of Texas."

The advertisements also describe the "Pine, Ash, Cedar and Oak in inexhaustible quantities; also the tall and beautiful Magnolia grows in abundance. In the vicinity are five quarries of stone."

But in the vicinity there was no saw mill. After the first clearings were made and for some time thereafter, it was necessary to import lumber. Colonel William Fairfax Gray—who was soon to start the task of bringing the Episcopal Church

1835. Texas proclaims independence from Mexico in convention November 1, and provisional government is formed.

to Texas—had trouble getting hauled from Galveston up to Houston his lumber which had been brought all the way from Virginia along with the Gray family's children, servants, furniture and clothing.

Mrs. Dilue Harris, writing of her memories of her girlhood near Stafford, said: "There was so much excitement about the city of Houston that some of the young men in our neighborhood, my brother among them, visited it." They came back disappointed to report: ". . . it was hard work to find the city in the pine woods, and when they did, it consisted of one dugout canoe, a bottle gourd of whisky, and a surveyor's chain and compass, and was inhabited by four men with an ordinary camping outfit. We had a good joke on the boys . . . we asked them at what hotel they had put up and whether they went to church and to the theater. They took our teasing in good part and said they were glad to get home alive. They said the mosquitoes were as large as grasshoppers and they thought they would have a nice clean bath but in a few minutes the water was full of alligators."

This was the city which the Allens—in their confidence and optimism—sold to the Republic of Texas as its first capital.

The *Telegraph and Texas Register* of November 19, 1836, commented, "We have received many communications respecting the future seat of government. And many places have been named such as Houston, Brazoria, Washington, Nacogdoches and others . . ."

And in the same issue the announcement: "We have at length and almost without the use of mathematical instruments, completed a plan for the CITY OF HOUSTON which can be seen at the Senate Chamber."

By this plan, the boundaries of the town extended "back from the bayou six squares and parallel that stream for twelve blocks."

Houston won the capital—and a temporary capital at that—by only twenty-one votes. But the vote insured Houston's future. The coup constituted, as Anson Jones said in his memoirs, ". . . a high testimonial to the shrewdness and sagacity of the promoters of the city of Houston. It marked the beginning of one of the few successful speculations of this time, so numerous in that day."

Congress adjourned December 22, 1836, with the vote to convene in Houston May 1, 1837.

Meanwhile, it had authorized the president to erect or cause to be erected, a building suitable for the accommodation of the Congress of the Republic, and "such other buildings as may be necessary," up to the sum of $15,000.

The Allens by this time had designated Court House Square, Congress Square, a Church Reserve and a School Reserve. The School Reserve was on the half block now owned by Christ Church.

They persuaded Francis Richard Lubbock to ship a stock of goods to Houston, and came with him on the steamer, *Laura,* to their new capital.

Passing Harrisburg, Lubbock wrote in *Six Decades in Texas,* "No boat had ever been above this place, and we were three days making the distance to Houston, only six miles by the dirt road, but twelve by the bayou. The slow time was in consequence of the obstructions we were compelled to remove as we progressed. We had to rig . . . Spanish windlasses on the shore to heave the logs and snags out of our way, the passengers all working faithfully.

". . . Capitalist, dignified judge, military heroes, young merchants in fine clothes from the dressiest city in the United States, all lent a helping hand."

Lubbock was describing the people who would become Houstonians, the kind of people from whom the Christ Church congregation would come.

1835. Cherokees cede lands for $5,000,000 and agree to cross Mississippi River.

Tired of the steamer's slow progress, Lubbock and a few others took a yawl and set out ahead to find the city. They passed it by entirely and only realized their mistake when they ran into White Oak Bayou and struck into the brush.

"We then backed down the Bayou, and by close observation discovered a road or street laid off from the water's edge. Upon landing, we found stakes and footprints, indicating that we were in the town tract. This was about the first of January, 1837, when I discovered Houston.

"For though I did not accompany Columbus when he discovered America, as is asserted, I certainly was in at the discovery of Houston, the *Laura* being the first steamer that ever reached her landing."

But Houston had already begun to grow. Walking up the freshly cleared dirt street, Lubbock found a few small tents, a large one used as a saloon, several houses being built, and logs being hauled in to build the first hotel.

By covered wagons, horseback and sidewheel steamboats, bringing their best clothes, their heirlooms or their bar equipment, their books or their Faro games, their slaves or tailor's needles, their carpenter's tools or medical kit, and often bringing lumber with which to build, Houstonians-to-be were on their way.

Brief Capital

General Sam Houston had been elected president of the Republic of Texas, and the government of the new Republic was in a position to give away vast tracts of land.

From the United States, France and England, people began to come to Houston as capital of the nation: speculators, investors, farmers and ranchers, builders of all kinds, black sheep and laborers, as well as doctors and lawyers, teachers and preachers came to the new city.

By April of 1837, Thomas W. Ward, construction contractor, managed to persuade enough carpenters to leave other jobs and the Round Tent bar to begin work on the capitol building. It was April 15, the day the Republic's archives arrived from Columbia. (In his contracting zeal, he even fought a duel before the capitol was completed in a burst of over-protectiveness toward his project.)

Lumber for the capitol was shipped from Maine and was slow to arrive.

It was springtime in Houston. The sound of hammers and sawing rang through the clear air, and the smell of new cut wood and fresh paint mingled with the smells of woodsmoke, lantern oil, saddleleather and whisky.

During that first summer, a steady stream of people poured into town. Uncountable tents stretched out on the open ground, some men slept in shelters made of thatch on poles, many slept in the open on beds of Spanish moss.

Few women came in 1837, and one of the first ladies to arrive was Mrs. A. C. Allen, whose money had been used in founding the city. As an old woman on her 89th birthday, she recalled that there was only one log cabin built at the time, and the men who occupied it moved out to let her move in. On the day after her arrival, President Houston escorted her on a ride to what was known as the Lamar camp—three miles from the bayou on the site of the present Commonwealth and Hyde Park intersection—and for a time they lost their way in the woodland, so new and unmarked were the trails.

There were many head of cattle, but no dairy animals. Butter was as high as 75 cents a pound, chickens a dollar apiece, and eggs a dollar a dozen.

Beef—fattened on prairie grasses—sold for 2 to 4 cents a pound.

Everything imported from the United States was expensive. Cloth, boots and hats cost from three to five times as much in Texas as they did in the States, and lumber sold for as much as $150 a thousand feet—a fact which would make it hard for any struggling young church congregation to build a simple chapel.

By April 20, 1837, Houston was a city of 500 people—400 of them male.

Houstonians celebrated San Jacinto Day with a parade, a flag-raising, speeches made in an unfinished but gaily decorated frame building.

And in the evening, President Houston donned a black velvet suit trimmed with gold cording, a ruffled shirt and a red waistcoat to lead the first cotillion with Mrs. Moseley Baker. His presidential party at the ball included the visiting British vice consul, Captain and Mrs. Baker, and John Birdsall.

The ball was held in a room which was scarcely more than a camp in the woods lighted by sperm candles in chandeliers hung from raw beams. But most of the guests were dressed as formally and as lavishly as guests attending any gala ball in a big city.

When Congress met in the new Capitol May 1, the building lacked a roof.

John J. Audubon, arriving in Houston at about this time, found drunken Indians "whooping and hallooing" as they stumbled about in the mud, and groups of dejected Mexican prisoners watching the antics.

The town he saw had houses, some frame, some log, many unfinished.

"I could not understand," he wrote in his diary, "where so many people could be lodged. I soon learned that the prairie was dotted with tents; these tents were partially concealed by the tall coffee bean weeds which were cut down just enough to make room for the tents."

It is possible for a perfectly accurate observer like Mr. Audubon to make a somewhat distorted inference. The Indians were a group of Cherokees who had come to Houston for a serious conference with President Houston.

"The chiefs," Francis Lubbock wrote, "consisted of some six elderly and very sedate, grave gentlemen, who were seated around a table and communicated through an interpretor. . . . General Houston acquitted himself with his usual tact. . . ."

On the day after the conference with President Houston, the Indians came into town and "to the sound of a drum formed by a dressed deerskin drawn over a skillet and the music of a nasal song which was drawled out by the whole party" did a dance.*

They seemed to expect payment for their dance, and the spectators gathered around each contributed something. The Indians promptly took their cash to the bar and soon the sedate, grave gentlemen of yesterday's treaty conference were, as Audubon said, running around whooping and hallooing—though some just went quietly off into the prairie to sleep it off.

Though this was still in President Houston's own hard-drinking days, he prudently sent word out to the tavernkeepers to give the Cherokees no more whisky.

To the astonishment and dismay of the professional gamblers, the Congress outlawed gambling. This did not, however, end gambling in Houston.

The Congress gave away public lands and sanctioned slavery.

As a result, planters poured toward Texas, bringing their slaves with them, and most of these people passed through Houston—staying for a few days, a few weeks or a few months. By June when Congress adjourned, Houston had two hotels on Main Street—each two stories high though still rudimentary in furnishings—several stores painted white, and on Main Street, the Long Row, a block

* *Texas in 1837* Andrew Forest Muir, Ed. (Austin: University of Texas Press, 1958)

of 10 stores in which the rent was $500 each.

Dr. Francis Moore, Jr., early member and frequent vestryman of Christ Church, is listed in many historical sketches as the first mayor of Houston. But James S. Holman, the Allens' agent and district clerk of Harrisburg County, was first mayor of Houston. Moore was second, elected in 1838.

In the summer of 1837, Houston was organized and incorporated as a city, and by the end of the year, it was a town of 1500 people.

Mary Austin Holley wrote of Houston at that time:

"The main street of this city of a year extends from the landing into the prairie—a beautiful plain of some six miles wide, and extending with points and islands of timber quite to the Brazos. . . . The Capitol [is] 70 feet front—140 rear—painted peach blossom about ¼ mile from the landing. . . . We kept our lodge in the boat. . . . The President . . . dined with us 2 days one of which was Sunday and gallanted us to the Capitol, in one wing of which is a gallery of portraits of distinguished characters of the last campaign."

The Allens, she thought, "a very genteel people and live well. Have a good house and elegant furniture (mahogany—hair sofas—red velvet rocking chair and all nice and new and in modern style.)"

This was the Houston which Colonel William Fairfax Gray, a life-long Episcopalian from Virginia, thought would make a promising home for his family.

And this was the foreign country which the Episcopal Church of the United States was beginning to see as a promising field for foreign missions.

Episcopal ministers had come to Texas by this time—none yet to stay.

The Rev. Richard Salmon, priest, came to Texas as early as 1836, and spent some time in Houston in 1838. The Rev. Chester Newell, deacon, came out to Texas in 1837 and to Houston the next year.

Salmon wanted to found a colony of Church families in Texas. Born in Connecticut in 1797 and ordained priest by the Rt. Rev. John Henry Hobart of New York, Salmon apparently had the approval of the New York Episcopalians for his colony, but was never authorized to act as missionary by the Board of Missions.

Salmon with 15 families—54 people—arrived in New York on their way to Texas in late 1835 or early 1836. Delays were caused en route in part by the unsettling news of the Mexican invasion of Texas.

"The colonists," Dr. Andrew Forest Muir wrote in his article on William Fairfax Gray in the *Historical Magazine* of December, 1959, "perforce lingered in New Orleans, seemingly at Salmon's expense, until June, when they moved up to Natchez where they had been tendered the use of some buildings by a former New Yorker who, a few months later, immortalized himself by laying out, with his brother, the city of Houston."

This friendship may have offered entree in the new Republic. The Rev. Mr. Salmon (with a Presbyterian minister) was elected chaplain of the Senate of the First Congress of the Republic of Texas then meeting at Columbia.

Mr. Salmon officiated at a number of funerals of those who had served in the Texian army, and on December 29, 1836, read the burial service for Stephen F. Austin at the Bryan-Perry graveyard at Gulf Prairie.

"Salmon may have visited Houston as early as September 9, 1838," Doctor Muir writes, "when a statement appeared in a local newspaper that Episcopal service was to be held at the Capitol."

Two months later, the *Telegraph and Texas Register* announced:

"Notice—School in the City of Houston—Mr. Salmon recently from New

1837. Victoria, 18, niece of William IV, becomes queen of England.

York and who has been practically acquainted with the important business of teaching, is now in this city (having been invited hither by several of our most respectable and influential citizens for the purpose herein specified) and ready to open a Primary School, so soon as a suitable room can be procured. Mr. S. will be happy to take charge of a class or two in the higher branches of science, should any of our youth be desirous of procuring such studies . . . a further and more particular notice in the papers of the ensuing week, in which the terms will be given. . . ."

Salmon's combination of teaching and the ministry was of a pattern followed by many of the Episcopal priests who came to Texas.

Partly this was due to the fact that the need for schools in the new Republic was desperate, and partly due to a general enthusiasm in the Episcopal Church of that period for parochial schools to shape the tree by bending the twig.

But Colonel William Fairfax Gray was *not* one of the "respectable and influential citizens" who had invited Mr. Salmon to Houston.

This was at a time when Colonel Gray was already writing urgent letters to the Episcopal board of missions in the United States asking that a minister be sent to Texas.

Though Salmon did open his school—the Houston City School housed in a new schoolroom near the capitol and supported by the city government—and though Colonel Gray had school age children, there is no record of friendship between the two.

They were surely acquainted: Salmon was secretary of the Houston City Council and Colonel Gray active in both national and city affairs.

Doctor Muir suggests the possibility that coming from Low Church Virginia, the Grays were not likely to feel en rapport with a priest from Hobart's High Church diocese of New York.

Newell too failed to attract Colonel Gray. From Massachusetts, Newell was a gradute of Yale and of the Virginia Theological Seminary. He served as missionary at Hermitage, Tennessee, and came to Texas in the spring of 1837.

He came first to Velasco where he advertised his plans for opening a school to teach children and youth the various branches of an English and classical education, and in April, 1838, he opened the sessions of the House of Representatives with prayer. But he was defeated for election to the chaplaincy of the house.

Newell was writing a history of Texas and, except for the opening prayers at house sessions, apparently performed no clerical duties. He did later write his history—one of the most complimentary views presented of Texas of the era.

Lawyer, Officer, and Gentleman

Chapter 3

In more casually researched histories of Houston, written from 1900 to the present, the Rev. R. M. Chapman is usually given full credit for founding Christ Church. And certainly he was a catalytic agent in that he gave Episcopalians a reason for the formal effort.

But Dr. Andrew Forest Muir places the credit squarely where it is due in his article "William Fairfax Gray, Founder of Christ Church Cathedral, Houston," which appeared in the December, 1959, issue of the *Historical Magazine.*

Son of William Gray and Catherine Dick, William Fairfax was born in Fairfax County, Virginia, November 3, 1787. As a young man in his early 20's, he was in the publishing business in Fredericksburg and March 21, 1811, Governor James Monroe commissioned him captain of a company of the Virginia Militia.

He was on active duty during the War of 1812, and by 1820 had reached the rank of lieutenant colonel, commissioned by Governor Thomas M. Randolph.

Colonel Gray was a member of St. George's Church, which had been founded in 1720, and owned and occupied Pew No. 8. He was elected to the vestry in 1816 and a year later, at 30, married Mildred Richards Stone, 17-year-old daughter of Mayor William Scandrett Stone. Of the twelve children born to them, six reached maturity.

These were days when the educated man and responsible citizen played many roles in a lifetime. Gray was postmaster of Fredericksburg, and while postmaster, was commissioned captain of a company in his old regiment. Though he was *de facto* commander of the Rifle Grays until 1834, Virginia law did not let him hold both a state commission and a federal office.

Gray was an active Freemason, and during his term as worshipful master of the Fredericksburg lodge in 1824, the Marquis de Lafayette visited Virginia. "On Sunday, November 21, the lodge escorted Lafayette to St. George's Church in a parade, of which Gray was both marshal and military commander," Doctor Muir wrote. "On the following day, Gray entertained Lafayette at dinner, after which the distinguished visitor left for Washington, D. C."

May 5, 1835, Gray was admitted to the Virginia bar—at the age of 47— too late in life to build quickly a career adequate for the support of a large family.

He therefore was willing to take on the commission of two Washington speculators to go and inspect lands in Mississippi and Louisiana, and in Texas—then a part of the Mexican state of Coahuila and Texas.

Colonel Gray left home October 6, 1835, and on his long journey kept the diary *From Virginia to Texas* which, "in part, is one of the most important sources for the history of revolutionary Texas."

Finishing his business in Mississippi and New Orleans, Colonel Gray crossed the Sabine River on January 28, 1836, and was at once caught up in the Texas Revolution. Four days later this lifelong Virginian voted in Nacogdoches—February 1—for delegates to the convention to meet in Washington-on-the-Brazos and on March 1 he went to Washington with a thought of getting himself elected secretary to the convention. "In this he failed," Doctor Muir said, "but in some cases his diary is fuller than the official minutes of the convention that, on March 2, adopted the Declaration of Independence and so initiated the Republic of Texas."

Gray accompanied the president and his cabinet from Washington to Harrisburg and there completed the business he had begun with Texas commissioners in New Orleans. In March, with a paper from the Secretary of State granting permission to leave Texas, he went home to Virginia.

Colonel Gray was a well established, obviously popular, member of one of the most graceful societies in the United States but he seemingly saw in Texas opportunity for himself and his children which Virginia did not offer. On his way home, he wrote provisional President David G. Burnet from New Orleans: "I shall return to Texas with as much speed as my affairs in the U. S. will admit, to make my future home among you."

When he arrived in Fredericksburg on the night of June 26, the Rifle Grays in uniform and with a band met him to escort him home. But his mind was made up to the move, and he had much to offer the new Republic.

"Gray was a cultured man," Doctor Muir wrote. "Besides playing the flute, he was a reader and accumulated a library of some 250 volumes. This comprised not only law reports and treatises, including Blackstone's and Kent's commen-

1836. The national debt of the U.S. is paid in full, but Andrew Jackson continues his war against the Bank of the United States.

taries, but also works of a more general interest. He had, as reference books, a set of Encyclopedia Americana and a number of dictionaries, including Samuel Johnson's and Pickering's vocabulary. There were biographies, among them Washington Irving's ' History of the Life and Voyages of Christopher Columbus,' some works on agriculture, philosophy, physics, military science and music, a lot of sheet music and a number of items on Texas. . . ."

Colonel Gray was back in Texas by February, 1837—this time to look for the best place to open an office and settle his family. He was admitted to the Texas bar in Brazoria, but the city of Houston had been founded and the government of the republic was now there.

Seeing Houston in spectacular boom, he understandably decided that this was the most interesting place in Texas to be.

Colonel Gray opened a law office in May and was elected clerk of the House of Representatives during the second session of the First Congress (May 4-September 26, 1837).

He had his office in a house on the east side of Travis between Preston and Prairie directly across the street from what Doctor Muir terms "the hovel occupied by President Sam Houston." Allan C. Gray, his son, remembered his father's office in a block which "was vacant except for the two buildings on the corner of Preston Avenue; but right near the middle of the block, and facing Travis Street, was a little bit of a building of two rooms, painted red, which was my father's office." Several Christ Church vestry meetings would be held in that office in the 1840's.

Colonel Gray leased for his family a house on the west side of Fannin Street between Congress and Preston and directly opposite the court house.

"According to the lease," Doctor Muir said, "the dwelling was a one story building that had in the attic a room 16 by 18 feet, lighted by dormer windows. Downstairs, in addition to an unspecified number of rooms, was a central hall with stairs going up to the attic. There were folding doors front and rear with transom lights, and the front door was flanked by shuttered windows. The walls were plastered and the woodwork neatly painted. The windows had Venetian blinds. The walls of the house were of tabby, that is concrete made of seashells. In the rear was a kitchen, separated from the house in order to reduce the fire hazard. . . . There was also a good and commodius privy with a sink under it at the back of the lot."

Mr. A. C. Gray, from his boyhood memories, "My first recollection of the court-house square, was: On the north corner a two-story building the first story of which was built of rock blocks from 10 to 18 inches square, constituting the jail. Above was one story wooden frame and weather boarded, painted red, which was the court-house. The balance of the block was vacant.

"My father's house was on the block between Congress and Preston and facing the court-house square. On the other side, on the corner, was a blacksmith's shop. Next to the blacksmith shop was the house of Leonard Perkins, cousin of Erastus."

Colonel Gray was secretary of the senate of the adjourned session of the second Congress (April 9 to May 24, 1838) and two years later was appointed district attorney of the first judicial district of the republic by President Lamar.

Between 1839 and 1841, he was one of the two first notaries public of Harrisburg County (by the end of 1839, Harris County).

And from his first coming to Houston, he worked with intelligence and a degree of passion to establish the Episcopal Church in his adopted country.

1837. Martin Van Buren takes office as the first Great Depression in America's history begins.

A Gentlewoman Pioneers

Like scores and hundreds of other gentlewomen, uprooted by enterprising husbands, Milly Gray was sad to leave Virginia—her birthplace, her lifelong friends, the endlessly ramified family connections, the comfortable charms of home. She was 38 years old.

"Tuesday Night, Nov. 20th, 1838 at 10 clock at night I went on board the St. Boat Rapphahannock at Fredericksburg with a heavy heart," she wrote in her diary. "Left Mr. Barton's house where were assembled all my beloved Sisters & Brothers and their children. . . . There was with me Peter, Edwin & Allan, Kate & Alice, Margaret Stone & our servants, Dinah, Lucy & John, Jane & her child & Armistead. Passed a restless, disturbed night. . . .

"Arrived at Baltimore about 8 o'clk. on Thursday Morn. 22d. The first time I have been here since 1817—Twenty one years—a long time & many many changes in it—How little did I dream then, that I should ever come here to take shipping for Texas—then a part of Mexico—

"Mr. Gray met us at the wharf, and soon had a carriage ready to take us up to Mr. Goodwin's Boarding House."

But Mrs. Gray—who in her diary expressed reluctance to make transitory acquaintances because of her deafness—was essentially a social creature, willing to like and be liked, and her diary is peppered with the names of old friends and new, of the comings and goings of innumerable friends and acquaintances who eased the trip to Texas by visits to the boat when docked.

And despite her understandable reluctance to leave Virginia, her natural buoyancy of spirit and interest in people soon revived.

After attending Sunday morning services at Doctor John's Church in Baltimore —"I was not particularly struck with him as a preacher. He is generally greatly admired"—they made their final packings Monday and after dinner, boarded "the Brig. *Delia,* Capt. Walker, for Galveston in Texas.

"We found the cabin of the Brig very neat, tho' small and soon made ourselves as comfortable as the confined space would admit."

They lay becalmed off Baltimore through Tuesday, but at last the breeze freshened, and they were on their way to a new world, a new country, a new city, a new life. It was a move as radical for Milly Gray as though some present-day vestryman should decide—at middle age—to move his family to a newly laid-out city in Alaska.

After days of gale and seasickness and a passage through beautiful blue waters off the Bahama Banks, they arrived off the Texas shore Thursday morning, Christmas week. "We were all charmed beyond measure to find ourselves at Anchor opposite some Town. We had suffered dreadfully the day and 2 nights previously from a severe gale & hoped our troubles were now to end."

Disappointingly, the town was Velasco, and they had to wait until Friday morning to anchor off Galveston, and until evening before the wind shifted and let them into Galveston Harbor. They had been at sea a month.

"We were agreeably surprized to find the Town much better in appearance than we had expected. There are some large houses & all better looking than we had been taught to expect—We are struck however with the singularity of houses without chimneys. They are all heated by stoves. The only house with a chimney is one at the Navy Yard, occupied by the Commandant, quite a good & respectable looking house."

She was referring, of course, to the Texas Navy—not the U. S.

1837. The first fatality in the history of railroading occurs on the Boston & Providence line. Trains travel 20 miles an hour, and "this great speed and irresistible momentum of the machines" terrifies beholders.

From the first moment of arrival, they began to meet former Virginians and New Yorkers whom they had known—or whose friends and relatives they knew. Texas was—after all—part of a small world.

In the warm, balmy days immediately before Christmas, they went ashore.

"All intercourse with the shore is by means of small boats, and even they cannot get in close. So we had to stop about 20 yds from the shore & walk on planks, supported on stakes—It seemed to me a ticklish passage—others did not seem to mind it—so I suppose I should soon be accustomed to it too.

"We found a gigg & a Buggy waiting for us.—the carriages quite handsome, the horses the roughest I ever saw, but very active and gentle. We drove across the Island (about ½ or ¾ wide here) to the Beach and had a charming ride—picked up a good many shells to bring to the little girls & when we returned, found that Dr. Jones had been & taken them ashore with him. They returned soon after we did. All highly delighted with our excursion. Peter returned to the Town with the young gents, after taking a lunch of bread & cheese & a glass of ale. We also shared with Dr. Jones, for we were all out at the usual dinner hour. Mr. Gray & Edwin dined at Col. Bowyer's (a boarding house) & came home exulting at their fine dinner."

A norther blew in, they were confined to their cabins, and on Christmas Eve, though Mr. Gray and Peter went ashore directly after breakfast, Mrs. Gray and the girls spent the day sewing, writing, and reading. "I have blessed dear Mr. Barton a hundred times for his Life of Sir Walter Scott."

Not until Dec. 30 could they at last say goodbye to the Brig *Delia* and take their steamboat to Houston. One on which they thought they had booked passage passed them by.

But on the morning of Dec. 29, "we heard the joyful tiding of 'a Steamboat coming in'—She proved to be the *Putnam*. Mr. Gray went on board of her immediately & secured a passage for ourselves & our furniture etc. but the Capt. will not take the Lumber—which we regret—it will add to our expense and we shall have to pay $25 per day every day after tomorrow that we keep it on board the Brig."

Even so, they found the *Putnam* a "very elegant boat. Superior to either of the others that run between this place and Houston. We found one Lady with 3 children on Board. Capt. Sterett very polite & gentlemanly. We had quite a party to dinner and a very handsome entertainment. [Four Galveston guests came aboard to dine with them. Steamboats apparently offered no threat of sailing away with the visitors.] "This Boat seems almost like a palace, compared to our Brig—and *my* appetite is really enormous."

Dec. 30. "We were grievously disappointed at not being able to go ashore today to attend Divine Service. The Rev.d Mr. Chapman is here & preached both morning and night but Mr. G. thought the difficulty of landing would be too great for us to encounter, the tide being very very low. We expect Mr. C. will go up to Houston with us.—"

As passengers came aboard, Mrs. Gray was increasingly cheered to see how many of the present or potential Houstonians were attractive, educated people.

Though on Monday, Dec. 31, Mrs. Gray was expressing expectations that they would be heading for Houston next day and would arrive by night, leaving Peter behind to fetch the lumber as best he could, she later wrote:

"We arrived at the landing of this precocious city, on Wednesday, Jan 2nd. between 10 & 11 o'clock in the morning, after a rather agreeable trip up the Bayou. But for the wet weather it would have been very pleasant indeed—We

1838. The Great Western *with 450 horsepower leaves Bristol, England, April 8, and arrives in New York City April 23.*

1839. America's first baseball game is played at Cooperstown, N. Y., and the first normal school is opened in Massachusetts.

were introduced to several persons on board, amongst them the Rev.d Mr. Chapman and Mr. Gray's friend Judge Birdsall (late Atty. Genl.) The former a very young looking man, but very prepossessing, plain & unaffected, but I fear too young & of course inexperienced for the station."

Though the Allens had been careful to lay their city out at the head of navigation, navigation was not necessarily easy. "The Bayou became so narrow at last that I thought it would be no difficult matter to jump ashore from either side the Boat. And indeed I feared several times we should get aground. Once we were in an ugly situation, a snag having got entangled in one of the wheels. It caused some alarm & might have proved a dangerous accident. After seeing the number of floating logs etc. in the Bayou I ceased to wonder at the one wheeled Boats I had seen—my only wonder now is how any escape. . . .

"The water is pleasant, *but muddy*—and after a while it is said persons dislike it very much. All who possibly can use cistern water. I don't wonder at all the clothes being spoilt that are washed in this water. It would be impossible to make them white I should think—(It may be cleared by a small quantity of alum dissolved in it.) Every body tries to get rain water—to drink at least. . . . On our arrival here, we were joined on board the Boat by Mr. Doswell and Mr. John Morris—who I felt rejoiced to see. He appeared like an old friend. . . . Young Mr. Harris procured a carriage to bring his Grandmother Mrs. Birdsall up to his Sister's, Mrs. Judge Briscoe, and very politely insisted on all our coming up in it to our house.

"We did so, and were agreeably surprised with its appearance. Eve was delighted to see a nice walk from the gate to the front door, covered with shells.

"It did not look clean & white very long, for I never saw anything like the mud here. It is tenacious black clay, which cannot be got off of anything without washing—and is about a foot or so deep—although everything looks better than I had expected, my heart feels oppressed & it requires an effort to wear the appearance of cheerfulness. I could (if I were a weeping character) sit down & fairly weep—and if asked for what I could not tell—merely because all is strange and I fear to look forward—and the poor servants are so uncomfortably lodged—such a barn as the kitchen is—and yet it is to the full equal to the larger part of the houses here—many are a great deal worse."

But Mrs. Gray was not a weeping character, and from the beginning, her diary reveals the comings and goings to which Houston of 1839 was subject.

Famous men came to Houston for a session of Congress or to do business with the executives of the new Republic, stayed a few weeks, perhaps set up a house of their own, closed that house down, moved as friends or as boarders into the Gray home, departed to the states or Mexico or Austin or Washington-on-the-Brazos or France.

Mrs. Gray may have had times of deep homesickness. But she was not lonely.

A clue to where the Grays managed to put their boarders appears in the memories of A. C. Gray—a child of eight when they arrived—as related by him many years later.

"My father's house was on the west side, very nearly in the middle of the square. It was a one-and-a-half story house—the first story made of concrete composed of shell, lime and cement. The second story was enclosed with weatherboard, ceiled on the inside, and was one large room in which there were probably ten or twelve beds. Downstairs there was one large room from the front door opening on the porch or gallery, and running back to the back door. That constituted the dining room. On the left hand side, as you entered

1839. Samuel Morse takes the first photograph ever made in the United States.

from the front, was the parlor or sitting room. Back of it was my mother's room, and a small room that my younger sisters occupied. On the other side were three bedrooms and what was called the "shed room." Back of that house was the servants quarters with kitchen, store room, etc."

Mrs. Gray—looking at a new house in a new land with the eye of one who has lived her life in Fredericksburg with its century-old church and pride of being the birthplace of George Washington's mother—saw this house as better than she expected, but still pretty bad: ". . . Such a barn as the kitchen is. . . ."

To young Allen, whose memories of Fredericksburg as an eight-year-old were pleasant but vague, and who had a lively enjoyment of swimming and fishing in Buffalo Bayou, the house had charm: "The house stood back from the gate some twenty feet, and in front of it was a flower garden, and on the south side also, in which were grown every kind of flower that was known in this part of the country. Right in front of the house was a red-bud tree, with a yellow jessamine vine growing all over it, and the effect of the red budded flowers in the Spring mixed with the yellow jessamine was very beautiful. In that yard were some eight or ten cape jessamine bushes, and that was the first place I ever saw them."

In 1838 to 1840—with so many lone men or couples without children coming into town, unsure of where they would live or how long they would stay—gentle folk opened their doors to their own kind with lavish hospitality. Some came briefly as guests, some stayed as boarders, all were treated as friends or family members. The children of Colonel and Mrs. Gray were thereby exposed to some of the most interesting people who came into Texas in their childhood.

The flow of Mrs. Gray's diary from January, 1839, to February, 1840, sounds like a perpetual houseparty:

After less than a week of unpacking and getting settled, she wrote "At night we went again to the Capitol when Mr. Chapman preached And it really did me good to hear our own familiar prayers and hymns. Mr. C. preached a very plain & sensible discourse.

"On Monday the 7th, our family was enlarged by the addition of the 2 Messrs. Morris, Mr. Doswell and Mr. James H. Davis, a Bro. of our Va. University Professor, who came to live with us. They came to supper.

"A good many Gentlemen have called to see us . . . Mr. G's dear friend Col. James Love, Mr. Allen the Presbyterian Minister, Mr. Chapman, Judge Birdsall, & Dr. Ashbel Smith. One day during this week, Col Love brought his friends Mrs. James Ryley to see us, a very pleasant sensible lady—a niece of Mrs. Henry Clay . . . [In fact, a grand niece.]

"In the course of a few weeks we were visited by several ladies—Mrs. A. C. and Mrs. George Allen, Mrs. Wharton, Mrs. Branch . . . Mrs. Lubbock, Mrs. Reid, Mr. and Mrs. J. D. Andrews from Virginia . . . After awhile we were delighted to hear that Col. Bee had brought his Lady to Houston. They called soon after, and we should soon have become good friends but for his appointment first as Minister to the U. States, and then to Mexico."

The Henry S. Footes spent 10 days and in that time the Gray girls were allowed to go to the Theatre with them once.

"On Monday, 14th, we rec.d at our table as Boarders (I name them being our first) Col. Love, Gen. Johnston Sec. of War, Gen. Hunt, Sect. of the Navy, Mr. J. G. Watson, Attorney . . . On the 17th February, President Gen. Lamar came to board with us, and Judge Webb who is Act. Sec.ty of State . . . His family arived early in April . . ."

So many came and went and came again that Mrs. Gray had to backtrack in her diary "I forgot to say in the proper place . . ." and insert these visitors (who may have stayed anywhere from one night to 10).

"The Rev. Mr. Chapman came to board with us on the 21st Feb. and continued with us until his return to the U. States . . . He left us the 9th of June, much to our regret, especially as he had been teaching our children & now they are left without."

Allan Gray—now nine—went to that school. "There was a little red house, one-story with two rooms, occupied by my father as his office. His office was in the front, and in the rear my brother and I and several other boys were taught by the first Episcopal clergyman who came to Houston, Reverend Mr. Chapman. Afterwards my father moved his office round on court house square . . ."

Chapman was not of course the first Episcopal clergyman. He was only the first with whom Colonel Gray chose to make close friends, the first to have any association with the Episcopal congregation once it began to take shape.

A Happy Worldly Abode

Chapter 5

Time and time again through diaries, sketches, letters and histories of Houston of 1838, the impression grows of just what a remarkable city this was in any era. Small town in number of residents, parvenu among cities in age, it yet was a neither small town nor provincial in attitude or atmosphere.

Its people were not only widely traveled—they rather had to be simply to get here from Virginia, New York, England, France or Mexico—but a remarkable number of them were also well dressed, well read, well educated.

This is evident in the beauty and clarity of their handwriting after 125 years, in their interests—they founded churches, philosophical society, schools and government—and in the ease with which they traveled farther.

Houstonians of 1838 apparently thought nothing of a jaunt to Galveston, though it took all day or more by steamboat. They were more cautious about trips north and west—chiefly because of the completely genuine dangers from Indians. And a surprising number of leading Houstonians of 1838-40 went off to Mexico City, Washington, D. C., Paris and London whenever given an appointment to do so by the Republic.

References to these trips were quite as casual then as they are now among business and professional men who commute between Houston and Paris and think this is a phenomenon of the 20th century.

Houston showed only its bright face under the flag of the Republic.

In a Houston newspaper of March 13, 1839:

"The Houston Jockey Club announced that races for the spring meeting will commence on Monday the 15th of April and continue 6 days. The First Day Sweepstake for colts and fillies, 2 years old, Mile heats, $250 entrance; forfeit $150. Second Day—Sweepstake for 3 year old colts & fillies, 2 mile heats, $500 entrance, $250 forfeit." Hedenberg and Vedder, 55 Main Street, announced that new goods received on consignment included 35 sacks of corn, 125 bbls. flour, 35 firkins butter, 100 sacks fine salt, 15 boxes raisins, 32 bbls. whisky, 3000 lbs castings, 12,000 lbs. bacon, 20 sacks coffee, 50 kegs pickles, 25 boxes lemons, and 25 bbls sugar.

George Fisher at the steamboat landing advertised that he had a few copies

1838-39. Young Italy is organized to bring all the kingdoms of Italy— now held by Austria and the Pope—under the rule of King Charles Albert of Sardinia.

1830-40. The Clipper Ships are at their peak.

of the English version of the *Civil Code of Louisiana*. Bibles and Testaments in various sizes, languages, and prices could be had at the depository at the Texas Bible Society. "For Sale: A negro man, for particulars enquire of E. Humphreys at the Telegraph office." W. D. and R. M. Lee had Havana Segars for sale. And E. S. Perkins & Company had just received a "Large assortment of VERY SUPERIOR ready made clothing and for sale cheap." Hosley and Perkins had a billiard table for sale, made by Penn of New York.

There was obviously much shuttling to and fro by steamer. These advertisements bore the stamp of confidence and success:

"For New Orleans, in Forty Hours, splendid low pressure steampacket Columbia, Capt. Wade, will leave Galveston Bay the 8th and 22nd of each month." Other steam packets advertised for Galveston and Mobile.

Thomas J. Rusk and James Reily, attorneys and counsellors at law, had their office with J. A. Newland, Notary Public. "Gen. Rusk is now in the East but will be in this city so soon as the Indian difficulties in that part of the Republic are settled."

On March 20, four days after the Christ Church agreement was signed, the newspaper carried a notice: "The citizens of Houston are hereby notified that the city school was opened on Monday last, the 11th instant. Tuition $3 a month. R. Salmon principal and president of the board."

There will always be a mystery as to why the Rev. Mr. Salmon was so thoroughly excluded from all proceedings incidental to the founding and development of Christ Church.

It was also in this week that the Senate tabled a joint resolution which would have approved the employment of friendly Indians and provided for their pay.

And the newspaper marveled over "A village lighted by Natural Gass. The village of Fredonia in the western part of the State of N. Y. A hole an inch & a half in diameter being bored through the rocks, the gas left its natural channel and ascended through this. One hundred lights are fed from it, more or less, at an expense of one dollar and a half yearly for each. The streets and public buildings and churches are lighted with it."

Sometimes ailing, accustomed to occupying herself largely in her own home—sewing, writing, reading *Nicholas Nicholby* to the children when they began to worry because Colonel Gray was several days overdue on a trip to Austin—Mrs. Gray nonetheless entertained in a year a stream of men and women, of a kind which any modern hostess would think quite remarkable.

In addition to the presidents, cabinet members, and diplomats of the Republic, she had as her houseguests—of course—Bishop Leonidas Polk and his party for three or four days when he came on his first visitation to this new foreign mission field. (This was, incidentally, the first visitation by a missionary bishop from the United States to any foreign field.)

After preaching two or three times at the capitol, the Bishop had family prayers with the Grays and a few friends. Mrs. Gray invited Erastus S. Perkins and his wife, and James Reily and his wife to join them.

Admiral Charles Baudin, commander of the French fleet "now off the Coast" and his two aides, Captain Couchard and Captain Eugene Maissin, "declined all public entertainment" but so enjoyed meeting the Grays at soirees at the Andrews' and the Allens' that some weeks later, he sent Mrs. Gray a basket of West Indies sweetmeats.

After a visit for a few days, Col. William Christy and his son from New Orleans "gave Mr. Gray the most complete little travelling apparatus I ever

1839. Nathaniel Haw-thorne is given a position at the Boston Customs House.

saw, containing a tumbler, spoon, knife & fork, etc., and to me he gave a writing desk equally complete." And such was the whirl that Mrs. Gray forgot to tell her diary that "August 9, three days after I came up, Margaret and Evalina went down to the Island where they still are." The newest comer in August was "a Mr. Hawthorn, a Scotchman, who we like."

Meanwhile Peter Gray, now 20, was employed by Albert Sidney Johnston, Secretary of War, to go to Nacogdoches and Natchitoches on government business—"as a part of the Country between here & there has been so recently the theatre of Indian War. Mrs. Andrews spent the evening with us. She has been with me frequently since the girls went away—and has moved up to Mr. [A. Jackson] Davis' house for a while—'til Mr. Andrews returns from the States, where he has been gone since May. Mr. and Mrs. Davis are also in the states." It is a picture of constant movement—from house to house, town to town and country to country.

No one could hope to claim, of course, that Houston was composed purely of quality folks and gentry.

In 1839, of its 2,073 people, 1,620 were male and 453 female. Of the females, some were "play actresses"—one set of them came up on the steamer when the Gray family moved to Houston—some were perhaps less acceptable. But a great many were women of good character, ranging from those of fairly simple education and social custom to a large number of ladies, in the 19th century sense of the word. But for every one gentlewoman in Houston at this time, there seemed to be two or three lone gentlemen, either bachelors or men waiting to bring wives and families to the new republic.

Historians who work from the diary of a gentlewoman and from the vestry minutes of a church are obviously limiting their research to a fairly narrow circle made up of gentle folk. The circle they reveal talks in terms of church services, prayer meetings, school building, tea parties, calls, and occasionally of balls and the theater.

Though Louis de France was in Houston, hoping to teach fencing, there were probably more men in town accustomed to fist, rifle or bowie knife.

Of the males, there were certainly a substantial number of the varied lot known as frontiersmen—some rough, some not, some transient, some settlers, roustabouts and day laborers, gamblers and bar tenders, knife toters and thieves, but also carpenters, bricklayers, printers, newspapermen, doctors, dentists, lawyers, and retired—or temporarily retired—military.

And then there was crime. In January, 1838, John Houston was found guilty of grand larceny for having stolen $780 and was sentenced to "39 lashes on his bare back and be branded on his right hand with the letter T."

Convictions for operating a gambling house and for gambling were common. Fines ranged from $125 to $1,000. First Chief Justice Andrew Briscoe was fined $500 for playing cards. Solomon Childs, a justice of the peace, was deprived of office for not suppressing a duel. And Peter Gray was fined $20 for smoking in court, and another $20 for sitting on the table in court.

Though most new Houstonians came from Alabama, Georgia, Tennessee, Kentucky, the Carolinas and Virginia, the city had not yet taken on the Old South atmosphere it was to absorb during and after the Civil War—its citizenry was too varied. But already Texans were trying to combat the notion abroad that Texans are a bunch of rough but simple Westerners—a fight they have not yet seemed to win.

Silas Dinsmore of Matagorda, vestryman of the brand new Matagorda

1839. The last great summer rendezvous of the fur trade, with traders, trappers, Indians and agents of the fur companies, takes place at Horse Neck Creek in the Ute Country. The rise of the silk top hat brings decline of the beaver trade.

Church, addressed himself to Bishop Benjamin T. Onderdonk—bishop of the Diocese of New York in the United States—in a letter recommending that the church send missionaries to San Augustine, Galveston, Houston, Matagorda, Austin and San Antonio.

"Houston is connected by indissoluble commercial relations with Galveston and the circumstances of the location for a time of the seat of Government at that place, gave to Houston an impulse and commercial importance which, as the population of the country is increasing, it will be likely to retain.

"Among the population of Texas," he continued, "are found natives of nearly every state of the Federal Union, and of every nation in Europe.

"The intercourse which they have had with the world and with each other has had the tendency to vanish bigotry and obliterate prejudices and most of them are able to estimate with little partiality, the pretensions of all, according to their merits. AS A PEOPLE," said Mr. Dinsmore in capital letters, "they possess superior intelligence.

"It is," he said, with conviction, "the enlightened who look abroad to ascertain in what region may be found the greatest advantages combined to contribute to a happy worldly abode. It is the strong and the courageous who exert their energies, and who hold in contempt the obstacles and dangers which they feel may be overcome by an effort. And thus it is that exposed frontiers are found to be inhabited by the brave and the enterprising—while the feeble, the timid and the ignorant cling to the land of their nativity.

"These suggestions will enable you to appreciate the character of the people of Texas in some particulars," Mr. Dinsmore concluded more benignly, "and you will be thereby enabled to select teachers possessing qualifications suited to the instruction of such a people—well informed in all subjects—except one— the most important of all—the CHRISTIAN RELIGION—a very great majority of the people of Texas have probably never seen a prayer book."

The letter is in the papers of the Board of Missions.

Whether it was the impact of Mr. Dinsmore's letter or the cumulative pleas of Colonel Gray or simply the natural flow of history cannot be said.

But within a few months, the Rev. Benjamin Eaton had arrived to divide his time between Houston and Galveston, giving Christ Church and Trinity one more nudge forward; by 1843, Christ Church had as rector a brilliant and driving young priest as well educated as Dinsmore could ask for, and by January, 1849, these two men would join with Matagorda's distinguished Caleb S. Ives to found the Diocese of Texas.

1830-48. Louis Philippe is king of France.

Chapter 6

Texas to Board of Missions

In the early fall of 1838, Texas began to figure regularly in the report of foreign missions and under the section on "Foreign Correspondence" in the *Spirit of Missions*—amid reports from West Africa, Constantinople and China.

The October issue presents "extracts from a letter addressed by a communicant of the Episcopal Church to his former pastor. The writer is well known and his statements cannot fail to interest." The letter is dated Houston, July 8, 1838. And the letter was almost surely written by Col. William Fairfax Gray, for one year and three months a resident Houstonian.

"I have for some time had it in my mind to write you on the subject of an Episcopal mission in this country. Or, perhaps I should more clearly express my meaning, by saying, the establishment of the Protestant Episcopal Church in Texas. I am, perhaps, more immediately impelled to the effort this evening from having just returned, for the second time today, from listening to a Presbyterian, who has been preaching for several months, and is establishing a foothold.

"We have had several Presbyterian preachers here—several Methodist—occasionally Baptists—and one Roman Catholic; all of whom preached zealously, and generally with respectable and encouraging congregations. But not once have I heard an Episcopalian preach, or the Episcopal service read since I left New Orleans in February, 1837.*

"But at, and during the revolution, there was literally no religion in Texas. I have known men here say, they had not heard preaching since they left the United States, some 10, some 12 or 15 years ago. The revolution has changed the face of everything. New people are coming in, and bringing with them whatever of religious, or moral impress, they may have received in more favored communities; and they feel the privation of the change.

"They who do not fall into the dissolute and vicious habits that are too general here, mourn over the privileges and social blessings they have left, and eagerly look for the time when they shall be received here. Those all eagerly flock to hear the itinerant preachers who come among us, and listen perhaps to inferior strains with more attention and delight, than ever they did in their more favored days; and the old settlers and their children go to hear them out of curiosity. To them it has the charm of novelty.

"In fact, I think this nation is now in precisely the situation that calls for a strong and powerful effort, to supply it with zealous and enlightened preachers. Preaching they will have of some sort, and if the right ones are not sent, the wrong ones will come. That is, I mean men not prepared by education, talents, and character to do the work as it ought to be done, will rush in where "angels fear to tread;" and the consequences will be seen in those wild and grotesque varieties, those burlesque perversions of common sense and decency, which are manifested in the doctrines and practices of some of the thousand sects of the western states.

"From this, I think we may be at least measurably saved, if the Church will send us an adequate supply of educated and sensible men to lay a good foundation. . . . Here at the metropolis we must have one. The older and abler the better. We can, with a good pastor, organize a good congregation here, in a little while. And if his elocution be attractive, he will have a *large* congregation. . . . At present, one might divide his labors between this and Galveston.

"With God's blessing, I hope to have my family here in a few months. And as for me and my house, we must have the offices of the Church with us. We may perhaps be the humble instruments of planting a church, which may hereafter stand upon a good foundation. I pray you look around, and find, if possible, a suitable pastor for the church at Houston; we must have, also, a good schoolmaster—a classical teacher. My two little boys are of an age to render that indispensable; and there are others here to make up a good school. The town proprietors give us the ground, both for a school and a church; and we shall be able, to erect a school-house next fall."

The reference to a gift of land for church and school is one of many such references of the period—all of which contributed to the legend that

1836-40. Franz Liszt, Hector Berlioz, Honoré de Balzac and Georges Sand add the young Frederic Chopin to their circle in Paris.

---

* Despite the early impetus of the Presbyterian Church in Houston, Christ Church Cathedral is the oldest religious organization in Houston, the second oldest parish in Texas. The First Presbyterian Church articles of association are dated March 31, 1839—15 days after those of Christ Church. And according to Dr. Andrew Forest Muir, "A claim for the priority of the Roman parish in Houston contains not a shred of evidence."

the Allen brothers gave Christ Church the land upon which it is built.

Though the lot was promised, the city map was still in a state of change. But the unnamed letter writer had captured the attention of the Board of Missions. A long and strong editorial entitled simply TEXAS appears in the November *Spirit of Missions*.

"Texas is now estimated to contain 100,000 inhabitants,* and the number rapidly increasing," the editors informed readers in the United States. "The eastern portion is represented as already settled, and presenting an aspect similar to occupied portions of the southwest of our own states. . . .

"Galveston, which a year since contained scarcely more than a single dwelling, is becoming an important port. Between this place and Houston, about ninety miles distant (sic) five steamboats are constantly plying, and two of a larger class connect it with New Orleans by four trips each month.

"The customs collected in the bay are estimated at $50,000 per quarter."

Describing the state in terms of seaboard, prairie, and hill country, table lands, the article goes on: "Religion and religious institutions are acknowledged by its leading inhabitants as important to the welfare of a state, and are therefore encouraged by the more prominent citizens of Texas, if not for their own sake. A desire is manifested for ministers of good standing."

Ministers, the *Spirit of Missions* said, are often given free steamboat passage, and though living is expensive—from $8 to $10 a week in the principal towns—"In Houston a lot for a church and school has been secured (sic) and expensive as living is at present, yet a year's board has been offered by a highly respectable communicant in the church, to any competent clergyman who shall be sent to that place." This offer was probably from Colonel Gray who expected to have his family settled in a good-sized house in Houston well before the mission board could assign a missionary to Houston.

"The Rev. R. M. Chapman," the editorial continued, "is also appointed to Texas—his station not yet fixed. Several of the younger members of the clergy are desirous of going out and establishing the institutions of religion.

"It may be asked if there are not one or two of longer experience in the ministry, who will go and uphold the hands of our younger brethren . . ."

The chief trouble was the old and eternal one: money. The editorial concluded with an appeal to "those who love a spreading gospel—whose hearts rejoice in a Church animated with the spirit of Christ—to come forward and give them ability to sustain her efforts."

Apparently only a few Episcopalians in the United States loved a spreading gospel. The Board of Missions had no budget to send out Mr. Chapman or Mr. Ives, and Americans were not overwhelming in their generosity to Episcopalians struggling to build a church in Texas.

The same issue of the *Spirit of Missions* carries the letter of a Methodist minister writing from Houston:

"Two theatres are open every night, but not a church yet marks the site, and no denomination of Christians has yet organized a society, though there are numerous individuals of the leading sects residing here. I have preached in the senate chamber to large and attentive audiences and there is an apparent interest for the means of religious instruction; but such is the pressure of business, and the excitement of speculation, and the want of money, that no successful effort for the erection of a church has yet been made.

"Building materials are extremely expensive. Houses are going up on every

---

* U.S. had 15,000,000 in 1835 and 17,069,453 in 1840.

street. Carpenters receive five dollars a day and are all employed. Houses for Galveston are actually imported from New York.

"All we can do at present is to secure sites for churches in the numerous new villages and cities. . . . The proprietors of the new towns are, in general, disposed to be liberal in the grant of lots for such purposes."

But before that edition of the *Spirit of Missions* could be mailed out and read by those comfortably at home in New York or Virginia or Connecticut, the picture had changed:

Houston had a church—the first to be formally organized.

The Rev. Robert Martin Chapman, who arrived in Texas while Colonel Gray was in Virginia moving his family, was the first missionary of the Foreign Committee of the Board of Missions to reach Texas.

Now 29, he was from a Virginia family—born in Petersburg—and had been made deacon in Pittsfield, Mass. July 1, 1838, by the Rt. Rev. Alexander Viets Griswold. Before his ordination he had written to Vice President Lamar in Texas saying that he thought of coming to Texas to establish an academy.

In October, the Foreign Committee appointed Chapman missionary—without designating a station and without salary—but Chapman was already on his way to Texas. He arrived in November, and from the beginning divided his time between Galveston and Houston.

In December, 1838, he was called upon to open the Senate of the Republic of Texas with prayer. In his report later to the committee on his half-year stay in Texas, Chapman said: "Most of that time I spent at Houston, and except a few unavoidable interruptions, I preached once a day and sometimes twice in the capitol, one of the large halls having been kindly afforded for religious meetings by the Secretary of State.

"Colonel Gray," he added, "rendered great aid in various ways. He circulated a paper for the enrollment of those who would become members of an Episcopal Society [March 16], to be established in Houston, and also another for subscription for building a church. On the second about $5,000 were subscribed. On Easter Monday a meeting of our friends was called, at which I presided, and we organized a church by the election of proper officers. I officiated at five marriages and nine funerals and baptized two infants."

Church Organized

On March 16, 1839, Col. William Fairfax Gray circulated a paper organizing a congregation:

"The undersigned agree to unite together as a Christian Congregation in the City of Houston—to observe the forms of worship, and be governed by the Constitution of the Protestant Episcopal Church in the United States of North America—" Twenty-eight men signed their names to the document which now rests in the archives of Christ Church Cathedral.

The original signers in alphabetical order were George Allen, Harvey H. Allen, Ambrose Andrews, John D. Andrews, Barnard E. Bee, George D. Biggar, John Birdsall, Henry H. Godfry, Peter Gray, William Fairfax Gray, John D. Groesbeeck, Paget Halpen, DeWitt Clinton Harris, H. E. Hartridge, M.D., Charles Hedenberg, Memucan Hunt, A. Kasson, Charles Kesler, W. Doswell Lee, Thomas Viscount Mortimer, George Moffitt Patrick, Erastus S. Perkins, Tod Robinson, Henry Thompson, James Webb, Arthur F. Woodward, Corodon C. Woodward and Andrew Janeway Yates.

1839. *The* Houston Telegraph and Texas Register *announces April 10 that the Rev. Jesse Hord, Methodist, will preach in the Senate Chamber Sunday, April 14, "at which time a church will be organized."*

Thus armed, the Rev. R. M. Chapman and Colonel Gray called a meeting of "the members of the Episcopal Congregation of the City of Houston." Announced Sunday, it met at 4 PM Monday, April 1, in the office of John Birdsall with Mr. Chapman in the chair, and DeWitt Clinton Harris acting as secretary.

This was an interesting group of men.

Birdsall, for instance, was a New Yorker from Chenango County whose family had immigrated to Texas about 10 years before. By 1837 he was a practicing lawyer in Houston and in August that year, President Sam Houston appointed him attorney general of the Republic. Birdsall—like Colonel Gray— was a charter member of the Philosophical Society of Texas.

Barnard Bee was from South Carolina, born in Charleston in 1787. Bee studied law and served on the staff of his brother-in-law, South Carolina's Governor James Hamilton, until he fell out with the governor for taking part in the nullifaction struggle of 1832.

Bee came to Texas in 1832, joined the Texas Army, was Secretary of Treasury and of State under provisional President David Burnet, and was one of three commissioners sent to accompany Antonio Lopez de Santa Anna to Washington. When Bee returned to Texas, he was Secretary of War under Mirabeau B. Lamar, and went to Mexico on an unsuccessful mission to secure recognition of Texas independence from the government of Mexico. He was minister from the Republic to the United States.

[The Congregation saw little of Bee from 1838 to 1841 when he was Texas minister to the United States. Bee County was later named in his honor, but he went home to South Carolina in 1846 because he opposed annexation of Texas to the U.S.]

D.W.C. Harris, 25, was another New Yorker, born in Seneca Falls in 1814. Son of Harrisburg's founder, John Richardson Harris and Jane Birdsall, he came to Texas with his mother in 1833 and in June, 1835, was a fairly innocent cause of the outbreak of hostilities between Texans and Mexicans: He and Andrew Briscoe were imprisoned by Mexican customs officials at Anahuac and the incident was the last straw.

Harris worked as a clerk for Briscoe, his brother-in-law, and as first county clerk of Harrisburg County (later Harris County) was a director of the Harrisburg Town Company and an elected alderman for the town, and through the years became contractor, conductor, director and secretary of the Buffalo Bayou, Brazos and Colorado Railway.

Memucan Hunt, 32, born in 1807 in Vance County, North Carolina, was a planter and business man when he moved to Mississippi at the age of 27. At 29, he volunteered to Texas and arrived just in time for the battle of San Jacinto. He was commissioned brigadier general by President Burnet to meet an expected invasion from Mexico in 1836, but when the danger passed, resigned his commission.

President Houston appointed him agent to the United States to go with William H. Wharton to gain recognition of Texas from the U.S. government, and when that was achieved in March, 1837, Hunt became Texas minister to Washington. He urged annexation but was turned down in Washington. Under Lamar, Hunt was Secretary of the Navy from December, 1838, to May, 1839, when he became the Texas representative on the joint U.S.-Texas boundary commission.

George Moffitt Patrick was a Virginian and a physician who came to Texas in 1827—at the age of 26. A volunteer fighter at Anahuac in 1832, he attended the Consultation as a delegate from Liberty in 1835 and was commander of the schooner *Flash* in 1836. In 1837 he had a home—Deepwater—in Harris County and the Texas Army camped there. He later moved to Grimes County.

James Webb, born in Fairfax County, Virginia, only four years after the birth of Colonel Gray, was taken in boyhood to Georgia but returned to teach school in Virginia, to work in the office of the county clerk and to study law. He, too, served in the War of 1812, and was admitted to the Virginia bar in 1816. He began his slow progress toward Texas: in 1819—Georgia; 1828—Florida; 1838—Texas. In Florida he was U.S. district judge under John Quincy Adams. He resigned this judgeship to come to Houston—but soon moved on to Austin as friend and advisor to Mirabeau B. Lamar. He became Secretary of the Treasury and then of State, and was Attorney General from 1839 to 1841. He was another original Christ Church member who was sent by the Republic to deal with the government of Mexico.

The remarkable thing which becomes apparent in the run-down of these biographical sketches is that Colonel Gray managed to get the 27 men in town long enough to sign that first historic agreement. He and Mr. Chapman must have felt at times that they were trying to hold together a congregation made up of swallows or a highly mobile school of fish.

But the congregation did come to the first meeting on April 1, 1839, and on the motion of Ambrose Andrews, portrait painter, resolved that this association be called the Protestant Episcopal Church of Houston.

On the motion of Memucan Hunt, it was resolved that there be elected 12 persons to act as vestrymen, and that from their numbers, the vestry should elect two wardens. The chairman appointed Hunt, Gray and A. F. Woodward as a nominating committee and the congregation elected these men as nominated:

William F. Gray, John Birdsall, M. Hunt, A. F. Woodward, James Webb, William Pierpont, Tod Robinson, E. S. Perkins, D. W. C. Harris, J. D. Andrews, C. Kesler, and George Allen.

Fortunately for Christ Church, the congregation elected not only some of its most famous members—most of whom would soon go off to Washington, D.C., France or Mexico—but balanced the slate with a solid group of Houston merchants. Though he was county clerk, Harris was also securely rooted in business here. Charles Kesler owned Kesler's Arcade. Pierpont, Andrews, Robinson and George Allen were all in the mercantile business. And Erastus Perkins had not only a flourishing business—pool tables to ready-made clothes—but also a house which faced Prairie and backed to the capitol with a large flower garden growing in the side yard. Here to stay and grow with the city, these men gave continuity and stability.

The new vestry was empowered to choose a name for the church—and though there is no record of when they did so, Christ Church was the name in use in the vestry minutes by June, 1844.

Meanwhile Colonel Gray had very practically circulated a subscription paper to raise funds for the proposed church, and got 45 names in addition to his own. The signers subscribed $2,890 in Texas promissory notes, $800 in building materials, 1,000 feet of lumber, a lot in Anahuac and another in San Leon, and the promise of half of block 55 in Houston for a church and school—the land where the church buildings now stand.

On April 3, the vestry met, elected Gray and Perkins wardens, and named

1830-40. James Fenimore Cooper is a favorite author in England and America, and the intellectual world is excited over Jean Jacques Audobon's Birds of America.

1840. The first antislavery party nominates a candidate for president of the United States.

Birdsall, Andrews and Gray to a building and lot committee.

The vestry went on record thanking the Rev. Mr. Chapman for "his clerical services heretofore rendered to the Community of the City of Houston," and invited him "to continue the same in cooperation with the congregation now formed until it shall be so firmly established as to enable it to make a more definite arrangement."

With this sound beginning—or a beginning which would have been sound in any less fluid community—the Rt. Rev. Leonidas Polk was completely justified in the tone of his letter written from Houston, May 17, 1839:

"The town of Galveston is situated on the east end of the island of the same name," he wrote, "lying in the Gulph, and opposite the mouth of the Trinity river. It is the place of deposit for all articles of merchandise imported into the republic, and from which their exports are shipped. . . .

"The number of inhabitants now there is estimated at 2000, and others are moving in daily. The population appeared to be highly respectable and would compare very well with that found in any towns of our own country of equal age. Many families I saw there were as respectable as those found in our country generally. . . .

"On the day after our arrival, we left in a steamer for this place. We left at 4 o'clock P.M. and arrived on the following day about 7 A.M., the route being through Galveston Bay, the San Jacinto and Buffalo Bayou. On the bank of the latter stands Houston.

"The country here is very flat, and the Bayou narrow; so much so, as to make it difficult for two steam-boats to pass each other.

"The town is well laid out, in the style of our new towns generally, and has the air of business. The census, recently taken, makes the number of inhabitants rather more than 2000. This being the seat of government, the state officers are here, and the residences of those who administer affairs.

"A change is shortly to be made in this particular and the Government to be transferred to Austin, on the Colorado. . . . This place however must always be one of considerable importance. Perhaps it will continue to be the second in the republic.

"There is a Presbyterian congregation organized here [the preceding March 31] and also one of our own church. Four or five thousand dollars also have been subscribed for erecting an Episcopal church. This will shortly be enlarged, and the building commenced, as I am assured."

Neither Bishop Polk nor the Christ Church vestry could foresee that the removal of the government would bring the removal with the government, and in all directions, of many of those who had signed the subscription. Nor could they foresee that yellow fever epidemics and new threats of Mexican invasion would collapse the boom of Houston's first two years.

The brilliant promise of the beginning soon gave way to seven long, hard, tedious, often heart-breaking years of work before the congregation would kneel in worship in its own small brick church.

And Colonel Gray would not live to see that church.

1839. The National Intelligencer *reporting on progress of morals in Houston April 18 refers to "Recently organized Episcopal, Presbyterian and Methodist denominations."*

Chapter 8

Woeful Check

"We have been woefully checked in our anticipated operations," Colonel Gray wrote the Foreign Mission Board October 31, 1839.

"Mr. Chapman's return to the north left us without a pastor, which we have anxiously but hitherto vainly hoped the Board would supply us with. . . .

"We have suffered much in sickness and death. The mortality has been greatest among the dissipated and worthless. Some poor persons, who deserved a better fate, have died for want of proper attention, being strangers in a strange land, and some of our best citizens have fallen.

"I mentioned in my last, the Hon. John Birdsall, one of our best citizens and a hopeful member of the Church. We have also lost the Hon. Henry Humphreys, presiding judge of the county court, a man of worth, whose family are members of the Church; also Dr. Edmund R. Anderson, my family physicion, who died in my house, having been removed hither two days before his death. He was a martyr to his professional zeal; having been exposed two nights in succession to long rides in the country, and by losing the road having had to sleep overnight on the open prairie. He was a fine physician and a gentleman. These three were all of my immediate circle and I feel their loss heavily.

"I am not accurately informed of the whole number of deaths, but think, for the last month, they will have averaged four or five a day, and that in a population now reduced probably to 12 or 1500. Very few females have died. Not one of any distinction. Indeed very few of them have been sick, and still fewer of children.

"The prevailing type of the disease seems to leave all our physicians at fault. Some call it *yellow fever,* others *cold plague.* Certainly it differs greatly from the descriptions of yellow fever that I have read of. In some of the most striking cases there has been but little fever, the seat of the disease seeming to be the stomach, which cannot retain the usual remedies. Some cases have terminated with the black vomit, which is the only characteristic of yellow fever about them, and that, I am told, is not an unerring symptom.

"We now indulge the hope that the worst is over. Some of the most conspicuous cases are recovering. This has been a much more fatal summer throughout the South than the last. The sickness has not been confined to Houston nor to Texas.

"I have cause of much thankfulness that my large family remains entire, and has had very little sickness—not more than might fairly have befallen them in Virginia in any summer. I have nine whites and nine blacks, large and small, of my own family, and have had an average of ten or twelve boarders during the summer. Dr. Anderson is the only one of them who has died, or had a very serious spell of sickness. My three youngest children were sick in the early part of the summer, who are now uncommonly hearty. Myself, my wife and elder children, have had excellent health. Indeed, my wife's health, which was delicate in Virginia, has decidedly improved here.

"I mention these particulars to show you and those who are thinking of a residence in this country, that although, as new comers, they must expect to undergo an acclimation, and take their chance for dying, as is the case in all southern countries, yet there is nothing peculiarly terrific in a residence in Texas, or even in Houston.

1840. Commander Charles Wilkes of the First U.S. Exploring Expedition finds the Antarctic Continent.

"I have resided nearly four years in Texas, two entire summers, and until the 7th of August, of a third, in this place; and I do not hesitate to pronounce it as healthy as any place in the same latitude that I have yet known; far more healthy than the same parallels in Louisiana and Mississippi, and in this opinion I am sustained by intelligent medical men.

"During the gloomy period that we have just past, we have been without the aid of any clergyman. The Presbyterian, who had been preaching here for eighteen months, has been irregular in his attendance through the summer, and has, I believe, gone to the new metropolis, the city of Austin, to reside. We have had no preaching for several months. Many of the dead have been buried without christian rites. Over several I have read our funeral service, and the same has been done by other laymen.

"We have at length come to the determination to open public service on the Sabbath. My brother Warden and myself, will attempt to read the service with such as will attend, and perhaps we shall be assisted by others. This may be deemed irregular, but in our peculiar circumstances, insulated from the rest of the christian world, and denied the ministrations of the ordained, it seems to be the only way in which we can keep alive *the forms* of the church we love among us. We hope it will meet the approbation of the Church, and the blessing of its spiritual Head.

"How long, my dear sir, shall we be left thus destitute?

"This country is to rise rapidly in the scale of nations. The English language, and the free institutions of the United States, are already here. The Church is yet to be built up; indeed the foundation is yet to be laid. The model and the workmen are with you? Will they deny us their aid?"

There were reasons for despair in Houston in the bleak autumn of 1839.

Milly Gray wrote in October "Sickness—Sickness—Sickness all around and many deaths. . . . Summoned early in the morning to see Judge Humphreys who is dying. Over there nearly all day. . . . Much occupied with Dr. Anderson who we had brought over here this evening. He is exceedingly ill. . . . poor Dr. Anderson breathed his last about ½ past 2 o'clock. We carried him to the grave this evening. . . . There are a fearful number of new graves. This was the 6th today. This is an awful disease and does not seem to be understood by the physicians."

In addition to the yellow fever epidemic, which claimed 240 of Houston's 2,000 residents, Houston was suffering the reduced circumstances of a city whose major industry—government of the Republic—has just been moved to another town. When it became known that Houston had lost the capitol, New Orleans merchants began to refuse credit to local merchants, and Texas currency depreciated to 10 cents on the dollar—taking with it the bulk of the Christ Church subscription fund.

The November meeting of the vestry was a depressing one from the outset, Still known as the vestry of "the Protestant Episcopal Church at Houston," it met in Gray's office with only four present—E. S. Perkins, William F. Gray, Wardens, and Memucan Hunt and Charles Kesler. "Owing to death and removal among the members, and the temporary absence of others," the minutes read, "It being found impracticable to procure a meeting of the majority of the whole number of the vestry, it was Resolved that the members present proceed to fill vacancies in their body . . . ."

James Reily was elected "in place of John Birdsall, Dec; Alden A. M. Jackson in the place of James Webb, removed to the city of Austin; William

Douglas Lee in the place of Arthur F. Woodward, gone to the United States."

This body then resolved that "inasmuch as the church is destitute of a minister and there is no immediate prospects of obtaining the services of one, it be recommended to the wardens to make arrangements for having the services of the Church regularly read by Laymen."

The vestry also recommended—futilely—that the building committee make an immediate estimate of how much a church would cost, and that the committee be appointed to correspond with the Board of Foreign Missions in the United States upon the interests of the Episcopal Church in Texas.

This was somewhat retroactive approval of Colonel Gray's correspondence begun a fortnight before.

By January, 1840, the epidemic was abating and Mrs. Gray wrote "The fever continued to be very fatal and a great many persons died. It is said one third of the population fell victims to it. It has prevailed through the whole southern country & was equally as fatal as it has been here . . ."

But "We are now all getting quite social and cheerful." And best news:

"We were very happy in having the Rev. Mr. Goodwin of Maryland with us a few days. He preached on Sunday the 29th both morning and evening in the Court House where we Episcopalians have determined to have worship in future until we can get a church built. This place is very pleasant now as to society but is changing every day."

Henry Gillett had arrived. "We sent our Boys and Kate to a young Mr. Gillett on Thursday the 2nd Inst. He is studying for the University & we like him very much so far . . .

"Thursday we commenced the Episcopal Sunday school." And in mid-January "Very warm. No fires & doors and windows all open."

The arrival of Henry Gillett gave the church a new member, and the children an excellent school master. The fortuitous arrival of Mr. Goodwin undoubtedly gave the congregation new impetus.

In February, 1840, the vestry minutes struck a happier note, though there was no quorum "by reason of the absence and sickness of members," but the minority nonetheless Resolved: That the thanks of the vestry be presented to the Rev. Henry B. Goodwin of the Diocese of Maryland for his acceptable ministerial services during his visit to this place.

"Resolved that the Rev. H. B. Goodwin be invited to accept the temporary charge of the Episcopal Congregation of Houston as Rector, during his sojourn in this country."

Mr. Goodwin accepted the cure pro tempore, and in March was presiding over a vestry meeting at which James Reily was added to the committee for procuring deeds, testimonials, etc. and John Pitkin and Gray were added to the "Committee for furnishing temporarily Seats in the C. House, each vestryman contributing Ten Dollars."

And the whole vestry became a committee "for procuring Subscriptions to the building of the church, to urge the same with zeal and activity."

It was perhaps after this March meeting when the vestry had resolved to "zeal and activity" that they added 11 new names to the original congregation—dated on the old document only "Spring, 1840."

The 11 were: Charles William Adams, Henry R. Allen, William Robinson Baker, Henry F. Gillett, Rawleigh B. Green, J. B. Houghtaling, Alden A. M. Jackson, Leonard S. Perkins, James Reily, George C. Temple and James West.

Also in that active Spring, they added another sprinkling of names and

1840. Population of the United States is 17,069,-453.

pledges to the subscription list.

Young Mr. Gillett was from Connecticut. He was a student of Trinity College, Hartford, when poor health prompted him to come to Texas to join his cousin, Ashbel Smith. He taught school in Houston, and after a period in Washington County, he returned to Houston in 1844 for another two years of teaching, bringing back with him a wife.

James Reily, a native of Ohio, had studied law in Kentucky and had married Ellen Hart, grand-niece of Mrs. Henry Clay, when he brought his bride to Texas in 1836 or 37. They soon moved to Houston. Reily became well known locally as captain of the Milam Guards in a campaign against the Indians, but he later became internationally known as a diplomat representing Texas in Washington, and as consul representing the United States in St. Petersburg, Russia.

Leonard Perkins was a cousin of the merchant and builder Erastus Perkins of the first vestry. And William Robinson Baker owned title to a part of the land now held by Christ Church Cathedral.

Certainly Colonel Gray's letter of June 22, 1840, to the *Spirit of Missions* is considerably more cheerful than his preceding one.

"We were favored from Christmas to Easter (with a few occasional absences) with the labors of the Rev. Henry B. Goodwin of the diocese of Maryland, who voluntarily came among us, and who has made himself very useful and acceptable. Could he have remained, our wishes as to a Rector would have been gratified."

Buried in a paragraph of the December, 1840, issue of the *Spirit of Missions* was a minor notice which meant that help was coming—not very much and for not very long. But in this period, every dollup of encouragement was important to keep this hard-luck congregation alive.

The item: "At a special meeting held on the 24th of October, the Rev. Benjamin Eaton, of Wisconsin, was appointed missionary to Texas."

1840. Five-year-old Samuel Clemens starts to school in Hannibal, Missouri.

Chapter 9

Reluctant Texan

Just as the Rev. Mr. Chapman has often been called the "founder" of Christ Church, which is not quite true, so has the Rev. Benjamin Eaton always been listed as one of the church's early rectors—from January 14, 1841, through about May that year—which is not quite true either.

Mr. Eaton came to this new nation as a missionary to Galveston and Houston. Born in Dublin, Ireland, in about 1806, he had been ordained deacon and priest by the Rt. Rev. Jackson Kemper, and had served as missionary in Mineral Point and Green Bay, Wisconsin.

As much to get away from the cold climate as anything else, Mr. Eaton was willing for the Foreign Committee to appoint him missionary to Texas in October, 1840.

He accepted, and in December, set out for Texas by way of St. Louis.

By all the laws of psychology or by any arrangement of present day aptitude tests and consumer reaction polls, the Rev. Benjamin Eaton and Texas should never have been got together.

In fact, the combination worked well.

Mr. Eaton was not the brilliantly educated man Mr. Silas Dinsmore had demanded for these cosmopolitan people, and Texas got off on the wrong foot with Mr. Eaton.

He landed in January in the middle of a severe norther, and, wrote Doctor Muir, "was told that the weather was unusual. (Weather in southeast Texas is similar to that of southern California in that no matter what its state, it is unusual, according to residents.)"

He also found business poor, and Galveston residents in reduced circumstances. He wrote grumpily to the *Spirit of Missions:*

". . . I have already seen, & heard enough of the republic to cool my Texas fever, and to make me fear that I have left a most promising field for one where my exertions will not be half so useful, or half so much thought of, and where I shall experience almost every privation that a civilized man can endure. I have already suffered more in Texas from destitution of comfort, and want of what I have been used to think common conveniences, than I did during the year I passed in Wisconsin."

Mr. Eaton had more or less planned to make Galveston his headquarters before he left Wisconsin, but meanwhile Houston was expecting him.

On January 19, 1841, he went to Houston and on Sunday, January 24, had morning and afternoon services in the courthouse. It was cold in Houston too, but the newspaper announcement of the meeting, promised that the room would be made as comfortable as circumstances permitted.

Somewhat retroactively, the vestry met on Monday, January 25, to receive the letter from the Secretary of the Foreign Committee announcing Eaton's appointment to Galveston and Houston.

At this meeting, the vestry resolved that it "felt much pleasure in the arrival among us of the Rev. B. Eaton, Missionary of the Protestant Episcopal Church in the U.S. and that we trust it will prove, under the blessing of Almighty God, the dawning of a brighter day for the Church in Texas."

The vestry also respectfully asked Eaton "to make his residence in the City of Houston and favor this Church with as much of his ministerial services as he can consistently with the duties of his Mission."

Technically, the vestry did not elect Mr. Eaton rector, did not call Mr. Eaton to be rector—and nowhere in the vestry minutes is he referred to as rector of Christ Church. But Mr. Eaton considered these resolutions and the accompanying letter an invitation to be rector, and without a doubt, had Mr. Eaton been willing to accept the invitation to spend most of his time in Houston, the vestry would have been quite willing to elect him officially.

Mr. Eaton preached in Houston three times and was inclined to think. Houston the more promising city for the development of a church.

He reported to the Board of Missions that Houston had some 15 communicants, of whom three or four were males. [This seems puzzling—there were *nine* vestrymen present at the meeting which welcomed him to Houston but in the 19th century, non-communicants were sometimes welcomed on the vestry by a struggling church].

". . . but I have never met with more indifference, generally speaking, on the part of those who profess attachment to the Episcopal Church than it has been my lot to find here. I hope, however, that before long things will wear a less discouraging appearance, and that God will so dispose the hearts & minds of this people that a large & pious congregation may be established amongst them in both places." Mr. Eaton may have been simply homesick for Wisconsin —he had been greatly liked there.

By April, he could write to the Foreign Committee that he had held services in Houston 13 times. He had celebrated Holy Communion on Palm Sun-

1841. First passenger train begins to run on Erie Railroad June 30.

35

day, and had given communion to eight persons, one for the first time.

But he had by now decided that he was spreading himself too thin by traveling between Houston and Galveston, and he would therefore devote himself to Galveston—paying Houston a visit when he could.

Mr. Eaton therewith abandoned Houston.

Four months later, he reported he had not been back since his April report. The Houston vestry held no more meetings in 1840 or 1841.

Its warden and founder had died—Colonel Gray.

Colonel Gray had not, perhaps, achieved the success in Texas which he had hoped to achieve when first fired by the vision of revolution, new republic and new opportunity.

He was not successful in his attempts to win a political office. But:

"His lack of success in politics," Doctor Muir commented, "probably benefited the community in that he was able to devote a greater portion of his time to nurturing law and order, religion and education in the raw community that was Houston during its early years. He served as a member of the police patrol of the city in 1839 when the local government collapsed . . . in 1840 he was one of the trustees of the Houston City School that provided instruction despite continuous administrative crisis. On occasions he served as election judge and for a while was a member of the committee appointed by the city council to prevent fires."

And throughout the long bare stretches when the Episcopal congregation was without a minister, Colonel Gray acted Sunday by Sunday as lay reader, and in the tragic epidemic of 1839, read the burial service over some of his closest and most respected friends.

In May, 1841, Colonel Gray formed a law partnership with his son, Peter—now 21—who had just been admitted to the bar, and then took on John Scott. Mrs. Gray referred to him in her diary as "deaf as I am—& a cripple."

But the unfortunate fact was that most of Colonel Gray's services to society were not of a kind to bring in money.

He was candid when he applied to President Lamar for the post as district attorney of the first judicial district. "My main object in seeking this office, is to endeavor to achieve, through a diligent discharge of its duties, a provision for my family which my present business denies."

He got the appointment on November 9, 1840, and the Senate confirmed the President's appointment November 30. Gray presented his commission to the district court of Harris County and went vigorously to work.

It was on official duty, when he went to Galveston for the spring term of district court, that he caught a cold. After his return to Houston, this developed in to acute pneumonia, and he died April 16, 1841—aged 53 years.

He left behind a widow—41 years old—who for the remaining 10 years of her life would work sincerely for the church he had founded. He left a son—Peter W. Gray—who would provide the stamina, the determination, often the cash to keep vestry and church on course for the next 24 years.

The congregation still had Mr. and Mrs. James S. Reily and Mr. and Mrs. Erastus S. Perkins—described from the beginning by Mrs. Gray as "zealous Episcopalians." Peter Gray was now an adult.

Names were becoming familiar in both church and city affairs: A. S. Ruthven, J. D. Andrews, W. W. Swain, Cornelius Ennis, Jacob Cruger.

Andrews was mayor of Houston and a popular one. Jacob Cruger was a newspaper editor. And Ennis—a vast man 6' 3" tall and weighing 275 pounds

—was Houston's first cotton merchant. His firm of Ennis and Kimball made the first shipment of cotton from the port of Galveston to that of Boston in 1841. And that year he married his partner's sister, Jeanette Ingals Kimball.

Mr. and Mrs. Ennis would be quiet, sure mainstays of the church in both Houston and Galveston throughout their long lives.

But Colonel Gray's death undoubtedly took the heart out of the Episcopal congregation in that period. The vestry held no meetings, left no records.

Yet the congregation held together and—for lack of something more substantial—held on to a sort of orphan-to-uncle relationship with Mr. Eaton.

In May, 1842, the congregation at last met again, "previous notice having been given from the pulpit by the Rev. Mr. Eaton."

N. B.—Not "the rector, Mr. Eaton."

The pulpit was probably that of an interdenominational meeting house which had been started in 1840.

At this meeting, the congregation unanimously elected Erastus Perkins and A. S. Ruthven, wardens; J. D. Andrews, E. J. Felder, William W. Swain, Cornelius Ennis, Peter W. Gray, L. S. Perkins, H. Evans, Jacob Cruger, James Reily and John F. Torrey.

Though Mr. Eaton was still a missionary from the United States and based now fairly firmly in Galveston, he was being held responsible for Christ Church by the Houston proprietors.

It was in this month that the Town Company—represented by James S. Holman—deeded the present site of the church to the Protestant Episcopal Church for $1 "provided that the Rev. Benjamin Eaton, rector, and E. S. Perkins and A. S. Ruthven, wardens, will build or cause to be built a good and substantial church. . . ." The legend that the land was given to Christ Church was strengthened.

In contrast to this highly if-and-when situation, the Galveston parish had received so much of Mr. Eaton's time and energy that by August of 1841, Trinity's first church—"a neat Gothic structure 40 by 70 feet was in progress, to be completed by the 1st January next, and not to exceed in cost $4400."

For Galveston, this was the firm beginning of a happy partnership—priest and parish. Mr. Eaton never married, he devoted his whole long, vigorous, earnest life to Trinity Church where he was much beloved—and he left the church the bulk of his estate when he died.

And throughout those years, he was a good friend to Christ Church, Matagorda, and Christ Church, Houston—his two senior parishes in the diocese.

1842. Roman Catholic Church is built at corner of Franklin Avenue and Caroline Street on the edge of a ravine.

A Résumé in Context

Chapter 10

Christ Church in its first four years was scarcely more than an idea struggling precariously for survival.

It means little unless viewed in context: the context of the raw, new Houston, the context of a Republic moving toward statehood, the context of a Protestant Episcopal Church only now regaining the ground lost in the American Revolution.

It could be argued that Houston had little hope of attracting a minister to stay so long as it was plagued every year or so by epidemics of yellow fever. Actually, it was as easy to catch yellow fever in New York.

Houston was no more bothered by the disease than most American cities

of the 18th and 19th centuries. Yellow fever occurred wherever there were mosquitoes and a yellow fever patient available for them to bite.

Ironically, Saint James Church, New York (founded in 1810), benefited from New York City's epidemics. In his history of that church, the Rev. James Elliott Lindsley quoted: "In the early part of the last century some of the wealthy residents of the city began to think that it was hardly safe to remain in town during the summer months. The yellow fever had, for several years in succession, caused many deaths. So it became desirable that those who could do so should build summer residences which might also be used in Winter, and so should not be far away."

Mr. Lindsley added: "There had been yellow fever epidemics in 1797-99, and again in 1801, 1803 and 1805, and it is clear that the rock studded northern end of Manhattan Island became known more and more as a refuge from contagion." And so, St. James was born on Manhattan Island, about where Hunter College now stands.

St. James was also fortunate, of course, in that it received considerable help from rich old Trinity Church in downtown New York.

It could be argued that living conditions—water, streets, fire protection, public health, city beauty—were yet too primitive in Houston for a resident minister to wish to come.

But in daily living, the difference between big old American cities and small new Texas cities was not great.

Most cities were still using water from cisterns and wells for drinking.

Few cities had sewage systems and few houses had indoor plumbing.

Few streets were paved. Streetcars were mule-drawn.

And as for civic beauty, Buffalo Bayou's banks were muddy but the water was clear enough for swimming, and magnolias still hung over the water.

Houston's tent city and shacks were probably no worse a slum than the area of the New York's Central Park which was "for the most part a succession of stone quarries, interspersed with pestiferous swamps. The entire ground was the refuge for about five thousand squatters, dwelling in rude huts of their own construction, and living off the refuse of the city which they daily conveyed in small carts, chiefly drawn by dogs, from the lower part of the city, through Fifth Avenue (then a dirt road, running over hills and hollows.) This refuse they divided among themselves and a hundred thousand domestic animals and fowls." (From *Memorial History of New York* by General Viele.)

To Texas—and to those drawn to Texas as Col. William Fairfax Gray was drawn—this was an exciting place to be: revolution, founding of a republic, development of a new country and a new capital.

But the years between the founding of Christ Church and the completion of its first church building were exciting ones everywhere.

Belgium and the Kingdom of the Netherlands in 1839 were separated by treaty and Belgium declared independent.

In 1840 the Antartic Continent was found by Commander Charles Wilkes of the first U. S. Exploring Expedition.

In 1842, the first use of anesthesia was tried by Dr. Crawford W. Long in Jefferson, Georgia, and Dr. William T. G. Morton in Boston.

In 1844, the first message traveled over the world's first telegraph line from the U. S. Supreme Court room in Washington to Baltimore, and Joseph Smith, Mormon leader, was killed by a mob in Carthage, Illinois.

And in 1845, Texas was—at last—ready for annexation.

That Texas was going to be annexed was apparent to almost everyone from the beginning—except for the few who opposed it. Christ Church Vestryman Barnard Bee went back to South Carolina in protest.

There was never in these years, for instance, any really convincing movement to establish a national Protestant Episcopal Church of the Republic of Texas—as there was to be under the Confederacy.

Much as the Allen brothers wanted Houston to be proclaimed capital, they did not call in any Major l'Enfant to design a nation's capital in the precedent established in Washington and since followed by Australia and Brazil.

And as soon as young Memucan Hunt got to Washington as Minister to the United States from the Republic of Texas, he began to campaign for the annexation of Texas.

The Episcopal Church in the first half of the 19th century was only getting back its strength from the damages done by disestablishment at the time of the American Revolution. A Johnny-come-lately of 1839, Christ Church was not so far behind the much older Episcopal churches of the eastern seaboard as the years between them would suggest.

Though William Fairfax Gray was baptized and confirmed into a church already a century old, the church in Virginia was at low ebb in 1800.

Far from meaning a legal separation of church and state, disestablishment to many newly independent American citizens meant total destruction of the Church of England. Some of the old Virginia churches were stripped of their furnishings, fonts were used as watering troughs, communion chalices were taken home to become loving cups.

In New York in 1811, when John Henry Hobart and Alexander Griswold were ready for consecration as bishops, it seemed at first impossible to get together the essential three bishops to insure apostolic succession and for a time looked as though again, the American church would have to go back to England for this consecration. (The few living bishops were seemingly unable to make the journey through illness, paralysis, or unwillingness.)

Hobart's diocese, the Diocese of New York, covered 50,000 square miles— from Long Island's eastern end to the Canadian border—and there were no railways. Griswold covered a similar amount of territory in the Eastern Diocese which included all of New England except Connecticut.

In North Carolina in 1816, with the death of Parson Blount, "there was not left surviving a single clergyman of the Episcopal Church in the entire state," and in 1823 Bishop Ravenscroft—newly consecrated—served without pay as rector of Christ Church, Raleigh, holding services in an abandoned theater. In 1835 in the entire United States there were 763 Episcopal clergymen —in a population of 15 million.

The struggles of Christ Church, therefore, told a story familiar to many of those still living in the older sections of the country.

Christ Church, Houston, is a part of that story which began in 1835.

That year, the Protestant Episcopal Church through its new Foreign Committee of the Board of Missions resolved "That the Committee establish a Mission Station in Texas."

Thereafter, reports from Texas—however irregularly—appeared in the *Spirit of Missions* section "Foreign Correspondence," often sandwiched in between reports from Greece or Batavia, or with notices from Western Africa, Crete, Constantinople or India.

The missionary effort had not been made before because until Texans

1841. Friedrich Wilhelm IV invites Felix Mendelssohn to take over the court orchestra and chorus of Berlin.

revolted against Santa Anna, Texas was a state of a Roman Catholic country, and as Dr. Lawrence L. Brown states in his new history, *The Episcopal Church in Texas from Its Foundation to the Division of the Diocese*—1838-1874:

"The Episcopal Church had never sent a mission to a land where the Roman Catholic Church was established by law, as had been the case so long as Texas was a part of Mexico." Though the Rev. John Wurts Cloud came to Texas in 1831, it was as teacher and planter in Brazoria.

The Rev. Richard S. Salmon with his colonists came in 1836, but not as a representative of the Board of Missions because "intimate and direct connection with a land company" made his appointment inappropriate *(Ibid.)*

The Rev. Chester Newell, deacon, came in 1837—but chiefly as teacher and as a historian collecting material on the new Republic for his envisioned book.

Until the summer of 1837, nothing more was done to put the Texas Mission into effect.

By 1838, Colonel Gray was addressing his pleas to the Board of Missions, and these were being published in the *Spirit of Missions*. And in the General Convention in Philadelphia that September of 1838, sentiment was clear that Texas should be sent spiritual leaders. Many of those present in Philadelphia had friends and relatives out in that new foreign land of Texas.

The Foreign Committee in New York, therefore, seized upon the election of the Rev. Leonidas Polk of Tennessee as Missionary Bishop of the Southwest as the solution: they asked him to supervise the mission in the Republic of Texas with Houston and Matagorda designated as stations.

At this point, Matagorda had the kind of luck—earned luck—which with all its efforts Houston had not yet managed.

The Reverend Caleb S. Ives of Alabama accepted an invitation of Matagorda residents to come and establish a school.

This put him in the position of being able to accept the assignment as missionary without pay.

He and the Rev. Mr. Chapman, who had volunteered to go as a missionary, were the first two missionaries appointed to Texas. Mr. Chapman—after helping Colonel Gray get the Houston church organized—did not stay long. But Caleb Ives gave his life to Matagorda. He must have been a truly intelligent, wise and attractive man.

Born in Vermont in 1797, he was the son of a not-very-prosperous Vermont farmer, who inclined to drink.

Yet, at the age of 29, he became so interested in the Episcopal Church that he entered Trinity College, Hartford, in 1826, graduated in 1830, and then enrolled in General Seminary for the three year course which prepared him to be first deacon and then priest.

Ives began his priesthood as a missionary in Alabama under the Domestic Committee of the Missionary Society. There Ives founded three churches in five years, got accustomed to the more primitive living conditions of small towns in frontier sections, and married Miss Katherine Duncan Morison in Tuscaloosa in 1834.

With his marriage, the Rev. Mr. Ives moved into Mobile and joined the faculty of the Mobile Institute as professor of ancient languages. He assisted his wife's brother-in-law, the Rev. Samuel S. Lewis, who was rector of Christ Church, Mobile, and of the church at Spring Hill.

Caleb Ives' diary of his life and work in Matagorda is a charming, revealing and informative book—unfortunately not in print.

Though almost every entry begins with a weather report, weather was, after all, more important in a time when rain meant impassable roads and no church, or drouth could wreck the congregation's finances, or when it simply got too hot or too cold for services if the Texas wind changed.

But even this preoccupation with weather has its charm to Texans in that on one visit back east, he complains in his diary of the heat.

Having traveled from Matagorda to Mobile to visit relatives, and then back to New Orleans and by boat to St. Louis, "St. Louis is now a large city and must one day, from its peculiar and favorable location, be one of the great cities of the United States," he went on by steamer to Louisville and from there by mailboat to Cincinnati and by steamer to Guyandotte, Virginia, from whence he took the stage for Charleston—"the stage agent has sent all my baggage on east without me . . ." and then went by stage on east "over the McAdamized road running from Staunton to Winchester" and finally to Baltimore and Philadelphia.

"The day has been dreadfully hot," said the Rev. Mr. Ives of Baltimore. Next day in Philadelphia: "A most excessively hot day, the thermometer standing, it is said, at 102 in the shade in the Parks. Attended St. Peter's Church A. M. and Christ Church P. M."

And the next day "Thermometer stood, in a counting room this A. M. at 9 o'clock, at 96 degrees. Left at 5 P. M. for New York.

And the day after "Dreadfully hot in New York."

Despite his devotion to weather, Mr. Ives could—and did—tell in his diary of the important things happening in his life and around him: The sudden madness and suicide of a brilliant Frenchman who was a fellow passenger aboard a steamship, and the suicide of an acquaintance, a love-lorn doctor. The fears of new Mexican invasions in town and the tendency of townsmen to start off valiantly to war, only to straggle home again for one reason or another. The joyous day that his father decided to give up drink, or that his baby son could stand alone. He chronicled the deaths of presidents, the annexation of Texas, the founding of the Diocese of Texas—all in an accurate and charming fashion.

1842. Massachusetts recognizes the legal right of labor unions to exist.

If his teaching was as accurate and as charming—and it apparently was— he must have done wonders with the youth of Matagorda of 1839 to 1848.

And despite the crop failures, the threat of famine, the rumblings of war, and the occasional revivals by traveling evangelists—which Mr. Ives felt to be most unfortunate as they inclined to unsettle the people—the Rev. Caleb Ives founded and built Christ Church, Matagorda, as the first in Texas.

By this act, he became the founder of the Episcopal Church in Texas.

Ordering a prefabricated building from New York, he had it raised by March, 1841, and that month baptized Albert Gervais Levy—age four months —the Church's first baptism.

In the United States, the Protestant Episcopal Church doubled the number of clergymen in the country between 1835 and 1850—from 763 to 1,558— despite a recession.

Church memberships were growing more rapidly still—from 36,416 communicants to 95,212. Part of this last gain came, of course, from Texas which had more would-be church parishes than it had ministers to fill them.

There is probably no single reason for the difficulties the Christ Church congregation faced those first critical years in trying to get a full-time rector and to build a church. The story throughout Texas was scarcely better.

But by 1841, Matagorda had both church and rector. By January, 1842, Eaton had his first church built in Galveston. And Houston's turn was long overdue.

Chapter 11

A Storm and a Petrel

"January 31, 1843: Last night about 10 o'clock commenced a furious 'norther' as it is here called. That is a north west wind. We are too near shore to keep on our course, and consequently tacked and stood off. After calling all hands and reefing sails, we about ship(ped) and drove ahead."

This first line in the diary of the Rev. Charles Gillett in Texas characterizes his whole career as a man, as rector of Christ Church, as stormy petrel but valiant and successful worker in the Protestant Epsicopal Church.

He was—to Christ Church members—first rector of Christ Church, Houston.

Neither he nor the Houston congregation knew anything about each other when the *Spirit of Missions* announced under "Intelligence—TEXAS: The Rev. Charles Gillett, a graduate of the Theological Seminary, Alexandria, and now in Priest's Orders, was appointed by the Foreign Committee, on the 11th of October, missionary to Texas. His immediate field of labor to be chosen after reaching that country."

Gillett was young, strong and well educated, and his picture—in his high white neckerchief tied in the fashion of the early 19th century—leaves no doubt as to his determination or vigor.

1843. Ulysses Simpson Grant is graduated from West Point.

Gillett—who in the course of his stay at Christ Church would become Gillette—was born in Hartford County, Connecticut, February 16, 1813. He attended Trinity College at Hartford, and taught in high school before entering the Virginia Episcopal Seminary at Alexandria. This period of teaching infected him with a life-long passion for founding and running and teaching schools. He was ordained priest by Bishop Meade in Christ Church, Alexandria, October 9, 1842. He was ready to give to his new mission the fresh optimism it so badly needed.

Already he knew some of the problems: At the suggestion of the Foreign Committee, he had attempted to raise money in the United States to help Mr. Eaton rebuild his storm-smashed Trinity Church, Galveston, and had found it far from easy.

"Early in the morning came to anchor off the bar in sight of Galveston, where we lay during the day. The wind blowing furiously during the day.

"February 1, 1843. Early this morning the pilots came off, and it took us nearly all day to beat into harbor, a distance of about 10 miles. After getting in, I went ashore in the boat and found the Rev. Mr. Eaton.

"He urged me to stay on shore during the night, but as he seemed not very comfortably located, and boarding, I chose to return on board the brig for the night with the promise to see him in the morning. It is very calm tonight and much milder than it has been either yesterday or today. The fires on the prairie are burning very bright in sight. As we came in, large quantities of sea fowl of various kinds were to be seen along the shore. The barking of a dog was fine music tonight, having heard nothing like it for a long time."

Landing in Galveston, he found himself in full sympathy with his new colleague—older by six years than Gillett, a bachelor, still without church or home of his own. Mr. Eaton's lovely church, which had opened in January, 1841, was blown down in September, 1842, while the rector was in the vestry room. Gillett promptly wrote the Foreign Committee:

"It is now nearly three years since he commenced his labors here—during all that time with the exception of a few weeks, during which he used his vestry-room, he has had no comfortable apartment for study, no place of retirement suited to the labors and preparations of a clergyman. Obliged to board at a public house, where the tranquility and order so necessary for his studies, preparatory to the duties of the sanctuary, could not be obtained."

Perhaps there was naivete in a later paragraph—the naivete of a city man from Connecticut and Virginia facing the frontier: "The original cost of the Church in Galveston was six thousand dollars—which is certainly very cheap, considering the cost of material and labor in that place."

Cheap it was by Eastern standards. But it would be two more years before Gillett could lay his hands on enough cash to open a simple, frame lecture room. $6000 would soon seem to him a fortune.

Next morning Mr. Gillett made calls with Mr. Eaton on his parishioners. "Far more refinement among them than I had expected," said Mr. Gillett in a tone which New Englanders have used toward Texas ever since. "Called at the custom house and got my permit to bring off my baggage. Went to the brig after dinner and got my trunk and saddle bags."

After a Sunday in which he went to hear the Presbyterian minister preach in the morning and preached in the Presbyterian meeting house "to a large and attentive audience" in the evening, he prepared for his journey to Houston.

By leaving Galveston at 4 in the afternoon, he arrived early in the morning at Houston. "Met by Mr. Perkins at the boat. Took leave of Mr. Cruger and Mr. Smith, two gentlemen to whom I had been introduced on board. Mr. Ruthven met me near the boat." Here were his two wardens who would serve on every vestry during his stay in Houston and at one time catch him between them in a prolonged and tedious squabble.

Before the week was out, Mr. Gillett had preached twice on Sunday "in the Presbyterian house of worship." He had a smaller crowd the following Sunday—"It was not generally known that I was to preach"—but now was sufficiently settled to start in on his pastoral calls.

"Monday. Went at night to visit some poor people, who are much attached to the church, being communicants. A poor man, who lives by his daily labor, said he wanted to sell two cows to help build the church, that he would consider that finishing his own house."

In a report to the Foreign Committee of the Board of Missions, Mr. Gillett described this incident more fully:

"I called some time since to see a poor man belonging to our communion. He has been struggling hard with the adverse times, and had at length succeeded in erecting the frame of a house containing only one room, and covering it, but had not been able to lay a floor. In this he lived with his wife and two little orphan girls he had undertaken to raise. He inquired of me if we intended building a Church?

"I told him we hoped to erect a lecture room soon.

"Said he, 'I have two cows I want to give you to help do it. It is true I have not been able to complete my own house yet, but *that* (meaning the Church) will be my house too, for I shall be there one-seventh part of my time.'

"I thought if some of our rich brethren could have *heard* this poor man's

simple remarks (for they lose all their power by being repeated or put on paper) they would have said to him 'You have enough to do to provide for your wife and those orphan children; keep your cows and we will build your chapel.' This man is always at Church, and though he cannot read, he has learned most of the responsive part of the Liturgy by hearing it."

At the time Mr. Gillett paid this call, which so moved him that he remembered it and referred to it in later years, he still had no idea just how long and uphill the road ahead was.

He thought then, for instance, that his congregation owned its lot.

"Tuesday, February 21, 1843. Went with some of the congregation to plant some trees about the Church lot, hoping by and by to have a building erected," he wrote in his diary.

At this point, the Rev. Mr. Gillett becomes a maddening diarist.

Setting out on his travels with the plan of reporting to the Board of Missions on the situation in Texas, he lapses into a jotting which not only gives 20th century readers no real picture of what he saw, but which could have meant little even to him a decade later.

". . . Stop-waggons—his watch—mules—my horse poor-fretting mule-spur prairie-cranes, geese,—cold ride—stop for the night."

Or, "Went to Washington. Called on Pres. Houston and his Lady—The Gen. stature, dress—appearance—his Lady—appearance—et cetera."

Whatever his virtues—and he had many—the Rev. Mr. Gillett was not an ideal reporter from the historian's point of view.

Occasionally he returned to sentences. "Saw the comet again, for it proved to be that which I had seen on Tuesday night. The tail was long, spanning nearly a third of the heavens."

The jottings do give a picture of a vigorous young man, riding long miles by horseback in the coldest and wettest of Texas weather, enjoying the abundance of wild game he saw, doing some shooting, talking old friendships and Yale with John Wurts Cloud, marrying the first couple of his clerical career, dining at the best houses of Washington and Independence and being welcomed warmly wherever he went.

Fortunately too, he still had reports to write to the Board of Missions. The Christ Church archives would later suffer for lack of these fuller explanations once the church could pay his salary and Mr. Gillett no longer owed the board an account of his doings.

Despite Eaton's irate letter describing the freezing weather in Galveston, the *Spirit of Missions* was freshly impressed by Mr. Gillett's account:

"While reading this account of Mr. Gillett we found some of the fancies of youth about the balmy airs and perpetual summers of the South fast disappearing and we discovered that the missionaries of the cross may have fellowship with an Apostle in physical suffering even in the genial clime of sunny Texas.

"The distance to Washington is about seventy miles and the journey is generally accomplished in two days. The road lies for the most part through the level and seemingly interminable prairies, with which the country bordering on the Gulf everywhere abounds. The climate during winter is subject to sudden changes . . .

"It was the fortune of the travellers to begin their expedition at the commencement of one of these 'Northers,' as they are there styled; and the road at that season being very bad, two days and a half were required to finish the journey. The cold and piercing wind blew directly in their faces and occasioned

1843. Enraged because President John Tyler vetoed Henry Clay's bill to repeal the treasury system and increase tariffs, Whig mobs storm the White House and Whigs in Congress demand Tyler's impeachment.

them an amount of suffering not often experienced in the winters of our more rigorous latitude."

A sudden norther and heavy sleet kept Mr. Gillett from keeping his engagement to dinner at the home of President Houston.

"March 17 & 18, 1843. Journeyed from Washington to Houston—prairie set on fire—river bottom—companion Home about 1 o'clock Saturday.

"Sunday, March 19, 1843—Preached at Houston at night.

"Sunday, March 26, 1843. Preached in morning.

"Tuesday, March 28, 1843. Mr. A. left for the States. Sent some letters by him."

April 7. Gillett caught the steamer for Galveston and the re-opening of Mr. Eaton's church. There he and Caleb Ives met for the first time. These three men were the only Episcopal ministers in the entire Republic of Texas, and shared a kinship of ideal and effort which made Galveston, Matagorda and Houston seem closer together than they seem to be today.

Ives—who had also seen the comet and marveled over its beauty—wrote in his diary: "Breakfasted with Mr. Tod Robinson, who came last night to the public house and introduced himself to me and invited me to do so. Rode to Galveston with Judge Andrews . . . Found Mr. Eaton busy, getting ready to reopen the church which was blown down last fall.

"8th. Rev. Mr. Gillett arrived from Houston this morning. Have never seen him before, and I am pleased with his plainness, simplicity and apparent worth." Coming from one of the oldest, best established sections of the United States, with more formality of education than Mr. Eaton's, Gillett and Ives struck it off at once, and understood the importance of setting up some rules by which they could shape the future course of the church in Texas.

Though Eaton was not always in sympathy, and though he was preoccupied with the more urgent problems of a parish which had built not one but two churches in two years and suffered a hurricane besides, he went along with the organizers:

"Mr. Eaton, Mr. Gillett and myself, being the only clergymen of the Church in Texas (Episcopal Church) held a consultation and adopted the following preamble and resolutions, and forwarded them to the editor of the *Churchman* in New York for publication:

"At a consultation of the undersigned missionaries, holden at Galveston, Tex., April 8, 1843.

"Resolved: That all communicants of the Episcopal Church in the United States or elsewhere, who shall hereafter remove to Texas, be requested to bring satisfactory testimonials of Christian character, and that they enjoyed the confidence of their rectors, at the time of their emigration.

"We feel constrained to say that we cannot hereafter admit any emigrants to the communion without such testimonials; and that we have come to this decision for the protection and welfare of the Church in Texas; and also to save ourselves the mortification to which we have, in some instances, been already subjected."

[This was Mr. Ives's idea, and written out by him].

After taking turns preaching and reading the morning and evening services for the reopening of Mr. Eaton's church, Mr. Gillett and Mr. Ives were ready to go home—Mr. Ives by horse down Galveston Island, Mr. Gillett by steamboat. Messrs. Gillett, Eaton and Merritt rode with Mr. Ives a good six miles on his way, and then returned for Monday night services.

1843. Henry David Thoreau is jailed in Concord, Mass. for refusing to pay poll tax.

1843. The first settlement of Vancouver Island is made at Victoria.

Mr. Gillett got back to Houston by Wednesday and on Good Friday preached to an 11 o'clock service and a pretty good congregation.

Easter brought its usual large turnout. "Administered the communion to 16."

On Easter Monday, the church's annual meeting day, Mr. Gillett moved into his new room. "Ladies very kind in fitting it up. Mrs. Reily, Mrs. Ruthven, Mrs. Lemaid and Mrs. Perkins."

Mrs. Reily reassured the young rector greatly, as he confided to his diary that she led him "to hope that my preaching yesterday had some good effect."

Gillett's first wedding in Houston by his Parish Record was performed on May 27, 1843: "Thomas, a servt of Mrs. A. C. Allen to Melinda, a servt. of E. S. Perkins." This marriage was recorded by the church but does not appear in the county court house records.

The year 1843 wore on for Mr. Gillett—a month of regular services interspersed with further travels in May, this time west and south through Richmond to Matagorda.

On his journeys north, Mr. Gillett usually rode in company of friends. Indians were still unpredictable. South and west, he often went alone.

How many young men—30 years old and freshly down from Connecticut or Alexandria, Va.—would today like to set forth by horse from Houston to Matagorda if they were given no map, no marking on the roads, nobody to ask directions from for a day or more at a time, no restaurant and no guarantee of a night's lodging on the way?

Though on the first night he made Richmond and pleasant quarters, on the second day his jottings conjure up a rather lonesome little scene:

1843. The Seminole War in Florida is now in its sixth year.

"prairie—lost the way-path-monotony—Mexican Travelers-sent across the prairie—empty hovel—lonely ride—enquiries concerning the road—crossing-San Bernard-prairie." But it all ended well. "Mr. Foster's-Mrs. Foster-sociability-supper-night."

The next night he had trouble finding a place to stop and the next day he even found Mexican goats and sheep worth mentioning, but the day took him to Matagorda.

On this particular trip—which sounds so bleak—he had traveled with "two pious ladies"—Mrs. Gray and Mrs. Reily. If young Mr. Gillett's willingness to undertake such a journey is imposing, the willingness of Mrs. Gray—widowed and 43 years old—and of Mrs. Reily is even more so.

The church in Texas had brave and doughty members.

Mrs. Gray and Mrs. Reily could not, of course, do anything official at this second meeting of the three clergymen. They were—after all—not male.

"Arrived today Mr. Gillett of Houston, with no lay delegates," Mr. Ives wrote in his diary, a bit reproachfully: "to attend the primary Convention of the Church in Texas. But he was attended by two pious and respectable Ladies, Mrs. Grey (sic) and Mrs. Riley (sic)."

After morning and evening services, including morning communion, in which the three rectors alternated in reading or preaching, they and their delegates met Monday.

Mr. Ives had prepared well for the convention and was ready with a preamble and resolution drafted by himself and a young lawyer in his parish.

Despite this formal beginning, and the legal dignity of the resolutions, the convention members realized that the best they could hope to do was to agree to keep in touch by forming a "Committee of Correspondence" made up of rector and one layman from each of the three parishes.

This sounds a bit superfluous or redundant—surely they would be writing each other from time to time anyway.

But seemingly Mr. Ives alone realized the importance of making clergy and laymen aware of their own historic significance as the beginning of the Church in Texas, of stimulating their sense of responsibility in planning toward a more complete church organization which could some day become a diocese.

Mr. Gillett—while in pleasant accord with Mr. Ives—was fairly casual in his diary references, and Mr. Eaton—Mr. Ives said in his more satisfying diary—left for Galveston "much displeased with the result of the Convention."

But the Convention was graced by a lunar rainbow to mark its closing.

The Puzzle of the Lot

Chapter 12

Legend—shaped by misleading documentary evidence—has held for a century and more that the Allen brothers gave the land upon which Christ Church Cathedral now stands.

But the fact is that the Christ Church congregation paid $400 for it at $200 a parcel. And the mystery is: why did they?

As a man who had had practical experience as a vestryman in his century-old boyhood church in Virginia, Colonel Gray knew the importance of money to flourishing piety. Therefore in the same month in which he obtained 27 signatures on his agreement to unite into a congregation—March, 1839—he circulated another paper for pledges and subscriptions to the new church.

"We the undersigned severally promise to pay to John Birdsall, William Pierpont and Wm. Fairfax Gray the sums hereto respectively subscribed by us for an EPISCOPAL CHURCH in the City of Houston—

"All sums of thirty dollars and upwards to be paid in three installments at not shorter periods than one month from each payment: sums under thirty dollars to be paid on demand. The funds raised to be appropriated under the direction of the Vestry of the Church—"

The first two pledges were those of Gray and Pierpont at $100 each, the largest Birdsall's at $200.

Paradoxically—Gray got 27 joiners, but 45 contributors.

The amounts pledged were handsome ones in any day, especially those coming from men who seemingly had no intention—yet at least—of joining this proposed Protestant Episcopal Church.

Captain Moseley Baker (whose wife led the San Jacinto Cotillion with President Houston) pledged $100.

Albert Sidney Johnston (Secretary of War) pledged $50—perhaps because he was a close friend of the Grays, and frequently a boarder at their house while in Houston.

Dr. Ashbel Smith, soon to represent the Republic as Minister to France, $50.

It was more to be expected that members of the new congregation such as Gray, Pierpont, Harris and Yates should pledge such amounts.

The original subscribers on the old document in the Christ Church archives, with their names here alphabetically arranged, were: Charles William Adams, Augustus Chapman Allen, George Allen, Harvey H. Allen, Henry R. Allen, John D. Andrews, Moseley Baker, William Robinson Baker, John Beldin, John Birdsall, Asa Brigham, Thomas Jefferson Chambers, George Campbell Childress, Robert H. Chinn, James D. Cocke, G. Copeland, Jacob W. Cruger,

1843. Congress authorizes the first telegraph line. The first message is sent in 1844 from the U.S. Supreme Court room in the Capitol by the inventor, S. F. B. Morse: "What God hath wrought!"

A. Jackson Davis, Alexander Ewing, W. B. P. Gaines, William Fairfax Gray, Paget Halpen, DeWitt Clinton Harris, Hedenberg & Vedder, Matthew Hopkins, Memucan Hunt, Albert Sidney Johnston, W. Doswell Lee, James Love, Thomas Massey League & Peter Wilson, Thomas Viscount Mortimer, William Pierpont, J. B. Ransom, W. Richardson, Tod Robinson, Thomas Jefferson Rusk, Safford & Woodward, Ashbel Smith, John W. N. A. Smith, T. W. Swete, Henry Thompson, James Webb, Robert Wilson, Corodon C. Woodward, Archibald Wynns, and Andrew Janeway Yates.

The last of the four pages of the subscription list is headed "In spring of 1840" and on this sheet, H. Houghtaling's pledge of one hundred dollars is marked PAID. Also marked "Pd." is a subscription "Mrs. Cowling's (a Widow's Mite) $10."

In 1840, an additional $1,380, in Texas promissory notes, was subscribed by Charles Bigelow, John Carlos, John V. Cowling, Mrs. Cowling, Joseph C. Eldredge, Cornelius Ennis, J. B. Houghtaling, Arthur Ikin, John W. Moore, Charles A. Morris, Erastus S. Perkins, Leonard S. Perkins, J. W. Pitkin, James Reily, John Allen Southmayd, Frederick Stokes, George G. Temple, C. W. Watrous, James West, and Edward H. Winfield.

It was on the original subscription list now in the archives of Christ Church Cathedral that the famous lot offer was made:

"A. C. Allen Four Hundred dollars in Lumber ($400). Also half of Block 55 for church and school—so long as it is used for that purpose."

Augustus Allen underlined his signature with a double looped flourish.

Perhaps it was because land was so plentiful, perhaps it was because a town could be founded, could flourish and be wiped out, all within a few years as Harrisburg had been, but whatever the reason, lots and their boundary lines were handed about with remarkable casualness in this period.

For instance, the story is told that on the first San Jacinto anniversary celebration, President Houston gave a sailor a town lot simply because he managed to get the flag up the flagpole when no one else could—thereby saving the ceremony and starting the parade.

Mr. William R. Baker bought Lots No. 1 and 2 in Block 55 in 1838, only to have the map changed on him so that under the new map, Lot No. 11 claimed by Christ Church overlapped his property to the extent of a strip 25 feet by 100. Fortunately nobody noticed the discrepancy for several years, and by the time it was discovered, Mr. Baker was far too thorough-going a church member not to relinquish his claim gracefully.

In 1839, Christ Church members obviously considered half of Block 55 theirs.

Bishops, missionaries and rectors mentioned the lot possessively in letters to the *Spirit of Missions,* and church members even went to plant trees and generally to beautify their property way out on the last street at the south edge of town.

But as the years wore on through the depressed and depressing months of 1839 and on into the 1840's, the city proprietors apparently used A. C. Allen's provision ". . . so long as it is used for that purpose" . . . to tie a stronger string to the lot.

A deed of May 28, 1842, shows that James S. Holman as trustee for the Allen brothers assigned the property to the Protestant Episcopal Church for $1 and "further for the high regard and advancement of the Christian religion and particularly the Protestant Episcopal denomination . . ." with the provision that "the Rev. Benjamin Eaton, rector, and E. S. Perkins and A. S. Ruth-

1845. Laredo, Texas, is 90 years old.

ven, wardens and trustees, will build or cause to be built a good and substantial church not less than 40' by 60' on the said premises within two years from the date hereof." Otherwise this deed "will be null and void and of no effect."

Looking ahead to that implacable deadline, Mr. Gillett found himself in a town struggling up out of depression, in a congregation whose strength was constantly sapped by the removal of members to Austin or Mexico or the United States.

In the spring of 1843, he wrote to the *Spirit of Missions*:

"A lot was given to us by the City Corporation, for the erection of a church, but only on the condition it should be a substantial building 60 feet by 40, and completed by the 28th of May next. The building of such a church at this time would cost six thousand dollars—labor and material being now about half their former value. But such is the pressure here that by any effort we could make, $500 in cash could not be raised for this purpose. . . .

"What, under these circumstances, could be done, we are now trying to do. We, in the first place, secured our lot by purchase for $200; this is paid for--and the deed, made to the Rector and Wardens of the Church, put on record." Christ Church had bought its lot—after four years of "owning" it.

But this was still not the whole of the historic half block.

The credit long given to A. C. Allen might perhaps better be given to William W. Swain.

May 10, 1843 (filed May 16), Swain bought the south section of Block 55— Lots 1, 2, 3, 4 and 5 long before pledged by A. C. Allen—for $1 and the cancellation of a debt owed him by Allen. The amount of that debt is not mentioned. On the same day—but not filed until June 10—Swain deeded the same property to the Trustees of Christ Church, for $200. This was at a time when similar property in downtown Houston was selling for more.

But the church builders were not satisfied with this first purchase, and October 16, 1843, William W. Swain bought for another $200 Lots 11 and 12. End to end they form a 50-foot stripe running from Fannin to San Jacinto across the rear of the total church property Lots 1, 2, 3, 4 and 5.

It is probable that the first school building facing Fannin stood on Lot 11.

On November 10 and recorded December 6 was the next deed whereby Swain transferred these two lots to Christ Church for $200—a total of $400 spent. The fact that W. R. Baker's property claim overlay Lot 11 seemed not to have been noticed by anyone. This is odd in that W. R. Baker, as clerk of the County of Harris, notarized every one of these property deeds* from May, 1843, on through to the final quit claim he himself gave June 6, 1846.

By releasing 25 feet of Lot 11, Mr. Baker gave to Christ Church free claim to its perfect rectangle.

Trial and Setbacks

Chapter 13

Times were hard in Texas.

The currency of the Republic was greatly depreciated—thereby reducing the subscription list left by Colonel Gray to a fraction of its face meaning.

The moving of the government from Houston had left Houston business men unable to gain credit in New Orleans and the east.

---

* Long time vestryman A. S. Richardson listed these deeds in a memorandum headed "Chain of Title to the Church property" and concluded gently at the end "From the above it appears that the Church holds by purchase for consideration and not by donation from the Allens." He affixed this memorandum to the collection of deeds which he received in 1898 from W. V. R. Watson for repository in the archives.
Both the deeds and the memorandum were largely waived in favor of the flourishing legend until research on this history got under way.

The crops which failed near Matagorda and the storm so destructive to Galveston had fringe effects upon Houston.

Throughout Texas generally, the panic which had begun in 1837 continued ruthlessly until annexation, reaching its worst in 1841.

Though Mr. Gillett seemed never quite to find in Houston the acute poverty which Eaton noticed on his arrival in Galveston, nor conclude at one point that he should have to send his family home to New England for lack of food supplies in the community, as Mr. Ives once did, still he found that it was exceedingly hard to get enough small amounts of money together to accomplish something permanent.

First had come the fear of losing the lot which had been given the church with the $1 deed by the town proprietors.

Mr. Gillett expressed that fear candidly in his account of the transaction written to the Foreign Committee.

"From the little experience I had in trying to raise a small amount for the completion of Mr. Eaton's church at Galveston, I was fully convinced that but very little could be done towards raising the required amount of means in the United States.

"What under these circumstances could be done, we are now trying to do. We, in the first place, secured our lot by purchase for $200.

"This is paid for—and the deed made to the Rector and Wardens of the Church, put on record."

The words ring with a sort of dogged satisfaction. Mr. Gillett had managed to buy and secure the first church property of his career in the church.

"We next determined on building a lecture room or chapel, large enough to hold 200 or 250 persons; this will accommodate our present congregation, and probably for some time to come. It will be a building some 40 by 25 feet." He must have planned standing room only.

"We have on our subscription which we can depend upon near $800; this by good management, we hope will be sufficient to put up the frame and cover it, and if we have means to do no more, we shall stop there and worship in it, in that state, as we are determined on no account to be in debt."

As the letter went on—expressing the hope that Episcopalians from the U. S. could find it in their hearts to help—Mr. Gillett confessed that of the $800 subscribed, "perhaps we cannot rely upon $200 in cash—the rest must be in lumber, labor and orders on stores."

This did not mean, he was quick to add, that Houstonians were not generous and willing. "The friends of the Church in this place are disposed to do all in their power, but the difficulty of raising means at this time can scarcely be imagined by those abroad.

"It is a difficult matter for some gentleman here (who would be accounted rich if lands were worth but a small price per acre) to get money enough to pay their taxes and do their marketing. We might have any amount of land subscribed [except for that precious downtown site] but we could make no use of it, as we could neither work it in as material for the building, nor make it turn to support labourers.

"Our present number of communicants is fifteen, and our usual congregation from 150 to 200." This, as Gillett said, included the usual meeting with Presbyterians "and at present it would be impossible to say what our congregation would be, if we had a place to assemble in by ourselves, though I think larger than any other congregation in town."

1844. The Jewish Cemetery is opened in Houston.

Taking this estimate, one could—in a generous mood—allow the Presbyterians 75 and the Episcopalians 85, or,—more pessimistically—decide that Mr. Gillett had on a good Sunday no more than 60 or 70 in his Episcopal fold.

"I have baptized five children during my residence here, married three couples—one of them colored—and was called to attend one funeral, so that all the baptisms performed by me in the country are seven, the marriages four."

This was written in 1843—July.

The removal of the government was not a total loss. Though it took with it attorneys general, secretarys of war and navy, and British consuls, it also took with it some of the speculative gamblers, land grabbers, and hangers-on.

Among Gillett's stalwarts at this time were James Reily, now in middle age; Peter W. Gray, 23 or 24 but not yet confirmed for lack of a visiting bishop; Erastus S. Perkins and Archibald St. Clair Ruthven, well established business men—even though they couldn't get along with each other.

Though Tod Robinson, 31,—with his obvious eagerness to make friends with Caleb Ives on the Matagorda trip—was still interested in the church, he was first off on the expedition against Vasquez and later moved to Brazoria. George Patrick had moved to Grimes County. James Webb followed the government to Austin. Memucan Hunt, now 36, continued to take part in church affairs whenever he was in town, but he was often away on prolonged missions for the republic. D. W. C. Harris, not yet 30, was a busy Houstonian.

Mayor Andrews, Cornelius Ennis, Reily and Gray were by 1842 in Houston to stay. Or were at least legal residents.

Born in Ohio and raised in Kentucky, James Reily had married Ellen Hart Ross, the grand niece of Henry Clay's wife, shortly before coming to Texas in about 1836 or 1837.

In 1839, Mirabeau B. Lamar had appointed Reily commissioner to negotiate for the sale of $1-million worth of Texas government bonds, and in 1841, President Sam Houston sent him to Washington as charge d'affaires to the United States.

With Reily representing Texas and Daniel Webster the United States, the Treaty of Amity and Commerce and Navigation between the United States and Texas was signed, but the U.S. Senate failed to ratify.

Reily opposed annexation, and after two leaves of absence in service of the republic came back to Houston thinking to stay. As a practicing attorney, he was one of Gillett's strongest and most generous vestrymen throughout most of the 1840's and 50's.

(Later he would be sent to St. Petersburg by U. S. President Buchanan, and later still would go off to the Civil War and fight for the Confederacy.)

Though still making trips to survey Texas for the Board of Missions, Mr. Gillett was settling more and more into the Christ Church cure.

The vestry meeting of June, 1844, at the house of E. S. Perkins, set up a building committee of Perkins, W. W. Swain and Thomas N. League; appointed A. S. Ruthven treasurer and H. F. Gillett corresponding secretary.

Mr. League—from Baltimore—was one of Houston's first settlers. He had come in 1836, brought his family out three years later, and was a merchant. In 1839 he was postmaster of Houston, and a year later a charter member of the Chamber of Commerce. Christ Church could see in the first Chamber of Commerce a number of its own first subscribers—all merchants: William D. Lee, Charles J. Hedenburg, John W. Pitkin, Charles Kesler, E. S. Perkins,

Henry R. Allen, and DeWitt Clinton Harris.

Though Mr. League had been one of the original subscribers to the proposed Episcopal Church in 1839, it was a year after his election to the vestry that he and his wife were baptized by Gillett and confirmed by Bishop Freeman. League continued as a member of the Christ Church vestry until 1846, but he had begun doing business in Galveston by 1842 and became one of the many transfers back and forth—laymen and clergy—between Eaton's Trinity Church and Christ Church, Houston.

The year 1843 had been a long one for one so young and busy as Mr. Gillett.

He and Mr. Eaton got together to urge parochial schools upon the Foreign Committee as well as upon their congregations. And Mr. Ives was asking for a few prayer books in German and French.

Bishop Polk came back for another visit—a year and a month after Mr. Gillett's arrival—and had the usual beneficial, reassuring and stimulating effect.

Vast and powerful whether as West Point cadet, Episcopal bishop, or Confederate general, Leonidas Polk seemed far more suited physically to the rigorous life of missionary bishop than either Bishop Freeman or Bishop Gregg who came after him.

All these gentlemen rode by horse, stagecoach, gig and wagon, thousands upon thousands of miles in every conceivable kind of weather, over every conceivable kind of road and trail, seeking always to find new potential sites for missions for the church and to strengthen the hand of missionaries already on duty. It was the custom for two local rectors to escort the bishop wherever possible, accompanying him in a system of relays.

After confirming 13 in Christ Church—"all except one are heads of families"—Bishop Polk set out for Matagorda accompanied by Gillett.

"The poetry of Missionary life consists in sitting quietly at home and talking and writing about it," Mr. Gillett wrote the Foreign Committee. "For when it comes to the real plain matter of fact, the romance vanishes.

"We were four days in performing our journey.

"The first during a very hard rain, and for the three following we found the prairies so covered with water and the creeks so swollen, that we were kept constantly wet, sometimes swimming our horses, at others riding with the water half-way up our saddle-skirts. We were obliged to sleep out one night in the prairie—or rather stay out, for there was not much sleep."

Cold and flood Bishop Polk could take. But the summer sun on the prairie was more than even he could bear. Once he came close to sunstroke. And so warned, he abandoned one prairie section of a trip which would have taken place in late July and early August. Sensibly he left the tropical sun for mad dogs and Englishmen.

Because Mr. Gillett knew how hard it was to raise money in the United States from his pre-Texas experience in behalf of Mr. Eaton, he was reluctant to undertake a begging mission back home. Because to the congregation of Christ Church, the $1,000 American dollars he had raised must have looked enormous, they urged it. And Bishop Polk concurred in the urging.

Against his better judgment, therefore, Mr. Gillett decided to go East—and then stated his rationalization for so doing in firm terms to the Foreign Committee: "When I came here," he wrote, "it was with the determination never to leave for the purpose of raising funds abroad for building a Church.

"From this resolution I should not depart, if things were at all, here, as they are in the United States—*even in the frontier and newly settled states*—but

1844. Sarah Bernhardt is born.

52

it is entirely different. In addition to all that men have to struggle with in settling a new country, we have had here, from the very commencement, continued 'wars and rumors of wars.'

"Not only the National Treasury has been exhausted, but individual property has been so far appropriated to public use that no man of any considerable means can be found in the country, unless wild lands may be accounted means, which certainly would not avail in erecting a Church."

He hated to leave. In the afterglow of the Bishop's visit, "a deep seriousness" pervaded the community. He could count 33 communicants and others expressing interest in becoming so. "Had we a permanent place of assembling, so that I might be with them during the summer, I have reason to believe that it would please God to add more . . . But as it now is, we are liable at any time to be called upon to give up our place of assembling."

Though he could not afford to lay a cornerstone for his building, he was still doggedly intent on building a school as well as a church—in keeping with the feeling he shared with Mr. Eaton that a parochial school was essential to the health and growth of the church membership. Ives, they felt, had proved the point in Matagorda.

Gillett spent the summer in 1844 in the East urging Americans to contribute money toward his mission church in Houston—but it was spring of 1845 before he reported on his trip to the Foreign Committee.

He had come home disappointed.

Meanwhile, Leonidas Polk, missionary bishop of the Southwest from 1838 to 1841, had become Bishop of Louisiana. And October, 1844, George Washington Freeman became missionary bishop of the Southwest.

For his first official visit to Houston, he arrived on Good Friday of 1845, the 21st of March. It was so rainy and muddy that Easter Sunday service— with the bishop assisted by Gillett—had to be held in a private house, attended only by those communicants who lived closest by. But with their continuous and unfailing kindness, the Presbyterians offered their church for the evening service and a large congregation came.

Monday night the bishop confirmed seven, among them Vestryman League and his wife, and was preparing on Tuesday to leave "but was detained, and two more, who were desirous of being confirmed, were added to the number, making nine." These last two were Mr. and Mrs. Peter W. Gray—vestryman and wife. They were confirmed at the home of Mr. Nichols. (Mr. Nichol's wife was Margaret Stone, Millie Gray's young kinswoman who had come down from Fredericksburg with the Grays.)

Jane Gray had come to Houston in 1842 as a young woman of 22. She was a Presbyterian who carefully moved her membership to the Houston Presbyterian Church when she came. But after marrying Peter Gray in 1844, she interested herself in the Episcopal Church and became a churchwoman of unusual interest, effort and generosity. In her quiet way, Jane Gray added as much to the Gray family tradition of service to Christ Church as any other member—and the day would come when her final thought of the church kept it from going under.

Having stayed over, the bishop held another evening service on short notice, and "by ringing a small bell," they gathered a good sized congregation. On Easter Monday of the bishop's stay, the congregation met in the office of W. W. Swain and elected E. S. Perkins and H. F. Gillett wardens.

New members to the vestry were William Marsh Rice and E. B. Nichols—

1844. Joseph Smith, Mormon leader, is killed by a mob in Carthage, Illinois.

1845. Withdrawing from the General Missionary Convention over the issue of slavery, the Southern Baptist Convention is organized.

both young men, already partners in the wholesale business which was to make them both rich.

Nichols had been a broker in New York City until in 1833 he let himself be persuaded by his brother-in-law, Abner Cooke, to come to Texas with a cargo of lumber. He soon got into the fighting against Indians and Mexicans, moving up from lieutenant to major in the process, and settled in Houston in 1838. Here he met and married Margaret Stone.

On this Easter Monday, 1845, the vestry accomplished the first major business it had accomplished in years: it adopted a constitution.

Resolving that this church shall be known by the name Christ Church, Houston, it went on to establish a vestry of 12 chosen from pew holders and to be elected by "resident male members of the congregation who are pew-holders on EASTER MONDAY or as near that time as convenient notice of said election being previously given by the Rector."

It also provided that the senior warden should be appointed by the rector, the junior warden, secretary and treasurer to be elected by the vestry.

There is something a bit tragi-comic about a church constitution based on pew holders for a congregation which had no pews nor even a temporary meeting house. But the building committee was given authority to build at their discretion—a euphemistic phrase.

Freeman found 40 communicants and 50 families in the congregation, and told the Foreign Committee that if somebody in the United States would send down about $1500, Christ Church could build a church. With a building of their own, he added pointedly, he thought the church would soon be able to support their minister without further aid from Missionary funds.

1845. Texas votes for annexation to the United States July 4, is admitted to union December 29.

The Bishop's visit had the usual salutary effect.

Mr. Gillett, who had taken a real beating in spirit in the United States, at last in April wrote his account of that visit to the Foreign Committee in tones which showed nine months of stored up outrage:

"Wherever I was permitted—to make known our wants, there seemed to be a generous sympathy enlisted," he wrote. . . . "Yet I found very many of our brethren of the clergy unwilling that the matter should be mentioned to their congregations at all. . . .

". . . I was sometimes pained and grieved beyond measure to find some of my clerical brethren, who placed over large and flourishing congregations, had never known what it was to want, either personally, or in any arrangement connected with their stated seasons of public worship, and who consequently could know nothing either of the *wants* or the *trials* of Missionary life, inveighing against such of their brethren as placed on the outposts, felt themselves called upon to make an effort to sustain and comfort their feeble parishes, by asking aid from those to whom God has given an abundance."

With several additional pages of reference to those who are not—after all— "calculating men of the world" but instead "profess to be regulating their lives by the precepts of Him who was meek and lonely, and who taught his followers daily self denial . . . that it was 'more blessed to give than to receive,' that 'whosoever giveth to the poor, lendeth to the Lord'—I say," Mr. Gillett continued, pausing only for breath, "among such I had expected to meet only with sympathy . . ."

And among some, he granted, he did meet sympathy.

"After all my efforts, I returned here having about $1200 to commence a church; some of this I brought with me, and some of it I left to be sent to the

Foreign Committee—the greater part of which I have not yet seen acknowledged." [The *Spirit of Missions* comments "Because not received."]

Coming home, with perhaps $600 in his pocket, Mr. Gillett found that a building which had been built for a city school some years before was up for sale. As one who had wanted from the first to start a parochial school, and who would keep on founding schools with a liberal hand for the rest of his life, Mr. Gillett found that second-hand school house irresistible.

"As we had no place for worship, the thought struck me that we might purchase it for a small amount, repair it for a place in which to hold service for the present, and eventually make it a school house."

They bought the school, moved it on to the property, fitted it up, and in late April, 1845, at last had a Sunday service in a room of their own possession. The whole project had cost about $500.

Ironically, the *Spirit of Missions* in this period ran a drawing of a handsome, big, sturdy log church—built on an octagonal plan—which its architect said could be built for about $500.

That it was possible in Houston to build log cabins, log hotels and log stores, but not possible—at any time between 1839 and 1845 to build a log church—was a paradox repeated by many missionaries of many different denominations. But none of them explained why.

The frame school building "was very much crowded," Gillett confessed, "and I fear will hardly accommodate an ordinary congregation.

"The $500 expended on this building is from the money collected by me while in the United States. My hope is to be able to replace this money before we complete our church which we shall soon commence.

"Under the circumstances, I did not see how we could do better."

This frame building was never considered by anyone a church—but rather a lecture room to become school room. It was never consecrated.

2 The first brick church, the ladies
sewing circle, and gentlemen's disagreement. 1845-1855.

The First Brick Church

Some men were clearing ground, surveying and laying out plans on the lot at the corner of Texas Avenue and Fannin Street one day, when a cattleman on horseback rode along Texas Avenue—herding before him his cattle. He paused and watched.

"What are you doing?" he finally asked.

They explained that they were getting ready to build a church.

The cattleman took his lariat from his saddle, roped a steer, pulled it in, and handed the rope to one of the churchmen.

"Here," he said. "Let me give you the first contribution toward your church."*

This story has been handed down since some shadowy beginning of Christ Church time, and came into this century when it was told to Ingham S. Roberts, lifelong Christ Church member and collector of church history, by the Rt. Rev. Charles M. Beckwith, when he stopped in Houston briefly in 1926. Bishop Beckwith said he had been told the story while rector of the church (1887-1892) by A. S. Richardson—vestryman from 1857 to 1899.

There is reason to believe that the story is true, but there is no record to show which church building was being laid out. The first church was started in 1845. The school house was moved to the back of the property, and the church was planned to face Fannin Street. Fannin Street at the time was a dusty or muddy street without gutters or sidewalks, and the settled part of the town stopped at about Texas Avenue. Most of the communicants of Christ Church lived between the church and the bayou—some in houses facing Court House Square, some along Prairie or Preston or Congress within the first few blocks off Main Street. The parishioner who lived on several acres of land near the present City Hall was a poor man living on the outskirts of town where land was cheaper.

In August, 1845, Mr. Gillett wrote to the Foreign Committee: "The brick for our church is now being hauled upon the ground. We shall go on with it until our means fail. I fear that we shall be in the condition of the man in the gospel, who undertook to build, but was not able to finish, not because we have not counted the cost, but because some of our good friends upon whom we had relied for help, have failed us . . . If the work fails in part or altogether, I have the satisfaction to know that it will not be because I have made no exertion."

Mr. Gillett had apparently worked too long and achieved too little at this point to have much heart left. He makes no reference to the building of this church in his diary, and tacked this information onto a letter on many subjects which began "There is no marked difference in my own congregation worthy of mentioning."

At the time—his diary shows—he was in the first of the annoying conferences trying to make peace between Mr. and Mrs. Perkins and Mr. Ruthven, and while he ignores every major event of his life from 1845 to 1849, he devotes pages to detailed reports on a four-year dispute over what he said, what she said, what he said to her, and what she said which was not true. Yet in 1846, Mr. Gillett again appointed Mr. Perkins senior warden.

In this interval—while the church building grew so slowly and painfully —the Republic of Texas had ceased to exist and Texas had become a state in the United States. Though members of the vestry and church were

*The steer's head on the Diocesan Seal commemorates this gift.

1846. James K. Polk sends General Zachary Taylor to seize disputed land settled by Mexicans in Texas.

keenly interested in this transition for reasons of business, ideology or politics, though some opposed annexation and some supported it keenly as active participants in international affairs between their republic and the United States, there is no reflection of this historic event either in Charles Gillett's diary or in the vestry minutes of the church.

With a livelier sense of history, Caleb Ives wrote in his diary: "Used the *collect for the President of the United States for the first time today.*" And on March 21st "Had today a second mail for this week. Our mails have now come into the hands of the United States government, and we are hereafter to have two mails a week." Presumably Mr. Gillett was experiencing the same changes, but perhaps when you're meeting in a borrowed meeting house, it's harder to feel historic.

At the June meeting, the building committee's report was approved. The vestry expressed itself fully satisfied "that the committee have fully expended the amount raised by them ($4,966.52) in the erection of the Church, and that there was another $1,600 to $2,000 needed to complete the church according to the original plans."

At this belated point, the vestry suddenly realized or discovered that they were building a church on land—or at least had placed their school house on land—which belonged—or might belong—to someone else. Ruthven, Perkins and Gray were appointed to call upon William R. Baker—their fellow churchman—and see if he would be willing to relinquish his claim. And Mr. Gillett volunteered to find 10 persons to give $100 each toward completion of the church.

For once, both committee and rector were successful: On June 27, 1846, Peter Gray reported that "on examination it appears that Mr. Baker in 1838 purchased from the town proprietors Lots Nos. 1 and 2 in Block No. 55—as designated on the original map of the city made by the Messrs. Borden by which map the lots had a depth of 125 feet back from the street. That afterwards the Town Proprietors changed the plan of that part of the city by laying off in Block No. 55 new lots of which the lots Nos 11 & 12 known as Key Lots were a part. That by this change, Lot No. 11 on the map now used overlapped on Lots Nos. 1 & 2 to the extent of 25 feet by 100 feet or more than half of Lot No. 11. That Lots Nos. 11 & 12 were conveyed by the Town Proprietors to Mr. Swain (under whom the Church now claims) according to the map last referred to and hence a conflict arises between the church claims and the above one of Mr. Baker." Mr. Baker, who had been a Christ Church member for some time now, "cheerfully and liberally agreed to release his claim by way of donation to the church," and the committee submitted the deed of release. Later the church gave Mr. Baker his pew rent free for quite some time in gratitude.

The building committee said they had plans for completing the belfry and parts of the interior of the church, Mr. Gillett said he had raised the $1,000 he had volunteered to raise, the vestry voted for the building committee to let a contract at the best terms they could get. And on this cheerful note, the meeting adjourned.

Despite the dirth of description, a picture begins to gather of that first church: It faced Fannin. It was of brick [brick given by Marian Roberts Dancy's great-grandmother Mrs. Philip Roberts]. It had a belfry. It had doors to its pews. It had a gallery. And before it was completed, it had amber glass, painted amber perhaps, in the windows and a melodeon which cost $150. The subscription for the melodeon at $5 to $20 amounts —the $20 was from E. B. Nichols, $10 each from the rector and such faithfuls as Gray, Andrews, Van Alstyne, Ruthven, Mrs. Reily and William Marsh Rice—is not dated. Also the church had a bell from New York— "from the exertions of the rector." Vestryman J. W. Cruger was appointed to have it hung.

In addition, it had a Sunday school of some 40 to 50 children in regular attendance, and by 1845, Gillett had instituted regular services for the Negroes every Sunday afternoon. "I am endeavoring to teach them by repeating and making them repeat after me. I have in regular attendance from 25 to 30. They have already learned the Lord's Prayer, several hymns and have nearly completed the Ten Commandments. My wish is to have an oversight of all the servants connected with the families of my congregation." But in December, 1846, the church was still not finished and $600 was needed. As chairman of the committee to raise it, James Reily settled the matter simply by taking out a loan, guaranteed by his own signature, with the understanding that when it was paid back, $50 should be deducted as his share of the donations. The vestry accepted this action and resolved to pay up.

Perkins, Nichols and Cooke were asked to draw a plan for the pews to be rented. By their plan of April 9, 1847, the church is shown to have a narrow vestibule across the rear and three banks of pews extending from vestibule to chancel—the central bank more than twice as wide as the two side banks but with a line drawn down the middle which divided each wide center pew into two sections to be rented separately. The back two rows, or eight pews, were *free*. The four front row pews would rent for $20 each; the next four for $25, the next 20 for $30, the next 8 for $25 each, the next four for $20, the next 8 for $15 and the final-but-not-free ones for $10 each a year. The pews were to be put up at public auction April 17, 1847. And they would bring in $1,220 a year. It seemed such a lovely plan.

By May 3, the vestry was in a hassle with the carpenter, Mr. Henry. He had contracted to do the interior finishing for $763, and now was charging $533 extra. The vestry offered $350. Mr. Henry was adamant. The vestry expressed itself in some indignation in the minutes. "We have no doubt that Mr. Henry ought not to have the amount asked by him."

Finally, triumphantly, in May, 1847, Christ Church, Houston, was completed. Leaving Mr. Henry's settlement to the future, the vestry drew up a deed of donation, engrossed on parchment, requesting the Rt. Rev. George W. Freeman to consecrate the new brick church. Bishop Freeman arrived with Eaton on May 3, and held services Wednesday, Thursday, Friday and Saturday nights. And on Sunday morning, May 9, the bishop—attended by the Rev. Mr. Ives, the Rev. Mr. Eaton and the Rev. Mr. Gillett "all in their surplices"—consecrated the new church by the name of Christ Church. Mr. Gillett read the instrument of endowment, Mr. Eaton the sentence of consecration, Mr. Ives Morning Prayer and the Litany. Sunday evening the bishop confirmed 31 persons, and on Monday night four more—35 new communicants on opening day.

Newly consecrated—Christ Church was already outgrown. And this was to be its somewhat difficult history: each church built was outgrown before completion until the final church of 1893. These poor rectors and vestrymen were experiencing in the 19th century the futility of trying to raise

1847. Brigham Young and Mormons reach Great Salt Lake.

standards of living in competition with a population explosion. Bishop Freeman wrote to the Foreign Committee "The new church at Houston, which has just been consecrated, is found too small, by at least, one half —the congregation having rapidly increased during the progress of building, and it must soon be enlarged."

He added euphemistically: "At Galveston and Houston, but recently Missionary stations, the Rectors are now supported comfortably by the people whom they minister, receiving a salary of $1200 each." That must have lifted a few eyebrows in Houston: those of Mr. Gillett, who had not been paid anything by anybody for a year, and those of the vestry which had only got around to offering him $1,000 per annum four days before the church was consecrated.

On this one major loop of his huge southwest missionary diocese of the southwest, Bishop Freeman traveled 665 miles by land, 6,530 miles by water —7,195 miles. In the light of all this—from winter travel escorting a bishop, to non-payment of salary and carpenter's law suits—it is somehow amusing to read Mr. Gillett's quite sincere letter to the Foreign Committee in which he urged that the church in the United States might make up its lack of missionaries in Texas by sending out the invalids.

This seemed to him, he wrote, a field "where many of our invalid and suffering brethren of the North would reap incalculable benefit from the climate. I know there are many clergymen who are in some cases entirely disabled, and kept from the performance of ministerial duty, by weak and infirm health; and I am perfectly satisfied that such individuals in this climate would recover their energies and be saved from a premature grave . . . they would rarely be subjected to fevers . . . I mention these things, hoping they may be inducements for those of our brethren of weak and consumptive habits, to examine, in selecting their field of labor, and see whether by giving them such a constitution, God has not given them a hint at where the path of duty lies." Mr. Gillett had apparently become a Texan. But forewarned by his earlier descriptions of northers, floods and Indians, surely the weak and infirm clergy decided that in giving them such a constitution, God wanted to call them unto Himself quickly and peacefully from their own homes.

Rector and Vestry

The vestry had been in session at Colonel Reily's when Bishop Freeman arrived in Houston. Notified in mid-meeting of the bishop's arrival, the Rev. Mr. Gillett excused himself, and leaving Colonel Reily's, went immediately around to Mr. Nichols' to see the Bishop. Given this opportunity, the vestry resolved to ask Mr. Gillett to continue his services as rector "which have been invaluable to our community since his coming among us," and further that "the sum of $1,000 be tendered as the sum which the church is able to afford him as the least which his labors are worth," payable quarterly, beginning with Easter Monday last. Immediately after the consecration, Bishop Freeman left to continue his visitation to Texas, escorted by Mr. Gillett.

Perhaps keyed up by the successful completion of the church, Mr. Gillett was now intense in urging that all the Texas churchmen meet during the bishop's visitation to consider forming a diocese. But in the general excitement, he never had time to explain his reasons to his vestry. While he rode trustingly from town to town with the bishop, therefore, the vestry met,

1847. Napoleon's widow, Maria Louisa, dies.

Chapter 15

dutifully elected delegates to attend a "convention of the churches in the state" as Mr. Gillett had left instructions for them to do. They elected Perkins, Andrews, J. D. Groesbeeck, C. Ennis, from the vestry; and James Reily and John P. Conger from the congregation.

Then, with the most honorable of intent they instructed their delegates to oppose the formation of a separate Diocese at this point, "it being in our opinion premature and in the present state of the church in Texas involving too much expense to pay a Bishop." With their brand new church already outgrown and a new one to be built before the pains of building the first one had eased, with a promise to pay the rector $1,000 a year and a carpenter already demanding that much for his unsettled bill, they acted with what they thought was simple gumption. And they got thoroughly chastised by their rector.

Called on the carpet June 1 at the office of Rice and Nichols, the vestrymen were presented with a letter by their rector, who then left them to read it and repent: "I have been grieved and mortified at the result of the late attempt to organize the church in this state, which result was brought about by the course pursued by the delegates from this place, who declared themselves bound to act in accordance with previous instructions given them by the Vestry. I am aware that in political gatherings, and in civil legislation, the right of instruction is claimed, and often acted upon; but such a thing in the church, I believe altogether unheard of; and I therefore more deeply regret that so unhappy a mistake should first have been made by us."

Granting that the vestry may have been laboring under misapprehension, Gillett then explained that they could organize a diocese in one of four ways: 1. They could elect a bishop, and ask the General Convention's approval, and the House of Bishops to consecrate. 2. They could organize and leave it to a standing committee to invite a bishop to come on visitation whenever necessary, paying his expenses of travel. 3. They might, after organization, place the diocese, under the jurisdiction of any bishop, giving him full control of the diocese, but again paying for his visitations, or 4. They might organize, and then place the diocese under the supervision of a missionary bishop, asking the Missionary Society to continue to pay the expenses of episcopal supervision until the diocese wished to take on greater responsibility.

It was this last which Gillett had proposed at Galveston—expecting that a diocese would be organized and Bishop Freeman would continue as their missionary bishop. The vote of the lay delegation to Galveston, Gillett felt, had swung the convention to its decision not to organize a diocese just yet.

Mr. Gillett was upset. His letter, which went on into four full pages in which the words *grieved and mortified* were frequent and underlined, concluded "The evil, which in my judgment has been thus brought upon the church in this State, cannot now be remedied." But it would help, he added, if the vestry would send resolutions to each of the other parishes in the state explaining that they had acted under misinformation. "This would in a measure, relieve me from the mortification and embarrassment of having been so openly and decidedly opposed at our late Convention called *principally,* perhaps *entirely* through my instrumentality." The vestry quickly passed the required resolutions and in the fastest action of its history, mailed them off to the other churches—to the bishop and to the rector—thereby giving the secretary, W. J. Hutchins, many a long letter to write.

It is hard to say whether it would have soothed Mr. Gillett, or affronted him, to know how casually everyone else had taken the whole business.

1847. The Mexican War continues. General Winfield Scott takes Vera Cruz with 12,000 troops March 27, captures Santa Anna September 17.

Bishop Freeman wrote of this meeting: "In the afternoon was held a meeting of the clergy and laity from four parishes, called at the earnest solicitation of one of the clergy, and by advice of the Bishop, for the purpose of considering the expediency of organizing the Church in Texas into a Diocese. The organization was opposed on the ground that it might involve the parishes in an expense which they were not able to bear, and was decided against by the non-concurrence of the two orders, one of the clergy voting in the negative, and the delegations from the parishes being divided."

Mr. Ives, who had from the beginning projected the idea of forming a diocese whenever it should become practical, wrote calmly in his diary "The organization of a Diocese was thought inexpedient by so many that the measure was not carried."

June, 1847, was a difficult month for rector and vestry. Three weeks after receiving their humbly worded apology and expression of devotion to himself and to Bishop Freeman, Mr. Gillett addressed the vestry again in stern tone:

"June 21: The Copy of a resolution of your honorable body was transmitted to me through your Secy. sometimes since, requesting me to continue my labors among you and also stating your Treasurer should pay me one thousand dollars in quarterly payments, commencing from Easter Monday. I had supposed from the tenor of the resolution . . . that it was the intention this payment should be made quarterly in advance. The first quarter is now about expiring, and yet your treasurer has no funds in his hands, wherewith to comply with . . . sd. resolution. I am therefore under the painful necessity of stating to the vestry things which I had hoped not to mention.

"... for the first three years of my labors among you, I received a Salary from the Foreign Board of Missions in the U. S. and . . . during the last year I have received nothing from that quarter. I have therefore been under the necessity of borrowing and paying interest upon money to meet my necessary expenses. A portion of this money is borrowed. I am now called upon to refund (at a season somewhat earlier than I had anticipated) and am compelled to raise within five days, a sum of not less than one hundred and seventy five dollars. Fifty dollars of this amount I borrowed about one year since to defray expenses while attempting to collect funds for this church in Louisiana.

"I am sorry to feel myself compelled to make these statements of my personal affairs to the vestry . . . But having been obliged to do it, I must beg an immediate answer."

The vestry promptly resolved that Peter W. Gray be appointed and Colonel Reily requested to act as a committee to raise $200, adding dubiously "or if that amount cannot be had, such sum less than that amount as can be procured, by subscription, or as a loan on four or six months." They agreed that they *had* meant for payments to be *due* at the beginning of each quarter, but again showed a lack of hope that they'd make it: "and will be paid at such time during the quarter as the same can be collected from pew rents."

Already the pew rents were proving themselves not the happily envisioned $1,220 a year, but rather an uncertain source of uncertain amounts of income. But the vestry and congregation held on to the pew rent system with unflagging optimism until well into the 20th century. Mr. Gray and Colonel Reily found it impossible to raise more than a few dollars by subscription, and therefore procured a loan of $100—a third each from Messrs. Perkins, Reily and Gray. This was the kind of generosity which was to bail Christ Church out many times in the coming century. Being a vestryman meant digging into your own pocket to provide the necessities or to save the church from embarrassment.

But the $100 still left Mr. Gillett $75 short, and nothing to go on for his current living expenses. By the end of July, Mr. Gillett had to write to the vestry again—a letter running to three long, closely written pages, sometimes repetitious, but of unmistakable sincerity. He had used the $100, he explained, to pay half his debts and get a 15-day extension on the remainder, "with the *assurance* as I supposed, that as a quarterly pew rents became due on the 4th, the money should be at once collected and laid over without fail. With this assurance, I promised others to raise money. When the 15th came, no notice was given me of my money being ready. Not wishing myself to become a 'dun' I waited until the 21st or 22nd of the month; still hearing nothing, I went to the treasurer (who informed me there was nothing in the treasury)— this evening of the 28th of the month he has sent me the sum of $20.—

"Now gentlemen," said Mr. Gillett in exasperation, "I am not disposed to find fault, but there seems to me something wrong in this whole matter. If the vestry could not raise the money as promised, it was at least proper and right that due notice should have been given me, that I might have had sufficient time to relieve myself from embarrassment by borrowing from some other source yet up to this moment, 13 days after the time specified, all the notice I have received is the small sum of $20, just sent me.

"I do not pursue this subject," said Mr. Gillett, pursuing it for another two and a quarter pages, "You are all of you business men enough to understand whether such things are right or just in any sense of the word." Mr. Gillett explained that he had other debts besides those being pressed for payment, including overdue accounts at Houston stores, and that if payed, he would willingly bear his share of church obligations. But if all pew rents were going to pay church debts and none to him, he could not be content.

"I have never shrunk from bearing with you the burdens . . . of a new parish and the erection of our church Edifice. We have been embarrassed, and are still, to some extent. And . . . I will willingly become one of 20, or 15 or even 10 to discharge at once all the liabilities of the church. But I cannot consent to take the whole burden upon my own shoulders, which is to all intents and purposes the case, so long as all the pew rents are applied to liquidating the church debt, and no other provision made for quarterly payments to myself."

Calling for a distinct understanding of where he stood, Mr. Gillett concluded "Gentlemen, if you want a clergyman to labor efficiently among you, you must supply his necessities, so that the fear of want may not prevent his turning his mind from the duties of his profession. You must *at least see* that he is paid *promptly* and punctually what you agree to give him." This was Mr. Gillett's first parish and he this church's first full time rector. Like the young father of a first-born son, he felt his duty to teach his vestry how to behave properly. "I trust, gentlemen, you will at once arrange this whole business, so as to prevent my ever referring to *this,* to me very disagreeable subject again. Your *immediate* action upon or neglect of this communication will *speedily* determine my course of action for the future."

William Marsh Rice moved that a committee be appointed to solicit donations to pay the rector's salary, and if possible the church debts as well. Rice and Andrews were appointed from the vestry, and John P. Conger of the congregation asked to work with them. Anyone reading the vestry minutes of the next few years soon senses a sort of rhythm: Someone says that they

1847. Johannes Brahms makes his concert debut in Hamburg at the age of 14.

must have more money, and the vestry promptly votes to pay up, and then appoints a committee to raise money for the payment. They never seem to lose faith that somehow the committee will raise the necessary money—even if it failed to do so last time and the time before—and that by so resolving, the problem has been met.

This time the committee did raise $120 which it paid the treasurer for the Rector's salary. And in October, Mr. Gillett called an extra meeting of the vestry to urge upon them again "the permanent support of the academy heretofore conducted by himself in the school house on the church grounds and for the employment of competent teachers."

Understandably the vestry postponed this extra obligation. The carpenter, Mr. George Henry, had filed suit in District Court against Messrs. Gillett, Perkins, Gray, Andrews, Hutchins and Couger for his account and now claimed $1,689.72—"being," the vestry report said indignantly "about $400 more than his account heretofore rendered and without allowing any credits."

For the first time—but not for the last—the vestry gave itself a shake and took itself in hand. It appointed a committee to try to find out just how much the church owed to whom, and found that it owed $773.01 (not counting the carpenter) including $325.80 now due Mr. Gillett, $165.77 to Rice and Nichols, $100 divided into three parts to the lenders Reily, Gray and Perkins, and $97.86 to J. D. Groesbeeck for paint and oils. The smallest item on the bill was $6 to Sampson & Co. and the vestry voted that of this total list, they pay the $6 to Sampson & Co.

But the rector was still urging permanent support and hiring of teachers for the academy, and forced into action, the vestry appointed a committee to study the subject. This insistence on a school was not purely theological enthusiasm on Mr. Gillett's part. Houston had now closed the one public school, begun by the Rev. Mr. Salmon as principal, and there was an acute shortage of schools in the town. Teachers and friends of education had met in the Methodist Church in 1846, hoping to set up an exchange center where those wishing to teach and those needing teachers could find each other. Mr. Gillett, the Rev. C. Richardson, and Peter Gray were among citizens there. That meeting went on record as favoring adoption of uniform text books by the private and public schools of Texas. But schools were slow to take shape. [By 1857, Houston still had only 10 small private schools, most of them with all the children in one room. Altogether these schools would not house 200 children, and Houston had 600 children of school age.]

In the thin state of Christ Church finance, Mr. Gillett's repeated efforts to start a school sounds foolhardy. Aware of how many children needed schooling, and of how many were actually being sent off to school, Mr. Gillett may have felt that the school would—once properly launched—support itself. The old two-story school house which Christ Church had bought and moved to the property in 1845 had received almost $250 worth of repair and refurbishing at the time. For the next two years it had been used not only for Sunday schools but for vestry meetings as well, and at some time in this period, the Rev. Mr. Gillett had—on his own—started regular day school in the building.

At last in 1847, Mr. Gillett managed to persuade the vestry to support his educational project. At an open meeting of Christ Church members held in the school house November 29, Gillett was called to the chair and Peter W. Gray—obviously sympathetic to the project—was made secretary. He reported

1848. Richard Wagner finishes work on opera Lohengrin.

the meeting formally to the vestry:

"Whereas we deem it of great importance to this community that the standard of Education among us should be elevated and are willing to make exertions for that purpose by giving our aid and support to schools—

"1st. Resolved that the congregation of Christ Church will at once take measures to support and maintain the male and female departments of the Houston Academy as a parish school, which has been established and carried on mainly by the exertions of our Rector.

"2nd. Resolved that we proceed forthwith to elect a Board of Trustees to consist of twelve members to take under their direction the said Houston Academy and to provide for the best interests of the same.

"3rd. Resolved that it shall be the duty of said Board of Trustees to prepare a Constitution for their own government and submit the same for approval to the vestry, by which when adopted they shall be governed and also to establish several rules for the government of the school, including a system of rewards and punishments for the scholars and the responsibility of the teachers; to provide able and efficient teachers; to regulate tuition fees and fix the salaries of the teachers and see to their payment . . ."

It was a valiant undertaking for men who had not yet managed to collect pew rents and pay the one salary of the one rector of their church. They elected as trustees E. B. Nichols, James Reily, William M. Taylor, W. J. Hutchins, F. Scranton, P. W. Gray, John P. Conger, Cornelius Ennis, N. T. Davis, J. W. Cruger, J. E. Wade and A. Cooke, Jr. And by May they had had another $599 worth of repair work done on the school house and—after only a minor contretemps—managed to pay the contractor's bill in full.

A Wedding, A Cemetery, and a Holly Day

Christ Church was a week late in holding its annual parish meeting of 1848. Easter Monday morning at 8 o'clock in Matagorda, the rector was married to Miss Mary Ann Wharton by the Rt. Rev. George Washington Freeman. The newly wedded pair then got on horses and rode with the bishop, a presbyter and a deacon, toward Houston, in continuance of the bishop's regular visitation. The bishop confirmed 20 persons in Houston and found that Christ Church now had 80 families, 90 communicants, and 35 persons baptized in the preceding year. This meant, of course, that the church was more crowded than ever.

"The Church and congregation here continue to increase," wrote the bishop, "and the building, erected with great difficulty and consecrated a year ago, is found too strait for the accomodation of all who desire to worship in it. It needs enlargement, and speedily too, if the congregation is to be enlarged. But how to effect this object, the worthy rector is wholly at a loss."

The vestry minutes of May 2, 1848, held one small item, the first hint of a great potential—help from the women of the church. "The committee appointed to raise money by subscription reported that the Ladies of the Church had paid to the Treasurer on account of Rector's salary the sum of $250." In addition, the money raisers had got subscriptions of $703.84, had already collected $553.84 of the promised sum, and using this had cleared off $407 worth of church debts and given the treasurer another $115 for the rector.

1848. Wuthering Heights becomes best seller.

1848. Gold is discovered in California, January 24.

This meant, the committee said happily, "that all the church debts were paid, except the following viz: "The Rector's salary to 4th April last $128.48. Allowance to be made to sexton say $40, and whatever Mr. Henry may recover by his suit for work on the church." The vestry agreed that the sexton should be given $40 and pew rent for his work of the preceding year.

The sexton, Mr. James West, was a communicant of the church and referred to always as "a good man" in Gillett's diary. Mr. West was the kind of frontiersman who shared what he had not only with the Lord, but with those in need around him. By account in Gillett's diary, Mr. West took on two orphan children to raise. It is possible that it was he who offered to give two cows to the early program of church building. But surely, it was he who offered to give to Christ Church the land for its cemetery.

Having agreed at their first meeting of the year to meet four times a year henceforth, instead of the once, the vestry gathered in October, 1848, to consider the propriety of procuring a burial ground. The rector stated that "Mr. James West had offered to donate a parcel of his land on the south bank of the bayou in the fourth ward of the city for the purpose; that the location was an eligible one, but suggested that, as Mr. West is a poor man, the ground would be laid off in lots and sold to the members of the church at suitable rates to pay a fair consideration for it & surveying & enclosing." E. W. Taylor, A. S. Ruthven, Thomas W. Clark and D. W. C. Harris were appointed to confer with Mr. West "as to the terms on which a part of his land can be procured as a Burial ground for the Church." And as usual, the vestry owed the rector money.

In December, 1848, the vestry and wardens of Christ Church received a circular letter from Bishop Freeman calling them to a meeting to consider organizing a diocese at Matagorda. This time the bishop spoke in forthright terms: he was urging diocesan organization because of the "great difficulty in effecting the Canonical ordination of ministers, as well as the admission of persons desirous of entering the ministry." And this time, the vestry approved the proposed organization *"provided,* however, that as a diocese, we do not assume the support of a Bishop, but that the Diocese remain as Missionary ground under the supervision of a Missionary Bishop and that the expense of episcopal supervision be defrayed by the Missionary Society." The vestry had learned well Mr. Gillett's sternly given lesson of the year before. They named Col. George Fisher and William M. Taylor delegates, either to act for both should only one be able to go.

On February 27, 1849, Mr. Gillett called his vestry together to announce that the Diocese of Texas had been officially organized, that Bishop Freeman had been invited to take charge as Missionary Bishop. The six charter members of the Diocese of Texas were Christ Church, Matagorda, organized in 1839; Christ Church, Houston, 1839; Trinity Church, Galveston, 1841; St. John's Church, Brazoria County, 1847; Christ Church, San Augustine, 1848, and Christ Church, Nacogdoches, 1848.

This new status in Texas prompted Mr. Gillett to another thought: "On suggestion made by the Rector, it was ordered that a Parish Register book such as the Rector approves be procured for the use of the Parish in which the Rector may keep a register of Marriages, baptisms, etc."

Christ Church was 10 years old—and now had its first Parish Registry. In the new parish record, Mr. Gillett apparently tried to go back and set down those baptisms, marriages and burials he remembered or had kept notes on.

But memory or notes were not always specific. Under burials recorded in 1849 was one which had taken place in 1846. "An English servt. March, 1846, Houston" is the unknown man's epitaph. And again . . . "A German Soldier, July 1, 1847." But he did remember that William Burgess, August 4, 1847, "died in jail on a charge of Murder." From the fall of 1848 on, he included place of burial but rarely included age except to scribble "child" "infant" "child."

At Christmas, "the Ladies of the Episcopal Church, Houston, desirous to decorate the House of God for the next coming Christmas in the style usual on such occasion," took up a subscription in sums ranging from 30 cents to $2. Among the subscribers were the familiar names including Dr. Roberts (whose wife had given the brick for the church), H. Sampson, L. J. Latham, W. J. Darden, C. Ennis and A. S. Ruthven. Rice & Nichols, and Bremond & VanAlstyne were the two $2 contributors. Filed by Peter Gray as a list of contributors "to decorate the Church for the Christmas holly days," this simple little sheet of paper would have been startling in many parts of the Episcopal Church of the United States where holly in the church at Christmas was still shockingly High Church.

In the 1840's in Houston, people in need turned to a minister without much regard for denomination. Though the first Roman Catholic Church had been built in 1842, and perhaps because the priest was out of town, Mr. Gillett was called upon "to bury a Mrs. Grant, who arrived in the place about five days since, from England, had been married only 5 months, husband in great affliction. Family all Roman Catholics."

Mr. Gillett performed many marriages in Houston. Some of the young people were members of Christ Church, some were not Episcopalian. Among them were: Thomas S. Lubbock and Miss Sarah O. Smith, Robert Lockart and Miss Anna R. Lubbock, Levi J. Parker and Ann Thompson, John Benson and Jane Wharton, Albert Wickes and Miss Alice Ann Wilson, Daniel D. Culp and Miss Elizabeth T. Thilman, William R. Baker and Hester Eleanor Runnels, John C. Hutchinson and Margaret Thompson, Robert Brewster and Miss May M. C. Andrus, John H. Brown and Miss Julia Elizabeth Baldwin, Henry B. Wiener and Miss Hannah Levy, Samuel L. Isaacs and Miss Rachel Caroline Levy, James W. Moore and Miss Elizabeth Cooper, Paul Bremond and Miss Mary E. Van Alstyne, Richard J. French and Miss Alice Ann Wicks, John Randon and Miss Charlotte M. Baldwin, Henry Sampson and Miss Catherine D. Gray, Sterling N. Dobie and Miss Mary J. Morris, Claudius W. Sears and Miss Susan Alice Gray. The Rev. Henry B. Goodwin had married W. Douglass Lee to Ophelia Morgan, and the Rev. Benjamin Eaton had married J. Temple Doswell to Evalina Gray before Gillett's coming.

Once the church was consecrated, the years had settled into something of a pattern: The pew holders were usually in arrears, various members were appointed to collect pew rents if possible, those remiss were threatened with loss of the pew, and at one point the collector was put on a percentage pay of all amounts he collected. As a sensible business man, E. B. Nichols saw that the pew rent system did not work and proposed giving it up for a subscription system, but was voted down. And the Rev. Mr. Gillett's salary was always in arrears. Diocesan meetings were attended faithfully, cemetery lots were sold at rates of from $10 to $50 each depending on size and location, outsiders unlucky enough to die in Houston were buried in Strangers' Ground of the cemetery, fences were built about the church lot, and in the summer

1848. Louis Philippe is dethroned in France and Second Republic set up February 26.

of 1850, Lindsey P. Rucker supplied at Christ Church during Gillett's summer absence. Mr. West drifted off the scene as sexton, probably because of illness, and two vestrymen, John P. Conger and Abner Cooke, Jr., died, earning resolutions of affection and loss.

In April, 1849, Peter Gray, acting as lawyer for the defense of the rector and H. F. Gillett against George Henry, carpenter, finally settled the suit by cancelling the $50 which Henry owed Gray, by having H. F. Gillett convey to Henry the lots that Gillett had long ago pledged as part payment for the carpenter's work on the church building, and by giving Mr. Henry $50 in cash. Gray advanced the cash.

The Rev. Benjamin Eaton came up from Galveston to solemnize the marriage of William Marsh Rice to Margaret Bremond. Born in New England, little Mr. Rice started earning his own living at 14 and landed in Galveston in 1839 as a young man 22 years old. Baptized a Methodist, he was not on the early subscription lists of 1839 and 1840, but became a member of Christ Church soon after arriving in Houston—probably influenced by his partner, E. B. Nichols. By 1845, both were on the vestry.

Their firm prospered, and expecting to live his life in Houston, Mr. Nichols began to build a house—a mansion. Legend has it that the building materials were originally intended for a warship. But the house was built of heart-pine timbers 18 by 24 inches with mortised joints, wooden dowels and handmade nails. The floors were two inches thick. Rosewood was used inside. Before this house could be finished, and at about the time of the Rice-Bremond wedding, Nichols and Rice saw how valuable it would be for one of the partners to move to Galveston to establish a branch. Nichols went—after six years on the Christ Church vestry—and in Galveston became a life-long pillar of Trinity Church. The newly-married Mr. Rice bought his partner's unfinished house and moved it to Congress Avenue, facing Court House Square. He had the house finished and it was considered one of the handsomest in Houston.

1850. William Wordsworth dies, and Alfred Tennyson is named poet laureate of England.

Chapter 17

". . . A Hundred Ties"

The year 1850 was a significant one to Christ Church, and to the Diocese of Texas. The first annual convention of the new diocese was held in Houston beginning May 9, and four new congregations were added to the original six. The four new ones were Trinity, San Antonio; St. Paul's, Washington; St. Peter's, Brenham, and St. Paul's, Fireman's Hill (now Cold Spring) Polk County. At the Houston meeting, the bishop pushed the importance of building at once a diocesan school to educate young men for the ministry.

In October, 1850, the Diocese of Texas was admitted to the General Convention of the Protestant Episcopal Church at Cincinnati. Texas was represented by Benjamin Eaton, Charles Gillett and John Freeman Young as clerical delegates, and by James Reily and Peter W. Gray as lay deputies. W. L. Sartwell, who had been named the second deputy, never got to the meeting. Peter Gray showed up a few days after it began, and because Eaton and Gillett were a majority of the diocesan standing committee, they simply elected Gray deputy.

Apparently the Houston Academy Male and Female Departments, which had been so robustly taken over by Christ Church in 1847, had been closed by 1851, because in January, the Ladies Sewing Circle wrote formally to ask permission to lease the school building for five years. "Our object . . . is to secure a permanent and comfortable place for the Sunday School as well as to obtain for the church an income from property which has hitherto been useless." This was a tactful way of taking the maintenance of the old frame two-story building off the vestry's shoulders, and the interchange of letters is exquisite. Mrs. Mary Gillett (presumably the rector's wife rather than the school master's in that the rector had married Mary Wharton) wrote the letter in a hand as delicate as a spider's web but easier to read 112 years later than at least half the vestry minutes. It was signed by Maria Van Alstyne and Jane Gray as well.

James Reily wrote the reply in his upright style "The vestry most readily and unanimously accepted the proposition . . . said school house with all its privileges and appurtenances hereto appertaining shall be the property of said Ladies Sewing Circle for the full term & period of five years, without charge, from the first day of the present month." The legality of phrase hints ever so slightly at tongue in cheek, but both Mr. Reily and the vestry were sincerely grateful: "The vestry appreciate the excellent motives which have induced your circle to take the lease of the house, and hope your most sanguine expectations may be realized." The realization of sanguine expectations was something the vestry was beginning to look upon as a luxury not to be counted upon. Peter W. Gray faithfully filed this "Lease of School House to Ladies Sewing Circle Jany. 8th, 1851."

Almost by the same mail had come a letter to the Vestry of Christ Church, Houston signed "M. R. Gray, Sec. & Treasurer of the 'Sewing Circle' of Christ Ch. Houston." Written by Mrs. William Fairfax Gray in her clear, and quite lovely handwriting, it reflects Millie Gray's quiet humor, and conjures up a picture of the somewhat run-down little brick church. The ladies, she said, were presenting a petition, praying that certain repairs and improvements be made on the church building—

"They respectfully suggest to the Vestry—

"First—that the Spire be taken down *for the present*, leaving the Turret, and repairing the same—and that the Bell be removed to some convenient place within the church inclosure, with a roof over it to protect it from the weather.

"Secondly—that the Gallery is exceedingly uncomfortable, and that it is very desirable to put it into better order—making the seats more commodious etc.

"Thirdly—that the Windows & Walls require to be repaired—and the windows to be repainted—or some other mode of keeping out the sun— Also repairs on the platform in front of the entrance door.—and

"Fourthly—that the Lamps now on the Reading desk and Pulpit, instead of giving light to the minister and people serve rather to blind the latter and throw darkness on the work of the former. They therefore, earnestly request the Vestry to enquire of Mr. Gillett how this evil may be rectified, so as best to aid him to enlighten the people.

"All which is respectfully submitted to the vestry—petitioning that they will carry into effect according to their best judgment the wishes of the 'Circle' on this point."

The letter gives the effect of demurely lowered eyelashes and meek proffering of a note. But its concluding paragraph has one final clincher: "The sum of one hundred and thirty Dollars ($130.—) is in the hands of their

1850. Vanity Fair *and* David Copperfield *are popular novels.*

Treasurer, subject to the order of the Vestry for this purpose. Very respectfully, M. R. Gray, Sec. & Treasurer of the 'Sewing Circle' of Christ Ch. Houston."

The ladies, with their efficient list and their convincing show of money, had their way with a promptness unusual in the records. A series of brief, prettily written vouchers—each one signed by one William Rosselle—tells the story. The first reads:

March 29—To taking down spire to church	$ 60.00
To taking down tower or Belfry	45.00
To laying platform & altering seats	15.00
	$120.00

The voucher of April 21, 1851, tells another story—of how these gentle, demure ladies raised money. In the tiniest possible handwriting at the bottom, there are a series of minuscule notations:

Col. Reily	5	
A. S. Ruthven	5	
P. W. Gray	5	$20
W. M. Rice	4	
P. Bremond	1	

The Ladies Sewing Circle was an almost forgotten forerunner of the Ladies Parish Association, and it did not survive. With his faithfulness to the record, Peter W. Gray added a notation on the back of the "Lease" which was Colonel Reily's letter of 1851—"Surrendered by Mrs. Van Alstyne to Dr. Eliot the Treasurer of Vestry June 16th, 1854—The Ladies Circle having gone out of existence." The circle may have, but the ladies had not.

In August, 1851, Mr. Gillett changed his name to Gillette. On August 13, he was still signing Gillett. And on August 30 and forever after he and his wife changed to Gillette. So did Henry F. Gillette, though there is no evidence as to whether he did so at the same time.

August 30, 1851, Mr. Gillette offered his resignation as rector of Christ Church. The Diocese was going to open an Episcopal School at Anderson, and had asked him to take charge.* Mr. Gillette had worked passionately within the diocesan organization to have a school established, but was sincere in his letter of resignation when he said: "The call upon me is so direct from the Convention; and in it may be traced so plainly, as I think, the hand of Providence, that I do not feel myself at liberty to refuse the work thus put upon me....so to separate myself from the strong ties by which I am bound to my first and only parish, requires not a little effort and sacrifice. But where the good of the Church and personal feeling or personal sacrifice come into contact, I have made it a settled rule of my life always to yield the latter to the former, remembering that 'we are not our own.' "

Gillette and Christ Church had gone through disheartening as well as satisfying times together. His vestry had sometimes failed to come up to the expectations he set for them and he had sometimes spoken with candor to his vestry—and he and his wife had left a child in the Episcopal Cemetery, which was the custom of the time.

Before leaving Houston, Mr. Gillette had two last sad duties. Within one fortnight in July, 1851, he read the funeral service for his brother-in-law, Henry Wharton, and laid him to rest in the Gillette lot in Christ Church Cemetery, and he read the service for Mrs. William Fairfax Gray—wife of Christ Church founder. It is Peter Gray's handwriting which added to the

---

*For full account of the Anderson School and Gillette's later career, read *The Episcopal Church in Texas, 1838-1874* by Lawrence L. Brown, The Church Historical Society.

record: "Episcopal Cemetery, Houston, 51 years 6 days. With her were also deposited the remains of her husband, William Fairfax Gray, removed from the City Cemetery—He died April 10th, 1841, aged 53 years, 5 mos. & 13 days."

At no time in Gillette's stay had the vestry passed any resolution reflecting awareness of or sharing his joy or sorrow, but on his resignation, it resolved: ". . . That the resignation of the Rev. Mr. Gillette should be accepted to take effect on the 1st Jan. 1852; but in so doing, they believe that this parish sacrifices its interest for that of the Diocese at large.

"That the growth and prosperity of the congregation of Christ Church, Houston, are mainly owing under God, to the pious, fervent, and faithful labors of Mr. Gillett its first Minister; and that the beneficial influence of his services will long be felt in this community.

"Resolved, that the Congregation of Christ Church Houston entertain for Mr. Gillett the warmest feelings of love and respect, both as a Man and a Christian Minister; that both in the pulpit and desk and in his daily walk and conversation whilst among them, his Ministry has been that of a faithful, pious and consistant Christian; and that when he shall part from them, the hundred ties that can exist between Minister and people, will be severed with regret."

New Rectors

The story of Henry Sansom is an odd one—a mixture of charm, tragedy, and teacup tempest which could have damaged Christ Church permanently. He was a deacon in April, 1848, when he was first appointed missionary to Texas, and assigned to San Augustine and Nacogdoches. He and his family arrived in San Augustine May 23, and that day their first and only child died of scarlet fever caught on the trip down. Sansom's first service in Texas was the funeral service for his child, and on the next Sunday, he began his ministry to the church.

Sansom was an Englishman of extensive education and high intellectual ability. He was considered a "sweet singer" and attracted many friends and admirers. He stimulated the kind of affection which made his vestry wish to have the dead child buried under the altar of the new church he and they built together. Bishop Freeman said "I was much pleased both with the Missionary, the Rev. Mr. Sansom, whom I now met for the first time, and with the members of the congregation, from whom I received many kind and hospitable attentions. Our Missionary has been well received, both here and in Nacogdoches, and all seem perfectly satisfied with him. He entered upon his duties, according to my judgment, in the proper manner, and in the right spirit . . . he moves on quietly, turning in accommodation to the prejudices of others neither to the right hand nor to the left; and while he sedulously avoids everything like fraternization with the various sects, being careful to abstain from any assault upon their peculiarities, and, in his private and social intercourse manifesting kindness of feeling and courtesy to all."

On this visitation, the bishop was accompanied on his journey west by Mr. Sansom who proposed applying for Priest's orders at some convenient point en route, where the presence of the requisite numbers of presbyters could be secured. It was a little like earning the priesthood through the labors of Hercules: "We traveled in the mail stage," the bishop wrote. "Starting late in the afternoon, the horses already being jaded and the roads bad, we were benighted before we had proceeded half a dozen miles and could only advance by holding a lantern before the horses' heads . . . We did not reach Douglas, the end of our first stage, only 16 miles, until 10 or 11 o'clock at night."

After journeying to Cincinnati on the Trinity River they reached Huntsville Sunday morning. They held services morning and evening in the Court House, a large, handsome brick building. "Mr. Sansom read Prayers. I read the Communion Service and preached. The congregation . . . though small, was attentive, and if not greatly edified," wrote the bishop, "were interested by the apparent novelty of our appearance and proceedings. The services of the Church had never before been performed here, and we appeared before the wondering people robed in the surplice and gown . . .no voices were raised in response but our own."

They traveled to Washington by stage and there Mr. Gillett took up the convoy while Mr. Sansom went to Houston to supply at Christ Church. The bishop and Gillett were caught up in floods, had to turn back and take a second night of former President Anson Jones' hospitality. After Brenham, Austin, Columbus, San Marcos, New Braunfels, San Antonio,—all in December weather of almost continuous wet northers—they had all planned to meet in Matagorda for a general meeting of the clergy and laity January 1, 1849—but the floods were so high that even the mail stage was stopped. The cold was excessive. Mr. Sansom, still deacon, was stuck in Houston.

At Matagorda they learned that cholera had broken out in Houston. Mr. Gillett left for home immediately. And on January 11, Bishop Freeman too went to cholera-stricken Houston, accompanied by John Freeman Young, Henry Niles Pierce and Lindsey P. Rucker. "Soon after our arrival, a violent storm of rain set in, which continued many days, rendering the streets nearly impassable, and preventing the assembling of a congregation for Divine Service. On Sunday morning, however, the church was opened, and notwithstanding the rain and the mud, a small congregation was assembled. On this occasion, the Rev. Henry Sansom . . . was admitted to the Sacred Order of Priest. He was presented by the Rev. Charles Gillett, who together with the Rev. Messrs. Young and Pierce, united in the imposition of hands."

Understandably in 1851, Mr. Sansom would feel that he had a link with Christ Church. He was eager to succeed Gillette. But a vigorous number of the vestry simply did not like or want Mr. Sansom. Having received Mr. Gillette's resignation in August—to take effect January, 1852—the vestry met in October, 1851. The secretary, J. H. S. Stanley, seconded by W. W. Stiles, moved that the vestry make a call to Mr. Sansom, "at present ministering in Marshall. After debate and opposition, it was *resolved,* that the motion be laid on the table."

In November, Stanley and Stiles withdrew their motion that Mr. Sansom be called, and the vestry unanimously voted to recall Mr. Gillette. In his letter of resignation, Gillette had been so loathe to cut off these ties abruptly that he had offered to go on a temporary basis for one year, though later in the letter he had recognized that this was not a wise measure. Apparently this lent hope to the vestry's motion to recall him.

With that remarkable confidence in the prestige and charm of Christ Church that the vestry was to continue to show through years of declinations, they blandly asked the secretary to "acquaint him with the same and to intimate that the stipend will be as before." In other words, a $1,000 a year—always in arrears? In fact they owed Gillette money at the moment. Mr. Gillette politely declined. His letter arrived for the November 11 meeting which

1851. Cornerstones are laid for the wings of the United States Capitol.

was attended by only 7 of the 12 members.

Promptly Mr. Stiles moved and was seconded by Dr. Francis Moore that Mr. Sansom be called. The vote carried and the secretary was instructed to communicate same to Mr. Sansom. A note in the margin of the vestry minutes—added by a different hand—comments: "Rev. H. Sansom called as the rector by vote of 4 ayes and 3 nays: 5 *absent*." However in fairness to Mr. Sansom, once he had a slim majority, the vestry was unanimous in offering him $1,000 should he accept.

By December 11, the vestry had its acceptance from Mr. Sansom in a courteous well written letter—"regarding it as an indication of the Providence of God and believing it to be in accordance with the wishes of the majority of the Congregation."

On the back of this letter, Peter W. Gray wrote in pencil, and signed, this wry editorial comment: "This letter bears no date of time or place. Mr. Sansom in *Houston* at the time it was written, and it was recd by the vestry Nov. 1851. Mr. S. *well knowing* the vacancy in this parish about to occur—left his parish at Marshall—came by New Orleans to Houston, and remained here some week or ten days before the Call was made. When made by the vestry, there were 7 members and 5 absent. Of those present, 4 voted for him, 3 against; and of the absentees, 4 were opposed to the call and Mr. S. *knew it when he accepted*." Mr. Sansom has had no chance in the record to offer denial or rebuttal, but he was off to an unfortunate start. Ten days before his arrival was due, the Rev. Mr. Gillette swooped back, called a vestry meeting, asked for the remainder of his "unpaid stipend," and departed.

The Houston which Gillette left was rather different from the one to which he came. The Gold Rushers of 1849 had passed through town, taking some Houstonians with them but buying their supplies from Houston merchants for the long trek from Houston to California. Cholera and yellow fever had come and gone again. By May, 1851, James House was selling ice in Houston and public health was good. Main Street stores offered "fine French cloth dress and frock coats, frock and sack gro-de-ta, Doe skin and gro-de-ta pants." The city limits ran from Live Oak Avenue along Lamar to Brazos, along Brazos to Buffalo Bayou, and along the meanders of said Bayou to Live Oak Avenue. There were some brick sidewalks.

Things went smoothly at first after Mr. Sansom's arrival. The vestry decided to raise pew rents, approved Mr. Sansom's suggestion of taking up a Sunday evening collection, and asked the rector to have work done to "render comfortable the approach to the Vestry." Then Mr. Sansom made his first upsetting mistake. Announcing the annual Easter meeting for election of vestrymen from the pulpit on the preceding Sunday, Mr. Sansom somehow gave the ladies the idea they were going to be allowed to vote.

The vestry minutes simply record that these vestrymen were elected: P. W. Gray, W. M. Rice, Dr. F. Moore, W. H. Eliot, S. Dupree, A. S. Ruthven, B. F. Tanksersley, E. W. Taylor, J. H. S. Stanley, C. Ennis, W. W. Stiles, and J. Reily. But after signing the minutes, "Stanley, Secy." Stanley, Secy. added: "Note! This election was held for the first time since the organization of the Parish, in the open church, in presence of the Congregation male & female—many of the latter, having cause, expecting to vote, in consequence of a notice to that effect, given the Sunday before by the Rector. The manner in which the election was conducted caused much remark and some dissatisfaction."

1851. House of Seven Gables *and* Moby Dick, *are published.*

At the April meeting, Peter Gray proposed free pews, and was voted down. And Doctor Moore, Mr. Rice, Ennis and Stiles, were elected delegates to the annual convention. Ruthven was the rector's choice for senior warden. The rector proposed that the vestry should instruct the delegates to oppose the election of a bishop—but the vestry took no action. By October, a number of the vestrymen were openly annoyed with the rector.

The secretary recorded the fact that eight members of the vestry had written the rector, October 13, asking him to call a meeting immediately, and that the rector ignored the request by calling a meeting for October 28. The letter of request had pointed out that all members of the vestry were then in town, and that they wanted to consider "the rectorship of the church for the ensuing year. *Your call to the Rectorship,*" the secretary copied in underline, "was understood to be for one year from the 1st of January last." Even with the delay, 11 of the 12 managed to be at the meeting with Mr. Ruthven and Mr. Stiles wardens.

Mr. Gray moved and Colonel Reily seconded that the rector be respectfully advised to resign. Ayes were Mr. Tankersley, Colonel Reily, Mr. Taylor, Mr. Gray, Mr. Ruthven; nays Mr. Dupree, Mr. Stanley, Mr. Stiles, Doctor Eliot, Mr. Ennis and Mr. Rice. Doctor Moore was voted nay, though absent in the country, because of a letter he had written giving his sentiments.

Then a document was presented expressing "entire satisfaction" with the rector and the wish that he be retained, signed by 37 members of the congregation. This could not, of course, be considered a legal vote of confidence because some of the signatures were from females, but it did indicate a healthy group of supporters. Whereupon, Mr. Gray handed in a letter of resignation "having in view the necessity of peace, and having done all in their power to effect that object by peaceable and honorable means without avail—and believing that harmony cannot be restored so long as the Rev. H. Sansom remains rector." It was signed by James Reily, P. W. Gray, Benjamin F. Tankersley, E. W. Taylor and A. S. Ruthven. This stripped the vestry down to no quorum—so it sensibly adjourned.

But the confusion had only begun: In November, the five who had resigned begged leave to withdraw their resignation, and their withdrawal of resignation was approved. The rector withdrew, the senior warden took the chair, and the vestry voted 7 to 5 to pronounce the rectorship of this church vacant after January 1. Doctor Moore and Mr. Stiles, both of whom had supported the rector, were appointed to tell him.

But by November 22, with the rector in the chair and his senior warden Mr. Ruthven beside him, Doctor Moore seconded by Mr. Rice proposed that vestry *reconsider* the vote approving the withdrawal of the resignation. This lost by a vote of five to six. And December 22—the rector called a meeting to protest Mr. Ruthven's vote—his senior warden's vote—on grounds that Mr. Ruthven had not been a pew holder at the time of his election in April, and therefore had voted unconstitutionally. He then announced he had dismissed Ruthven and appointed Doctor Moore senior warden.

Mr. Sansom was fighting a last ditch fight right up to his January 1 dismissal. Immediately after the November 22 meeting—it was explained on December 22—the rector had written Mr. Ruthven dismissing him as senior warden on grounds that he had been informed "within a few days past" that Mr. Ruthven was not a pewholder in April when he was elected vestryman. "Mr. Stanley the Secy. stated that the rector knew that fact when

1852. The General Sherman, *Houston's first woodburning locomotive, lands by steamboat in Galveston.*

Mr. Ruthven was appointed by him, as S.W.—that he had informed him so. Mr. Sansom replied by asking *'whether he had informed him officially.'* These matters," Secretary Stanley wrote at the bottom of the vestry minutes, "produced bitter feeling and controversy in the vestry." The rector's party was in brief ascendancy. Stanley resigned as secretary and Stiles was appointed. Tankersley tried to resign as vestryman but was tabled. Gray and Ruthven obviously tried to continue the meeting as though nothing untoward had happened. But on December 24, with Moore in the chair, on motion of Rice, seconded by Ennis, the action declaring the rectorship of Christ Church vacant was rescinded. And the rector's letter of resignation was accepted.

It was a polite letter, in which the rector tried to save face for everyone —himself and the vestry: "Since I have been among you the good of the Church of the Redeemer has been the object which has always lain near my heart, and it is in view of this that I have been led to the conclusion that the relations existing between us must be severed. Hoping that the spirit of peace and unity will guide you in your future deliberations and aid you in the selection of a pastor I hereby respectfully resign, the 31st of December, 1852."

The vestry assessed themselves $15 each to pay the rector's deficient salary. But this was not quite the end: A committee of Rice, Ennis, Stiles, Gray, Ruthven and Moore were appointed to find a new rector. And January 5—inexplicably—this committee reported with the move that the Rev. Mr. Sansom be called as rector of Christ Church. And—though Gray and Ruthven were among the 4 voting no—this motion was carried. Mr. Sansom *was* called, and had the extremely good sense to decline.

Clerical Letters

Perhaps as a result of tensions which had built up during Sansom's stay, perhaps because the vestry was feeling like passengers on a rudderless ship, in the early spring of 1853, tempers, which had been held in check during the controversy over Sansom, blew up over nothing. J. H. S. Stanley had been secretary-treasurer through 1852, and the committee, appointed as custom, went to his office to take the books for annual audit before turning them over to the new treasurer.

"He refused to give them up unless the Committee would examine them immediately in his office beforehand, and give him a certificate of their correctness, which they declined to do because it would take a long time." Peter Gray wrote in one of his familiar notations. "Mr. Ennis then attempted to take the books away without examination. Mr. S. resisted and a small fight ensued, in which Mr. S. was worsted. But they were separated, and Mr. S. retained the books. This I learned from both parties afterward." This was brave if not foolhardy on Mr. Stanley's part because Cornelius Ennis was 6' 3" and now in his 40's at the peak of his 200-pound plus might. The matter was solved by the appointment of Gray and Dr. W. Henry Eliot as a new and more soothing committee to call upon the touchy retiring treasurer. The books were found to be in order.

Houston in 1853 was pushing out its horizons. Edwin Fairfax Gray, once a midshipman in the Texas Navy, went off to sea as a lieutenant in the U. S. Navy, and served under Commodore Perry on the historic trip to Japan. In 1853, W. M. Wood's invention—a steam wagon—was hauling cotton over

1852. Louis Napoleon is crowned emperor of France. Daniel Webster, Henry Clay and the Duke of Wellington die.

Texas roads without horses. A new record was established by stagecoach from Austin to Houston in 36 hours, and the stage from Washington made the trip to Houston in 10 hours. These runs, compared to routine travel, were rather like the run of the four minute mile as compared to usual rates of pedestrian travel down Main Street. As late as 1857, Bishop Freeman could write: "I determined to trace my way back to Houston (from Austin) by the shortest and least fatiguing route. Accordingly I joined the Rev. Mr. Eaton in hiring a rough wagon—it *was* a rough one indeed, but the best we could find—and proceeded directly to the terminus of the Houston and Texas Central Rail-road. This we reached on Saturday, May 30, and same day by rail, 35 miles, arrived in Houston."

With telegraph and railroad lines being projected for the future—as they were in 1853—Christ Church decided to go out of the diocese for their next rector. The first call went to the Rev. Meyer Levin in Jackson, Mississippi, and Mr. Levin declined, admonishing a bit unfairly that "a Parish of such importance to the Diocese of Texas as Christ Church, Houston, ought not to go to waste, which I fear it is in danger, if it remains vacant much longer."

Having been a major force in letting Mr. Sansom go, Peter Gray rose to the occasion by finding an excellent candidate for his replacement—Joseph J. Nicholson. Peter Gray—who attended the General Convention in Cincinnati when Texas was admitted (1850)—was well acquainted with many laymen and clergymen of the national church by the time he went to the General Convention in New York in October, 1853. He therefore scouted for possible rectors, and after Levin's declination, Gray reported to the vestry that "no one pleased me so well as the Rev. Joseph J. Nicholson of Waterford, New York, who had been very highly recommended by letter to Mr. James Ennis, which he showed me...I went to hear him preach in his own parish and got acquainted with him. He preaches well and in a popular style, is a sound churchman, and enjoys a high reputation both as a Minister and as a Man. He is a married man, having a wife and four children, is about 35 years of age, [Peter Gray's own age] agreeable and gentlemanly in his manners, and seems active and zealous. He is a native of Maryland and is highly spoken of by Bishop Whittingham who ordained him and also by gentlemen from Maryland whom I met. He made a favorable impression also on several of our Texas clergymen who met him at the Convention." This is the first instance of the now-established custom whereby vestrymen go visit a priest in his own parish before the church issues a call.

The vestry issued the call, and Mr. Nicholson accepted with flattering promptness—wanting, Gray said, "to change his residence to a more southern latitude both for health and social reasons." Mr. Nicholson was highly thought of in his own time, and has been called "this great priest" in recently written histories. But his letters are nonetheless amusing.

Each one to the vestry was written, he said at the beginning, in the middle and at the end, in great haste—haste which he was sure, he said in his next letter, must have been evident. But each one, however hastily written, ran on—or scurried—for pages and pages and pages. In the first letter to Peter Gray from Rectory, Grace Church, November 29—which ran to more than 1200 words—Nicholson expressed joyous Christian hope mixed with frank economic fears, and he did his mental arithmetic out loud:

"The expense of removing out will come, I think, from that data that I have, at least near $300—If in addition to this I am obliged to pay the

1853. December 30, James Gadsden negotiates purchase of 29,640 square miles of land from Mexico for $10,000,000.

76

rent on our house, say $200, it will leave only $160 for my support the first year. And I apprehend *that* in your new country will be a small provision. Mrs. Lyn, my wife's mother, sent me a letter from Mrs. Ritchie a few days ago, & which was written without any reference to my movements (for she was wholly unacquainted with them) of Galveston in which she says everything there was very high all the summer. Flour as much as $14 to $15 a Bbl at one time, chickens 5 to 6 dollars a dozen, eggs 30 to 50 cts. per doz. Butter, when it could be had, 40 to 50 cts. lb. Good reason then have I to be apprehensive. And yet I can not see how these prices could have existed unless during the panic when everything was at a stand—These can not be permanent rates."

In this letter he refers to the newest dispatches yesterday "that the yellow fever still lingers about Galveston & Houston"—also "that it has broken out afresh in Louisiana within the past week." To the practical 20th century eye of the Christ Church financial secretary, Jean Shepherd, this reference to newspaper accounts in the east of yellow fever coupled with the request for additional money looked like "ecclesiastical blackmail."

In calling Nicholson, the vestry planned to pay $1200 a year, and offered an advance of $300 for the expenses of moving—collected at $50 apiece from the vestry and issued on a New York bank through Henry Sampson. The vestry election was little more than a formal recognition of a fait accompli. Obviously Gray had made a tentative approach to Nicholson, received his provisional acceptance, and was sure of vestry approval before the vestry meeting ever took place—because when the secretary's letter reached Nicholson, he simply wired Gray: "Will you pay my rent first year. Letter on way."

The nearest telegraph line was in New Orleans, and J. T. Doswell— once of Houston and Gray's brother-in-law—handled Christ Church telegrams from New Orleans east and relayed answers by mail. The query about the rent came to the vestry at the same time the grapevine informed them that Mr. Nicholson had also been offered Grace Church, Baltimore. This turned out later to be erroneous, but had a quickening effect upon the vestry: they not only wrote Mr. Nicholson an agreement to pay the year's rent, but wrote again to Doswell in New Orleans to wire this promise to Mr. Nicholson in Waterford, N. Y.

Thereafter Mr. Nicholson peppered the vestry with telegrams and letters reporting progress: a telegram December 15 "Coming as fast as possible. A letter is on way," was received in New Orleans December 17, and in Houston December 25. The letter did come. Letters of November 29, December 1, December 14 and January 3rd all came—warm, voluble, revealing, almost breathless in tone. And all had to be copied in the vestry minutes in long hand by the secretary. But on learning just as he was leaving Waterford that Houston was in a panic for fear he might accept the call to Baltimore, Mr. Nicholson very sweetly wired he was coming, and then wrote—en route—"I regret that you should have been so troubled about the report of my call to Grace Church, Baltimore, and especially that you should have been disposed to attach so much importance to me. And I hasten not only to relieve your mind of all anxiety but also to regain my humble position. I beg of you not to set your mark too high, lest the reaction should prove detrimental to my work . . . I was *not* called to Grace Church . . . It is not so desirable a post as you imagine. I assure you I am highly satisfied in advance with Houston & feel that so far as my own wishes are concerned that position is all that I ask. My

1853. Franklin Pierce, youngest president in U.S. history at 49, names Jefferson Davis Secretary of War.

77

1854. *Texas and Red River Telegraph Company builds first line from Shreveport to Houston.*

1854. *Charge of the Light Brigade at Balaklava is ordered October 25, and 400 of 607 are killed.*

only anxiety is that this rumor should have given you too high an opinion of so humble a man as myself."

Mr. Nicholson had Col. John D. Andrews as his senior warden, W. W. Stiles junior warden, Dr. Henry Eliot treasurer and Peter Gray secretary. He soon found that the year without a rector had reduced the congregation to 46 (some pewholders had argued in that dismal year that if there was no rector they saw no reason why they should pay pew rent). But Mr. Nicholson reopened the parish school, took an active part in diocesan affairs and was named secretary of the new Society for the Diffusion of Christian Knowledge at the 1854 convention. Within the first year his salary was raised to $1500.

Poor Mr. Nicholson. After all the great expense of words, letters and true emotion, he should have been allowed by fate to live out his life in constructive peace at Christ Church. Instead he acquired what may have been amoebic dysentery, and after scarcely more than a year, was compelled to resign explaining "It is known to you that since my residence in Houston, I have with slight intermissions been afflicted with an affection incident to the climate or change of climate. From the first I had hoped it was merely an acclimating process, and that it would in time go away. On my return from a trip across the Gulph in the spring, I found myself, as I supposed, entirely restored. But of late it has returned upon me with more virulence . . ."

The vestry regretfully accepted the resignation "solely in deference to his wishes" . . . and assured Mr. Nicholson that he "enjoys the good will and esteem of the congregation as a zealous pastor, and that his talent and services as an eloquent preacher of the faith of Christ and his church are highly appreciated and valued, and that he and his family will carry with them the good wishes, sympathy and regard of the vestry and people." Mr. Nicholson moved to Mobile, Alabama, where he became rector of St. Mary's Church. He returned to Texas in 1865, this time to San Antonio where he opened St. Mary's Hall, a girls' school. And within another year he was dead—one of the first victims of a cholera epidemic.

Slow growth of the second church through
epidemic, war, and diversities of opinion. 1856-1885. 3

Because of the yellow fever epidemic in the long summer of 1855, Christ Church vestry made no effort to get a new rector until December. Yellow fever may have been Houston's chief attraction to the Rev. W. T. D. Dalzell —who throughout his long life was eager to help communities stricken by the deadly epidemics. But it took Christ Church months to find him.

The vestry issued several calls. One went to the Rev. Edward A. Foggs in Bordentown, New Jersey, who replied contentedly, "My people will listen to nothing with regard to the matter and the vestry will not accept my resignation."

One went to the well-to-do Rev. A. Cleveland Coxe of Baltimore, who was, at the same time, being invited to become Bishop of Texas. Mr. Coxe replied by having printed up two "Private Documents"—one addressed to Reverend Father in God (the formal address printed across the bottom indicated that this was Bishop Freeman), and one to Reverend Brethren and Gentlemen ("The Rev. Messrs. Chars. Gillette, E. H. Downing, and J. W. Dunn; and W. L. Sartwell and A. S. Richardson Esqs. Committee etc. etc. etc.") These two nicely printed letters had across the top in small type "A limited number of Copies printed to avoid the labor of transcribing; and for private use exclusively." Only a copyright number is missing. Mr. Coxe sent a copy of each letter to the Christ Church vestry by way of saying no, though the letters actually explained in elegant terms why he did not feel called upon to accept the Episcopate of Texas. [The Rev. Mr. Coxe was later generous in offering to help subsidize the salary of any bishop the diocese might elect by unanimous vote.]

A third call went out in March to the Rev. C. H. Albert who seemed in his reply to be trembling on the verge of acceptance though explaining, "I have indeed no dread of the fever (yellow fever) *personally,* but it is rather an unpleasant thought . . ."

This prompted from the vestry a letter which was unusual in the first 100 years of the church's history—one describing the parish as it was, and telling what the minister being called might expect to find in Houston.

"The present state of this parish we regard as unsatisfactory—while the people are reasonably harmonious and anxious to have the regular services of the Church, there is a want of that zeal and life which only the active services of a minister can infuse. Yet we keep our Sunday school, with eleven teachers and from 30 to 40 regular scholars. The Ladies also have been active in making repairs in . . . the church, painting, rearranging pews, etc. We have a good brick church edifice sufficient to accommodate about 300 persons—some 50 families who attend the Church; and 40 to 50 communicants. At last Convention Rev. Mr. Nicholson reported 62.

"The parishioners generally are not wealthy. Yet most of them in comfortable circumstances. The population of our town is from 4,000 to 5,000 and the character of the people reasonably fair. We believe they are reputed to be rather more church going people than usual in the Southwest.

"The yellow fever has visited us annually for three years last past—but this is unusual. We have no expectation of it this year, but feel strongly assured it will not appear. It is indeed a severe and fatal disease, frequently, yet there are many of our people who have lived through it for years, and our congregation have been singularly spared.

"With the exception of the epidemic, the health of our city is universally admitted to be good. And the county about us is always healthy."

Admitting that many planters keep their families out in the county and board in town during epidemics, the letter continued, "Board in town varies from $20 to $30. We have no parsonage and rents usually are high—from 12 to 30 dolls. a month. There is a small but convenient dwelling, formerly occupied by Rev. Mr. Gillette, in a pleasant locality which you can rent for $150 per year as we are told. Educational advantages here are small, and much needed. In fact there is good opening now for a first class Academy. There is an old School house belonging to the church on the same lot. It is a frame building, 2 stories high, much out of repair, and unsightly in its present condition. But with repairs of some $300 it would answer a good purpose and a good school could be maintained. Mr. Nicholson established one & had about 30 male scholars when he left."

Mr. Albert apparently did not have the Rev. Mr. Gillette's weakness for schools, nor was he reassured by the suggestion that yellow fever killed only non-Episcopalians. He wrote: "Being a Northern man I have greater fears of the Yellow Fever than those accustomed to it." And in his next, "When I take into consideration that I was brought up in a cold and exceedingly healthful climate and that in consequence the danger would be so much greater in my case, I feel as though I cannot." Which put him right back to his March 7 letter in which he had said, "I felt that it could not be my duty with my little family to throw myself into danger." It had taken him six weeks and several hundred words to say no.

And after that, Christ Church got a rector who plunged toward yellow fever as a horse heads into a burning barn: The Rev. W. T. D. Dalzell —doctor and priest. William Tucker Dickinson Dalzell was born of English parentage on a sugar plantation in St. Vincent, Windward Islands, in the British West Indies, in June, 1828. At 14 he was sent to London to school, and while in England, he studied and practiced medicine, and studied theology. He returned to the West Indies as a missionary for the Society for the Propagation of the Gospel. In Jamaica he was ordained first deacon and then priest by the Bishop of Jamaica.*

Doctor Dalzell was a man who moved in wide sweeps across the globe in a time when travel was not particularly fast or easy. He went to Charlotte Amalie, St. Thomas Island, as rector of All Saints' Church which was under the British Bishop of Antigua, though the island was Danish territory. It is believed that on a visit to Demerara, British Guiana, where his sister lived as the wife of a British Naval Officer, he ministered as priest and doctor to those dying in a cholera epidemic.

In 1854, newly called to Trinity Church, Columbus, Georgia, he went on an emergency mission to Savannah to serve in his dual capacity in a yellow fever epidemic. Savannah looked upon him as a ministering angel. The Rt. Rev. Stephen Elliott Jr., wrote, "From . . . about the 12th day of August until the middle of November, I was confined to the city by the fearful pestilence which ravaged it, and exposed its congregations to nauseous disease and rapid dissolution. In this work of duty I was assisted by the disinterested labors of the Rev. Mr. Dalsele, (sic) then recently called to the Rectorship of Trinity Church, Columbus; and it affords me much pleasure to record thus publicly my own gratitude, and that of the congregations of Sa-

*Courtesy the Rev. Frank MacDonald Spindler.

1855. Houston has 4,690 oxen, pulling 670 wagons and drivers.

vannah, for his self-sacrificing attention to the sick and the afflicted, and for his excellent judgment and good sense in suggesting and carrying out various plans for the benefit of our suffering city."

The Rev. Henry Hopkins, Jr., after praising Bishop Elliott and his wife for *their* disinterested—or selfless—work, added, "I cannot forbear to mention the noble conduct of the Rev. Mr. Dalzell. When he heard of the existence of Yellow Fever, he hastened to Savannah." A year later Doctor Dalzell accepted a call to the Church of the Ascension in Philadelphia.

Bishop Freeman had been hunting a rector for Houston for some time, and at last in December, 1856, he wrote, "There is a clergyman in Philadelphia. . . . He is the Rev. W. T. D. Dalzell, rector of the Church of the Ascension. He is, I think, from the West Indies, and, accordingly acclimated. His wife is the daughter of the Rt. Rev. H. U. Onderdonk, and is represented to be a fine woman and well suited to the position of a Clergyman's wife. I have not heard him preach, but learn that he is respectable in that line. He is a tall, good looking man and may be about thirty or thirty-five years of age." [He was 29.] Nobody stopped to think that young Mrs. Dalzell from Pennsylvania might *not* be acclimated.

The vestry resolved to call Doctor Dalzell, and to ask the Rev. R. B. Croes, in Texas temporarily from the Diocese of New York, to officiate at Christ Church until a rector could be acquired. They offered Dalzell $1,200—which was less than his predecessor had received—and Croes $75 a month.

With the arrival of Dalzell, Christ Church not only gained one of the most interesting rectors of its history, but also its first High Churchman. Perhaps the credit should go to the liberal breadth of its bishops, perhaps to the fact that clergy and bishops were too busy building any kind of church they could build to bother with differences of opinions as to how services should be conducted within those churches. But whatever the cause, neither Christ Church nor the diocese had been caught up to any painful degree in the great controversies over ritualism which stormed through the Protestant Episcopal Church during most of the 19th century. The church in Texas was never so Low Church in its services as the ardent evangelicals would have demanded: both Bishop Polk and Bishop Freeman wore surplices. And services were seldom so High Church as the Anglo-Catholics would have liked: it is not easy to have an altar, to have cross, flowers or candles on the altar, or to have a cross at the head of a choir procession, when services are being held in a court house.

But Doctor Dalzell made his position clear from the start. He was a reasonable rather than a rigid or dictatorial man. His ministry throughout his life was marked more by enthusiasm, by love for the Church and for people, than by the strong opinion which sometimes had prompted the Rev. Mr. Gillette to admonish the congregation with youthful but professorial vehemence. But he believed that principles clearly explained in words and example will endure. In his first talk to the vestry, he expressed his pleasure in being offered this new field of endeavor. He reminded them that his interest was not monetary in that he had come for a lower salary than he had been receiving in Philadelphia. [Which does support the theory that yellow fever was one of Houston's charms for him.] He then proposed, the vestry minutes say, "to hold church services twice on Sunday, to have morning prayer on Wednesdays and Fridays, and service on the Holy Days recognized by the Church. Also that he designed taking collections systematically for church institutions and other purposes. In Advent for Domestic Missions. At Epiphany for Foreign Missions. On Trinity Sunday for Diocesan expenses and Missions. And that he desired the approbation of the vestry to his taking collections at other times for such occasional objects, connected with the church, as might present themselves."

This was spanking-new language to the Christ Church vestry of 1857. Up until that time, the church had subsisted—or tried to subsist—on pew rents. Ten years of futile struggle to collect pew rents, recourse to paying the treasurer a commission on all he could collect, constant indebtedness and frequent compulsory rescue by individual vestrymen—none of this had shaken faith in the pew rent system. Though E. B. Nichols and Peter Gray had once each proposed free pews, at no time had the vestry thought to pass a collection plate regularly in church. The vestry was quite pleased to approve Doctor Dalzell's program, but in the same meeting, went on to appoint A. Keech, Jr., to help rent pews and to go out and seek funds from "friends of the church." It ordered the treasurer to be allowed 5 per cent commission on any rents he could collect. And it voted to give Pew No. 4 for the use of the rector and his family.

The arrival of a new, vigorous, handsome and well educated rector with a charming wife who was a bishop's daughter stimulated the vestry "to procure a rectory building by building or purchase." On request, the rector named Col. John D. Andrews, Peter W. Gray and A. Keech, as the committee to raise funds by subscription. The vestry worked rapidly and well. E. W. Taylor became chairman of the building committee. Subscriptions mounted: "William J. Hutchins, $500; J. D. Andrews, $250; P. W. Gray, $200; Judge B. P. Buckner, $100; E. S. Gentry, $100; F. A. Rice, John Dickinson, A. M. Gentry, Henry Sampson, $50 each. And from young Ben Botts, $25." And when they came up short, they dug again a year later; "W. J. Hutchins, $500. James R. Ennis, $100. B. P. Buckner, $100. F. A. Rice *in lumber,* $50. J. Dickinson, $50. J. D. Andrews, $250. James Reily, $100. P. W. Gray, $100. F. Scranton, $200. I. S. Roberts & Co., $50. W. H. Eliot to be paid from Comms. as Treas. of Vestry $75. O. L. Cochran $40. E. S. Perkins, $100. Henry Sampson, $50." And young A. Keech, Jr., and young Ben Botts, $25 each.

The new rectory, the contract with Bering Bros. stated, was to be built behind the church and facing Texas Avenue. The "Main House" was a two-story rectangle with a 16-foot-square room on each side of the central hall and staircase. A gallery ran across the front, upstairs and down, and on pleasant days a hammock would swing across the upper gallery.

The "Wing" was the leg of an L running back from Texas Avenue on the church side of the house. It was more poorly finished—thinner plaster, simpler baseboards, fewer coats of interior paint. The backmost of the wing rooms was the kitchen, and the one closest to the front of the house was usually the rector's study. A back gallery ran along the inside of the L to connect the kitchen with the front part of the house. The tin gutters were all constructed to pour into the cistern—a large one, "10 by 16 feet with a good wood cover." Patrick Fox charged the vestry $8.25 for 5½ days' work spreading cistern earth and sand on the rectory lot at $1.50 a day. The privy had two rooms, "one to be ceiled and neatly finished." This was a $3,000 house at mid-19th century.

On his last visit to Houston before his death, Bishop Freeman was en-

1856. The city of Dallas is incorporated.

couraged to find "Mr. Dalzell very acceptable to the congregation, who were already projecting the building of a Rectory and the enlargement of the church. I trust he will be eminently successful in uniting and edifying this important congregation." Outsiders always seemed to look upon Christ Church as "important"—however hard the struggle or frail the structure sometimes seemed to those at home.

Doctor Dalzell soon became a well known and popular Houstonian. He was invited to speak at school commencement programs, and when on trips, wrote back charming, sometimes teasing, but informative letters to his friend who edited the Houston *Tri-Weekly Telegraph*. He spread himself as far as he could—to found Calvary Church, Richmond, on the base laid by the Rev. Hannibal Pratt, and to found St. Bartholemew's Church, Hempstead. Exhausted by the chore, Hannibal Pratt wrote gratefully to the *Spirit of Missions* "Brother Dalzell of Houston kindly volunteered to supply Richmond, thus relieving me . . . of 120 miles of stage travel, by night, monthly." And St. Bartholomew's still reflects his influence.

But before the vestry could make all its collections for the rectory, the first "monetary difficulties" which foreshadowed a coming depression cropped up. And before the Dalzells could move into the new rectory, the rector had to read the funeral service in the Episcopal Cemetery for the infant Jeanie, one of the twin daughters born in Houston. Eight-year-old Spencer Dalzell died in the autumn of 1858, and six-month-old Henry Onderdonk Dalzell died the next August.

Peter W. Gray had been recommending for some time a revision of the constitution, and his new constitution was adopted at the Easter Monday meeting of the congregation in 1858. To comply with Texas law on the appointment of trustees to handle corporate lands and properties, the constitution provided that the vestry would be the Board of Trustees of the congregation. It reduced the number of vestrymen to nine, "to be chosen from among the male members of the congregation entitled to vote for vestrymen, and to continue in office for one year. All persons who reside in or near Houston and who are Communicants or worshippers in the church of this Parish are members of this Congregation; but only the male members, being either Communicants or Pewholders, or else Worshippers and annual contributors to the support of this church, shall be entitled to vote for vestrymen." In other words, to be a vestryman, one had to be male, a contributor, and fairly faithful in attending church services. Neither baptism nor confirmation were required for membership to the vestry.

Doctor Dalzell raised money among the parishioners to buy an organ to replace the old melodeon, and hired Miss Payne* as organist "for such amounts as might be received at collections to be taken in church on the third Sunday evening of each month." He was trying quietly to get the congregation accustomed to the idea of some contribution from everyone, and the vestry agreed to declare the pews free for the annual convention of the diocese. But at the same vestry meeting, the vestry raised pew rents for the year under the happy conviction that though lower pew rents could not easily be collected, higher ones would solve all their financial problems.

---

* Miss Payne was probably Keziah Payne who would some day become the founder of De Pelchin Faith Home. J. J. Nicholson referred to her in his notes on church offerings: "April, 1855. $30 devoted to aid of Bohemian widow and 6 children. A case of real need; all ill of typhoid fever, nursed by Miss Keziah Payne . . ."

The 1859 Church

The first brick church facing Fannin Street had been outgrown before it was paid for. But in September, 1858, rector and vestry faced the fact that it was no longer even safe. The committee appointed to look into the task of building a new church proposed a four point plan. The first recommendation was "that it is expedient to erect a new church of much larger dimensions than the present, such as will cost not less than $16,000." And the fourth was "that the church be made a Free Church if possible or practicable after a fair trial."

Doctor Dalzell wrote the *Church Journal* of New York for help:

"On taking charge of this Parish in the last year, I found a tumbling-down church, which has now become so bad that it is hardly safe to worship in it. I am now making an effort to replace it with a new and larger one, which I design to make, if possible, a Free Church. I have already obtained $10,000 toward this object in this town, and hope to raise $1,000 more, either before commencing to build or while the building is in the course of erection. . . . such a church as will supply the growing necessities of our town will cost at least $18,000, and then will not be larger than one which, with you, would cost 40 per cent less than that amount."

Free churches, Doctor Dalzell added, seemed particularly needed in Texas.

"The Church here has always been mainly supported by a few, while the many have done little or nothing; and although since I have been here I have instituted a weekly offertory, it has not proved as successful as I could wish, or as it would otherwise be, on account of the pews being rented, that being sufficient plea with many for not giving, and a source of fear with even some of my vestrymen that people are bored by the plate passing around.

"Add to this that the Church has established the reputation here which she elsewhere frequently sustains, of being aristocratic and exclusive, and that therefore many who would attend her services do not for fear of intruding on private property, and we make out a cause for a free church.

"With a free church, those who have always given largely can only, if necessary, continue to do so, while many who now give *nothing* will give *Something* . . . and many will be led to join the congregation who will never do so, except occasionally, while the rented pew system prevails."

One of those rare and reasonable men able to see that he might be wrong, Doctor Dalzell added, "I am persuaded of the *truth* of the principle, and feel strongly assured of its success here if it is fairly tried. Yet I might be mistaken. If it can work here, with God's blessing it shall. But if we find that it is impracticable, I wish the Rector and vestry to be at liberty to change from it to the present system; and I explicitly state this that none who contribute to the building shall misunderstand the matter." Texas, he concluded, needed and deserved help from the Church of which it was a part. "Without a Bishop; with a very small staff of clergymen; with only two or three respectable church buildings; with little or no money; the things that remain are ready to die. Yet . . . we are not in despair. The Church has here a glorious work to do . . ."

Doctor Dalzell sent his letter and then prepared to go east to ask for help in person in Washington, Baltimore, Philadelphia, New York, Boston, Columbus, Ohio; Cincinnati, and Louisville.

This young man of many parts was now traveling as a Texan, and February

1859. Charles Gounod's Faust *has its premiere at the Théâtre Lyrique in Paris March 19, and Victor Herbert is born in Dublin.*

1860. Abraham Lincoln is elected 16th President of the United States, and South Carolina secedes from the union.

23, 1859, he wrote to the Houston *Tri-Weekly Telegraph* from the Steamer *Express* about 30 miles from Memphis:

"Leaving Galveston on 29th Dec., I crossed the Gulf, then smooth and placid as some fairy lake, in that best of boats, the *Texas,* and one worthy to bear her name. At the St. Charles, New Orleans, I found that self-interest, if nothing more, secured me every attention and comfort. Less than two years ago, I had spent a few days of the greatest discomfort at this same hotel. But then I was registered as a Philadelphian, whereas now I was a Texian, in which difference I was told, was to be found the true reason of the change. Texas travel (as it is now called) having now become of such consequence and so remunerative, that the proprietors are anxious to attract it to their house. Hence much attention and politeness.

"Need I tell you that one hears of nothing now but President making, acquiring Cuba and the revival of the Slave trade?

"As to the slave trade, the views of the people North differ widely from yours, Mr. Cushing; all are opposed to its revival. That they oppose it on true principles I am not ready to assert; but that their opposition is unconstitutional [sic—possibly an error in newspaper type setting] and lawful we must admit: and until the laws of the United States shall be altered; until the war cruisers of European powers shall be withdrawn; until the horrors that for ages past have attended the slave trade will not longer exist; until everything that can prevent a cargo of Africans from enjoying the same ease and immunity that belong to any other ship load of emigrants going from one country to another shall be removed, I hope that the voice of the opposers of the traffic will be heard . . ."

1859. Charles Darwin publishes his Origin of Species.

Doctor Dalzell's letter—which could almost as easily be run in a present-day newspaper—concludes: "Let me only add, that everywhere Texas seems to be looked to as a State of richest promise and that I have heard but one opinion expressed in reference to her future. That future, all prophesy, is to be one of greatness. With us who are already in the field, it remains to develop that greatness social, political and religious. To this end, Mr. Editor, may you and I, and all of us who have any influence at all to wield, whether it be at the polls, in the school, through the press, or in the pulpit, wield it in the fear of God for the good of the Community."

On that trip north—while in New Orleans—he stopped for a visit with Bishop Leonidas Polk and there met again Bishop Elliott of Georgia—his old comrade of the yellow fever days in Savannah. Both bishops knew of the long, drawn out search for a bishop being made by the Diocese of Texas. Both knew well and admired tremendously the little known Alexander Gregg of Cheraw, South Carolina. From this conversation, Doctor Dalzell discovered and gave in nomination to the diocese a great bishop—one of his finest contributions.

1860. Garibaldi invades Sicily. Francis Joseph I becomes king of Hungary. First embassy from Japan reaches Washington and is received by Buchanan.

Doctor Dalzell had expected to be gone several weeks but stayed almost three months. Like Gillette before him, he found his colleagues and fellow Episcopalians in the east disappointing in their response to his enthusiasm for the new land of Texas. He came home with $1,100 in cash and $1,000 more in pledges. But on his return to Houston, he urged that a beginning be made at once on the new church, arguing that the sight of the work being done would inspire further contributions.

Edwin Fairfax Gray, now state engineer, presented his plans for a charming little church which he and the rector thought could be built for $14,000— if they gave up the basement. They had $12,000 in subscriptions, they thought. And it was now imperative that the congregation stop using the old building which was markedly unsafe, and move their services once again to the Court House. The vestry agreed. The new church would, it resolved, "be of brick with Tower and steeple, and of dimensions 52½ feet by 87 feet deep . . . to have a vestry room in the rear."

This church would be the first on the site to face Texas Avenue. Benjamin A. Botts, still one of the fairly young members, was appointed chairman of the building committee. As time for signing the contract drew near, rector and vestry faced the fact that they actually had only $8,000 in hand and doubted if they could collect more on their subscription list any time soon. And so they ordered $8,000 worth of church. They commissioned John Trenton to build walls, roof, enclosed windows and—if possible—a tower "to the extent of $8,000."

September 7, 1859, the cornerstone was laid by the Rev. Dr. Dalzell, Peter W. Gray and Dr. W. H. Eliot, wardens; W. J. Hutchins, E. W. Taylor, Alexander Keech, Robert Brewster, Owen L. Cochran, B. A Botts and A. S. Richardson, vestrymen. They deposited in the cornerstone "a copy of the *Journal of Convention* for 1859, the last copy of *Church Journal* published in New York, last Copy of *Banner of the Cross* published in Philadelphia; one copy each of the last numbers of Houston *Telegraph* and Houston *Republic,* Various coins of the Union." And the work began.

Dalzell Finds a Bishop

One month after the corner stone was laid for a new Christ Church, the vestry minutes record: "The Revd. Alexander Gregg of Cheraw, South Carolina, who was elected to the Bishopric of Texas by the Diocesan Convention on the Sixth of May last, *was duly consecrated* as *Bishop of Texas,* in the Monumental Church at Richmond, Virginia, during the General Convention of the Church."

Though the Diocese of Texas was established in 1849, it had no resident bishop for the first decade. The Rt. Rev. Leonidas Polk—that vast man who would found the University of the South and die as General Polk in the cause of the Confederacy—was named missionary bishop of the Episcopal Church in the same year of Christ Church founding. Fortunately young and powerful at 33, he took on all of Alabama, Mississippi, the Indian Territory, Louisiana and Texas, and in two years, made three visitations from one end to the other of his vast area—traveling by horse, by wagon, by oxcart, by boat, preaching, baptizing, marrying, burying and confirming as he went. When in 1841 he was elected Bishop of Louisiana, he agreed to oversee Alabama and Texas until Alabama could elect a bishop and Texas could become a diocese.

In 1844, the Rt. Rev. George Washington Freeman was elected missionary bishop of Arkansas and the Indian Territory, with special charge of the missions in the Republic of Texas. By 1845 Texas had entered the union, and on his first visitation, Freeman found 200 communicants in the entire state and most of them in Houston, Galveston and Matagorda. He was not a strong man physically, and he was 55 years old when elected, but he gave to Texas 15 years of dedicated Christian service. His trips through Texas accompanied in relays by the young missionaries and clergy along the way, were feats of pioneer steadfastness and endurance. His earnestness and wisdom, his readily

given praise and reassurances, helped each one of the early congregations and rectors to try harder under the bishop's leadership.

When the Diocese of Texas was formed at Matagorda in 1849, Bishop Freeman was urged to move from Little Rock to Texas. In Texas at this time, there were a tremendous number of good people who—though willing to accept or eager for religious instruction—had had no church training of any kind. "The field is white for the harvest" was a favorite sentence among church builders and missionaries. Undoubtedly some missionaries— regardless of denomination—were tempted to try to be all things to all men, to provide so broad and general a church in theology and service as to attract all. Bishop Freeman saw this tendency as a danger which could weaken, damage or destroy the Episcopal Church.

In one convention address, Dr. Lawrence L. Brown writes, Bishop Freeman made two points.

"First, the clergy must set forth the whole Gospel, as they had received it. There must be no compromise, no holding back for fear of prejudice, in presenting the Church 'as a divine institution, as apostolic in its character and organization, as Catholic as well as Protestant in its doctrines, and as the Body of Christ of which all who would be saved must ordinarily become members.'

"The services of the church must be conducted in strict obedience to the rubrics of the Prayer Book. To omit portions, to make changes as some were disposed to do, was to violate the vows of ordination, the Bishop believed, and further, was to gain nothing at all, for the liturgy in its integrity commended itself to people better than watered-down versions.*"

When the Diocesan Convention urged Bishop Freeman—whom they loved —to move from Little Rock to Texas, he saw that his first duty was to organize the work in Arkansas and the Indian Territory. He advised the Texas Convention to prepare themselves to support a Bishop, and then to elect one.

In 1852, the convention unanimously elected Freeman bishop of the Diocese of Texas. In 1853 he arrived in Austin prepared to decline. By this time, Freeman was well past 60 and feeling increasingly frail. He knew that he must say no, but the clergy were so eager to have him that they persuaded him to delay his decision for a time. It was therefore not until 1854 that Bishop Freeman finally declined the bishopric which Texans had been offering him in one form or another for almost five years. And it was 1855 before the Diocesan Convention could regroup and conduct another election.

Thereafter the convention invited four different men—one each year— to become bishop of the Diocese of Texas and each one declined. Texas did, however, receive an offer—through the Rev. Arthur Cleveland Coxe in Baltimore—to support a bishop of Texas at the rate of $1500 a year for three years *if* the diocese would offer him $1,000 and traveling expenses. After that, Coxe would give $1,000 a year if the diocese would pay $1,500. Coxe was acting for a group including New York, Philadelphia and Baltimore clergymen [*Ibid.*]. The Texans agreed to the matching funds offer, but still had no bishop. After four refusals, the diocese was in a predicament.

At last in 1859, nominated by Doctor Dalzell of Christ Church at the convention in Galveston, Alexander Gregg of Cheraw, S.C. was elected on the fourth ballot and then unanimously. Uniquely—he accepted. And almost nobody, except Doctor Dalzell, had ever heard of him.

* *The Episcopal Church in Texas,* 1838-1847, by Lawrence L. Brown, p. 47.

1860. First Pony Express starts with 80 riders, 420 horses, 190 relay stations, and a change of horse every 10 miles between Sacramento, California, and St. Joseph, Missouri.

1860. Houston's first Methodist church falls down Sunday morning 25 minutes after the congregation is dismissed.

Born in 1819, Gregg was from a rich planter background—Baptist—and was already a well established young lawyer at 22. He fell in love with and married Charlotte Wilson Kolloch, a devout Episcopalian, and soon after his marriage, he was baptized and confirmed in the Episcopal Church. Immediately after that, he gave up law and set himself toward the ministry. It wasn't easy. There was no theological seminary in South Carolina, and he began a course of reading under Bishop Gadsden. Retiring to a farm he owned, Alexander Gregg studied Hebrew and Greek, as well as theology, and after three years passed his examinations, and was ordained. At St. David's Church, Cheraw, his ministry showed concern for all human kind, regardless of color, nationality or pocketbook. Under Gregg, St. David's congregational offerings for diocesan, foreign and domestic missions usually exceeded those of many churches much larger, and Bishop Davis reported ". . . the congregation appears to be in advancing condition. The Rector has devoted himself with faithfulness and success to the very poor members of his parish." As bishop and slave owner, the Rt. Rev. Alexander Gregg would show the same warm interest in the spiritual education of the Negroes in Texas that young Charles Gillett of Connecticut always showed.

It was not easy for either Mr. or Mrs. Gregg to leave South Carolina—a rich, and gracious land peopled with gentle folk who were their lifelong friends and relatives. But they recognized the real desperation and the plight of Texas. Equally devout in their church and in their sense of duty, they agreed that Alexander Gregg should accept the call. The Diocese of Texas was represented at his consecration in Richmond, October 31, 1859, by the Rev. W. T. D. Dalzell, Judge Peter W. Gray of Houston, the Rev. Benjamin Eaton, and Col. Isaac E. Nicholson of Galveston.

When Bishop Gregg made his first visitation to Houston on New Year's Day, 1860, the congregation was meeting at the court house. Bishop Gregg preached and administered communion in the morning, and preached and confirmed nine persons at night. This was apparently a high point in warmth between vestry and rector, for next day without Dalzell's knowledge, the vestry voted to seek a subscription among members to raise his salary to $1,500—the amount paid his predecessor—and to pay $400 toward the bishop's salary. This, they planned, would leave the collections at church services to go to other expenses and church purposes.

It was characteristic of the times that men who served the church were likely to be substantial citizens active in city and business affairs. Several Christ Church vestrymen took terms as mayor of Houston: Francis Moore, Jr., was mayor in 1838, 1843, 1849, 1850, 1851, 1852. John D. Andrews was mayor 1841, 1842. W. W. Swain was mayor in 1845. B. P. Buckner was mayor 1847, 1848, Cornelius Ennis in 1857, W. J. Hutchins in 1861. Christ Church vestrymen who were elected aldermen at various times were A. S. Ruthven, E. S. Perkins, E. B. Nichols, T. M. League, B. A. Shepherd, J. W. Cruger, Robert Brewster, W. A. Van Alstyne, E. W. Taylor, William M. Rice, Henry Sampson, T. S. Lubbock, F. S. Rottenstein, F. A. Rice, Alexander Sessums.

It is hard to understand why both rector and vestrymen felt unable to raise enough money in Houston to build the church. The year 1860 was the richest year commercially the city had had up to that time, with both exports and imports reaching a new high. The railroads had begun to develop. The Houston Academy had opened its new $20,000 building, part of Main Street had been covered with shell, the Houston and Texas Central Railroad shops

1860. The Rev. Zacharias Emmich, Houston's first Jewish rabbi, comes to Congregation Beth Israel.

1861. Battle of Bull Run. Son of Barnard E. Bee who signed the first Christ Church document, Brig. Gen. B. E. Bee shouts "There is Jackson standing like a stone wall!"

had begun. By 1860, the Texas Telegraph Company had opened service to Galveston. The time would soon end when Christ Church had to send its telegrams by mail to New Orleans. Dick Dowling's famous saloon—"a bank at the corner of Main Street and Congress Avenue for the purpose of dealing in the exchange of liquors for gold, silver and bank notes"—opened. And a newspaperman, looking out from the roof of the new, not yet completed Hutchins House, saw "In every direction new houses . . . while nearby stately brick stores are rising on every block."

Cotton was being shipped in at such rates that bales had to be stacked on sidewalks. W. J. Hutchins was rising steadily in business, Peter W. Gray—now 40—had been district attorney under President Sam Houston, had represented Harris County in the first meeting of the state legislature, and by 1856, was judge of the district court. Like William Marsh Rice and E. B. Nichols, Cornelius Ennis was doing well in his cotton business—one of Houston's oldest, and like Paul Bremond he was getting into railroading.

But the omens of the mounting crises in the nation were already evident: Harriet Beecher Stowe's *Uncle Tom's Cabin*—first printed in 1852—had become a best seller. As Doctor Dalzell had written the Houston newspapers, the talk was of nothing but the controversy over the slave trade. As early as 1858, a lyceum debate on "Is it to the interest of the South to dissolve the Union?" stirred such interest that it had to be carried over for five nights.

In June Doctor Dalzell's young wife—not yet 30 years old—died. Bleakly he called a meeting of the vestry. "After prayers, the Rector stated that in consequence of his bereavement by the death of his wife (Mrs. Helen Dalzell) it would be necessary for him to take his infant daughter to her mother's relatives in Philadelphia . . . as soon as he could make the necessary arrangements for leaving." In the custom of the times, perhaps, the vestry minutes make no reference to any resolutions of sympathy or condolence. Doctor Dalzell—who had lost three children and a wife in three years—suggested that because of his unusual expenses, he be allowed to rent the rectory, reserving a room for his own use. The vestry approved and then asked the rector to solicit further subscriptions toward paying for the church.

The vestry had contracted for $11,800 worth of work to be done on the new church—by this time getting a bit weathered though incomplete—and had managed to pay only $8,017 of this debt—though the builder had given a discount of $355 and allowed $400 on materials from the first church. At this point, honor was saved when "The Committee would state in this connection that they received as a loan from the Ladies of the Parish Four Hundred Dollars, which amount they are now using for payment to Builder . . ."

By fall, the normally buoyant Doctor Dalzell was thoroughly disheartened. He mentioned the discouragements of his three years in Houston, and expressed the doubt that he was fitted for success in this field. He asked the vestry's opinion and got no answer: "The subject was talked over, individual views were expressed, but no formal action was taken." Dalzell went on with his work. He helped to found the Diocesan Missionary Society which met at St. David's Austin with Bishop Gregg presiding. Doctor Dalzell preached a sermon at this meeting, and the first annual report shows him and Mr. E. S. Perkins as the only annual members from Houston. Of the two paid-up life members, one was Col. Robert E. Lee of the United States Army.

Colonel Lee was busy in Texas at the time conducting the Army's experiments to see how camels performed on the Texas deserts in compari-

1862. After 57 rehearsals, singers of the Vienna Court Opera declare Tristan and Isolde *impossible to learn.*

son to the army mules. It was possibly the army experiment with camels which prompted an Englishwoman to import 40 of them to Harris County— using then as a cover-up for blackbirding operations.* She boarded them for a year on Governor Francis Lubbock's ranch on Sims Bayou near Harrisburg. In the years before the Civil War, camels from this herd cooled themselves in the water of Buffalo Bayou and sometimes lumbered into town and down Main Street.

Among those married by Doctor Dalzell in his short career at Christ Church were Edwin Fairfax Gray and Miss Rosalie W. Taylor, Charles E. Gregory and Augusta R. Stone, Frank B. Wright and Mary J. Roberts, Samuel K. McIlhenny and Sarah Goldthwaite, J. H. Wickes and Dida Barry, John H. Foushee and Mrs. Martha Ann Nickerson, James H. Evans and Cora W. Taylor, Charles E. Caswill and Catherine J. Clarke, Robert T. Flewellen and Eugenia Andrews, W. Browne Botts and Mattie E. McIlhenny, Curtis A. Darling and Sarah A. G. Lubbock, Thomas R. Franklin and Julia E. Hadley.

Funerals were more numerous than weddings . . . The ages ran 1 month, 8 years, 2 years, 3 months, 8 years 6 months, 9 years, 66 years, in 29th year [Mrs. Dalzell] a few days, 23 years, 61 years . . . At the end of the parish list of funerals, Doctor Dalzell wrote "The above were parishioners of Christ Church. I have attended many other funerals of strangers . . ." Of the 12 parishioners he buried, four were of his own family.

Finally in May, 1861, Doctor Dalzell resigned.

"It is not necessary that I should dwell upon the causes . . . you are already fully in possession of them and they are of such nature as to impress me with the necessity of considering the good of the parish and my own prospects of usefulness, for resigning into your hands the care of the parish . . .

"I have been with you, Brethren, over four years. During that time I have been called to meet heavy trials and to endure much suffering. Let me assure you that this last trial of leaving this parish, as I am now about to do, is not by any means the lightest of these borne here, nor the least portion of the consequent suffering.

"From the outset, I discovered that I had entered in a peculiar field of labor. I have desired & endeavored to do my duty. I am . . . painfully conscious that I have come short in many things, but I ask you, . . . to accept the good intention & mercifully to forgive the shortcomings . . ."

The 20th century could wish that Dalzell *had* been willing to list his reasons. Certainly four deaths had not helped his spirits. Certainly the continuing failure of the community to pay for and complete the church for consecration had disappointed him.

Doctor Dalzell had been largely reared and educated in England. Britain abandoned slavery in the kingdom in 1772, and had outlawed it throughout the British Empire in 1834—paying 20 million pounds for the 700,000 liberated slaves. From his letter to the editor, it is obvious that he was not in sympathy with a continuance of slavery in the United States, and from his indications of character, it is probable that he stated his position reasonably, with humor, but quite frankly. Differences in so simple a thing as phrase can mean much in time of controversy and highly sensitized feelings. Mrs. William Fairfax Gray in her diary and even the Connecticut

* Source: Dr. Andrew Forest Muir.

1862. The first Presbyterian church burns, and regular services are suspended for the remainder of the war.

born Gillette always referred to "servants." In fact, Gillette's church records show no difference between a free "English servant" or a "poor white woman, servant" and the unfree Negro. But Dalzell in letters and records referred flatly to slaves. In a city which was soon to vote rousingly for secession and shout down even their beloved Sam Houston, this might not have made for universal rapport.

The vestry voted to accept the resignation and Benjamin Botts wrote him accordingly. "The vestry duly appreciate the many trials you have encountered during your sojourn with us and regret the necessity that compels your separation from us. Permit me to avail myself of this opportunity to express my individual wishes for your future success and happiness." This is the only kind word on record for Doctor Dalzell.

There are many elsewhere. Doctor Dalzell became rector of St. Mark's, San Antonio. After the war he went to Shreveport where he spent the remainder of his ministry—except for his various forays against yellow fever in any nearby state whenever needed. He became nationally known as the years went on and was a trustee of the General Theological Seminary, and of the University of the South at Sewanee. When he died, a Shreveport account said "One who knew him well once remarked . . . that it was almost incomprehensible that a man who could give such vehement utterance to his honest convictions, could also minister in his pastoral relationships with surpassing gentleness . . . Dr. Dalzell loved humanity with something like the love of Him who gave His life for men."

Chapter 23

War

The War Between the States brought excitement, controversy, glamor, profiteering, movement, and losses to Houston and to Christ Church. The mayor authorized Gen. W. P. Rogers, Henry Sampson and A. N. Jordan to organize a home and coast-defense battalion. Houston men drained out into the Confederate army at a fast clip. Captain Benjamin A. Botts's Bayou City Guards were scheduled for service in Virginia. Capt. William Gentry's Volunteers, Capt. Ashbel Smith's Bayland Guards, Capt. Hal Runnell's Van Dorn Infantry, Capt. E. F. Gray's Sumter Guards, Capt. J. H. Manley's Houston Artillery, Capt. F. Odlum's Home Guard, Capt. P. W. Gray's Texas Grays, Capt. D. McGregor's Home Guards, and Capt. A. T. Morse's Houston Cavalry, were ready for duty. Dr. W. H. Eliot, druggist, fitted up machinery to make printer's ink—no longer available from the states.

By Christmas, 1862, Galveston was in enemy hands but the *Bayou City* and the *Neptune*, took on cotton at the Houston wharf at the foot of Main Street, and behind the bales, carried a load of artillerymen and sharpshooters. They sailed down the bayou, followed by the *Lucy Gwinn* and the *John F. Carr* loaded with infantrymen. In the New Year's Day Battle of Galveston, the *Bayou City* and *Neptune* attacked the U. S. gunboat *Harriet Lane*. The *Neptune* was sunk, but the *Bayou City* rammed and captured the Federal cruiser. She returned to Houston with the *Harriet Lane's* ensign at her masthead. Houstonians watched 350 Yankee prisoners march down Main Street.

Bishop Gregg spoke out sternly against profiteering—against charging such extortionate prices for essentials, simply because they were rare, that only the rich could afford shoes. And Bishop Gregg had reason: some merchants asked

$100 for a pair of boots, $30 for a pair of garters, and sold milk at $1 a quart, flour at $50 a 100-lb sack.

Houston became the military headquarters for the Confederate District of Texas, New Mexico and Arizona. Christ Church, which lost many of its members to the movements of war, gained many refugees from Galveston. Saloon-keeper Dick Dowling became the town's hero when he and his Houston Irishmen manned six guns to repulse the attack of four Federal gunboats and the landing of 5,000 northern troops. But Col. James Reily—one time diplomat, a Christ Church founder, and first Lay Deputy from Texas at a General Convention of the Episcopal Church, was killed in action on the Bayou Teche in Louisiana as commanding officer of the Fourth Texas Cavalry.

Both Christ Church and the Diocese of Texas faced up to the dilemma of resolving their loyalties to the Confederacy and to the Protestant Episcopal Church of America. As a South Carolinian, Bishop Gregg naturally inclined toward the South's cause, but was too fair-minded a man, too devout a churchman, to be a bitter partisan. On the principle that the church always shaped its units of organization within national boundaries, he believed that without any break in the Anglican Communion, there must yet inevitably be a Protestant Episcopal Church of the Confederate States. But in appointing a committee to study the matter, he included the Rev. Charles Gillette, that Connecticut Yankee, and the Rev. Benjamin Eaton, who had come to Galveston out of Ireland by way of Wisconsin. The committee's majority held that it would be premature to form a new national organization at the first meeting called in Montgomery, but by a fairly narrow margin, the diocesan concensus went against the committee. Though the Diocese of Texas agreed to accept the constitution of the Confederate Church, because of distances and blockades, Texas was never able to take a very active part in the efforts to form a Confederate Church.

The chief controversy came between Bishop Gregg and Gillette over the wording of the bishop's prayer. Gillette objected to the phrase "this unnatural war which has been forced upon us," and rebelled against praying it in his church in Austin. In an exchange of a barrage of letters, Gillette carried the theological battle on throughout the war, and Bishop Gregg held his ground, though trying to make allowances for Gillette's feelings. Two things resulted: Bishop Gregg was inspired to write his "Primary Charge to the Clergy of the Protestant Episcopal Church in the Diocese of Texas" on the subject of the separation between church and state and deliver it in Christ Church Houston, May 9, 1863.* And on accumulated anger, Gillette at the war's end left the diocese he had helped to found, and spent the last days of his life working for the Freedman's Bureau. One of the most vigorous and colorful ministers in diocesan history, he died suddenly in Baltimore at the age of 51.

After the war, Bishop Gregg used his same principle to assume that the Protestant Episcopal Church must again follow national boundaries, and he was the first citizen in Austin to swear loyalty to the United States. Texas was the first southern diocese to return to the General Convention. To Gregg, the division had never meant a schism in the Anglican Communion. Though he was criticized by some of his more hot-blooded neighbors in Austin (as

1863. Abraham Lincoln issues the Emancipation Proclamation January 1 freeing slaves in 11 Southern states.

---

* Published in *Historical Magazine of the Protestant Episcopal Church,* Vol. XXXI, No. 2, pp. 165-203. Dr. Lawrence Brown commented "The moderate, thoughtful and theologically sensitive way that he used his knowledge of history and political interpretations of the Christian's duty to each contain thoughts which would well be pondered in our own time."

he had undoubtedly been criticized by some of his more cold-blooded ones at the beginning of the war) Bishop Gregg—by his example—speeded the return of unity between state and nation, and made it easier for other southern dioceses to come back into the Episcopal Church of America.

Meanwhile throughout the war years, Christ Church was host to every convention of the diocese—and going through a series of clergymen. When Doctor Dalzell left, the vestry asked Bishop Gregg to come and serve the parish both as rector and bishop. This was not unusual at the time, but Bishop Gregg—after first accepting—realized he could not do justice to both parish and diocese, and declined. The rectors who accepted the church call were fine men. But none could stay long enough to finish building the church or get it consecrated, and in the fluctuations of the times, Christ Church started on a general downhill trend which was not to be reversed until 1875.

The first rector to come was the Rev. Edwin A. Wagner. Mr. Wagner was, like Bishop Gregg, born into a well-to-do South Carolina plantation background in Charleston, and was a graduate of Charleston College. He was "of the highest culture and refinement and of a womanly delicacy and tenderness of feeling." After study at the General Theological Seminary in New York, he was ordained in South Carolina and after only two years as a minister, was among those nominated to become bishop of the state. In 1859, a month ahead of Bishop Gregg, he came to Texas and became rector of Trinity Church, Marshall, then the fourth largest town in Texas with 4,000 people.

On calling Mr. Wagner, the Christ Church vestry asked the ladies to raise $2,000 in subscriptions to pay the minister's salary, the portion of the Bishop's salary, and other expenses. The senior warden appointed Mrs. Tankersley, Mrs. Harriet Perkins and Miss Eva Harris to the committee and within three months the ladies had $1,782 in subscriptions. This so encouraged the vestry that they ordered a chimney for the parsonage, a new vestry room built, and a new church bell. Mr. Wagner came to Christ Church on New Year's, 1862, when war and the issues of the Confederacy pervaded the community.

Soon after, A. S. Richardson's younger brother, Walter, who had begun his study of theology in Anderson under Gillette, returned to Houston. When war broke out, he was a student at Berkeley Divinity School, Middletown, Connecticut. He managed to get through the lines and make his way back home. He was ordained deacon at Christ Church February 23, 1862—the first native Texan to enter the ministry of the Episcopal Church—and at Christ Church two years later, was ordained priest.

War may bring terror and heartbreak to many, but it also brings excitement and adventure to the young and carefree. During the Civil War, several Houston girls in their teens—Libbie Randon among them—were sent with their chaperone to school in Paris. They went by buggy or stage to Matamorros, and from there to the coast to set sail for France. On arrival in Paris, they were greeted by young Will Palmer of Houston, who was in school there, and after one look at their clothes—which were not only behind the styles but made under wartime, blockade conditions—Will urged their chaperone not to let them be seen in Paris until somebody could get them proper dresses to wear. But the young girls were so eager to glimpse the world's most glamorous capital that they slipped out and started out on their own—only to find Parisians transfixed at the sight of them. People stared, then turned to follow, and the Houston girls fled home again to obey Will Palmer's ruling. After her Paris schooling, where she learned excellent French, Libbie Randon

went to Edinburgh to study music, and for the rest of her life, made evenings gay for her family and friends by the light, delightful way she played the piano for dancing and singing.

During Wagner's first year, he married Adolphe DePelchin and Keziah Payne, and he buried Col. Thomas S. Lubbock, Alex Keech Sr., Alex Keech, Jr., Edward R. Flewellen, Elizabeth Grainger, and Walter, the two-year old son of Mr. and Mrs. A. S. Richardson. But he was obviously preoccupied with the Confederacy. Mr. Wagner, in contrast to Gillette, shared Bishop Gregg's feelings about the war, and undoubtedly embraced the prayer as one coming from his own heart.

In the front flyleaf of the Parish Register begun by Mr. Gillette and carried through 1873, Mr. Wagner wrote a "Record of baptisms performed elsewhere than in the parish of Christ Church, Houston, but during my Rectorship of the same." But in writing the record, he got carried away and added not only a bit of current history but an editorial opinion as well:

"1862. February 26, while on a visit to Eastern Texas I baptized 'Gabriella' daughter of Gen. G. J. Rains & his wife Mary Jane Rains, the child was born at Newburgh, N. York State, May 7, 1861 . . . also,

"Charles Rains, son of Chas. Henry Randell and Leila George Randell his wife. This child was born at Nachitoches, La. Febry. 26, 1862, while his mother & grandmother with their families were flying from the inroads of Federal Soldiers who had occupied Nashville, Tenn. where they were residing. The grandmother, Mrs. G. Rains, & Mrs. John Gregg being sponsors.

"It is worthy of record as one of the evils of this 'unnatural war which has been forced on us' that the male parents were ignorant of the place of refuge to which their families had flown and Lieut. Randell also ignorant of the birth of his first-born child. Both of these parents being in the Confederate Army and communications being infrequent and uncertain."

In his emotion Mr. Wagner spelled the family name Rundell in two places and carefully corrected it to Randell in another. And it is to be assumed that he visited Nachitoches February 26 rather than that mother and hour-old son continued their flight from Nachitoches to Eastern Texas.

In May Mr. Wagner asked and received permission of the vestry to offer himself as chaplain to the Confederate Army, and in November he went to Augusta, Georgia, the only representative from the Diocese of Texas to the General Council of the Protestant Episcopal Church in the Confederate States of America. The Rev. Benjamin Eaton supplied for him during his absence. On Wagner's return he married J. Charles Evans and Julia A. Clingman, Col. W. R. Bradfute and Miss Georgia Anderson, Col. George W. Baylor and Miss Sallie G. Sydnor, and buried in Christ Church Cemetery, Mrs. Marie M. Lanier, 39; Mr. Frank Lewis's child; Emily (colored) 18 mo.; Alpha Morse Hall, 40 years; Willie Lubbock, 13 years; Lodowick Latham, 6 years. On one of Wagner's absences, the Rev. Benjamin Eaton conducted funeral services for Mrs. William Marsh Rice. The dangers of war were still no greater than the dangers of living at home in the average city of 1863.

After the Easter Monday elections, Mr. Wagner wrote a long letter of advice and instruction to the new vestry. He called for monthly meetings of the vestry hereafter, and said that the church must return to renting pews or prepare to have an offertory at every service held in the church. But, he added, "if the church is to be supported in its annual expenses by contributions from citizens generally, who are favorable to the church, then some

1865. General Lee surrenders 27,805 at Appomatox Court House, Virginia, April 9.

1865. Houston is occupied by federal forces June 20 and Reconstruction begins.

. . . official should be appointed to attend to it.

"I cannot," said Mr. Wagner, "but enter my protest against the *informality* of our female members being called upon to perform this office."

Mr. Wagner's wife and children had been in South Carolina for some time, and his worries about them had increased steadily. At last he proposed to rejoin them, to bring them back to Texas if possible. He suggested that if he had not been heard from for three months the vestry consider his resignation. In the spring of 1864, the vestry declared the pulpit vacant and called the Rev. J. M. Goshorn.

Mr. Goshorn, who was ordained deacon in Pennsylvania and priest in Indiana, had come to Texas in 1859—first to Gonzales and then to Columbus. He was soon invited to be a trustee of the University of the South and a member of the Standing Committee of the Diocese. He was rector of Christ Church throughout the summer of 1864, and baptized Mr. and Mrs. Frederick Allyn Rice, but he declined to extend his stay because he felt needed in Galveston. "He officiated there," the vestry minutes say, "among the people remaining in the city, and the soldiers stationed on the Island, until he died of yellow fever in the fall." His wife died with him, and they were buried in the Episcopal Cemetery in Galveston by a regretful Trinity Church.

For a few weeks after he was ordained priest at Christ Church, June, 1864, young Walter Richardson supplied in the parish and while there baptized Mr. and Mrs. Samuel E. Allen and their children Rebecca, Jane and Charles.

The arrival of the Rev. J. M. Curtis and his family from Arkansas in 1864 seemed to bring fresh energy to the parish. From the beginning he served a wide area. Within a few weeks after coming, he began to hold services one Sunday evening each month in Harrisburg until he had securely established the Nativity Mission of Christ Church there. After Easter of 1865, he began to go two evenings a month. He supplied for Eaton in Galveston, held occasional services in Liberty, and on two different occasions, he went to Calvary Church, Richmond: first to marry his vestryman Capt. Hugh Trann Scott to Miss Emma Victorine Milby, and Mr. Edwin Hobby to Miss Dora Pettus, and on the second trip, to marry Mr. Charles C. Bass to Miss Laura Pettus. In Houston he married John Collins and Mary Hallett (colored) in the quarters of Colonel Clark, U.S.A.; William Williams and Viney Winters (colored) at the residence of the bride, and William Kennedy Jr., and Miss Annie Lubbock were married at the residence of Mrs. Lubbock. Dr. M. Perl and Miss Mary J. Allen were married in Christ Church. The last war and early postwar years were wedding years with a boom.

Not long after the war, Mrs. John Dickinson decided to go abroad. She had never met her husband's family in Dundee, Scotland, and taking their several children with her—including Ella, Nannie and small John—she went off for a year of touring Europe and England, having French and dancing lessons for the children and visiting the senior Dickinsons in Scotland. Elizabeth Dickinson's friends and relations were shocked. Not because she left her husband for a year—because he was beautifully tended by her mother, Mrs. J. D. Andrews who lived across the street—but because to make this extended tour, she had "dipped into her *principal.*" Mrs. Dickinson never seemed to regret that wonderful trip, and her daughter Nannie, who married George Clark, became an early member of the Altar Society.

1865. John Wilkes Booth shoots President Lincoln in Washington April 14.

Chapter 24

And Aftermath

By 1865, Houston was a city of mixed feelings and mixed population. Un-reconstructed rebels passed through on their way to a new life in Mexico or Brazil. But many leading Houstonians swore allegiance to the United States and were readmitted to citizenship. On the fourth of July, the United States flag was flown. The first Juneteenth celebration came a year later when freed men and their wives gave a big banquet and invited their former owners to come as guests of honor. And by the end of that year 25 brick buildings were rising downtown.

The rectory was in good condition because Wagner had put into repairs all the rent he had received for it during his family's long stay in South Carolina. The vestry worked up a subscription list to pay the salary of the rector, organist and bishop which ran to 52 names in amounts from $5 to $75. Currencies were changing so rapidly in this period that nobody was quite sure how much money he was offering or how much it would be worth when delivered. James R. Masterson, L. J. Latham, Hugh Trann Scott, were among those who paid in currency. William M. Rice, H. Fleishman, H. E. Loebnitz and H. W. Benchley (grandfather of Robert Benchley)* paid in specie. And some promised half and half. J. D. Andrews pledged currency, $25, "when I sell my cotton." H. E. Vaas, organist, received $15 in gold each month. Somewhat wistfully, Mr. Curtis wrote in his church accounts January 1, 1866, "Remark: Up to date the varied changes in Currency and con-fusions of the times have prevented a regular account of offerings & their ex-penditure during the incumbency of—J. M. Curtis."

But the war was over and the vestry felt more optimistic. The vestry or-dered from Henry M. Congdon of New York $1,961 worth of furnishings for the still unfinished church, including an altar with a marble top, a stone font, a bishop's chair, lectern and a chancel rail 30 feet long. With the diocese meeting annually at Christ Church, they undoubtedly felt the need. In the spring of 1866, they closed the church for two months to get it painted in-side and the new furniture installed in time for the next diocesan convention.

The editor's sketch on Christ Church prepared for the Houston city di-rectory of 1866 said "The present church is of brick; built in the early pointed style of architecture—with nave 63 by 42 feet in the clear and chan-cel 30 by 10 feet—and when completed, which will probably be accomplished the present year, it will be one of the most beautiful churches in the state." And it was already too small. The congregation had raised $5,320 toward church repairs and furnishings, but still had an unfinished church, one not yet consecrated, and one—as a visiting minister commented—"quite too small for the wants of the place." Shifting currencies, and the need to offer fairly clean and comfortable quarters every single year to the convention, had prompted the Christ Church vestry to put not-very-good-money after bad in an effort to maintain a decent status quo.

In September, 1866, Mr. Curtis resigned "for your welfare," and went to Marion, Alabama. For the next six months, services were conducted by A. S. Richardson, Peter Gray, and R. M. Elgin as lay readers.

Dr. Joseph Cross came to Christ Church from the Diocese of Tennessee. When called, he wired back "I accept & will come tomorrow." Doctor Cross was apparently an agreeable, adaptable sort of clergyman in contrast to the

*Dr. Andrew Forest Muir, associate editor, *Journal of Southern History.*

1865. On June 19, in Galveston, Gen. Gordon Granger, U.S.A., issues proclamation that all Negroes are free, mark-ing the first Juneteenth.

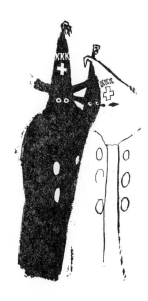

stern, tutorial Gillette and the confident, forceful Dalzell. He asked the vestry its pleasure: would they or would they not like services during Lent?

Though the church had gone back to pew rents, the vestry soon found itself marvelously lacking in money. It was being sued by John Brown for $2,000 owed him on building the church, and was paying to have the organ repaired only to find it could not be used until someone else could be persuaded to tune it. The Ladies of the Parish put a muchly needed fence around the Episcopal Cemetery. Doctor Cross married Samuel C. Timpson and Miss Hattie G. Bremond, William M. Rice, and Mrs. Julia Elizabeth Brown, Charles S. Marston and Miss Louisa M. Noble, Lawrence L. Cohen and Miss Savannah Crawford, John C. Chew and Miss Carrie Fisher, Robert M. Elgin and Mrs. Mary E. Shegog.

Robert Elgin—pronounced with a hard G rather than a soft one—was born in Tennessee in 1825, the son of Dr. and Mrs. William B. Elgin. His parents died during his childhood, and at 16, he came to Texas in a covered wagon with his uncle and aunt, the E. D. Tarvers. There were 10 in the party, and it took them 40 days to make the trip. "Every day of the journey was a delight" to the boy. After a period in Austin as clerk in the general land office, Mr. Elgin came to Houston just after the Civil War as commissioner of the Houston and Texas Central Railroad.

Doctor Cross's record for confirmations and attendance was good. But 1867 brought to Houston its worst yellow fever epidemic. There had been scattered cases and lesser epidemics in previous summers. In September, 1864, Mr. Curtis had recorded under Baptisms "This child was baptized at the residence of the parents, the mother being already sick with yellow fever and the child nursing, it was deemed prudent to baptize it before it was attacked." But 1867 brought back the grim days of 1839.

In the city—congested by soldiers and transients—16 people died one day, 29 the next. Before the epidemic ended that year, 492 men, women and children died of yellow fever. It claimed all nine members of one family, seven members of another, and killed eight doctors—including the city health officer. Between May 19 and Nov. 23, Christ Church lost 41 members of the church—including its retired vestryman, W. A. Van Alstyne; young Capt. Hugh Trann Scott, vestryman and not too long married, and 14-year-old Marianna Cross. Marianna may have been the rector's daughter—a probability suggested by the fact that under this name alone of the 41, the rector drew one long, tender line. Many northern soldiers died, and great vats of tar burned in the army camps and around town as a preventive against whatever poisonous airs or mists might be carrying this plague.

In 1868, R. M. Elgin and W. D. Cleveland came on the vestry for the first time. On his visitation, Bishop Gregg wrote serenely "The Church here . . . is greatly blessed in the ministrations of Dr. Cross. He has come, I rejoice to say, to give his heart and life to the work in Texas." But only for one year. By 1869, Doctor Cross had left Houston and the diocese. By 1869 spirits were on the rise. Trotting horses were so popular that speed limit ordinances had to be reprinted, and several well known gentlemen were brought into court on charges of driving at a gait faster than a walk.

March 30, 1870, Texas was readmitted to the Union. Despite the irritations of the carpetbag government, Houston was beginning to blossom. The residential sections were stretching way out south of Christ Church, and Rusk Avenue on each side of Main Street was becoming the loveliest residential

1867. At the age of 34, Emperor Maxmillian of Mexico is executed by the Juarez party June 19.

1867. Secretary of State William H. Seward commits "Seward's folly" by paying 2 cents an acre to buy Alaska from Russia for $7,200,000.

street in town. Judge and Mrs. Peter Gray moved out to Rusk. Mr. and Mrs. Cornelius Ennis moved to Galveston for a few years, and like Leonard Perkins a decade before, Ennis promptly joined the Trinity Church vestry.

The aftermath of the Civil War left Houston very Southern in tone. So many people of quality from the old South—from Virginia, Kentucky, the Carolinas and Tennessee—had come to Houston that the social life was purely Southern. In that extravagance of spirit which often follows a war, some of the social whirl was lavish to the point of absurdity—but great fun. Plantation parties became popular. Gentlemen came on horseback wearing velvet doublets, hose and plumed hats and "jousted" for the honor of selecting a queen by picking the most rings off with their lances while riding full tilt. Ladies came riding sidesaddle in picture hats and sweeping skirts which almost touched the ground. Ballets at the Hutchins House and grand balls where the Virginia reel and minuet were danced in colonial costume were climax of the party.

Between the departure of Doctor Cross and the arrival of Mr. Trader, two marriages were performed by the Rt. Rev. Alexander Gregg. The first was that of the Rev. J. B. Link to Mrs. Ada Miller. The second was that of young W. D. Cleveland. After the Civil War, Mr. Cleveland had come to Houston to seek his fortune, and soon met and fell in love with Justina Latham—daughter of L. J. Latham, one of Houston's leading furniture dealers. The successful business man was not at all interested in the court being paid his daughter by this unknown young man, and apparently would not permit any discussion of future plans. Finally one May day in 1869, Mr. Cleveland wrote to Mr. Latham a note in which he said, in effect, "I will be at your gate tomorrow morning at 7 o'clock, and with me will be a minister. If Miss Justina comes out, and I think she will, we shall go to Christ Church and be married. We should like to have your permission and blessings." The minister was Bishop Gregg, Miss Justina did come out, and the three of them walked over to Christ Church in the early morning of May 26 where the young couple were married.

The next rector was T. R. B. Trader, an ardent Southerner. He had come to Texas from Louisiana during the Civil War, crossing and recrossing the enemy lines—as he once wrote a friend—until he could join General Braxton Bragg as a Confederate chaplain. Mr. Trader was born in Salisbury, Maryland, on the old Trader farm in Wicomico County. He attended the General Theological Seminary in New York, was ordained deacon in 1846 and priest in 1848. His first parish was the Old Stepney Church in Tyeskin District, but he came south in 1850. A tall vigorous man, and a bachelor, Mr. Trader had a strong personality. He accepted the vestry's offer of "$2,000 coin without the parsonage, or if he wished the parsonage, then the rent of it to be deducted from his salary." Mr. Trader's acceptance so cheered everyone that the entire congregation and Sunday school adjourned after his first evening service to Gray's Hall "where a *Christmas Tree,* with presents and refreshments were exhibited and distributed."

The vestrymen were asked to serve as ushers for the year ending Easter Monday, 1871, on the theory that it might be helpful to the increasing number of newcomers and strangers to be guided to the proper pew. Mr. Trader saw at once that the present church was too small, and presented a plan for enlargement which would call for 375 thousand bricks and $10,000 in cash. The vestry agreed that this needed to be done, and authorized Mr.

1867. Karl Marx publishes Das Kapital.

1868. Louisa May Alcott publishes her most successful book, Little Women.

1869. Houston Ship Channel Company is organized to dredge the bayou to a minimum of nine feet. The Suez Canal opens November 17.

99

1867. The Dominion of Canada is established July 1.

Trader to seek subscriptions. Meanwhile the vestry had $489 worth of repair and repainting done to the rectory to make it worth a higher rent. The rectory was rented to newcomers from Matagorda—Mr. and Mrs. William H. Kirkland and her four children. Mrs. Kirkland's 17-year-old daughter, Rosa Elizabeth, joined Christ Church and continued as a communicant for the next 80 years. The Kirklands' son, William Hines, was a year old when they came to live in the rectory.

Mr. Trader performed many baptisms, funerals, and weddings during his stay at Christ Church. Among the many, he married Lewis Bryan and Mrs. Elizabeth Harper, E. D. Lynch and Sarah A. Shepherd, William Selkirk and Louisa Manly, David Lubbock and Alice London, C. F. Laigling and Mrs. Celestine Pillot, J. M. Kirkland and Mary McRae, L. T. Noyes and Rosa E. Kirkland, G. L. Porter and Libbie A. Randon. And among the many he baptized Benjamin A. Botts, son of Mr. and Mrs. W. B. Botts; Alice, daughter of Mr. and Mrs. W. D. Cleveland; Hines, son of Mr. and Mrs. W. H. Kirkland; Ingham, son of Henry and Laura Roberts, James and Edward, sons of Mr. and Mrs. James R. Masterson. In May, 1871, he baptized an adult William D. Cleveland, one month after his reelection to the vestry of Christ Church. A. S. Richardson and R. M. Elgin were sponsors. And a year later, Mr. Trader baptized Mr. Cleveland's new son, Alexander Sessums.

Now 42, A. S. Richardson was still only entering the second decade of his 40 years on the vestry, moving up from junior warden to senior. His parents had been pioneers in Austin's colony, and he was born in what is now Austin County near the Brazos River. At 42, he had already lived under four flags—Mexican, Republic, U. S. and Confederate—and was a well established, practicing attorney. Elgin and Cleveland were, of course, only youthful beginners on the vestry. But these three men were at the start of a lifetime partnership in service to Christ Church.

During her stay in Galveston, Mrs. Cornelius Ennis had been impressed by the splendid support given the aging Benjamin Eaton by a Trinity Church organization of women of the parish. Undoubtedly remembering the achievements of the Ladies Sewing Circle as well, Mrs. Ennis—with the approval of Mr. Trader—called together a group of outstanding Christ Church women. The first meeting was held in the church on her 49th birthday, September 4, 1871, and after a prayer by Mr. Trader, the Ladies Parish Association was founded. The 17 charter members were Mrs. Robert Brewster, Mrs. Rufus K. Cage, Mrs. Thomas H. Conklin, Mrs. Ella Connell, Mrs. Robert M. Elgin, Mrs. Ennis, Mrs. Lizzie E. Fall, Mrs. Thomas R. Franklin, Mrs. George Goldthwaite, Mrs. Peter W. Gray, Mrs. Kate W. Groce, Mrs. E. H. Harrington, Mrs. Henry House, Mrs. G. B. Mitchell, Mrs. J. R. Morris, Mrs. Dr. Robert Rutherford, Mrs. Elizabeth S. Tracy. The new membership elected as its first officers Mrs. Cornelius Ennis president, Mrs. Rufus K. Cage, vice president, and Mrs. Sarah M. Perkins, secretary and treasurer. In its first year, the Ladies Parish Association grew from 17 to 50 members.

In her history of the Ladies Parish Association Mrs. Lizzie Fall quoted from the first annual report: "The City was divided into 7 districts, and committees of two ladies visited in each district more or less regularly. Parents and children who have been absenting themselves from Church and Sunday School have been sought out and induced to 'return to the fold;' and the sick and needy have been regularly visited and relieved. Reference is made to this *system of work,*" Mrs. Fall added, "because of the fact that at that

1868. The first horse car begins to run on the Tap Railroad.

time very much of all the charitable and relief work among the poor and needy of Houston was done by the Ladies Parish Association of Christ Church and by the Ladies Aid Society of the First Presbyterian Church."

Pointing out that the church was so much too small that 30 families were being left out each Sunday morning for lack of pews, Mr. Trader pushed enlargement until the vestry agreed to the plan—if the money could be raised. But in July, 1872, the vestry owed Mr. Trader $1,847 of the $2,000 annual salary, and as usual, pew rents were not coming in. A. S. Richardson proposed that they narrow the church aisles, tuck in an additional 40 pews next to the wall—small ones, say four feet wide—thereby giving not only more seats but more pew rents. Always beguiled at the thought of pew rents, the vestry was delighted. "The above idea struck the Vestry very forceably, and they propose to take early action on it, provided means can be raised for the purpose."

But pew rents were not enough. Patience grew thin. The warmth between rector and vestry lessened and in 1873, three and a half years after coming, the Rev. Mr. Trader resigned—"to take effect when the amount due for past services is paid." It was a fair offer. The vestry tried to meet it fairly by paying up.

Next, the vestry hoped for the Rev. Hamner Cobb of Alabama, and then addressed themselves to a succession of prospects, but the pulpit was vacant from 1873 to 1875. Lay reading went on. The church grew shabby. And Judge Peter W. Gray died.

Peter W. Gray

Peter Gray had served Christ Church generously and intently for all his adult life. He first went on the vestry at the age of 21, when he had not yet been confirmed, and he resigned from the vestry only at such times when absence from Houston would have made him a poor servant. In 30 years, his contributions to the church probably went well beyond the tithe.

Born in Fredericksburg, Virginia, in 1819, he came to Houston at 18 and studied law under his father—who was a lawyer, clerk of the House of Representatives of the Republic, clerk of the Supreme Court, and district attorney at the time of his death in 1841. At 21 Peter Gray was commissioned captain in the Second Brigade of the Texas Army under Secretary of War Albert Sidney Johnston. At 22, Peter Gray succeeded his father as district attorney of the first judicial district on appointment by President Mirabeau B. Lamar, and two years later, President Sam Houston appointed him district attorney of the same district, now renamed the sixth.

In 1846 Gray was elected to the first state legislature of Texas, and he was the author of the practice act which led to the shaping of law pleading and practice in Texas. In 1854, he became district judge of the Houston district of ten counties, and Chief Justice Oran Roberts later said "the very best district judge that ever sat upon the Texas bench."

Gray represented Houston in the Confederate States Congress. Jefferson Davis appointed him fiscal agent for the Confederate government in the Trans-Mississippi Department. He was a volunteer in Major General J. B. Magruder's staff in the battle of Galveston, January, 1863. Peter Gray financed Henderson Yoakum's publication of the first comprehensive history of Texas. Gray County, Texas, and Gray Avenue, Houston, were named for him.

In his church, he helped Christ Church to build two new buildings, he

1870. Doctrine of papal infallibility is adopted by the Ecumenical Council in Rome July 18 by vote of 547 to 2.

Chapter 25

1870. Texas re-enters the Union March 20.

1870. Napoleon III, provoked by Bismarck, declares war on Germany.

helped the diocese to organize, he helped the diocese enter the General Convention, he helped the diocese to obtain Bishop Gregg.

In 1874, he was appointed to the Texas Supreme Court, but after two months he resigned—realizing that his health was too poor for him to serve. Six months later—quietly and after a brief illness—he died of pulmonary tuberculosis, October 3, 1874. He was 54 years old.

It is ironic that on his death—as at the death of his father—there was no rector of Christ Church in the city. The funeral service was read by the Rev. Albert Lyon of Galveston, master of the Trinity Church Parish School. The pallbearers were W. J. Hutchins, H. T. Garnett, Cornelius Ennis, W. G. Webb, J. B. Likens, E. W. Taylor, George Goldthwaite and Major J. T. D. Wilson. Several hundred people followed the casket from the house to Christ Church and 3,000 gathered at the church for Peter Gray's last service under that roof.

The vestry's last gesture was to close, with his death, the first book of vestry minutes Christ Church ever had—the big, leatherbound journal which had begun March 16, 1839, in the days of William Fairfax Gray, over which Peter W. Gray had spent so much time and in which he had written so many pages. The last page is his—in memoriam.

Chapter 26

1871. Verdi's Aida *is given its premiere at the Cairo Opera House December 24.*

From Cornwall to Texas

The coming of the Rev. J. J. Clemens to Christ Church in 1874 meant the right man at the right place at the right time. After a decade of postwar difficulties and of reconstruction, Houston was ready to boom. The railroad age, which had begun for Houston in the 1850's, was in full sway; by 1861, there were 357½ miles of railroad centered in Houston; by 1876 there were to be 1,503 miles. The Houston Gas Works had been established in 1867, and it was now known that "the light furnished their patrons is of superior quality." In 1874, Houston had a street railway system with turntables at the Fairgrounds near Main and McGowen, on Main Street, at the Market House, and at the Union and Central Depots. The Houston *Telegraph* reported "There were twenty-three persons on the car which was drawn by one mule with perfect ease at the rate of fully ten miles an hour." The Fire Department had 300 volunteers in service. The young Ladies Seminary, under Professor Horace Clark and Mrs. Clark, was one of the leading schools. And Doctors David Stuart, Josh Larendon and Thomas J. Boyles had built the Houston Infimary "above the machine and car shops on the Houston Texas Central Railroad having commodious buildings, healthfully located."

This was the Houston of 1874 to which the young Rev. Mr. Clemens brought his wife and small son Scott. This dark eyed, dark haired Englishman was an exquisitely tooled instrument of the Lord: slender, well made, with a pleasant voice and a delightful use of language. He was a talented musician, and a man of such totally unaffected sweetness of spirit that he was equally at home in the pool hall, fire house, or house of God. He was tied to Houston by those threads of family and marriage which seemed always to run through from one community to another in those days of small towns flung far across the growing nation.

Mr. Clemens' mother had died not long after his birth, and he spent his boyhood with an aunt and uncle in Cornwall. When he was about 16, his father sent for him to come to America where the senior Mr. Clemens had made a home in Germantown, Pennsylvania. The rector there became the boy's good friend and to the disapproval of his father, Julyan Clemens grew interested in the ministry. When after graduation from Kenyon College in Ohio, he decided to study theology, his father disowned him. But his stepmother always managed to tuck money into the books she sent him at the seminary.

Presumably, Julyan Clemens' early background was High Church or he had felt the influence of the movements to elevate the church in England and restore the old usage of Prayer Books and choir robes. Though the Virginia Seminary was at that time so Low Church that it would be many decades before a cross could be placed on the seminary altar, Clemens seemed to have studied there profitably and well. As a seminarian, he played the organ at Christ Church, Alexandria, where both Washington and Lee had worshipped, and he supplied in the Fredericksburg church where William Fairfax Gray was once a vestryman. In Fredericksburg he met Miss Sue Scott, a relative of the Gray family, whose father usually invited visiting clergymen to his home, and after Clemens' graduation, they were married. His first church was on the Eastern Shore of Virginia, but the bishop of the diocese was so Low Church that the young priest was uncomfortable. It upset him, for instance, for the bishop to throw the consecrated elements out the window after communion service rather than to consume them. He accepted a call to St. Paul's Church in Selma, Alabama. He was there when Christ Church was casting about for a minister. Ben Botts and Browne Botts had come originally from Fredericksburg, and they liked the young Englishman who had married their cousin Sue. They offered his name.

The vestry agreed, and Clemens came to Houston. J. J. Clemens was 29 years old. And he gave to Christ Church the finest, and the only full decade of his ministerial life.

1872. The United States begins to use postcards.

Christ Church stood facing a wide, unpaved avenue. A long line of tall trees ran along its Fannin Street side between sidewalk and street. Behind the church stood a large white house, still the residence of E. L. Coombs, the jeweler, and across Texas from the rectory stood the big house with art glass windows of Dr. David Stuart.

The rectory had been added to during one of the spasms of improvement, so that it had additional rooms above the study and kitchen which had started out as a one-story wing. At the back of the upstairs hall, it had one of Houston's first bath rooms with a tub and wash basin which drained out through a pipe and down a little brick gutter. Though the city was thriving, Christ Church was not. The church was so run down that the chancel and altar were stained where the rains had come in. The church yard between rectory and church was a black mud puddle.

Mr. Clemens started his work with the enthusiasm of youth and ideal. He found that the Ladies Parish Association, founded in 1871, had continued work and were ready to share his plans and follow his lead with a carefully accumulated organ fund and a nucleus of a chapel fund.

The vestry minutes of Mr. Clemens' period at Christ Church have been lost. Fortunately for history, Mr. Clemens left exquisitely penned notes of major events in his Parish Record Book in his first five years in Houston.

"Nov. 15, 1874: The Rev. J. J. Clemens assumed the rectorship of Christ Church, Houston, on the 14th of November, 1874—succeeding the Rev. Mr. Trader, who resigned in July, 1873. The Parish was found in a most disorganized state, rendered more disastrous by the recent death of P. W. Gray, Esq. one of our most prominent and zealous vestrymen.

"Jan. 24, 1875: To the Glory of God, and to the honor of the Congregation, I record this day that the old debt of $3,500.00 was paid in response to my appeal from the pulpit. And I also record the fact that this was largely due to the liberality of Mrs. P. W. Gray, Col. W. J. Hutchins, and Maj. B. A. Botts, although they were nobly seconded by many others."

While setting the parish finances in order, Mr. Clemens also tackled the lawn. He landscaped the mud puddle to make a circular rose garden with white shell walks. He was too much of an Englishman not to have a rose garden in the church yard. Events moved at such an exhilerating pace that the *Church Journal and Messenger* reported "On the Fifth Sunday in Lent the Bishop of the Diocese administered the Apostolic Rite of Confirmation in Christ Church, Houston. There were 25 confirmed, and the Bishop stated that it was the largest class ever confirmed by him in this parish. The church is growing vigorously in Houston, now numbering over 230 communicants. An old debt of $3,600 has been paid, a new organ costing $2,500 has been ordered, and all within four months."

"The new organ," Mr. Clemens wrote in his Parish Record, "was opened on the 7th of August, 1875—the Rt. Rev. Alex C. Garrett, D.D., missionary bishop of Northern Texas, preaching the Sermon, and Mr. C. H. Preston of Boston acting as organist. It was a day never to be forgotten. Laus Deo!

"September 26, 1875: The assistant minister and principal of the Parish School the Rev. Adrian Zimmerman, B.A., LLB, officiated today for the first time." Unfortunately Mr. Zimmerman stayed only half a year.

Mr. Clemens conducted the Sunday school himself, either playing the organ for the children to sing, or strolling up and down the aisle, leading their hymns in his pleasant baritone. And perforce, he did the same for the congregation in his first years. Despite the efforts of Doctor Dalzell, the Christ Church congregation had settled into a fairly Low Church position by the time Mr. Clemens arrived, and in this frame of mind, considered a choir in procession as nothing short of papist.

This was not remarkable, for in the United States at mid-century, an altar cross, flowers and candles, and a vested choir led by a processional cross were all symbols of the High Church movement. And to a true Low Churchman, a communion table with four legs was preferable to an altar. But the surplice and gown—rare in many dioceses in the 1840s—had always been used by the bishops and clergy of Texas, and Christ Church had a marble topped altar. Mr. Clemens wore the white surplice and cassock, and he often played the organ and led hymns during services.

His main energy at this moment was directed toward enlarging the church. Turning to the same Henry Congdon of New York who had designed and delivered the church furniture, he obtained architectural plans which would extend and enlarge the chancel, and change the entire scale of the church. "May 26th 1876: Ground was broken for enlargement of the Church after plans of Congdon's in New York." The Congdon drawings are the earliest in existence of any Christ Church building.

In this period, Mr. Clemens acquired a colleague of his own sort, but sorrowfully October 4, 1876, he wrote, "The organist, Mr. James Bray, was buried today. A loss the Church can never repair. An Englishman, a Mason, a thorough gentleman, and a devoted Christian. God's holy will be done."

1876. Gen. George A. Custer and 276 soldiers are killed June 25 in Battle of the Little Big Horn, Montana, in Sioux Indian war.

On the first Sunday in November, rector and congregation could see what the church was going to look like: "Today entered our New Church, everyone pleased with the enlargement, and the Rector returned thanks—next to God— to the Lay Members of the Building Committee." Thanks—and a stern call to duty. In a notebook, he wrote out this talk in a miniature handwriting. It fills four inches in the notebook, but can be transcribed into no less than two and three-quarter typewritten pages.

"When I first became rector of this parish two years ago," he wrote, "it was burdened with a debt of nearly $5,000 and . . . I found no adequate accommodations either for priest or people. The church was in need of much repair. There was no organ worthy of the name, the very Altar was weather stained and the walls cracked under the weight of the mortgage. To God be all the glory, and today we can say that all this is changed. The debt is paid fully and honourably; an organ was built . . . whose tones you heard today, which cost nearly as much as the original debt. This also, thanks to our good women, was paid for as soon as delivered . . ." He pointed to repairs and the enlarged chancel. ". . . even in its present unfinished condition, it is infinitely better for every purpose than the old Church. It is incomparably better for sound. It looks more like what it is intended to be, a house of God, and the increase of pew holders proves that cheaper pews was just what we needed. But the debt must be paid, and money raised to complete the task.

"Brethern, . . . as members of the congregation, you are the persons who reap the advantages. It is your property that has been improved, and from your purses must come the funds to pay the debt . . . this money has been borrowed on the faith of your ability and willingness. . . . I believe fully in your willingness—how can I doubt your ability? There is enough wealth in this congregation."

1876. Pablo Casals is born December 30 in Spain.

He may, of course, never have delivered this minutely written sermon. But . . . on Christmas Eve: "This day a gift of $2,500 was made to the Rector for the Church on the conditions that no one should ever know the name of the donor, but his record is in heaven. We thus hope to have our church completed by Easter, 1877." And "Easter Day, 1877: The church *was* completed, the chancel being well decorated and for the 1st time in Texas, the Easter music was rendered by a *Male Choir!*" Mr. Clemens must have sung his own jubilate that morning.

But he was not always saintly. His smile must have been impish the day he wrote, "Prof. Horace Clarke was ordained to the Diaconate. A blow for the Baptists!"* And six months later, "Rev. H. Clarke was ordained Priest in St. David's Ch. Austin, and became assistant minister to this Parish." In this period the Rev. William Dinsmore Sartwelle was ordained deacon in Christ Church, and Bishop Gregg mentioned the event at the 29th meeting: "*Second of all the clergy* who has been connected with the diocese, during my Episcopate, born and reared in Texas! Of the 2,000 boys baptized and brought up within the pale of the Church here, but *two* consecrated to her ministry," England was filling the gaps Texas failed to fill. During the second half of the 19th century, a great many Anglican ministers came to Texas. So did organists, choir singers and communicants.

Mr. Clemens had his share of clerical adventures. One day, two gamblers

---

* Prof. Clark was not only head of the Young Ladies Seminary, but also listed in the 1877 City Directory as pastor of the First Baptist Church.

got into a fight over cards and one shot the other. The dead man's friends wanted him to have a Christian burial; his enemies did not. Two of the friends came to Mr. Clemens to ask if he would come read the funeral service, explaining frankly that if he did so, they would have to guard him with pistols. Mr. Clemens agreed to come at once. Putting on his cassock and surplice, he went to the saloon and to the upstairs room where the body lay. With the two gamblers standing on either side of him, pistols drawn, he not only read the burial service, but delivered a little sermon on the evils of gambling and violence.

This led to a permanent friendship between Mr. Clemens and Bill Perry, one of the gamblers. Once in Toronto on his way to England, Mr. Clemens was spied by Perry on the street and swept off to have tea at his mother's house. Perry was greatly pleased for his mother to see what good company he kept in Houston. It was on this trip, perhaps, that Mr. Clemens brought back the ivy from Westminster Abbey and planted it at Christ Church.

The rectory, after so many years of transient families and vacancies, had become a pleasant place. Between Sunday school and church, the teachers often came over to the rectory to freshen up, and to small Elizabeth Clemens, they all seemed young and wonderfully pretty. The parlor at the front of the house had a black horsehair sofa, and small rectory children were sat upon it to learn their catechism. The Clemens had five children to be born in their years in Houston: Elizabeth Julyan born in 1875; Fannie, Frank, Fred and Mec (America). Scott, the oldest was fascinated by the firemen across the street, and once when he was quite sick, Mr. Clemens went across to the station and asked the firemen if they would come to see their little friend. They put on full uniform to present themselves at Scott's bedside, and Mr. Clemens always thought that this marked Scott's turn for the better.

Friday Carr had become a permanent part of the Christ Church close by that time—as sexton, major domo, and valued friend. There was no ice in the rectory, and on hot days, Mr. Clemens would ask Friday to fetch ice from a saloon on Main Street for the family tea. [Butter and milk were stored on a ledge half way down the cistern wall.] When small Elizabeth took a hard tumble from a high perch, it was Friday who picked her up. To two generations of children in Sunday school and boys' choir at Christ Church, Friday Carr would be the great big man who fished them out of difficulties, shared their labors at the organ pump, told them stories to keep them in order before service could begin. And when Mr. Clemens baptized the sexton's baby, it was in all good faith and English upbringing that he should write "Ivory Kerr, son of Friday and Tina Kerr."

Despite the new elegance of the church, this was still a parish of close, personal attachment between parishioner and church. On the Saturday morning before Easter, the ladies always began to collect flowers in great tubs of water in the church yard. Almost everybody lived within walking distance or a short drive to the church so that it was an easy move from garden to church yard. All day they worked, making elaborate and intricate decorations for the church for Easter Sunday morning. The Lubbock family usually hung a cross or an anchor of flowers in memory of their son who had been killed in a train accident. (These were the Theodore Uglow Lubbocks, adopted son of Governor Francis Lubbock.) Another family always made a crown. And some ladies made an entire church decoration out of yucca blossoms. On Easter morning, the chancel could scarcely be seen for the profusion of flowers which

1877. Sir Arthur Sulli-van writes the music for The Lost Chord

adorned it in the full enthusiasm of Victorian taste.

The Charles J. Graingers lived on Texas Avenue with their daughters Miss Eliza, Alice, Georgia, and Fannie, and little Sue and Lily. Dr. and Mrs. Perl lived over on Travis. The W. D. Clevelands had moved out to Rusk and San Jacinto. The F. A. Rices, the T. M. Shirleys, the William Fultons, and the S. L. Hohenthals had all moved out to Rusk not far from Mrs. Peter Gray. But there were still many living near, and north or northeast of the church. The R. M. Elgins were on Texas and Austin, the Frank Cargills lived on Congress, Mr. and Mrs. Cornelius Ennis still lived on Congress but had moved farther east to the block between Jackson and Crawford. But the E. E. Coombs still faced Court House Square in the house which backed up to Christ Church. T. W. House with his wife and three daughters, lived way across town on Capitol and Smith. Busy in what seemed to be half the business corporations in town, he contributed to Christ Church but did not serve as vestryman. The J. Waldos moved from Congress to the big mansion on Rusk and Caroline which occupied a quarter of the block between San Jacinto and Caroline on which the main downtown post office was later built.

The big old mansion of Col. and Mrs. W. J. Hutchins stood on Franklin Street at LaBranch in a part of the section known as Quality Hill. And in the middle 70s, the whole family was living there—Mrs. Ruth Harris, (Mrs. Hutchins's mother) W. J. Hutchins Jr., Rushmore, Leigh, Mrs. Ella Hutchins Stewart, Miss Eva, small Spencer and Arthur Hutchins. Mrs. Stewart was a highly educated woman who spoke several languages and translated books—well—for publication. She had caused quite a stir some years before by marrying Lord Stewart of England. The "black diamond" once owned by Mary Queen of Scots was the groom's gift to the bride. But with the passage of years, old friends and old Houston came to regard the title more in affectionate amusement than in awe, and she later married Seabrook Sydnor—for whom Seabrook was named.

1878. First commercial telephone exchange is opened in New Haven, Connecticut.

In the *Houston Morning Age,* which reported under "War in the Orient" that the Russians had crossed the Danube, there was an announcement by Sam S. Ashe that the Spring Races of the Houston Jockey Club would be run over the Texas State Fair race course continuing for four days. On the same page, the City Bank of Houston, capital $500,000, announced its officers as B. A. Botts, president; B. F. Weems, cashier; and directors W. J. Hutchins, A. J. Burke, Cornelius Ennis, and W. M. Rice. But it was at about this time that Mr. and Mrs. Rice moved east, coming to Houston for their winters, still available in moments when Christ Church needed their financial help.

The handing back and forth of names in family relationships and in friendships too becomes increasingly evident with each new generation in the Christ Church records—and increasingly confusing. William Marsh Rice, Jr., for instance, was not the son of William Marsh Rice, but his nephew. Willim Marsh Rice and Frederick Allyn Rice married sisters: Elizabeth and Charlotte Baldwin of Baldwinsville, New York. Though they were from a distinguished New York family, both girls were married in Christ Church, Houston. In 1847, Elizabeth Baldwin married John H. Brown, and two years later, as a very young girl, Charlotte Baldwin married John Randon. The Rev. Charles Gillett performed both ceremonies.

1879. Mary Baker Eddy organizes the Church of Christ, Scientist.

The Randons had one daughter, Libbie, named for Mrs. Randon's sister. Mr. Randon, a large landowner in Texas at the time, died shortly after the birth of his daughter, and young Mrs. Randon apparently went home to Baldwinsville. But Fred Rice had been her husband's best friend, and by 1854, the Christ Church list of communicants shows "Fred Rice and lady." Libbie Randon became Fred Rice's daughter and the beloved oldest sister to the many Rice children. She was especially dear to the oldest son, Jonas.

Margaret Bremond Rice, who had married William Marsh Rice in 1850, died early in the Civil War, and in 1867, William Marsh Rice married Elizabeth Baldwin (now herself widowed and listed in the marriage registry as Mrs. Julia Elizabeth Brown.) It is for her that the city park on Elgin between Crawford and Chenevert and the literary society at Rice University are named. William Marsh Rice had no children—a source of deep disappointment to him.

The Fred Rices, in contrast, had many: among them Jonas Shearn Rice, William Marsh Rice (customarily known as "junior" rather than as "the second," perhaps as an added gesture of affection for a childless brother.) Baldwin Rice, David, Minerva, Fred, Lillian, Benjamin, George and Nettie. Others died in infancy, and Nettie in childhood. Libbie Randon married George Porter, Minnie married Henry Holt Lummis, and Lillie married Paul Timpson. David Rice grew up and had many children, but William Marsh Rice, Jr., never married, and like his namesake uncle, had no children. All this may have contributed to William Marsh Rice's deepening determination to give his name to something—to a living something, like a school for the young people of Houston.

Christ Church vestrymen and members were stretching out and expanding into a variety of business ventures. A. Groesbeeck was vice president (under President W. E. Dodge of New York) of the Houston and Texas Central Railway. A. S. Richardson was secretary, F. A. Rice treasurer, J. Waldo general passenger agent. F. A. Rice was president of the Houston Savings Bank with Benjamin A. Botts vice president, and on the board, were George L. Porter, J. Waldo and W. D. Cleveland. Rice and Botts were also directors of the National Exchange Bank of Houston, and of the First National Bank officers, B. A. Shepherd was president; A. P. Root cashier, and L. J. Latham on the board. George L. Porter was president of the Houston Board of Trade and Cotton Exchange with T. W. House and S. K. McIlhenny among the vice presidents. The Young Men's Real Estate and Building Associates had S. M. McAshan president with Romney Greene as treasurer. And son of a longtime vestryman, Owen L. Cochran, young Owen, had his insurance office at 30 Main Street. He lived just around the corner from the W. J. Hutchins with his widowed mother until his marriage, and after.

Marriages were numerous at Christ Church. Among them: W. H. Autry to H. L. Cruger; Theodore Dumble to Fanny Gray; (at the house of A. C. Gray); O. L. Cochran to Alice Shepherd (at the home of B. A. Shepherd); Romney Greene to Caroline M. Evans, George W. Cleveland to Eva H. Richardson at the home of Mrs. A. S. Richardson with the ceremony performed by the Rev. Walter R. Richardson of San Antonio's St. Mark's; R. H. Culpepper to Mamie Kate Clark at the residence of Prof. Clark, J. Martin Lee of Montgomery to Rosa M. Jordan in Christ Church. The memorable wedding was that of Georgia Grainger to Alfred Ryland Howard, October 18, 1875. The Grainger house was directly across the street from Christ Church, and the father of the bride closed off all traffic on Texas Avenue to lay a red carpet from his own front door to the front door of the church. He did this for all his daughters, one by one.

If baptisms were an indication, the parish was growing robustly. On April 14, 1876, Clemens baptized Mary Lubbock, Adele Lockart Lubbock, Ella Hutchins Botts, Mec Mellinger Botts and Eva McIlhenny Botts. Among the many baptized during Mr. Clemens' first five years were Joseph Milton Howe, Charlotte Rice Porter, Elizabeth Julyan Clemens (by the Rt. Rev. Alexander Garrett, missionary bishop of north Texas) Susie M. Patillo, Patterson Patillo, Maurice Ennis Lombardi, Amanda and Annie Byrd, George Henry de Lesdernier, Samuel Oliver Noyes, Bessie Kirkland, Tina Latham Cleveland, Lena Grosbeeck Latham, Annie Kate Winston, Mary Elizabeth Dreaper, Matthew Jules Bujac, Milby Porter, Sallie Ashe, Helen Louise Autry, Bettie Ford Elgin, the four children of Capt. F. A. Rice (George Converse, Benjamin Botts, Lillian and Frederick), Curtis Blakeman Quarles, Clemens Perry (colored), Millie Gray Dumble, Sarah Venable Weems, the three children of J. Waldo, Wilmer, Cora and Mary; and Catherine Dreaper. John Dreaper was one of the last Mr. Clemens baptized before leaving, but his baptism is a part of the lost records of Christ Church. Frank Clemens was baptized by Bishop Gregg.

Mr. Clemens' records on burials are the most interesting of any rector's since Mr. Gillette's, because he gives the causes of death: Inflammation, Fever, Consumption and Congestion were rife in the community. But some causes of death were more remarkable: Erysipelas, Spinal Infection, Asthma, Drunkenness [this man died at 30], Dysentery, Shot [the victim was 40—the gambler?], Cancer, Carbuncles, Dropsy, Old Age [81], Debility [age 9], Worms—[age 45], Meningitis, Heart Disease, Apoplexy [a Lutheran minister], Paralysis, Pneumonia, Accident.

The infant of J. Tryon died at 1 day, and less than a week later, Mrs. J. M. Tryon died of Childbirth. She was 24. The young English organist was one of five persons who died within a few days of each other, all of "Congestion." Three of the five, including the organist, were 29 years old.

But before a reader can linger too sadly in conjecture, he hits the bottom of that page with a bump: "L. W. Daly, buried Glenwood, Cemetery, Dec. 13, 1876. Cause of death—Spiritualism."

A Fire and A Mission

"Feb. 28, 1880: After a regular Service, the Rector placed upon the altar the Memorial Cross, in memory of Mrs. Abbie Latham Tryon, the gift of Mrs. W. D. Cleveland." And this is the last record made by the Rev. Mr. Clemens in his exquisite handwriting in the History Section of his Parish Record. It is probable that he started a new book at that time, and that this was the book which went out on the hurricane with the Rev. Henry Aves' house in Seabrook.

It is also true that the rector was feeling strangely unwell. Everyone said that he had worked too hard—that the toll of morning and evening sermons, of baptisms and funerals, of mission forays in all weather in his phaeton, of good deeds around town, had tired him out. Mr. Clemens had such a sweet disposition that he was routinely imposed upon by the not-always-deserving. And so in the summer of 1880, at the urging of his congregation, Mr. Clemens went home to England to rest and recuperate.

The *Houston Post* reported "The Rev. J. J. Clemens: The many friends of the much loved rector of Christ Church will be pleased to learn that the

1882. New York City opens its first power plant during the summer, and Houston opens a power plant December 17.

1883. Long distance line connects Houston and Galveston.

Chapter 27

reverend gentleman has reached England in safety. His health is much improved, and he hopes to return home shortly, entirely restored and ready to push his work with vigor." The reverend gentleman was at the time 35 years old. He was half way through his decade at Christ Church. Few men have accomplished so much in five years.

Houston was continuing to grow with comparable vigor. In 1880 it got its first electric arc street light and its first scheduled train to New Orleans. Some 5,000 Houstonians turned out to greet former President and former General U. S. Grant with shouts of welcome. Hutchins House feared that the balcony would break under the weight of his admirers. W. D. Cleveland's sale of 3,071 bales of cotton to A. H. Lea for $150,000 was pronounced "the largest single cotton transaction ever made in Texas." W. J. Hutchins and T. W. House were on the board or president of an incredible number of corporations ranging from banks to railroads. W. L. Foley was advertising flannels, jeans, blankets, sheeting, ticking, Canton and flannels at 41 Main Street.

"Europe! Through Tickets. From or to any point in Great Britain or the Continent of Europe via the Houston and Texas Cent'l Railway." Russia was "sounding Japan regarding a joint occupation of Corea," and the *Post* each morning reported what had happened in the House of Lords and House of Commons in London. L. J. Latham "Keeps constantly on hand House Furnishings and Goods in Great Variety. Ground Floor 50 x 100 feet. Largest Store in Houston." And under "Edison's New Engine" was a subhead "—relative to the success or failure of the electric light of Professor Edison." The newspapers published each week a list of letters undelivered at the post office— or rather two lists. The letters to ladies were carefully separated in print from the letters waiting for gentlemen.

In Mr. Clemens' absence in England, his good friend Bishop Garrett had supplied for him, staying at the home of the Sunday school superintendent, W. D. Cleveland. It all should have worked out so well. But while Mr. Clemens was in England and the rest of his family was in Fredericksburg on a visit to Mrs. Clemens' family, 8-year-old John Scott Clemens caught diphtheria and died. The Clemens had lost their second son as a newborn in Selma, Alabama. But for an Englishman to lose his first born—a promising and beloved eight-year-old, was extremely hard for him to bear.

There was still work to do, a parish he loved, pleasant days to live. Mr. Clemens was not resting on his laurels. After Christmas in early 1880, Mr. Clemens opened the Chapel of the Epiphany in Fifth Ward, and soon settled down into a regular schedule of services there—going himself by phaeton, or assisted by the newly Episcopal Rev. Horace Clark, by laymen, or by such visiting clergy as the Rev. Edwin Wickens. In May, 1882, a telephone was installed in Christ Church to enable parishioners unable to attend service to hear the sermon and music, presumably on some sort of party line.

In December, the big old stove which stood near the entry was burning at such capacity that its sparks set the roof afire. Though the Fire Department (volunteer) was only across the street from Christ Church, all the firemen were away trying to put out a dangerous fire in the International Cotton Compress. Volunteer volunteers ran across to the firehouse, found an old hose, wrenched an honorary silver nozzle off its handsome mounting, and hitched them together. The first man on the roof with that make-shift hose was Bill Perry, the gambler. He was not, he said, going to let Mr. Clemens' church burn down. The roof was of slate, and Mrs. Ernest Humphrys (Elizabeth Clemens) remembers that little damage was done "except to Mr. Perry's suit."

Houston was filled with the English accents in the 1880s and 1890s. Most of those young Englishmen who came were in the cotton business. Alfred Lawrence-Toombes, whose children would take their places in Sunday school and choir, was a leather merchant. Many Englishmen were of the clergy. The choir of Christ Church grew strong on those voices. Willie Brattan came out from England for a few years as Christ Church organist and choir master, and when he returned to England in 1883, George C. Collins took over for a year. But the rectory children grew up saying *cyard* and *gyarden* in the fashion of their Virginia-bred mother.

The Rev. Edwin Wickens was to give Mr. Clemens one of his pleasantest friendships. Only a bit older than Clemens, Wickens was born in Surrey and was once an Anglican missionary in South Africa. He was ordained priest by Bishop Quintard of Tennessee, and on coming to Texas, was assigned to be a general missionary to the diocese, with a rectorate at Hempstead. When Mr. Clemens was away or ill, Wickens often helped out. And in 1882, Clemens and Wickens conducted a teaching mission—first in Christ Church, later at St. Bartholemew's, Hempstead.

A letter to the editor of the *Houston Post* described the mission:

". . . stirring sermons were preached twice daily . . . No great flights of oratory, but simple exposition of the truth, plainly, candidly and honestly put forth; no urgent, begging appeals, no loud calling on the audience to rise up en masse if they desire not to go to the certain hot place not mentioned in Houston polite circles, but . . . a plain, manly statement of facts . . . the church was crowded at each service."

From Hempstead when the vestry wrote to thank Mr. Clemens for his part in their mission, the letter said ". . .you have by the suavity of your manner, the eloquent teaching appeals to our consciences in your sermons, won a warm place in our hearts." These were apparently the first of the week-long teaching missions which were to become an annual part of Christ Church programs in the 20th century.

1881. Alexander II, Czar of Russia, is assassinated by Nihilists, and Disraeli dies.

Called "Doctor Clemens" by a variety of simple people, rolling up namesakes which is a proof of humanity as well as prestige, Mr. Clemens continued to go and to serve wherever he was needed. And he was thoughtful in many ways. He loved the seafood from the bay. Once when a colleague was in town, a missionary from West Texas whose budget was slim and whose distance from the seashore great, Mr. Clemens brought home 50 fresh oysters to be roasted over the fire of his study. The missionary, small Elizabeth noticed, ate 49. Her father saved out one for her. Mr. and Mrs. Clemens enjoyed the feast through the pleasure of their land-locked guest.

Mr. Clemens often used the vestry room over at the church to write his sermons, and Elizabeth often played quietly near him as he wrote. One evening he asked her to fetch him a hymnal from the nave. But it was dark, and she was afraid. He put down his pen, and taking her by the hand, strolled comfortably up and down the aisles of the church, as at home in the dark as in morning service, explaining that this was God's house—home—and she need not be afraid.

Not yet 40, Mr. Clemens grew more frail, more tired. He could not throw off the cough he had picked up. This big downtown church with its

The Rev. Charles L. Fitchett apparently served as assistant to Mr. Clemens at Christ Church during 1881 and 1882, Dr. Andrew Forest Muir said, on the basis of weddings recorded in the Harris County Court House.

many demands was too much, everyone theorized. He must seek something quieter. By a logic impossible to follow with modern eyes, Mr. Clemens agreed to accept a post as diocesan missionary to a widely scattered group of small, impoverished missions in Mississippi. Charmingly his dear friend, the Rt. Rev. Hugh Miller Thompson, wrote him from Oxford, Mississippi:

"This work will be a sort of bishoping. I want to make a Deanery. . .The idea of having you in Mississippi is just lovely to me. I think a year of missionary at large will help you. How I will work you when I get you!"

The parish which had been—up to now—his whole life's work, must let him go. He resigned. He had not intended to preach a farewell sermon. He did not believe in emotional displays. But after a few sentences, he suddenly fell to his knees in the pulpit, tears rolling down his face. The congregation knelt on the same tide of emotion. Together, they offered their separation as a sacrifice to a greater good to the honor and glory of God. A year in Mississippi, two in Rhode Island chosen for its cold and therefore "healthful" climate—and the Rev. J. J. Clemens was dead of tuberculosis at 42.

Churchmen Lost and Gained

Chapter 28

1882. Oscar Wilde makes a lecture tour of the United States.

The Rev. William C. Dawson came to Christ Church in the spring of 1885, bringing with him his family. One year later he died. His last service in Christ Church was Easter, 1886, when "With the shadows of impending dissolution already closing around him, he invoked in whispered accents upon us and upon our children the richest blessings of our Father and our God." An inspiring man with "rich stores of information," Mr. Dawson in his year of life and death stirred the congregation to affection and to a vivid appreciation of the Church. He was buried May 5, 1886, near Poplar Bluff, Missouri.

Bishop Gregg's cry for priests must have had effect. At Christ Church alone, ordinations occurred with frequency throughout the Clemens, Dawson and Beckwith rectorships. W. G. W. Smith was ordained in 1876. John Davis and William Dumble were ordained along with Horace Clark in 1880. Reginald Collisson and Davis Sessums were ordained in 1882, and Thomas Chalmers and Harry Cassil in 1886. In 1888, Mathew A. D. Brewster, son of Vestryman Robert Brewster, was licensed a lay reader and by 1890 had been ordained.

But Christ Church and the diocese had losses. At about the time Clemens left for Mississippi, W. J. Hutchins died. He had been elected a vestryman in 1847 just as the first brick church was being readied for consecration under Charles Gillette, and as his business flourished and his business affairs grew more complex, gave increasing amounts of time and money to the church. Between 1847 and 1882, he had served for 33 years on the vestry, often as senior warden and lay delegate, and as an elderly gentleman, he became a lay reader. Bishop Gregg said of him "Col. W. J. Hutchins from an early period in the history of the Parish has been one of its most active and liberal supporters. For years it was understood that when funds were wanted, it mattered not how much, he would give one-fourth of the whole. For a quarter of a century he was a member of the standing committee."

1885. First electric street railway in the United States opens in Baltimore.

And in that same year, Christ Church lost another Gray. Edwin Fairfax Gray was reared in the church, and his wife Rosalie was the daughter of E. W. Taylor, early vestryman. They were married by Doctor Dalzell shortly after young Lieutenant Gray returned from his Naval expedition to

Japan, and in 1857 and 1858, he designed the second church which was—with alterations—still standing 25 years later. But after he came back from the Civil War as a lieutenant-colonel and set up an office in Houston as civil engineer, he drifted out of the church. After his wife's death in 1874, he was no longer listed as a communicant. Mrs. Gray died at 37 within a few weeks of her brother-in-law, Judge Peter Gray. Colonel Edwin Fairfax Gray died in 1884, and was buried beside her in an unmarked grave in the Taylor lot in Glenwood Cemetery. He was 55.

Mrs. Benjamin A. Botts had died in 1880, and in 1886, Mr. Botts died. Bishop Gregg said of him "Few of our laity were ever so well versed in our canon law and history. Generous, true, faithful in all relations, Major Botts was confided in by all classes." Bishop Gregg read the funeral services for Major Botts as much out of old friendship as because of the fatal illness of Mr. Dawson.

W. V. R. Watson became a licensed lay reader, and Bishop Gregg commented "Lay readers and Sunday school teachers had cheered their declining rector by most earnest and efficient efforts to prepare young people for the Laying On of Hands." Mr. Dawson's approaching death moved and inspired the people of the church. "There is," the bishop said, "an active interest and religious life such as I have not seen before in this parish . . . Few men have made such an impression as he did upon the people whom he served after so short a connection. He spoke to me again and again most tenderly of their love and continuous devotion to the last." But after a year of accumulating sorrow, another year without leadership is hard to bear.

Chapter 29

New Life Infused

Lean, bald, vigorous, forthright and strong of will, the young Rev. Charles Beckwith hit Christ Church with the fresh breath of new life after a year of sadness. A man of many talents, he was one of those forceful personalities who inspire great admiration and love—and some dislike. But there is nowhere in Christ Church archives any record of his five years in Houston.

Though the archives are laden with letters from ministers who came and ministers who declined the call in 1845, 1859, 1865, and 1870, though there are vestry minutes and parish records dating back to 1839 and 1843, all parish record books of the Beckwith period seemingly went with the wind of 1900. Even the Beckwith memorial window is a recent copy; the original one was destroyed by fire. It is as though man and nature had conspired to wipe out all evidence of his rectorship.

Mr. Beckwith was 35 when he came to Christ Church in October, 1886. The Beckwiths were Yorkshiremen who had settled in Old Lyme, Connecticut a century before the Revolution. Born in 1851, Charles Beckwith was the youngest son of Dr. Thomas Beckwith, a Yale graduate who practiced in Petersburg, Virginia. Mr. Beckwith was baptized by the Rev. Charles Minnegerode, who gave his name to this baby without consulting the parents. Beckwith always said that he had been claimed from the beginning by the church. Charles Beckwith's older brothers fought in the Confederate Army, and as a teenaged boy, Charles carried messages between the lines and supplies to his brothers and their friends. Twice, he said, he was "treed by Yankee sharpshooters." He went to the prep school at Virginia Theological Seminary where "he pumped the organ in chapel and slept soundly through the sermons," and after receiving

1885. The Mikado by Gilbert and Sullivan opens in London March 14.

his B. A. degree from the University of Georgia, he taught at the University of the South and became headmaster of the Sewanee Grammar School [now the Military Academy]. He was 28 when he entered Berkeley Divinity School, Middletown, Connecticut, and 30 when he graduated with his B. D. In 1881 he went to Atlanta where he was ordained by his uncle, Bishop John W. Beckwith. He became rector of Saint Luke's Church, Atlanta, and was soon known for his energy in starting missions. He married, and a year later his wife and new born son died. In 1886, Charles Beckwith came to be rector of Christ Church.

Houston was, at the time, perhaps half the size of Atlanta. But it was a progressive city. When Mr. Clemens left, there were 200 telephones in Houston—one of them at the Christ Church rectory—and there was a long distance line to Galveston. The old and well established Houston Gas Light Company had two miles of mains laid and 15 hands at work. The new Houston Electric Light and Power Company, scarcely two years old, had 100 lights, "distributed through every ward in the city," and 10 miles of copper wire and 600 poles and cross-arms standing. It had contracted with the city to furnish 32 lights to burn all night on the public streets and bridges. "The company will light the city by placing the electric lights on 30-foot poles at the various intersections of the streets to be designated by the City Council, so that in a short time Houston will be brilliantly illuminated at night. The lights used are the same kind used to light up the Brooklyn bridge."

Houston had a water works. Before 1877, all Houston depended on underground cisterns for drinking and fire protection. But in 1879, the first water reservoir was built and a dam was put across the bayou to shut off tide water. Nobody expected to drink this water—but it was nice for fires. And before Mr. Beckwith left Houston, the city would have artesian wells all around town to supply drinking water.

Hunter, fisherman, athlete, musician, writer, inventor and tinkerer with gadgets and machines, Mr. Beckwith had his own way of dealing with a saddened and neglected congregation. He took on the choir with joy. He established a boys' and men's choir, and as the boys grew toward the day when their voices would change, he taught them to play instruments—wind instruments or violin. He got about a lot on bicycle, and whenever he saw boys playing baseball, he was likely to park his bike, shed his coat and join the game. He tackled missions with the same vigor he gave to choir and baseball, and took up with enthusiasm the mission work begun by Mr. Clemens at the Chapel of The Epiphany. He had as his mainstays in the vestry R. M. Elgin and W. D. Cleveland, wardens, Rufus Cage, clerk, and W. V. R. Watson, treasurer.

In Lent, 1887, Bishop Gregg reported: "Catechized the children, more than 200 who responded well. Preached and celebrated the Holy Eucharist at night, preached and confirmed 36 persons, the largest class ever presented here. After long and sore trial and privation, during the ill health and extreme weakness of the late lamented Rector, and also distressing financial losses in the Parish, it has been greatly blessed in securing a Rector who has infused new life and given an impetus, with God's help, to every element of growth and development which will tell largely in a year or two on its advancing prosperity. The people I found rejoicing indeed, and abounding in Thanksgivings to God for his mercies."

Beckwith realized that the church—so recently enlarged under Mr. Clemens—was already outgrown, but he valued the charm of the building and hated

1886. Geronimo, Apache Indian, is captured by U.S. troops March 21.

to waste the money so recently invested in its enlargement. He devised a plan whereby a new church would be built connected to the old one and facing on San Jacinto Street. The two could be used together on special days such as Easter and Christmas. He instituted a system of birthday pledges by which every communicant could pledge and pay a part each year on his birthday.

Easter Day a year later, Bishop Gregg confirmed 37 and reported that in the evening, "the Sunday school children had a joyous time, leaving comparatively little room for members of the congregation, many of whom were anxious to be present. The surpliced choir here, consisting of about forty, has been brought by the Rector to a high state of proficiency and deserved special notice and commendation."

Mr. Beckwith rapidly became a part of the community, and in 1888 in Christ Church, he married Lucy, daughter of Dr. William Irby Cocke, a former Virginian who had brought his family to Bellville. Two of Miss Lucy's brothers lived in Houston, William and Richard, and she had been confirmed in Christ Church by Bishop Gregg during Mr. Clemens' rectorship.

After three years, Mr. Beckwith could look back in his parochial report to the diocese and say:

"It is a pleasure to report Christ Church Parish is in a prosperous condition, growing in the number of its communicants and advancing in the devotional character of its services. The rector on taking charge of the Parish in October, 1886, found this a peculiar people: wonderful in its devotion to the Church and Christian principles where the Church had taken hold of the individual life, unmistakable in its lukewarmness where such was the individual characteristic. The late Priest, long sick, had died in harness, and the Parish left vacant had so remained a year and a half. Through all these trying times earnest Laymen kept the Church open and read the service to a congregation whose faith was being tested. If October, 1886, presented a scattered flock, it also presented an absence of all Diocesan claims. Every assessment had been paid in full, leaving a longstanding parish debt. This, in October, 1886, amounted to $5,850, bearing interest at 7 per cent."

1886. Dr. A. Conan Doyle publishes the first Sherlock Holmes story, A Study in Scarlet, *in December.*

Mr. Beckwith then corrected his council report of 1886 in which he had listed 444 communicants, stating that in his newness to the city he had included some since removed or dead. "Today we have 523 communicants. The debt on the Church except about $100 has been paid. We pay our assessments in advance. And we have laid by as a permanent building fund $2,252.95," (through his birthday plan). He gave credit to the Ladies Parish Association and the Christ Church Choir (composed of 40 to 50 young men and boys) "who by voice and instrument lead the song worship of the service. This, too, is a free gift, our boys receiving no pay for their labors."

But Mr. Beckwith's greatest interest throughout his church career lay in missions. As soon as one could become self-supporting, he was immediately ready to start another. The mission work in Harrisburg had been fluctuating with a shifting population and changing rectors. Curtis began mission work there and T. R. B. Trader had revived it. Mr. Clemens went to Harrisburg often. When Beckwith came, there was a good sized colony of Englishmen— railroad technicians and workmen of one kind or another—who had come to Harrisburg where the Galveston, Harrisburg and San Antonio Railway had its main shops. Then when the G. H. and S. A. merged with the Texas and New Orleans Railway to form a division of Southern Pacific, these shops were moved, in 1888, into Houston between North Main and Hardy Streets. Many of these

1888. Wilhelm II becomes emperor of Germany, and Peter Ilyitch Tchaikovsky conducts his own compositions at the opening of Carnegie Music Hall.

Episcopalians transferred to the Mission of the Epiphany, swelling its congregation. The 1884 city directory lists as Houston's second Episcopal church "Mission of the Epiphany—Northwest corner of Hardy and Conti streets. Rev. J. J. Clemens, rector. Sunday school services 3:30 PM." [It had been opened—according to Mr. Clemens notes—"in Fifth Ward, second Sunday after Christmas, 1880."]

Under Mr. Beckwith, the Epiphany Mission had Rufus Cage as its superintendent. The Rev. John Finlay served the Christ Church mission for two months before going home to die, and in the summer of 1887, services were conducted by a student at the University of the South, M. A. D. Brewster. At council meeting in 1888, Mr. Beckwith asked that a missionary be sent to the chapel, and by 1890, the Rev. Matthew Brewster was back as missionary. By 1891, Epiphany Mission had become St. Mary's Church with a full time rector and an independent congregation. This was Christ Church's first permanent contribution to the Episcopal Church in Houston.

But Beckwith was already talking in council of a mission Sunday school started the year before in Third Ward. "By the generous gift of an old communicant, added to by smaller donations, we have been enabled to erect a churchly building, known as St. John's Mission in this ward. The children of the Mother Church Sunday School at Easter gave $474 toward the purchase of a suitable site in the Fourth Ward (north) or the First Ward for another mission." He still held occasional mission services in Harrisburg.

He valued church property at $40,000. In 1891, he listed 699 communicants, $1,400 received at church offerings, $3,874 from pew rents, and so on for a total of $8,458.36 in contributions. Of this, $202 had gone into church improvements, $4,908 to salaries, light, fuel and incidentals, and $633 out through the offices of the Ladies Parish Association. He also had a subscription for church extensions from the Birthday Fund of $6,638, and from individual subscription $31,300. And $1,000 had been given to the Ladies Parish Association for charity by William Marsh Rice.

In 1891 he listed the seating capacity at 485, the number of church buildings as 3, and the value of them as $53,500. Without vestry minutes or financial statements to go by, it is hard to say why the value of the church property had gone up from $40,000 in May, 1890, to $53,500 in 1891. So far as Christ Church records now go, the property still contained only the 1859 church as expanded in 1876, and the 1857 frame rectory somewhat enlarged, with probably some kind of Sunday school room or vestry or choir room at the back of the property between the two. It is possible that Mr. Beckwith was including Christ Church's holdings on mission sites. With St. John's Mission well begun out Leeland Avenue way, Christ Church used the fund started by the Christ Church children's Easter fund to buy lots five and six on Bingham Street from T. W. House in June, 1892. This was the first site of the mission known as the Church of the Good Shepherd, Clemens Memorial, and was the mission in "first or fourth ward" which Beckwith had envisioned.

In 1892, he reported 610 communicants—and women outnumbered men three to one. And though in May, 1892, Mr. Beckwith was still listed as rector in the Diocesan Council and presumably was there to make his annual report, Mr. Beckwith was in fact gone. He had resigned October 9, 1891.

Mr. Beckwith's resignation was rather a long drawn out affair. As a man of strong will, decided opinion and vigorous plans, Mr. Beckwith cut across the feelings of some in the congregation who by their own strong wills, decided opinion and vigorous plans, had found it easier to follow the gentle, reasonable leadership of Mr. Clemens. It can be noticed that in his first report to council, he expressed his pride rather pointedly that the fine record for clearing the debt had "left us nothing to regret. No fairs, no chances, no accumulations through doubtful means in sweet charity's name. Every cent has come at the cost of hard labor, self-sacrificing, saving and cheerful gift." Was he here taking a shot at bazaars? Or egg rolls?

Certainly since 1871, the Ladies Parish Association had worked hard in every means acceptable for ladies of the nineteenth century to earn money, and by so doing they had bought the organ and built up a handsome fund toward the permanent building Mr. Beckwith wanted. They had also given a number of entertainments. In 1891, they gave *Scrap of Paper,* a French drawing room comedy, for the benefit of the Christ Church Building Fund. Mr. and Mrs. Nelson Munger, Mr. and Mrs. Arthur Livermore, and Mr. E. K. Dillingham were in the cast.

But at some time in Mr. Beckwith's fourth or fifth year, they planned to give the *H.M.S. Pinafore* at Gray's Opera House which faced court house square and was owned by Sweeney and Coombs. Mr. Beckwith was away on one of his prolonged summer vacations at the time, and when he returned, he vetoed the production with his usual firmness of phrase. The Ladies—according to those who remember that production—gave it anyway.

It was an exciting event. They had two casts to take full advantage of the abundant talent. Massie Dolan, who later entered the Episcopal ministry, and Nelson Munger, who had a deep bass voice, had leading parts. Mrs. Munger played Buttercup. The church choir boys were sailors in the chorus, and John Dreaper was one of the youngest members. "My sisters," he remembers, "were the sisters and the cousins and the aunts."

1889. Little Lord Fauntleroy *sells 100,000 copies.*

The theater was lighted by gas, so that half an hour before the performance, the janitor would have to turn on the main gas switch while he and assistants raced through the opera house, lighting lights as rapidly as possible. Once they were all lighted, they could then be adjusted—raised or lowered to the needs of the play. But when first lighted, the whole opera house smelled of gas and had to be aired out before the audience arrived.

"The boys' chorus sang afternoon and night," Mr. Dreaper remembers. "After our song, they always led us down under the stage where there were some acting bars and the like—I suppose to keep us quiet. They ran us down there one night, and I noticed for the first time a great big four-inch pipe sticking right up in the middle of the floor. It had a nut on it, and a monkey wrench on the nut. I pushed the monkey wrench a little, and then a lot, and every light in the house went out! My sister called to me and said 'Johnny come quick over here by me or they'll think you did it.' I knew dern well I did it, but it didn't seem the time to say so.

"Along came a fellow with a lantern, and they had to throw the big switch and light all those gas lights again, and the whole opera house smelled like gas, and it was 15 minutes before the show could go on again.

1890. Vincent van Gogh dies at 37.

"*Pinafore* ran three nights and two matinees, and they made some money. Mr. Beckwith resigned, but we had our *Pinafore.* At the time it seemed worth it."

The *Pinafore* incident was probably only one of several factors which contributed to hostilities between Mr. Beckwith and a group within the church membership. In October, 1891, he wrote to the vestry offering his resignation to take effect July 31, 1892. "This day is chosen so as to give you ample time to fill the vacancy and embarrass the Parish as little as possible. In the mean time my duties will be discharged as though the letter had not been written." Expressing profound sorrow and disappointment, he said that some members of the parish had expressed disapproval of his taking long summer vacations outside the diocese. "My physical capacity has a limit, and under the ordinary circumstances of general health in our city, I must leave the Diocese each year for a summer's rest. This is unfortunate, and more so because of the difficulty of securing . . . ministrations that shall be acceptable to the people. I learn that our congregation is not satisfied with the course I have deemed . . . and with a dissatisfied people left behind, absence could be no rest.

"I yield to another my place," said Mr. Beckwith, "not in the affection and esteem of this congregation but in the pulpit and chancel and government of the Parish. The former I trust shall be mine forever . . . . Your affectionate friend, C. M. Beckwith." The vestry protested, attempted to dissuade their rector, and at last accepted his resignation with a publicly stated regret in strong terms.

The Beckwiths had been married at this time more than three years and had one son, Edmund Ruffin, born in Petersburg, Virginia, in 1890, on what must have been one of Mr. Beckwith's summers out of the diocese. After his resignation but before it was due to take effect, Mrs. Beckwith died of typhoid fever in Houston, January 25, 1892. Mr. Beckwith had many who loved him dearly, and Mrs. Beckwith had been included warmly in the friendships of the parish—working with the Ladies Parish Association, busy with her baby. The congregation gave a memorial window to Lucy Beckwith.

"Mr. Beckwith used to teach us Easter carols all through Lent to sing on Easter Sunday morning," Mr. Dreaper said. "He was strict, and scared you to death, but you couldn't help but love him. There was no compromise in Mr. Beckwith. He was very determined, very direct in speech, a good preacher."

He was obviously respected and liked by his colleagues. In May, 1891, for instance, while still rector of Christ Church, he was elected assistant bishop of Texas to help the ailing and aging Bishop Alexander Gregg. He declined, pleading that he felt himself not ready for a bishopric of any kind. A year later he was one of the two clergymen sent to induce the Rev. George Herbert Kinsolving to accept the post. And one of the first actions of the Rt. Rev. Mr. Kinsolving after his consecration was to wire Beckwith, urging him not to leave the diocese, but rather to come to him as a diocesan missionary. This Beckwith accepted, leaving Christ Church for the work he loved best— starting new missions. He next became rector of Trinity Church, Galveston, and then fourth bishop of Alabama.

Perhaps the vestry hoped Mr. Beckwith would change his mind, or perhaps it was uncertain how soon a replacement could be found. To span the gap, Christ Church invited Dr. Benjamin Andrew Rogers to come down from Grace Church, Georgetown, and continue the work of the church as rector pro tempore.

Nearing the retirement age, Doctor Rogers was a distinguished churchman. Originally from the Diocese of Pennsylvania, he had come to St. David's Church, Austin, in 1865 during what was thought to be the temporary absence of the Rev. Charles Gillette, who had gone east for the General Convention to which he was a deputy. Doctor Gillette at first extended his stay, and then recommended to the vestry that it offer the St. David's pulpit to Doctor Rogers. By superior tact and Christian spirit, Doctor Rogers managed to keep together a parish made up of recent Confederates, Yankees and Reconstruction government appointees, all of whom sought to worship God under one roof.

He was the first to move—in 1868—that the Texas diocese be divided into several, and when Bishop Gregg was too sick to attend the Council of 1892, Doctor Rogers was elected president pro tempore—thereby presiding over the election of George Herbert Kinsolving as assistant bishop.

One outcome of Doctor Rogers' four months in the Christ Church rectory was a meeting between his daughter, who sang in the choir, and a handsome choirman, J. Arthur Tempest, an architect who was to supervise the building of the new parish house. The Houston Blue Book of 1896 shows that Mr. and Mrs. J. Arthur Tempest lived at 609 Elgin, and that living at this same address were the Rev. and Mrs. B. A. Rogers.

During Doctor Rogers' stay, the vestry appointed A. S. Richardson, William V. R. Watson, R. L. Pollard and S. K. McIlhenny a building committee for the proposed parish house. The committee called upon Silas McBee from out of town to design the building and J. Arthur Tempest of Houston to be architect in charge of construction. In September the building committee signed a contract with G. T. Macon, who agreed to build the parish house—with its present cloisters—and finish it by April 1, 1893, for $29,495.

By the time Mr. Aves arrived, this work was just about done. This same contract called, however, for "certain alterations and additions to the church building." The new parish house stood where Mr. Beckwith had expected his new church addition to go. The vestry had followed his plan and once the parish house was done, intended to move into that while the alterations and addition were made to the old 1859-1876 church which would let the two buildings connect and be used as one whenever more space was needed. But their intentions crashed about their ears.

1891. William Marsh Rice establishes an endowment fund of $200,000 for an institute for the "Advancement of Literature, Science and Art."

4 The good old days of church picnics and Easter
Sunday parades to controversy and depression. 1885-1933.

The modern era had begun with the opening of the Paris Exposition and the Eiffel Tower in 1889. By 1890, Houston had become the rail center of Texas, and Texas ranked third in railroad development among the nation's states. Twelve companies ran 234 trains to and from Houston each day.

Nice people in Houston were getting rich off cotton, lumber, railroads and land. Business men grew excessively genteel and wore tall silk hats to town when they drove in their velvet-upholstered carriages. Offices were often handsome with red plush chairs. Victorian houses with marvelous turrets, balconies, circular rooms, ballrooms and indoor tennis courts were beginning to go up. But many streets were still muddy, and Adele Looscan remembered that her husband once wore boots to a reception given by James Stephen Hogg shortly before he became governor in 1890. Christ Church members were at the heart of all this—still for the most part living within easy walk or a short streetcar or carriage ride from the church.

Henry Aves was a newcomer to this southern life. Mr. Aves was born in Huron County, Ohio, in 1853. After graduation from Kenyon College with a bachelor of philosophy degree, he studied at Cincinnati School of Law. A sermon by the Rev. George H. Kinsolving stimulated his interest in the ministry, and he transferred to the Theological Seminary at Gambier, Ohio, where he earned his bachelor of divinity degree. In 1883, he married Miss Mary Gertrude Smith of Kenton, Ohio. Aves was ordained priest in 1884, and his first church was in Mount Vernon, Ohio. He had spent seven years at St. John's, Cleveland, when he accepted the call to Christ Church, Houston, in 1892. He came in December, happy that Kinsolving was new assistant bishop.

There is a tendency among writers and historians to magnify their heroes by explaining what a terrible mess he was handed by his predecessor. One historian, writing in 1912, said that when Henry Aves came to Houston, he "faced a church debt of $30,000 and Christ Church had only one church society, the Ladies Parish Association;" that in 10 years he had wiped out the debt and founded seven church organizations, a parish school and three mission chapels "all the results of the Rev. Dr. Aves personal efforts." Actually, of course, Mr. Clemens had founded the first of those chapels and Mr. Beckwith the second. And the debt came later and suddenly. Mr. Aves' contributions to Christ Church were large. But he did not start at quite the rock bottom the learned gentleman pictured.

Mr. Aves arrived to find a healthy subscription built up toward the proposed church improvements, and to find the new parish house half way to completion. The alterations which would connect church to parish house were too minor to be listed in the building contract. The parish—at the time of his arrival—could be expected to stay comparatively free of debt.

In his newness, Mr. Aves of Ohio innocently provoked one of the most vividly remembered incidents of Christ Church's lighter vein of history. Christ Church had always had some Negro members. For instance, Eliza Wilson born in the household of Captin John J. Atkinson, had lived her life at the Atkinson home, and she came every Sunday to Christ Church. And that ardent Southern aristocrat, Bishop Gregg, had for years held fast to the conviction that the best possible way to serve the Lord was for Negro and white to worship under the same roof.

Until the Civil War, this had worked out well, because white masters simply

brought their household servants to church—having them baptized and married by the rector, and buried from the church when their time came. After the Civil War, Bishop Gregg was forced by events to abandon his theory: The Episcopal Church got very few new members from among the freedmen. In Christ Church, a confirmation class of 54 was remarkable if one of the 54 was Negro. And so Bishop Gregg was compelled to start developing Negro churches and Negro clergymen. These Episcopal Negro rectors had always come to Christ Church for annual council meetings, and had always marched in procession at council.

When Mr. Aves walked into church one Sunday morning with a Negro minister beside him in procession, the congregation thought nothing of it. But when after the sermon hymn, it was the Negro rector who took the pulpit, the congregation was astonished. Mrs. Sam S. Ashe, long time Sunday school teacher and always prominent in church affairs, regularly sat near the front with her children by her. By her side was Nora, the Ashe family maid's child, who had always attended Christ Church Sunday school and who was known by her own family as well as everyone else as Nig Ashe. When Mrs. Ashe looked up and saw a Negro rector in the pulpit, she stood up, took Nora firmly by the hand, and in tones audible throughout the church said "Come, Nig, this is no place for us," and marched out.

Some of the congregation went with her. But by the next Sunday, the incident was closed and life went on at Christ Church. Mr. Aves had simply not yet learned the intricate gerrymandering of the color line in Christ Church of 1892. There is no record to suggest that this was the cause of the east wall caving in.

In the early spring of 1893, when the contractor cut into the church building to connect it with the new parish house, the east wall began to crumble. The old church was not up to another extension or enlargement. With a seating capacity of 485, the old church had been outgrown years before. On big days like Easter, women and children might get inside but most of the men and boys had to stand outside and listen through the open windows. The crumbling wall simply forced the inevitable to happen a little sooner. And the 1859 church, designed by Edwin Fairfax Gray, was razed.

But this meant that Mr. Aves and the vestry were precipitated into building the biggest church of Christ Church history when they had just spent $25,029 on the parish house and when they had used most of the building fund accumulated during Mr. Beckwith's rectorship. On Good Friday, 1893, the corner stone was laid for the new church by the Rt. Rev. George Kinsolving. And this was the last service at Christ Church blessed by the presence of the Rt. Rev. Alexander Gregg. It was the custom at the time to lock the organ on Holy Thursday, and keep it silent until Easter morning. But for the corner stone ceremony, a melodeon was rolled out to the site, and played to accompany the choir as it marched from parish house to the waiting corner stone, singing "The church's one foundation...." Many parishioners were shocked at this flagrant violation of tradition.

The corner stone held "copies of Houston newspapers, of the *New York Churchman*, the *Southern Churchman*, the *Galveston News*, a copy of the papers included in the cornerstone of 1859, landing of Columbus, a $100 Confederate bill, constitution and by-laws of the Ladies Parish Association and of the Daughters of the Church, a photograph of the Bishop Gregg, a photograph of the Christ Church choir of 1893, a gilded horse shoe from the Protection

1892. Dr. Rudolf Diesel patents the internal combustion engine using pulverized fuel and air compression.

Fire Company (across the street) and a historical sketch of the parish by A. S. Richardson." It also held "The Holy Bible and church hymnal, books of common prayer of 1789 and 1892, constitution of the diocese and journal of council 1892, clergy list United States 1892, list of chief executives, federal, state and city, population of city of Houston as follows: 'On this Good Friday, A. D. 1893, Grover Cleveland is president of the United States; James S. Hogg is governor of Texas; John T. Browne is mayor of the city of Houston; population of the city of Houston, according to the directory, 58,513'." This report comes from the *Galveston Daily News* account which ran to two and a half newspaper columns.

In his historical sketch, Mr. Richardson listed the founders. "Fifty-four years have gone, and of those 39 persons, but one now survives and he, Mr. Henry F. Gillette, the last remaining link between the present and original congregation, is with us today." At 77, Henry F. Gillette could look back upon a life given to school building in Texas. He had come back to Houston from Polk County during the Civil War, and in 1866 was one of the founders of the Bayland Orphans' Home which he managed for 15 years. Now retired and living on his Galveston Bay estate, he came into Houston to see another church begun on the site he had known so long.

Richardson then described the building of the first church, begun in 1845 and completed in 1847, when Charles Gillett was rector and the vestrymen were E. S. Perkins, Abner Cooke, wardens; John D. Andrews, Jacob W. Cruger, Cornelius Ennis, Peter W. Gray, Thomas M. League, E. B. Nichols, James Reily, William M. Rice, A. S. Ruthven and W. W. Swain. "Forty-seven years, nearly half a century, has elapsed since then," Mr. Richardson said, "and of that band of workers two, William M. Rice and Cornelius Ennis, still remain, and by their presence here today make this occasion still more impressive." At 77, big Cornelius Ennis with his Prince Albert side whiskers was living in Houston in the pleasant company of his children and grandchildren. His oldest daughter had married Alfred H. Belo, publisher of the *Galveston News* and *Dallas News*. His second daughter married Frank Cargill, and his youngest was Mrs. Cesar Lombardi. The Cargills and the Lombardis lived in Houston. Little William Marsh Rice, 77, had long since given up his Houston house but spent enough time here that he and Mrs. Rice kept an apartment in the Capitol Hotel annex.

The laying of the corner stone began a year of incredibly complex chores for W. V. R. Watson, chairman of the building committee. Again Silas McBee and J. Arthur Tempest were the architects, and G. T. Macon builder. Leafing through scores upon scores of letters, receipts, specifications and memoranda exchanged, one gathers that Silas McBee did most of the designing down to each detail of roodscreen and altar, and Tempest handled supervision.

McBee seemed never to be there. His letters peppered in upon Mr. Watson from Lincoln, North Carolina; Sewanee; European Hotel Rozier in St. Louis; Brotherhood of St. Andrew Indiana State Assembly in Indianopolis; Hotel Aragon, Atlanta; Sewanee; the Richmond and Danville Railroad; St. Denis Hotel, New York City, and London—all these between June, 1893, and January, 1894. He wrote joyously of how beautiful the chancel was going to be, and regretfully—but reassuringly and hopefully—on hearing that the rood screen did not fit: "I take full responsibility, but thought it would be more beautiful...."

Meanwhile Mr. Watson was having letters from Mr. Cleveland who was in New York, toiling away two hours at one financier's office, three at another's,

1892. Development of Houston Heights is begun.

trying to raise a loan to cover this handsome new church. Mr. Tempest was having to stand as buffer between Mr. McBee's plans, Mr. Macon's performance, and the demands for more precise specifications from furniture makers, stained glass window designers and vestry. But Mr. Watson carried the heaviest load. He was the ultimate coordinator and boss.

"Dear Sir: Certainly it is not worth thirty-nine dollars and eighteen cts. for adding six inches of glass to these lights. Furthermore Mr. Macon charges us . . ."

"Dear Sir: The glass is made for iron ventilators, and in order to set it in wood we would have to make it all over...."

"Dear Sir: We would consider it a favor if you would kindly tell us what has been done with reference to the balance of our bill..."

"Dear Sir: We are anxiously awaiting your reply to our letter of Feb 21...."

Payments. Receipts. "Paid S. J. Westheimer, $7.50" for hauling glass for the new building. Unfortunately, much bigger bills were unpaid and mounting.

Finally in late August, the vestry faced up to the task of asking Bishop Kinsolving's permission to borrow money to pay for the church—and his reaction was rather that of a stern father told of his son's gambling debts.

"Sept. 15, 1893: My dear Mr. Watson: Your communication has been such a surprise to me that I am not prepared to become a party in such a transaction unless I can be made to understand the matter differently than from what it appears at present.

"I will be in Houston Wednesday or Thursday of next week.

"Yours very sincerely

G. H. Kinsolving."

But this was a case of necessity. The bishop agreed—protesting. November 18, 1893, the vestry reorganized, reincorporated for its next fifty years, and mortgaged the Christ Church property—Lots 1, 2, 3, 4, 5, 11 and 12—to the United States Mortgage Company for a loan of $20,000 in gold coin. They agreed to pay 8 per cent a year interest, in semi-annual payments, and to repay in full five years from the date. This was the debt which burdened the first several years of Mr. Aves' cure, and almost cost Christ Church part of its land.

The new church—still standing today—probably cost $36,971.

First services were held in the new church Christmas Eve of 1893—and there were two weddings, one before the other.

Miss Rosa Allen, daughter of Sam Allen, was engaged to Robert Stuart and had planned for her wedding to be the first in the new Christ Church. As a choir boy at the wedding, John Dreaper remembers the preparations.

"They would always play Mendelssohn's wedding march, but Miss Rosa wanted us to sing Lohengrin. So Miss Caroline Fraser, who was the organist and in charge of us choir boys, worked out words 'To Thee O God Enthroned on High...' and we sang it as a processional.

"Everybody used to get married on Wednesday night. *Nobody* could marry on Saturday—I don't know why—wed-nesday maybe—and it was positively sacrilegious to marry on Sunday though some who didn't know any better did it. But Sally Ashe gave up Wednesday and took Tuesday to be the first bride in the new church. She was going to marry Charlie Fitch. She took the same program of music that Miss Rosa had planned, and so for two nights in a row, we sang 'The Voice that Breathes Over Eden that Glorious Wedding day, and 'To Thee O God Enthroned on High....'

"The brides were in white, the men in tails, and the whole choir met the bride at the front door and led her down the aisle."

The Allens had a big wedding dinner party at Hutchins House after Miss Rosa's wedding—the second held in the new Christ Church. And apparently Rosa Allen Stuart and Sally Ashe Fitch remained friends.

The church gleamed with newness. Mrs. William Marsh Rice gave chimes for the new tower. There was the new brass and carved oak pulpit in memory of Jane Gray, the new memorial window to Lucy, wife of Charles M. Beckwith, and a window given by the builder, George Macon, showing Christ in Joseph's carpenter shop. Beloved old Bishop Gregg had died in the summer, and on Easter the children of the Sunday school gave a carved oak bishop's chair in his memory. But some things had come over from the old church: the cross on the altar in memory of Abbie Latham Tryon, who had died at 24, and the tablet in memory of the young English organist who had died at 29.

Gas lights gleamed. And Friday Carr had to light them.

Friday used to ring the bell—the first bell 30 minutes before service, the second bell for the choir to march in. At the end of the five minute ring of the first bell, Friday would toll it 12 times, and conclude with three short strokes.

"Why do you do that Friday?" asked John Dreaper.

"The 12 times is for the Apostles," Friday explained, "and the three times is for the Trinity."

Johnnie Dreaper's job was climbing up the ladder to the tower to ring the chimes between the first bell and the second. The choir master had taught him how, and the only drawback was that so many hymns had "one blooming note too many for the 11 pipes."

Friday had to ring the first bell, light the gas lights—with a candle hitched to a fish pole—go back and ring the second bell, and then hurry to the sacristy to pump the organ. Choir boys and ex-choir boys spelled him some times. But they also imposed other duties. "To keep us quiet until the service could begin," Mr. Dreaper remembers, "Friday would tell us stories. He tried to hitch a moral on it if he could. Often they were ghost stories, and he would have us so scared we could scream—but at least we had breath left to sing, which was what he wanted."

The year 1893 not only saw the opening of the new church, but the beginning of many lasting institutions in Christ Church. Ladies had been doing altar work for years, Mrs. George Clark among them. But in 1893, the Altar Society was formally organized with Mrs. L. T. Noyes president; Miss Lottie Porter (later Mrs. E. K. Dillingham) secretary; and Mrs. G. Felton, treasurer.

To provide a home for old and friendless women, the Sheltering Arms Association was organized by Mr. Aves with Mrs. W. J. Briscoe, Mrs. Ella Hutchins Stewart, Mrs. H. D. Aves, Mrs. George L. Price, Mrs. W. C. Crane, Mrs. William H. Crank, Mrs. J. H. B. Price, Mrs. R. L Pollard and Miss Rosalie McIlhenny as charter members.

And because Keziah Payne DePelchin had been one of the church's angels of mercy since before the Civil War, Christ Church felt it had a link of responsibility to her last great work—Faith Home.

Born of English parents in the Portuguese island of Funchal, Madeira, Keziah Payne was 13 when she moved to Houston and with her mother joined Christ Church. She played the organ for the church, and was one of Houston's first public school teachers in 1877. She was 34 when she married Adolph DePelchin, a Belgian musician, in Christ Church, but the marriage proved not to be a happy one. Mr. DePelchin moved to Matagorda where he faithfully

1894. Captain Alfred Dreyfus is found guilty of betraying French army secrets December 22 and condemned to Devil's Island.

served Christ Church, Matagorda, as lay delegate to council meetings.

In 1892, the aging Keziah Payne DePelchin organized what she called Faith Home to take care of the children of working mothers. She charged 10 cents a day or 75 cents a week, but financed her home out of her own slim earnings, walking to save streetcar fare to have more for her needy children. When she died in 1893, her niece and sympathetic citizens decided to carry on the work in her name, and it was announced that:

"The ladies of Christ Church have organized a building association for Faith Home." Houstonians of every faith felt a similar impulse, and Mrs. Charles Dillingham and Mrs. B. F. Weems were named to the first Faith Home board.

On St. Matthew's Day, 1893, the Rev. Mr. Aves called the organizational meeting for the Trinity Mission.

Houstonians had begun to move out to the remote suburbs. D. D. Cooley built out in the new Houston Heights—a lavishly Victorian house which the developers used as an illustration of the charms of the new section.

Many other Christ Church members had moved out as far as Milam and Holman to the new Fairgrounds Addition. The nearest streetcar to that section ran on McGowen, and parents found it hard to get the children dressed and downtown to Sunday school by 9:30—especially on muddy mornings.

Planning a mission of cottage services and Sunday school, Mr. Aves held the first service in the house of Mr. and Mrs. George W. Polk at Smith and Tuam. The new Mission of the Holy Trinity had Mr. Polk and Judge Norman G. Kittrell as Sunday school superintendents. Mrs. Kittrell, Miss Mary Bolms, Mrs. Henry Jonas, Mrs. E. H. McCullough, Miss Kate Jackson and Mrs. Walter Torrey were teachers. Within a year, the mission was moved to an old school house near Louisiana and McGowen, and Mrs. Kate Botts Carrington gave to Christ Church a lot in the Fairgrounds Addition to be the site for a future church.

Trinity was, from the beginning, a healthy off-shoot of Christ Church.

Chapter 31

Hard Times and a Proposed Sales

Christ Church was growing physically and socially—but the national economy in 1893 was beginning to sag. The United States entered a period of severe depression, marked by the march of Jacob Coxey's army on Washington and by the big railroad strike of 1894. As a railroad center, Houston was affected.

The state of the nation may be reflected in the fact that not only was Sheltering Arms established by Christ Church, but so was Houston's first Associated Charities which opened a Friendly Inn for the indigent.

Instead of beginning to reduce the $20,000 debt made in 1893 in New York, the vestry found itself in 1894 borrowing additional money from T. W. House in Houston to finish paying off those who had built the new church.

Mr. Aves, who had hoped for a new rectory to replace the vintage frame house, abandoned that hope if he could be allowed electric lights and some tightening of the window frames.

Mrs. Peter W. Gray died in early 1894 at the beginning of her twelfth year as president of the Ladies Parish Association. She was 74, and had lived in her own home at 610 Crawford. But Allan C. Gray, Judge Gray's younger brother, and Mrs. A. S. Richardson, Jane Gray's niece, lived close by and had cared for her as she grew more frail. The Christ Church vestrymen were her pallbearers, and several groups attended in a body, including the Ladies Parish Association, the Ladies Reading Club of which Mrs. M. Looscan was president, and the Daughters of the Republic whose president was Mrs. J. R. Fenn.

In death as in life, Mrs. Gray remembered Christ Church, and the vestry soon learned that she had left the church $8,000 for a parish school. The vestry obtained permission from Alice Gray Sears to use this money on a new rectory instead, but it became gradually apparent that the legacy would have to be made in land rather than in cash.

The Ladies Parish Association was asked to commit itself regularly for the annual interest due on the big loan, and Miss Caroline Fraser was asked to add to her duties as boys' choir director that of fund raising.

Corporately and singly, the ladies agreed.

Christ Church members were striving to pay their debts. The archives have a sheaf of penny postcards printed "T. W. House, Banker: Credited your account. . . . Amount. . . ." All were mailed from the House bank to W. V. R. Watson, and each had a notation in pen: "I. S. Roberts—$78." "Genevieve Johnson—$9.75" "F. R. King—$12.50" "G. B. Mitchell— $102.50." Because of the odd sums, these notations or deposits probably stand for a variety of collections ranging from a personal penny-a-day bank to collections made whenever and wherever they could be made for this good cause. But times grew darker. In 1897, the vestry accepted the fact of inadequate funds "making imperatively necessary a curtailment of its expenses for the present, which necessity it is hoped may be of short duration."

It proposed: To cut Friday Carr from $40 a month to $30. To pay Miss Fraser $50 instead of $62.50. To discontinue the services of Anton Diehl as choir master. (Diehl was Houston's most ubiquitous teacher of music and accompanist wherever needed.)

The rector "who had already voluntarily signified his concurrence, be and is hereby requested on and after July 1, 1897, to accept in full from the treasurer for his services such reduced sum below his fixed salary as he may deem compatible with his own needs and the necessities of the church."

The position of assistant rector was discontinued. The assistant was the Rev. A. R. Lwyd—whose name seems to have been pronounced Lloyd— and he had been living at the rectory. Considered very British by many Houstonians and presumably Welsh, Mr. Lwyd had conducted services at Trinity Mission throughout 1895, 1896 and half of 1897.

Miss Carrie Fraser was from Canada, and for reasons of health had been spending her winters in Houston, living at the A. S. Richardson house, and her summers in Canada. A small, confident young woman, she not only kept the choir boys in proper order but eager to sing their best. Miss Fraser permitted no nonsense in the church or parish house. But boys will be boys.

Small Georgie Cleveland, angelic in surplice, marched in procession one Sunday morning with a black eye, given him after choir practice one night by Johnnie Dreaper in a fight held under the streetlight on the corner, and promoted and refereed by older choir boys. And there came a time when

1895. Sidney Porter (O. Henry) goes to work for the Houston Post.

the choir boys, who did not like Miss Fraser's successor, crossed the reins on his horse so that when he started home, a pull on the left rein turned his horse to the right and almost into the ditch.

The dark days of debt are not reflected at all in the *Houston Blue Book* of 1896. In it, Christ Church shines as a center of happy, constructive, social gatherings.

The Christ Church Choir was accompanied by an orchestra: Mr. Alf Elgin, Mr. Tom Humason, Mr. Fred Root, cornets; Mr. Harvey Dumble, alto horn; Mr. Ernest Hail, clarinet; Mr. Albert J. Hail, tenor horn; Mr. William Crank, flute; Miss Cardwell, Miss E. Cardwell, mandolins; Miss Carrie Fraser, organist, and Mr. Fred F. Dexter, choirmaster.

William Hines Kirkland and Massie Dolan are remembered for their beautiful tenor voices. I. S. Roberts, W. D. Cleveland, Jr., and Charles Fitch were bassos.

The *Blue Book* lists the Ladies Parish Association, Sheltering Arms, Altar Guild, Daughters of the Church, and Cadets of St. Andrews meetings. And it gives a page to the Ladies Reading Club—"oldest of the existing ladies literary clubs . . . being now in its tenth year." Meeting Tuesdays at 4 PM in the Christ Church parish house, it had finished two years of Shakespeare and was planning to take up "the dialect writers of New England."

The Z. Z. Club was composed, the *Blue Book* said, "of the elite of the city" and it gave a cotillion once a month during season. Gentlemen of Christ Church were among the elite: Spencer Hutchins, son of the late W. J. Hutchins and a bachelor whose slightest attention was enough to insure a debutante's success for the season, B. R. Latham, J. J. Atkinson, A. S. and W. D. Cleveland, Jr., and S. T. McIlhenny.

Christ Church members appear in almost every kind of civic work. The Houston Philharmonic Society was organized in 1893 with 30 members. Rufus Cage was president; J. A. Tempest, vice president; J. McEnnis, secretary; and Professor Anton Diehl, musical director. Like their founders, Col. William Fairfax Gray and A. S. Ruthven, Christ Church men continued to be active in Masonic orders. To give their achievements as Masons would mean to write another book. At various times, R. M. Elgin was president of the Bayland Orphans Home Board, and the school board had as members H. B. Rice, president; C. Lombardi, Rufus Cage, and on the board of examiners, T. J. Patillo. Mr. Aves was vice president of the Humane Society. In the Ladies Choral Club, Mrs. W. H. Kirkland was president, Mrs. M. E. Culpepper, vice president and Miss Cara Root, treasurer. And Miss Genevieve Johnson was president of the Houston High School Library Association.

In 1899, Mr. Aves solemnized the marriage of small, dark haired, dark eyed Elizabeth Clemens—so much like her father but with her mother's Virginia voice—to a red haired young Englishman, Ernest Humphrys. Mec Clemens and young Emily Scott were junior bridesmaids, and the Cadets of St. Andrew were there in uniform.

Aware that the $20,000 note was due in 1898, the vestry began to dig deep. They had contributed money when needed throughout the past five years. Now 26 churchmen, including the vestry, agreed to pay from $250 to $500 each—$12,500 among them—in November, 1898, if this would make up the total needed. And $250 or $500 is a lot of money in a year when the country is in depression and when you can buy a

1897. The first demonstration of a horseless carriage is held in Houston.

child's school dress—size 6 to 14—at Foley's Store for 25 cents. The pledges were signed by W. M. Read, J. W. Jones, M. E. Howe, J. C. Hutcheson, P. K. Ewing, R. C. Hodges, G. A. Riley, C. H. Lucy & Co., Sam McNeill, I. S. Roberts, Hahl & Rudor, Mrs. Bettie Bryan, Rufus Cage, O. L. Cochran, Mrs. Latham, C. B. Shearn, J. H. Kirby, R. Tillbrook, J. B. Bowles, W. H. Kirkland, W. V. R. Watson, William D. Cleveland, L. T. Noyes, H. D. Aves, E. Cargill and R. M. Elgin.

In August, 1898, they managed to pay the annual interest of $800. Of this the Ladies Parish Association had given $200. W. M. Mitchell had gone out on his own and collected $150 in sums like $25 from T. W. House, $15 from Jake Hornberger, and varying amounts from J. E. McAshan, Philip Carson, Theo Pillot, the Levy Brothers, Stuart Drug Company, and others. (Whereupon the vestry sensibly elected Mitchell to take its one vacant chair.)

Finally in March—four months late—the church paid off its $20,000 note. They made it by the Ladies Parish Association's raising a heroic $4,398.50, by William Marsh Rice giving $3,000 on direct appeal by the rector, and by collecting $12,225 in a vestry canvassing job of grim effort. This brought them up to a total still $883 short, whereupon W. D. Cleveland, William M. Read, and Rufus Cage handed over personal checks for $294.35 each. But they still owed T. W. House $1,862, and $450 on paving the sidewalk, and $1,916.50 simply "due and unpaid."

They were strapped and penniless.

As the treasurer put it: "The Revenue for the support of this parish is derived from 132 people only and in sums ranging from $5 to $187.50 each per year. During the past six months, 43 persons have withdrawn the support and cancelled their subscriptions."

By 1900, Christ Church was still in debt $4,000—and so the vestry made a resolution which could have marked the beginning of the end of the church on its historic site: They resolved to sell the entire rectory corner at $250 a Texas Avenue front foot if the buyer would not use the property "for any purpose that would interfere with or be obnoxious to the Vestry of Christ Church."

The 50-foot lot they proposed to carve out of the half block would have brought them $12,500. This may have seemed like a fortune in 1900, as $1,000,000 for the whole block would later seem in 1926. After all they had just mortgaged the entire half block for $20,000.

They apparently had hopes of selling the lot to a library. Andrew Carnegie had promised the Women's Club $50,000 for a building if the city would provide a suitable site.

Fortunately the city found a cheaper—if not better—offer: The City Council on June 18, 1900, bought the east corner of the First Presbyterian Church property (at the corner at Travis and McKinney) for $7,880 and there the first Houston Public Library was opened. Though the vestry may have been disappointed at the time, this was one case where the Presbyterians' gain was Christ Church's salvation.

The vestry seemed unaware of the fact, but forces were working to restore the parish: buyers were slowly gathering to take up bit by bit and parcel by parcel the scattered lands inherited by the church from the estate of Mrs. Peter W. Gray. This money began to come in—incredibly small amounts of money for the land received by the standards of 1963,

1898. Madame Curie in Paris announces the discovery of radium.

1900. Sigmund Freud publishes The Interpretation of Dreams.

sometimes $1 an acre for good ranch land, which today could not be bought for $200 to $300. No one has cared to ask whether any of this land turned out to cover oil deposits. They managed to sell one lot, originally to be sold for $10 cash and $30 payable with interest at 8 per cent, by knocking $5 off the asking price. But at $80 here, $1,400 there, gradually the church became solvent again.

Meantime A. S. Richardson died after 40 years on the vestry, and after 13 years as organist and director of choir boys, Miss Carrie Fraser resigned to go home to Canada for good—receiving a tribute in the vestry minutes which no vestry of the previous century would have granted a bishop. The vestry adopted formally a resolution of respect and devotion to A. S. Richardson, and planned to place in the church a bronze plaque to his memory.

The 1900 storm at Galveston—most brutal in Texas history—killed 5,000 and destroyed Trinity Church. Four-year-old David Rice, staying with his aunt Mrs. S. K. McIlhenny, was lost in the storm. Christ Church expressed its sympathy in resolutions, in funds, and in accepting refugees as all Houstonians were doing.

But Christ Church had suffered a loss too: Henry Aves was not so well organized a man as either Mr. Clemens or Mr. Beckwith. When he married or baptized or buried, he made a note on a slip of paper and stuffed it in his pocket. He meant to write them all down when he had time. He took the notes and the Parish Record down to the house at Seabrook, intending to catch up on his sins of omission. The storm hit, and 25 years of Christ Church parish records went with it.

It is doubtful that the missing vestry minute book shared this fate. There is no reason for the rector to have taken the vestry's record of 1875-93 from church to bay in 1900. There is always hope that this book may yet reappear from some old family library or second hand book shop.

1900. William Marsh Rice is murdered in New York City September 24.

A Consecration and a Bishop

In September, 1901, President McKinley was shot.

Under "HONOR TO THE NATION'S DEAD," The *Houston Post* said: "The horror that filled the minds of the people of Houston over the attempt on the life of President McKinley; the intense sorrow that has filled every heart at his tragic death, and the sympathy heart-felt and universal for Mrs. McKinley, have crystallized into movements looking to outward and visible manifestations."

Mr. Aves announced memorial services at Christ Church. All military units of Houston took part, forming at their own headquarters, and in full uniform without side arms, marching to the church. The Houston Light Guard, George B. McClelland Post No. 9, G. A. R., Dick Dowling Camp, United Confederate Veterans; Troop A Houston Cavalry, Veterans of the Spanish-American War and Sons of Confederate Veterans, all took part. The Rev. Henry J. Brown, assistant rector of Christ Church, conducted the memorial service, and Rabbi Henry Barnston paid tribute to the late President.

No reference was made to the Cadets of St. Andrew in the newspaper. They were a military-religious organization of small boys who met the first and third Wednesday of each month at Christ Church. Mr. Aves was director. The

1901. The discovery of oil at Spindletop January 10 begins the oil era on the gulf coast.

cadets were: J. D. Bright, Walter Black. S. Briscoe, T. H. Botts, T. Bryan, W. D. Cleveland Jr., William Condell, A. Crary, Fred Clemens, B. Dammond, Johnnie Dreaper, Fred Hart, George Hart, Sam Harrison, Robert Holman, Maxie Heyde, F. Lambert, H. Pruesser, Ingham Roberts, A. Scudamore, R. Schneider, A. Swingle, William F. Tarver, T. C. Tarver Jr., and C. Weems.

By this time the widow and children of the Rev. Julyan Clemens had moved back to Houston to live. In one year in Rhode Island, Mrs. Clemens had lost not only her husband but twin children as well. A few years later, her friends and relatives persuaded her to return to Houston, and not long after her return, she added to her household her niece and nephew, Emily and John Scott, whose parents had died. The Clemens children and the Scotts grew up within the close family of the Christ Church parish, gaining from it in childhood, serving it and strengthening it as adults.

February 2, 1902, Christ Church was consecrated by the Rt. Rev. George Herbert Kinsolving. By 1902, better times had come. This is not only recounted in the published report of 1902-03, but exemplified by the fact that the vestry felt it could afford to have a 53-page illustrated report printed.

Church property was valued at $100,000 with five buildings, including mission chapels. Each Sunday, Christ Church celebrated Holy Communion at 7:30, had Sunday School at 9:30, morning prayer and sermon at 11:00. Evening prayer and sermon were at 8 PM April to October, 7:30 PM October to April, and Holy Communion first Sundays at 11:00 and Saint's Days at 7:30 AM. Litany was read every Friday afternoon.

Monday through Saturday there were no fewer than two meetings a day of some Christ Church group, usually at the church. Gray Grammar School classes met Monday through Friday from 9 AM to 1:30 PM under Professor E. L. Hallock, and had 34 boys. E. Cecil Seaman, Mrs. E. N. Gray and Miss Katherine Aves were teachers, and Capt. Wallace O. Breedlove was drillmaster. Of the 34 boys, one pupil was being prepared for the Massachusetts Institute of Technology, three for the University of the South. "The moral tone of the school is pure and wholesome." The school adopted a West Point cadet uniform for drill, taught Latin, German, French, English literature and composition, rhetoric, history, algebra and geometry. Arthur Hartwell was captain of the Gray Grammar School cadets and other officers were Delano R. Aves, first lieutenant; William W. Price, second lieutenant; Stanley Beard, first sergeant; Worden Fenner, Q. M. sergeant; Henry Black, second sergeant; Stewart Stanuel, third sergeant; Bartlett Chew, first corporal; Pringle McCraven, second corporal; Albert Bowles, third corporal.

With the opening of Gray Grammar School in the parish house, the Christ Church had met—in spirit at least—with the wishes of their great benefactor, Mrs. Peter W. Gray. She had left a major portion of her estate with the expressed hope that it would go for a parochial school at Christ Church. The money had been used instead to save the church from financial destruction. Nobody doubted her willingness to have it so used. Grays had been saving Christ Church from financial destruction for 60 years. But it did seem appropriate that any school operated on that site should be named Gray Grammar School. By 1902 Mr. Aves even had hopes of building a two-story brick building back of the new rectory to accommodate the school. But the hope and the school gradually went out of existence.

The big achievement was, of course, the building of a new and handsome rectory in early 1902. The old frame house of 1857 vintage was not torn down—it was sawed in half, sold, and taken off to continue life in two parts on other lots in the neighborhood. The new 15-room rectory was begun May 15, 1902, and completed November 1, for a cost of $11,000. "For the style and general plan of the new Rectory, which have been so greatly admired, we are indebted to the late Mr. J. A. Tempest of blessed memory, the architect of the Church and Parish building, and to Mr. George E. Dickey who so skillfully modified the original lines to meet the requirements of the building committee."

Once again, W. V. R. Watson led the building committee which included J. B. Bowles, William D. Cleveland and Frank Cargill. The house was big, lovely, standing in the middle of a large and pleasant residential section of Houston, and Mr. and Mrs. Aves promptly opened the doors in their usual and casual fashion.

In 1902, the Rev. Robert S. Stuart was Aves' assistant, devoting himself largely to Clemens Memorial Chapel of the Good Shepherd. Trinity had flourished under the Rev. Mr. Brown and a succession of Sunday School superintendents from Christ Church including I. S. Roberts, J. Massie Dolen, B. P. Bailey and A. S. Dyer, and Miss Lucy Bird. And in 1902, Trinity had decided to declare its independence, acquiring its own rector, supporting its own parish, and agreeing with Christ Church vestry on a boundary line between the two parishes. The Kittrells, Reynauds, Cushmans, Aikens, Dumbles, B. P. Bailey and Massie Dolen went with Trinity.

Though Trinity suggested Webster as the boundary and P. B. Timpson of the Christ Church vestry favored McGowen, Christ Church and Trinity finally agreed on a boundary between the two churches to run east and west along Hadley Street. It could not have occurred to any of them that before long, the automobile would have criss-crossed and blurred all parish boundary lines, that by mid-century a Christ Church rector might pay a parish call in New York, and that some parishioners would drive regularly from Galveston or the outer reaches of northwest Harris County to Sunday morning services at downtown Christ Church.

Looking back over his decade, Mr. Aves wrote, "To us who have felt the strain of united effort, and who know pretty well by experience how nearly the limit of our resources has been reached at times, figures which tell of hard tasks accomplished will carry a meaning that is even eloquent.

"According to our past ten Eastertide reports, our Parish has received and expended: For Church improvement . . . $104,452.31. For current Parish expenses (including charities and missions) . . . $88,168.48. For objects outside the Parish . . . $22,519.96. Total . . . $215,140.75."

As rector, Mr. Aves had seen the building anew of every permanent structure on the property: parish hall, church and rectory in that order. "Over the ten years last past, seven hundred and fifteen souls have been received into the ark of Christ's Church by Holy Baptism. Five hundred and seventeen persons have ratified their baptismal covenant and received the laying on of apostolic hands in confirmation. Six hundred and seventy-two have given and pledged their troth before God and in His Church in Holy Matrimony. And four hundred and fifty-one times, the Church's sad, faithful words of committal and prayer have been spoken in the burial of the dead."

The next few months were tranquil, troubled only by a protest from the Daughters of the Confederacy and the City Health Officer over neglect

1901. Marconi signals letter S across the Atlantic from Cornwall to Newfoundland December 12.

of the old Episcopal Cemetery. Friday Carr's wages were raised to $40 a month. Massie Dolen and Harris Masterson Jr. presented themselves as candidates for holy orders. Memorial plaques went up to Mr. and Mrs. Cornelius Ennis—she who had founded the Ladies Parish Association and he, that vast man who had served Houston as mayor, had helped build the railroads, and served as vestryman in both Houston and Galveston off and on for 60 years. The plaque was raised by their oldest daughter, Mrs. Alfred H. Belo. Sheltering Arms reported that it had cared for 14 women and three children in time of grave need, at a cost of $12.48 a month each. In its comfortable—if temporary—affluence, Christ Church received $2,455 from Elizabeth B. Rice's will, in the compromise settlement with the estate of William Marsh Rice.

In November, 1904, the Rev. Henry Aves resigned to become missionary bishop of Mexico. His consecration at Christ Church was the first of any Episcopal bishop in the state of Texas.

The Rt. Rev. Alexander Charles Garrett of Dallas presided over the ceremony, and eight other bishops came from far and near to take part. They were the Rt. Rev. Francis Key Brooke of Oklahoma and the Indian Territories; the Rt. Rev. Peter Trimble Rowe of Alaska; the Rt. Rev. George Herbert Kinsolving of Texas; the Rt. Rev. William Montgomery Brown of Arkansas; the Rt. Rev. Frank Rosebuck Millspaugh of Kansas; and the Rt. Rev. Davis Sessums, bishop of the diocese of Louisiana. Bishop Sessums, a one-time Houston boy who had been ordained deacon at Christ Church, stayed with his old and dear friends, the W. D. Clevelands, while in Houston. The Rev. Charles Aves of Trinity Church, Galveston, brother of Henry Aves, and the Rev. Thomas B. Lee of St. David's, Austin, were the attending presbyters who vested the new bishop in the habit of his order. And young Rev. Thomas J. Windham of Trinity Church, who had begun his theological studies under Bishop Aves in the rectory, acted as master of ceremonies.

Christ Church had not had to look for a new rector in 12 years, and the vestry put off all effort to do so until Mr. Aves had been consecrated and had gone off to Mexico. The time between his resignation and consecration was not great—from November 3 to December 14—and the vestry had many duties in getting invited guests from other cities to suitable quarters, in arranging for a luncheon to be served by the Ladies Parish Association and the Sheltering Arms Association. Those invited were assured that "many trains arrive at every hour," so the depot committee was particularly busy.

At the first vestry meeting called after Bishop Aves' departure, December 17, the vestry were inclined to think they could get a new rector for about $2,500 and an assistant for $600 or even $900 if necessary. Mr. Aves had been so undemanding where salary was concerned that the vestry was not quite aware of the costs of living in 1904 in Houston.

They had the happy idea of inviting an assistant to Christ Church at this low salary with the provision that when the vestry had selected a rector, if the rector did not like the assistant, he would be dismissed with 30 days' notice. This was the offer they made to the Rev. Stephen Moylan Bird, Jr., who was rector of his own parish at Taylor. In courteous terms, Mr. Bird told the vestry that no one could live in Houston and assume the role of rector pro tempore of Christ Church on a salary of $750, nor would anyone look forward to a post which might end as soon as begun.

1902. First International Court of Arbitration opens in The Hague in October.

1904. James M. Barrie writes the play Peter Pan. *Puccini's* Madame Butterfly *is given its premiere.*

133

Thus re-educated to the economics of 1904, the vestry was better able to appeal to a permanent rector once he could be found. Meanwhile Bishop Sessums suggested that the Rev. F. B. Nash of Albany was in a position to supply in Houston until permanent arrangements could be made.

Chapter 33

The Good Old Days

Despite depression, debt, and the war with Spain, the years from 1885 to World War I were the Good Old Days in Houston and certainly the Good Old Days at Christ Church.

These were days of Easter Egg Rolls on the Court House lawn, May Fetes in the Christ Church yard, annual church picnics by bus or barge or train, and long summers at the Aves place at Seabrook. Every Christ Church member who has any memory of even a few of these years gets an instant glow on his face at that memory.

The church was not only at the heart of town, but still in the center of its own parish residential section. Young people met in the choir and married—J. A. Tempest and Susan Rogers, Jesse Andrews and Celeste Bujac —and in the long years of church work and church play together, families were more and more closely knit in a pattern of thriving business, community service, marriage, and good friendships which resulted in name sakes and god-parenthood.

1900. Carry Nation crusades against saloons, swinging a hatchet, and Sarah Bernhardt tours the United States in Hamlet.

The same men and women who were building Christ Church were also building Houston government, Houston business, Houston welfare, and Houston culture. Though it may have made for in-family disputes, it looks from the perspective of 65 years, a time of beautiful harmony and much fun.

Henry Aves was ideally suited for this period. Not a particularly brilliant orator, no great shakes at raising money or consolidating financial gains, Mr. Aves shone in his ministry largely through his human qualities. Many men now executive citizens of Houston and of Christ Church remember boyhood summers spent—all summer long or for a week or two—with the Aves at Seabrook. All of them say ruefully that Mr. Aves never really got all the money due him, that little Mrs. Aves had a hard life trying to make ends meet—first in the skimpy old rectory, then in the handsome new. But Mr. and Mrs. Aves loved young people, loved boys in particular, seemed to enjoy all human kind in quantity as well as high quality.

Mr. Aves was a practical joker. He managed to keep this tendency under discipline in town, but gave it full play at the bay. Little boys who, in town, thought Mr. Aves a tremendously serious gentleman as befitted the cloth, knew that on the bay, almost anything might happen. One of his favorite tricks, Albert Bowles remembers, was to invite a guest to hold out his plate to be served and then, with an innocent expression on his face, let hot mush land on the thumb of the hand holding the plate. As frequent and long standing guests, the little boys were prepared, and waited with a gleam of anticipation for the next unwary newcomer to the inner circle to get *his* thumb burnt.

As a small boy, Albert Bowles didn't swim very well and was shy about trying in front of all the natural fish of the Aves family. When he said he couldn't swim, Mr. Aves put it to the test one day by levering him out of a row boat with the oar. "Thought you said you couldn't swim!" he called delightedly as Albert dog paddled to safety.

John Dreaper remembers the day that the Cadets of St. Andrew—all visiting in Seabrook at the Aves house—were told they'd been invited to Sunday dinner at Mrs. T. U. Lubbock's—but that she wanted them in uniform. They put on their woolen uniforms, walked over a mile in the summer sun, and then in snappy formation, marched to the house. There was a veranda full of people, all down from town for the day, all invited to Sunday dinner —by a hostess who had no knowledge of the invitations. Mr. Aves had planned the elaborate prank, mailing the invitations from the bay in her name.

His greatest trick, perhaps, was played on a guest who had come down for the day, wearing the full regalia of Victorian gentlewomanhood—big hat, huge sleeves, corset, tucked and ruffled waist, peplums, petticoats, sweeping skirts. It tickled Mr. Aves' funny bone and at the same time raised his hackles to see someone come down to the bay all dressed up as she would be in town.

Taking the lady and others out for a ride on the bay, Mr. Aves got them a good way out from shore and then said: "There's something wrong with this boat. You will all have to get out immediately and let me take a look." The captain had spoken, and everyone got out into the knee-deep or hip-deep bay water while Mr. Aves turned the boat upside down, gravely examined its caulking, righted it, emptied it, and let them get back in again. And the lady had to go back to the house, and presumably back to Houston, showing the signs of her wade.

Gradually on the stories of those who knew him, a picture grows of a wide-hearted man who enjoyed life thoroughly, who saw the church as the center of all sorts of good things, from new missions to outdoor summers at the bay for growing boys and city-bound ladies.

"Mr. Aves got up the first May Fete," Mr. John Dreaper says. "He planned it and called us boys to a meeting and showed us some handbills. We were to distribute the handbills and in those days, the streetcars were the best place. I'd get on Main Street and hop on one streetcar at a time. I'd ride a block and hang a batch of handbills up on a string. I didn't know I needed a permit and I guess the conductors thought I had one.

"Then Mr. Aves said 'You boys run the chili stand and have a Mexican dinner.' Jesus Torres made the best tamales in town, and I asked him for a price on 300 to 500 tamales. Seven for a nickel was his regular price, but he said if I'd buy 200 at that rate, he'd give me 100 free. That was our profit. We set our prices the same as those on Market Square: 7 tamales for a nickel, 4 with chili for a nickel.

"Mr. E. C. Crawford had a store, and I told him we were having a party at Christ Church and how much coffee would he give me? He gave me two pounds. He had a grinding machine you know. This was more than I had expected on first try, and that encouraged me to try others. The ladies made the coffee for us, and Mr. Aves told us to dress up like Mexicans so we wore white shirts, our regular pants and red sashes. Mr. Aves gave us sombreros he had. I remember we sold out and had to go buy some more from Jesus.

"That was in 1899," said Mr. Dreaper. "I remember, because my mother died April 7, 1900, and the second May Fete was right after that and my sisters wouldn't let me go."

Katherine Aves was queen of one of the first May Fetes and wore a crown

1903. Orville and Wilbur Wright make successful flights in a heavier-than-air machine at Kitty Hawk, N. C., December 17.

made of roses from the rectory garden.

The Easter Egg Roll was the earliest of the big outdoor spring parties for fund raising, and was always held on Easter Monday.

"The Ladies Parish Association held the egg roll on the old court house lawn because the old court house had a fence on all four sides and four gates. They could put a lady at each gate and charge 10 cents to get in. Then it cost you several dollars to get out because you'd buy a lot of stuff. They had a fish pond, grab bag, all sorts of things to entice your money. People going to the court house on business got in free of course; the ladies had to use discretion on who not to charge.

"The egg roll went like this: They'd put a long line of eggs on the ground, and then line up all the kids and call one two three go! We had to run to the eggs and whoever grabbed the most won. Once on my birthday, Mr. Horton bought me a brown derby. I was 10, and they cost $1.25. So I wore my derby Easter Sunday, and next day I wore my derby to the egg roll. I was running to the eggs when I fell, the derby fell off, and a fellow stepped on it."

The Court House Square was in the 1870's Houston's only park, and in the 1890's it was still a pleasant one: planted with trees, encircled by an iron fence but open until midnight, well lighted with gas lights, with benches pleasantly placed in the shade. Everyone went there to stroll, to rest, to see friends.

The May Fete began as an addition, not as a replacement, to the Egg Roll, and the Baby Show was one event which carried over from one to the other at some time during their overlapping history. A Houston newspaper of about 1905 gave more than half a column to it: "Large Throngs on Christ Church Lawn Yesterday Afternoon. Many Pretty Little Ones . . . Judges Discussed Awarding Prizes to Amiable Mothers Whose Babies Didn't Win." Prizes were given in 20 categories ranging from the prettiest, through heaviest and on to youngest mother with most children. Despite the great amiability of mothers, one wonders how the parents of the finest baby under six months (prize, talcum powder) felt when the finest boy from six months to a year got a spoon from Lechenger Jewelry Company or the most decided brunette (boy or girl) won a ring from Sweeney's Jewelry Company. And there are lingering rumors of the time a baby with beautiful curls lost out to a totally bald baby who was wearing a fetching ruffled bonnet. At least once—perhaps during the building of the 1893 church or the 1902 rectory—the Egg Roll was held on the big lawn of George A. Gibbons, whose house stood on Fannin Street at Lamar where the First Baptist Church now stands.

For years the Christ Church May Fete was the only one in town, and often other churches would be invited to send a Duke and Duchess to the court, or dancers for the program. The May pole was always where it stands now in the church lawn but there used to be a vacant space back of the rectory. There, every year, ponies would be brought to walk round and round in a ring for the children to ride during the May Fete.

In those good old days, Easter Day was worth remembering, and everyone who ever took part in one of those Sunday school parades remembers it vividly.

Mrs. Sam Ashe taught the youngest children of all, and her little Nig went to Sunday School along with the others. It was taken for granted that she

1903. Enrico Caruso makes his debut at the Metropolitan Opera House in New York.

should, inasmuch as her mother, Mrs. Ashe's slave-born maid, had been a baptized member of the church.

Miss Carrie Cargill was one of the most popular teachers in Mr. Aves' day. Willie Robertson taught the boys' class for a while. Willie was the adopted son of Mr. and Mrs. William Robertson, and adopted grandson of old Mr. W. J. Hutchins. He ultimately became an Episcopal priest and had a High Church parish in Nashville where—as Father Robertson—he never married. Matt Brewster, son of vestryman Robert Brewster, taught Sunday school during his summers at the University of the South and before entering the ministry. And E. Cecil Seaman, who taught both in the Gray Grammar School and as a Sunday school teacher, became a minister and later an assistant rector at Christ Church.

It is impossible to give any proper chronology to the Sunday school teachers of that day from which no records were preserved.

But living Houstonians of various ages, from varying periods in their childhood and youth, remember these teachers with affection: Mrs. Sam McNeill, Mrs. Bonner McCraven, Miss Elizabeth Clemens, Miss Helena Wilson, Mrs. Louis Bryan, Miss Genevieve Johnson, Miss Carrie Cargill, Mrs. F. M. Law, and Mrs. Harris Masterson.

Miss Genevieve held her class in the Christ Church transept and among her boys at various times were Albert Bowles, Palmer Archer, Fritz Dyer, DeWitt Dunn, Lindsay Dunn, Frank and Fred Clemens, Tom Taliaferro, Edward Palmer (who later drowned in a regatta), James Adair and John Scott. Miss Genevieve and John Dreaper transferred to Trinity Church in its early, growing days, and built the Trinity Sunday school program along the lines of the familiar Christ Church Sunday school.

And Mrs. McNeill's former Sunday school scholar—Miss Nancy Flewellen—taught a Sunday school class in Mr. Sears' day which included Ella Rice, Audrey Thompson, Lila Godwin, Maydell Swisher, Alice Gray Sears and others. They used to have a candy pull at Doctor Flewellen's house at 410 Austin and they have memories of the crape myrtles blooming in that Austin Street front yard.

Miss Laura Rice taught Sunday school and is remembered by one of her pupils as being "so beautiful. Every Sunday morning she seemed to wear lilies of the valley and be escorted from Sunday school to church by some tall, handsome beau." She later married Richard W. Neff.

For several weeks in Lent, the Sunday school and the boys choir were always in a spasm of preparation for Easter. Mr. Beckwith, for instance, would gather the boys choir together every Sunday afternoon during Lent to teach them Easter carols not in the hymn book—waving his clarinet as a baton. Then on Easter Day at 9 A.M., the whole Sunday school had to gather to practice the march they would make in the afternoon.

W. D. Cleveland was superintendent of the Sunday school and W. V. R. Watson was assistant superintendent. Tall, still handsome, wonderfully gentle, and with a great sweetness of spirit, Mr. Cleveland typified Christ Church to the children. Ministers came and went, and some of them even died, but Mr. Cleveland was—to them—eternal. And on Easter afternoon, they felt what Mark Twain called the pure Glory of being the outstanding boy or girl for one reason or another in the Sunday school.

"You got points," Mr. Dreaper explained, "Each Sunday, you got one point for being present, one for being on time, one for knowing the lesson,

1904. The Moonshine well, near Humble, is brought in November 6, opening the first big oil field in Harris County.

1905. Albert Einstein publishes his Special Theory of Relativity.

one for remembering the offering, one for behaving yourself. It was possible to get five points a Sunday. In each class, whoever had the most points by Palm Sunday was named Banner Scholar for Easter. Whoever was Banner Scholar carried the banner for his class, and whoever was runner-up carried the Lenten missionary money.

"We would form a double line down at Turner Hall at Caroline and Prairie, behind Mr. Cleveland and Mr. Watson who would lead the way, followed by all the classes starting with the infants class.

"The banners were made of satin and silk in beautiful colors and lettered in gold and they said things like *Little Workers* or *Christian Soldiers*. *Workers in the Vineyard* had a bunch of grapes and a cross on it, I remember, and *Wise Virgins* had an Aladdin's lamp on it. Once a bunch of teen-age boys got hold of the *Wise Virgins* banner, and it upset Miss Genevieve Johnson just *terribly*. She was mortified.

"We'd sing 'Onward Christian Soldiers' and march from Turner Hall up Prairie to San Jacinto, and when we got to the church, the choir met us at the front door and led us into church."

Banner scholars were given books as a reward for their "general excellence" —good books like *Four Years Before the Mast, Robinson Crusoe* or one of the James Fenimore Cooper novels. And they were given gold medals.

Arthur Dwyer won gold medals in Beckwith's day, and John Dreaper won gold medals four different years during Aves' cure. There was one drawback to winning the medal, Mr. Dreaper said. "Afterward, you had to wash your face, and put on your Sunday suit, and go downtown and hunt up the old, dignified business man who had given the medal, and thank him for it."

But all these were nothing compared to the Christ Church annual picnic.

"We dated everything from the picnic," said Mr. Dreaper. "We would say 'That happened the first Sunday after the picnic.' Or 'the third Sunday before the picnic.' (The early ones were at the old fairgrounds. The entrance was at McGowan and Milam. It had a baseball park and a race track.) The first picnics I remember were at Merkel's Grove on Buffalo Street and German Street. (Now St. Charles and Canal—German Street was changed during World War I.) Merkel's Grove had a big grove of trees and a dance pavilion.

"We would all start out early in the morning with a big picnic basket, *full*. We'd walk or take the mule car down to Christ Church. And there we would catch the omnibuses about 9 o'clock. The omnibuses were big, fancy, round, pretty-shaped buses painted bright colors with a baggage rack on top. Baldwin Transfer Company had a whole raft of them. The picnic wagon with fringe on top was the one the band rode in. The infant class went in the four-horse bus, other classes in the bus behind. We would start at Texas, go to Main with the band playing, then out Congress and on to Merkel's Grove.

"Next we used to go to Volkesfest Park which adjoined Merle Merkel's Grove. The Houston Packing Company is where Volksfest Park used to be."

One year in this period they went by water. Captain Atkinson owned the Houston Direct Navigation Company which ran cotton barges down to Galveston. The barges were always idle in the spring. "Captain Atkinson would run a fence around a barge, hang a tarpaulin over the top, and let the choir boys invite a girl and their families to go on a picnic. We'd get

on at the foot of Main Street and were towed down to Clinton. There we'd have lunch and some of Frank Vance's ice cream, and run around a while, and then we'd be towed on down to the battleground. I remember the year Mr. Cleveland's warehouse burned, the water was awash with wholesale groceries washed down by the fire hose. That year, the church used the barges for the annual picnic.

"Next came Magnolia Park." Magnolia Park had been opened on the bayou at Constitution Bend in 1890 and reputedly had 3,750 magnolia trees all blooming at once. The Houston Belt and Magnolia Park Railway established a service to the park which was known as the dummy line. It was also known as the angel-maker because of its tendency to kill pedestrians. Christ Church began to use the dummy line for its picnics at Magnolia Park. "The dummy line started at San Jacinto and Commerce, and had several open cars—like street cars—back of a little locomotive. It was built to carry its own coal, and had a funny jacket over the boiler and I guess that's where it got the name.

"People would cook for one or three days before the picnic, and we would spread out on big tables in the park. Sid Mitchell was in his glory. He was a bachelor, so he would visit from table to table. The band played dance music. Milton Baker, who was a Negro, owned a flying jenny which he always brought to the picnic. Two powerful Negro men would turn the crank to make it fly, and there were rings, and if you grabbed a brass ring you got a free ride. I *never* got a brass ring in my life, but you could swing out. They had straddle horses for the boys and carriage boxes for the girls. Milton lived on Fannin and Jefferson and he was rich.

"Frank Vance made the best ice cream. He had white chin whiskers and lived on Caroline and Pease behind his ice cream plant. He sold ice cream biscuits for 5 cents. Frank always came to the picnic. A dish of ice cream was 10 cents or a biscuit for five. At Dawson's it was 25 cents for two dishes. But at the picnic, everyone was given a ticket for one free biscuit.

"To make ice cream, you put a bucket inside a washtub filled with ice, and turned the bucket in the ice, back and forth with both hands. When the first freezers came out and they advertised 'WILL FREEZE ICE CREAM IN 20 MINUTES'—*amazing!*" said Mr. Dreaper.

"After Magnolia Park came Sylvan Beach. Christ Church would charter a train of railroad cars from the Houston, LaPorte and Northern Line. They were the old fashioned cars with vestibules. Everybody would swarm aboard, we'd pack those cars full, and there'd be a dozen kids on every one of those open vestibules. It's a wonder nobody ever got killed. We'd go down to Sylvan Beach for the day, and when the picnic ended, and it came time to go home, every boy rushed, and the first on held seats for their mothers or their friends.

"Frank Clemens was a young man then, and one picnic he came on board our car with his girl but every seat was taken. I got up and gave her my seat. Next time we went to cadet meeting, Fred Clemens said 'Frank wants to see you after the meeting.' And Frank took me to Polemenakos's candy place—for an icecream soda. Nobody had ever bought me a 10 cent drink before.

"I said why. And Fred said 'Frank's paying you for giving his girl a seat on the picnic train.' "

To small Lois Cleveland, who got in only on the last few picnics, the lemonade made in the big black barrel and with lemons floating on top, was

1907. Shearn Methodist Church on Texas Avenue is sold for $115,000.

the best lemonade ever made. There has been none like it anywhere at any time since.

The Southern Pacific bought the old H.L.P.&N., and would rent Christ Church a whole car without asking how many people or children you packed in. But when World War I came along and the government took over the railroads, it expected one ticket per person, and the rate was 3 cents a mile. This meant $1.50 a child per picnic. Neither Christ Church nor its members felt they could afford that kind of money, and it brought an end to the church picnics.

Chapter 34

Colonel Gray's Grandson

Christ Church has always shown a strong continuity—an interweaving of past and present and future. When Bishop Aves went to Mexico, he did not actually leave Christ Church. His bay home was still here, in times of need he turned to his successor and his old congregation to help his Mexican people, he would come back to Houston for a long and happy retirement as the fishing companion to a new generation of rectors and churchmen, and when he died, his casket would be carried by men he had known as boys in the church.

The Rev. John Julyan Clemens from Cornwall married into a branch of the Gray family which had founded Christ Church. After his death in far off Rhode Island, his wife and children came back to Houston—back to friends and relatives in the church, contributing their energies, their talents and their children to the church as it grew.

Old families move away and come back, sometimes married and under a different name. Young men who leave here as Sunday school teachers or aspiring theologues come back decades later as visiting bishops. Rectors in moments of latterday sorrow come back to Houston as the place they stayed the longest and feel most at home. And always Christ Church is in the same place. Always there are those who will remember the good old days—whenever they were—that the visitor is seeking to touch again.

Thus when Bishop Aves left for Mexico and the church called the Rev. Peter Gray Sears of Meridian, Mississippi, it was the reappearance of another thread in this pattern of continuity. Mr. Sears' parents were Claudius W. Sears and Susan Alice Gray who had been married in the home of Peter W. Gray in 1853—the last wedding performed in Houston by Dr. Charles Gillette. Doctor Gillette apparently came back to Houston for that wedding because of his long friendship with the Gray family. Mr. Sears' grandfather had sired Christ Church, and Peter Gray Sears was named for his uncle. These facts influenced Mr. Sears in his decision.

Peter Gray Sears' father was a West Point graduate who had been on the faculty of Tulane University, had fought in the Confederate Army, and after the Civil War, taught mathematics at the University of Mississippi in Oxford. Peter Gray Sears was born in Oxford in 1866, and was graduated at the University of Mississippi before entering General Theological Seminary in New York. The Gray family had always leaned toward the legal profession, but Sears' mother influenced him toward the ministry. In 1890, he married Fanny Elizabeth Archer, a young Baltimore girl recently graduated from school in Washington. Sears' first church was in Holly Springs, Mississippi. Old St. Thomas Hall there had burned during the war, and as rector, Sears rebuilt the school. James Lockhart Autry and William Stamps Farish, who later moved to Houston, went to the school as boys. After three years at St. Andrews, Jackson, the Sears moved to St. Paul's in Meridian, and it was there that Mr. Sears received his call to Christ Church, Houston. At about the same time he was offered Trinity Church, New Orleans, and a large church in Brooklyn. Mr. Sears accepted the call to Houston, arriving in March of 1905, in time for the annual Easter Monday meeting that year.

Mr. Sears was a slender man of only average height with fair hair and gray blue eyes, and he threw himself into life with all the passion of one who thinks, feels, believes and cares strongly. He was a man of eloquence, and of wide reading. Though his parishioners were never aware of notes, Mr. Sears worked hard on every sermon, often spending a week in preparation for the Sunday to come. When the sermon was delivered in tones of gentle reasoning and almost conversational ease, no one realized how carefully each point, each quotation, each phrase had been planned and made ready for linking to the next. Like the Grays of Virginia, Peter Gray Sears was primarily a Low Churchman. He might—or he might not—wear the clerical collar in town. In his rectorship, he reached out to all denominations and faiths and entered into a dozen phases of community and civic work in Houston.

The Houston waiting for him was a pleasant one. From the corner of Main and Texas Avenue Houston seemed a city of churches. Their spires rose at regular intervals in each direction. Main Street had the First Presbyterian Church on the corner of McKinney, the Central Christian Church at Bell, the Second Church of Christ (Scientist) in the block now occupied by the First City National Bank and the Second Presbyterian Church at Dennis. The First Baptist Church was at Fannin and Walker.

Texas Avenue was a wide, gentle, unpaved street of churches. The streetlights hung over the street from tall stands shaped like shepherd's crooks. Shearn Methodist Church, a lovely church with towering spire, stood at 809 Texas Avenue, Christ Church between Fannin and San Jacinto, the First German Evangelical Lutheran Church at Texas and Caroline, and Church of the Annunciation at Texas and Crawford, on land formerly owned by Peter W. Gray.

There were still gas lights standing on the corner by Christ Church, and a lamp lighter came each evening to light them. As Alice Gray Sears (Mrs. Frank Akin) remembers, the rectory was a house of 14 or 15 rooms with high ceilings. The doors were of leaded glass. There was a big porch across the front, and another at the side. She and her friends used to play jacks on the tile stoop of the front porch. "There was a tremendous stove at the back of the house in the big center hall. The parlor was on the left of the hall with Papa's study behind it, and his study opened into a yard which led to the cloister and parish house."

On the right was the library-living room, and back of that was the dining room and back of that the butler's pantry and kitchen which opened onto the back porch. There was still a cistern in the yard, and in the back yard was a small house where the rectory maid lived. Upstairs were five bedrooms and two baths.

Across San Jacinto facing the rectory was the big, imposing Central Fire Station with a domed roof. Cater-cornered across from the rectory was Mrs.

1905. Norway and Sweden dissolve the union between them.

1906. San Francisco earthquake and fire April 18-19 kill 452, leave $350,000,000 damage.

J. A. Flake's house. And across Texas Avenue was Earthman Funeral Home—the Earthmans lived upstairs—and the Cozy Theater, a hot spot of vaudeville with amateur nights thrown in. If the amateur acts were poor, the audience would shout "Give 'em the hooks!" by which a long shepherd's crook would yank the offenders off the stage. The rectory children, playing with the Earthman children, could sometimes get a free peek at the show.

Though the Central Fire Station stood on the corner, there were private homes north of the station on San Jacinto, and on Prairie behind the church.

By 1907, Houston had a Y.W.C.A. operating a dining room and parlors. William States Jacobs had come to the First Presbyterian Church. Mr. Sears had A. S. Cleveland as his Sunday School superintendent and among the teachers were Miss Helena Wilson (lovingly known as Miss Nellie), Miss Nancy Flewellyn, Miss Genevieve Johnson, Miss Adelaide Radetzky, and Miss Maude Leman.

Mr. Sears was rector of both Clemens Memorial and St. John's Chapel of Christ Church on Leeland. He had George G. Linck in charge of the Clemens Sunday School and Oscar M. Longnecker at St. John's Sunday School. St. Mary's Episcopal Church, still at Hardy and Conti Streets, had the Rev. James B. Snowball rector, and J. B. Muir as Sunday School superintendent. And the Rev. T. J. Windham was rector of Trinity.

The Parish Meeting of that Easter Monday typifies the parish as Mr. Sears found it. This was an era when Christ Church looked at first glance as big as it does now, and had a quite remarkable proliferation of organizations—each with a representative at the annual meeting to make a report: Choir Chapter, E. H. Hellen, secretary, reporting. Junior Branch of Girls Friendly Society, Mrs. Katie De. L. Hartwell, working associate. Women's Auxiliary Christ Church branch, Mrs. A. L. Gribble, secretary-treasurer. The Junior Auxiliary, Miss Irma Morse, secretary. Sheltering Arms Association, Mrs. W. V. R. Watson, treasurer. St. John's Guild, Miss Jessie B. Tharp, secretary. The Ladies Parish Association, Mrs. Florence N. Dancy. And the Rev. F. B. Nash, recently the supplying rector. Not to mention various vestry committees.

But at that parish meeting, there were only 22 members present. Mr. Sears re-appointed R. M. Elgin, small and dignified with a patriarchal beard, senior warden, and the vestry elected tall Mr. Cleveland, junior warden. The parish was fairly free of debt—thanks largely to the generosity of a few parishioners living or dead. Money was still coming in over the years from the sale of lands left by Jane Gray's estate.

Mr. Sears liked to select his own hymns to tie in with the theme of the morning lessons and sermon, and soon after his coming, he encouraged the efforts already being made to buy a new organ. The vestry signed a contract with the Hutchins Votey Organ Company of Boston to pay $6,475 for a new organ. It would have a water motor with a minimum pressure of 20 pounds. F. M. Law was agent for the company in Houston.

Not long after his arrival, Mr. Sears seemed to follow the Gray family-Christ Church tradition by permitting Miss Jenny M. Eichler to open a school in the parish house. A German woman from Oyster Bay, New York, Miss Eichler soon had three primary classes in operation. Among the children attending were Howard Hughes, Elizabeth Dillingham, Elizabeth Law, Alice Gray Sears, Dudley Sharp, Thomas William House, Ella Rice, Marion

Spencer, Helen Wicks, Minnie Gates, Tommie Rice, Louise McClain, Lila Gates, and Dudley Colhoun.

Miss Eichler was very strict with her small people and referred often to the importance of *character*. Her pupils loved her dearly, and if bending the twig is important, she played a significant part in shaping those children. The little class of thirteen children produced an internationally known aircraft and motion picture executive, a Secretary of the Air Force and a successful playwright for television and the London theater, as well as an unusually high percentage of citizens with charm, intelligence and ability.

As a newcomer, Mr. Sears offered no opinion on church financing. But he apparently was looking into the matter, because at one vestry meeting, a report was presented which showed that 68 pew holders were in arrears on pew rent in amounts from one month to more than two years. These delinquents were well established church members. They didn't mean to be delinquent. They just had not yet got around to sending in their rent. Mr. Sears was prepared, and by the time of his second parish meeting, he had persuaded his vestry that pew rents were not the answer to the problems of the church budget. High Churchmen and Low—lifting single voices—had tried to get this point across for half a century, and at last with Peter Gray Sears, Christ Church abandoned the pew rent system upon which it had depended, and which had proved so undependable for so many years.

To this meeting, Robert M. Elgin sent a letter of resignation after 38 years as vestryman. "My right hand has lost its cunning, my limbs can no longer bear the weight of the body, and it may be that in the wreck of the body, the powers of the mind have no escape," he pleaded. But he was not to be released from service. John Charles Harris moved that Mr. Elgin be elected to the vestry for the coming year by standing vote, and the parish stood in an upsurge of sentiment to elect him by acclamation. They swept in with him the retiring vestry of William D. Cleveland, Presley K. Ewing, W. V. R. Watson, Rufus Cage, J. B. Bowles, Sam McNeill, A. S. Cleveland, and M. A. Westcott.

Harris Masterson, Jr., was recommended as a candidate for holy orders, Mr. Law was paid the first $5,500 on the organ, and everyone agreed that the music as directed by Mr. Horton Corbett was so beautiful that the rector and vestry must give a party for the choir at the rectory.

The partnership between Mr. Sears and Mr. Corbett, so soon established, was from the beginning a tremendously successful one. Edith Lawrence-Toombs joined the choir as a school girl, and she said "I always felt I got my real education from sitting in the choir listening to Mr. Sears' sermons. His services were simple but very beautiful, and by the time you'd heard Mr. Sears in the pulpit and Mr. Corbett on the organ, you went home on air."

The Rev. E. Cecil Seaman, moving from deacon to priest, became Mr. Sears' first assistant. Teacher in the Sunday school and the Gray Grammar School in his youth, assistant at Christ Church at the start of his ministry, Seaman ultimately became second missionary bishop of North Texas. Mrs. Frederick Allyn Rice died, and at her funeral, her seven sons carried her casket. In 1907, P. B. Timpson represented her children to ask that they be allowed to place a window to her memory next to the Ennis window.

Another four lots of Jane Gray's legacy were sold for $1,200, and members of the finance committee were busy writing letters to all the com-

1907. The United States fleet makes its first round-the-world cruise with 16 battleships and 12,000 men.

municants and former pew holders and members explaining the new system of financing. Presley K. Ewing's letter said "The subscriptions range from $6.00 to $200 per year, covering various intermediate amounts. It is left to each to conscientiously determine what to give." The five members of the finance committee were—it seems—conducting unaided an every-member canvass by mail.

By the spring of 1907, the vestry felt able to raise Mr. Sears' salary to $5,000. Mr. Sears insisted that this be taken to the congregation, but the congregation heartily concurred in the vestry decision.

The balance of the organ debt dragged on for several years. In 1908 Rufus Cage had a treasurer's report printed which showed that in the past year, total receipts had amounted to $9,301.67, total expenditures had amounted to $9,043.61 with a cash balance of $258.06. But there was $1,454.15 balance due on organ and $1,000 due W. D. Cleveland & Sons for advance payment on organ. This caused a good bit of correspondence, and must have been hardest on Mr. F. M. Law, caught between the company in Boston and Christ Church in Houston.

In 1908, standing in the big bay window of Doctor Flewellyn's house at 410 Austin Street, Miss Nancy Flewellyn married Dr. A. Philo Howard, and her sister Bessie Clark, married Thomas A. Helm, in a double ceremony solemnized by their grandfather, the Rev. Horace Clark. Not long after, Mr. Clark read the ceremony for another granddaughter, Miss Mamie Culpepper, who married Clark Campbell Wren, a young Houston attorney. With her beautiful red-gold hair and delicate profile, Miss Mamie must have been the epitome of the Gibson girl, and she loved to remember in later years that to make her debut at the turn of the century, a young lady needed to have only a few good skirts and a great many pretty blouses.

Mexico, swept by floods in the autumn of 1909, was hit by an unseasonable frost. Mr. Sears received an eloquent letter from Bishop Aves in Monterrey. "I need your help," he wrote. "There is great suffering and impending famine among the poor (which means the bulk of the mountain population throughout the central mesa of Mexico.)" The frost had destroyed $20 million worth of crops in the mountains, and though wages were normally 25 centavos a day (12½ cents) now there was "no work, no money, no food." "I am asking," said Bishop Aves, "for a carload of corn from Houston which will ward off threatening famine." Mr. Sears told this story quite simply from the pulpit, and the carload of corn was soon on its way to Mexico.

Though secure in a country which felt itself independent of other continents, Christ Church parishioners gave often to missions in Alaska, to Armenians and Syrians, to the Near East, and after the earthquake, to Japan.

Mr. Sears saw Christ Church as a home to those of many denominations. He liked to have ministers from other churches speak, and visitors from other denominations often came to hear Sears preach on Sunday morning. In February, 1910, Mr. Sears offered Christ Church to a group of 50 persons wanting to organize a Greek church. A Greek Orthodox priest from New Orleans, presided over this meeting, and Nick Xanthos, James Condos and A. D. Polemanakos were among the Houston leaders.

In 1911, Charles Norvell Love, editor of *The Texas Freeman*, wrote to invite Mr. Sears to sit on the platform at the Booker T. Washington lecture at the City Auditorium, because, the Negro editor wrote, "you are deeply concerned in all the people. Mayor (H. Baldwin) Rice has consented to welcome Dr. Washington in behalf of the city." He courteously offered as his references: Mrs. Eugenia Flewellyn, 410 Austin Street; Mr. W. D. Cleveland, and Mayor H. B. Rice. "Mrs. Flewellyn," he added, "who is a member of your church, had much to do with my training."

In 1908, there was a major baptismal service. When Laura Kirkland, Tina Cleveland, and Lila Godwin were all born in 1908—the daughters of three close friends—the families used the occasion to catch up on all their past omissions. So three Kirklands, three Godwins, and one little Cleveland were all baptized that day. Little Bill Kirkland was old enough to invite Mr. Cleveland and Mr. Godwin to be his godfathers.

At this time the Kirklands lived on Polk, the young A. S. Clevelands on San Jacinto, and the Herbert Godwins at 916 Crawford. This was the pleasant, easy distance to live from town. The Sterling Myers lived at 1617 Main Street, and big Victorian houses had been built on either side of Main well out past Polk, past Leeland, past Jefferson. But many Christ Church members lived way out—the Arthur Lawrence-Toombs at 2110 Caroline and the Henry St. John Waggamans at 2218 Caroline. D. D. Cooley still lived in Houston Heights, as did his son Denton.

In 1910 Ella Cage married Mr. Dallas Tourtellot of Kansas City. Rufus Cage gave his daughter in marriage, Mr. Sears read the ceremony, and amid the many attendants, Chaille Cage and Virgilia Chew were flower girls.

These were tranquil years. Times were good, and Houston was growing. In 1907, $892,000 was spent on building private residences in Houston, and in 1911, $1,200,000. In the decade ending in 1912, $9 million went into house building, one historian reported at that time, "in homes of all kinds from humble cottages to palatial mansions. Some residences have cost $50,000 to $75,000." The historian didn't say how many humble cottages could be built for nine million if several cost $75,000. The new Y.M.C.A. was built on Fannin Street at McKinney in 1907-08 at a cost of $200,000.

"Probably the most interesting group of ecclesiastical buildings in Houston is the Christ Church group," B. H. Carroll said in his history*—"the church proper, the parish house and the rectory—perpendicular Gothic executed in red brick and sandstone. Incongruous as are their surroundings," he continued urbanely from the viewpoint of 1912, "the vine covered church and rectory with the deep cloister of the parish house, form an architectural group that has no superior in Houston." The incongruity came from the bustling metropolitanism of the city.

In 1912 the Carter Building soared upward to the skies: 16 stories with a roof garden and four elevators which ran at a speed of 600 feet a minute. "The building has a vacuum cleaning system all over, its own artesian well which produces 300,000 gallons daily, its own heating and electrical plants." The Beaconsfield was built out in the residential section of Main Street beyond Leeland, and nudged out the Savoy Flats as Houston's most elegant apartment building—a place it was to hold for 50 years and more. By 1910, Main Street was 2,313 feet long—the paved part.

Houston Heights was still a separate municipality, and Westmoreland was Houston's handsome new residential section. It was such a source of pride that in 1910, all Westmoreland, Emerson, Flora, and Garrott were paved while throughout the city, older streets were left to dust and shell.

The Automobile Club of Houston had been reorganized in 1909, and

* *Standard History of Houston,* by B. H. Carroll, Nashville, 1912.

1910. Halley's Comet spreads its tail 93 million miles across the sky, and Mark Twain dies.

1910. Ground is broken in July for the first building of Rice Institute.

E. R. Spotts was its president. C. C. Pillot and W. D. Cleveland, Jr., were on its board of governors, and James L. Autry an active member who, in 1910 was driving a Winton Six. The Houston Launch Club, founded in 1906, held its meetings at Harrisburg, and sailed out of the turning basin. The city directory of 1910-11 reporting on "Marvelous Increase in Water Traffic" said that "The tonnage carrying capacity has nearly doubled. The membership of the Houston Launch Club own over two hundred boats, mostly for pleasure." Several of these were ocean going yachts, and social notes of the day referred to the parties aboard for the cruise—Christ Church members were often among those aboard. But already the United States Congress had voted "At Houston's solicitation," $1,250,000, matched by Houston bonds, to make a 25-foot channel and a bigger and deeper turning basin. The Houston Country Club had been founded in 1908, and in 1911 its officers were W. M. Rice, Jr., president; E. B. Parker, vice president; P. B. Timpson, secretary-treasurer. Dr. Robert R. Knox, Edwin R. Spotts and E. K. Dillingham were chairmen of house, grounds and finance committees. And Presley K. Ewing was president of the Z. Z. Club.

By 1910 two telegraph companies in Houston were handling a 3,500,000 messages a year. By 1912, the Houston Electric Company had 13 rail lines with 191 cars running on them. And in September, 1911, the Houston-Galveston Interurban was running. The 50.5 miles of track had been built for $2,500,000, and the trip took one hour.

In October, 1911, Edith Lawrence-Toombs married W. Ernst Japhet in Christ Church with the Rev. Mr. Sears reading the service.

William V. R. Watson died in 1908 after 32 years on the vestry and decades as Sunday school superintendent. By his own force of will, character, and patience, he got the parish house, the church and the rectory built between 1892 and 1903.

Christ Church had—by the city directory of 1910-11—1,200 communicants with 200 children in the Sunday school. It had 2,000 baptized members. The vestry decided tentatively to elect three new or different members to the vestry each year, and after one year cancelled the by-law. Christ Church built a rectory for the Clemens Memorial Church of the Good Shepherd for $2,130, and the vestry insisted that their rector, whose service had "for the past several years been untiring and continuous," take a three month vacation.

The pressures were less in those pleasant days. From time to time the vestry would urge upon Mr. Sears a two-months vacation. The vestry sometimes failed to meet all summer, and in one year skipped three meetings in a row—October, November and December—for failure to achieve a quorum. But Mr. Sears always arrranged for excellent ministers to supply in his absence and the church seemed to cruise along during those months without vestry meetings. Young Harris Masterson supplied one summer, and the Rev. Stephan Moylan Bird, another. Mr. Bird was highly thought of at Christ Church. He had in his seminary days sometimes played the organ at weddings—he played well though he had only one hand—and he was twice called to the church as assistant. He could never accept the call, but he did come and supply one summer when needed.

The Rev. Thomas J. Windham was in and out of Christ Church in various capacities for years. As rector of Trinity, he had agreed to help Mr. Sears with the Clemens and St. John's missions without any payment from the vestry, and when he became rector of Clemens, he was employed by the Christ Church vestry which agreed to pay $50 a month toward his salary. Gentle, bright, witty, and of great sweetness of spirit, the Rev. Mr. Windham was one of those pure Christians who had no idea of money and no thought of himself. What he had, he gave to anyone who needed it, whether it was his overcoat or his services. He became the marrying and burying parson of Houston quite simply through this eagerness to go and to serve as needed—oblivious to lines of denomination and faith. He had snow white hair as a comparatively young man, and a face which was youthful throughout most his life.

The Rev. Stephen F. Power came to Christ Church in this period as assistant to Mr. Sears. Uncle of W. S. Farish, Mr. Power was known as Uncle Steve to almost everyone.

On October 13, 1912, Mr. Sears and the entire congregation of Christ Church were invited by Dr. Edgar Odell Lovett to take part in a religious service at the City Auditorium marking the formal opening of the William Marsh Rice Institute. Doctor Lovett, as president of the new institute, later wrote his thanks for the vestry's cooperation "in our efforts to establish in the minds of our citizens a permanent impression that the new institution is to have a spiritual as well as an intellectual significance in the community."

In December, 1912, William D. Cleveland died after 44 years on the Christ Church vestry and 38 years as junior warden. No layman since Peter Gray had done more for Christ Church in terms of time, of love, and of uncountable gifts of money, than Mr. Cleveland had done throughout his life. Mr. Cleveland was born in the same year that Christ Church was founded, and he was buried on Christmas afternoon, 1912. The Sunday morning service of January 12, 1913, was a memorial and the sermon a tribute to him. He and Mr. Sears had become good friends in the seven years of their association, sharing laughter over good jokes as well as work on plans which interested them both. Mr. Sears' sermon reflects a deep affection and respect.

"Of royal will power, of lionlike strength and manliness of deed, of incorruptible integrity, of woman-like gentleness of manner, of sympathetic and charitable consideration for all, of generosity of thought and speech and act, of broad-minded liberality in all things—a Christian gentleman. He was never anywhere or at any time or under any conditions anything else or less."

The Y.W.C.A. by 1913 was searching for a site upon which to build, but the vestry decided that "at this time it would not favor giving to the Y.W.C.A. the site now occupied by the present Rectory for its building site."

William D. Cleveland, Jr., was elected to the vestry, and Mr. Rufus Cage succeeded Mr. Cleveland, Sr., as junior warden. In 1913, Mr. Robert Elgin died. Mr. Elgin and Mr. Cleveland had joined the vestry together in 1868. Older by 14 years, Mr. Elgin had stood as Mr. Cleveland's sponsor at his baptism. A frail, small gentleman of 88 with a long, frosty white beard, he must have missed his young friend in that last year of his life. He had been active in many charitable and civic organizations, and he left to the church his children—Robert, Betty, and Hettie (Mrs. M. A. Westcott) and his grandchildren. His granddaughter, Miss Daisy Elgin, grew up to have a beautiful singing voice which gave Houston concert goers great pleasure, and his grandson, Mark Westcott gave Christ Church one of its light anecdotes.

One day Mr. Sears was in the pulpit in mid-flow of his morning sermon

1911. Captain Roald Amundsen, Norwegian explorer, reaches South Pole December 14.

when he saw Mark Westcott's dog coming down the center aisle. He paused and said firmly, "Mark, get that dog out of here!" and went on with his sermon. Mark got.

Christ Church at that time was a much lighter, airier-looking building than it became after the fire and reconstruction of 1938. It had windows on the Fannin Street side of the chancel, where organ pipes now are, and on any pleasant day of the year, all the windows were opened—letting in more light as well as air.

In 1913, the city proposed to pave Texas Avenue with wooden blocks. The pavement was an agreeable one. It ended forever the dust and mud of Texas Avenue, and it gave a soft and pleasant clop-clop sound under the hooves of carriage and dray horses. Its drawback was that after every rain—and Houston is not a city often plagued by drought—the blocks would swell and buckle. Street repairmen went about over the city to hammer the blocks back in—often having to split one block in half or knock off a third to get it back into its place.

Miss Frances Sears and Rufus Cage, Jr., were married in a ceremony by the bride's father. In Mr. Sears' first decade, there had been many Christ Church weddings: John Dreaper to Elizabeth Lemon, Elizabeth Yeager to John Gus Blaffer, James House Bute to Clara Robinson, William Gray Sears to Bettie Bringhurst Gaines, Dolores Pearl Guion to John H. McClung, Emily M. Scott to Joseph W. Evans (at the residence of Mrs. J. J. Clemens), Alma Cleveland Daily to St. George L. Sioussat (at the residence of W. D. Cleveland), Katherine Elizabeth Aves to George H. Harborat (with Bishop Aves officiating), Herman Hale to Dorenda Nolan, Libbie Randon Rice to William Stamps Farish (at the residence of David Rice), Kate P. Rice to Hugo Victor Neuhaus, Arthur Hartwell to Elizabeth Haskins, Daphne W. Palmer to Edwin L. Neville, W. Ernst Japhet to Edith Lawrence-Toombs, William Leonard Aves to Helen T. Wilson, Mary Louise Ayers to Louis Arthur Stevenson, Dr. Charles M. Aves to Ruby Linn Arnim, Ashley Newton Denton to Rosine Ryan Huston. The choir's soloist Florence Marian Kent and William Hogue were married, and the vestry sent them a wedding present.

The hurricane of August 16-17, 1915, swept into Houston with force. It blew out the front windows and walls of the church, damaged the Sunday school organ, blew out windows in the rectory, and the ceilings of three rooms of the rectory fell, including the one in Alice Gray's bedroom. Fortunately the Sears family had not returned from their summer vacation in Colorado. The Clemens Memorial Chapel was severely damaged. The repairs took weeks to complete, more than $5,000 in cost, and the vestry resorted to a bank loan until an extra subscription could be raised.

The beginning of World War I in 1914 found no reflection in the vestry minutes of the year. In 1915, Christ Church agreed to pay $600 a year toward the salary of a rector of St. Mary's Church in Fifth Ward. That year Christ Church members were—as usual—active in many civic affairs. John T. Scott was president and Mrs. Presley Ewing vice president of the Humane Society. Mrs. Elliott Cage was president of the Faith Home board. Mrs. Robert Godwin was president of the Y.W.C.A. John F. Dickson was president; T. W. House, vice president; and P. B. Timpson, secretary of the Glenwood Cemetery Association. Dr. A. Philo Howard was vice president of the Harris County Medical Society. The Rev. Mr. Sears delivered

the Rice Institute baccalaureate sermon—the first of many through the years.

Mrs. W. V. R. Watson planned a memorial window to her husband to be placed—appropriately—next to that of Mr. W. D. Cleveland.

In the winter of 1916, the Autrys' maid Tap died. Born Lucy Waller in Virginia, Tap had spent so much of her life with the Autrys that she and they considered her a member of the family. She was especially devoted to young Jimmie Autry, and caught her death of cold standing in a cold rain on a street corner with a raincoat for Jimmie hoping to keep him from getting wet when he got off a trolley car.

On the day of her death, she dictated to Judge Autry her will. "I hereby give and bequeath to James L. Autry, Jr., . . . all property of every kind owned by me—having known and loved and lived with him all the days of his life, and he having been always a joy and happiness to me, having watched his growth with pride and pleasure." Tap's funeral was conducted in the parlor of Judge Autry's house at 5 Courtlandt Place with the burial service read by the rector of Christ Church. Jimmie and five of his friends were her pallbearers, and her flowers came from some of Houston's most distinguished people.*

In late 1916, the rector began to plan to move out of the downtown rectory, and the vestry suggested that when the move should be made, the rector and his assistant should establish their offices in the rectory and maintain fixed office hours.

Christ Church was contributing regularly each month to War Sufferers— more than $500 in 1917, more than $600 in 1918. The church had a flagpole in the center of the lawn between church and rectory, and the vestry asked Andrew Dow and J. B. Bowles to fit up the Sunday school room as a club room at a cost not to exceed $25, with reading and writing materials provided. Taking a soldier home after church to Sunday dinner became the parish custom. Sterling Myer, Jim Dow, Henry Cortes, William D. Cleveland, Jr., and A. W. Pollard were the committee to entertain the soldiers. Major Frank Clemens went off to war, and the vestry voted to keep him as an honorary member to be returned to the vestry on his return from the army. W. D. Cleveland, Jr., was appointed to a national Church War Commission, and Christ Church gave $700 to the commission for its work overseas.

During the war years, the marriage registry shows many weddings between two young persons from out of town and out of Texas, and the groom often held military rank. But it also shows familiar family names: Marian Seward Roberts to Hibbert Henry Dancy, Lelia Tudor Torrey to Fitzhugh Carter Pannill, Mary Augusta Fraley to Ralph Clarkson Cooley, Marian Holt Seward to James Robert Neal, Georgiana Radetzki to Claudius W. Sears, Mary Bowles to Fritz M. Dyer, Frankie Carter to Robert Decan Randolph (lieutenant Naval Aviation Corps, Washington) Marguerite Kate Neuhaus to Leonard Franklin Hilty, Stella Root to James Royston Williams, Mathilde Booth to Wharton Ewell Weems, Camille Waggaman to Roy Stuart Brown, St. Clair B. Sherwood to Arthur Stockdale, Lottie Kathleen Blakeley to Browne Botts Rice, Audrey Christian Thompson to Martin Tilford Jones, Mary Damerel Aves to Ulysses Henry Berthier, Marguerite Pillot to Max Otto Bock.

The Rev. Clinton S. Quin, new rector of Trinity Church, and Mr. Sears conferred about the possibility of pooling resources to support a rector for St.

*Dr. Andrew Forest Muir.

Mary's Mission. A. E. Schaeffer, treasurer, took up the plea earlier offered by Rufus Cage that the church should have an every-member canvass, "not only to reach additional subscribers, however small, but to request those who are able to give, to increase their subscriptions."

In 1918 Rufus Cage died. He had first been elected vestryman when the Rev. J. J. Clemens was rector, and except for an interval 1899-1904, when he was out of Houston, had served on the vestry continuously. In his 30-year span on the vestry, "he was a straight-forward, upright, practical, earnest-minded Christian . . . and the fineness of his soul and force of his mind were equally evidenced by his rounded character and nobility of spirit," the vestry recorded.

And October 31, 1918—after only 16 months at Trinity Church—the 35-year-old Clinton Quin was elected bishop coadjutor of the Diocese of Texas to help Bishop Kinsolving in developing missions. He was the youngest Episcopal bishop in the United States. Clinton S. Quin had first started work as a teen-age boy, which enabled the Houston *Post-Dispatch* to say that he had been a successful businessman for 10 years in Kentucky before entering the ministry. He had had 10 years between diaconate and bishopric. Looking at this young man charging so energetically through life, many wise old heads were wagged, and it was murmured that this youth would surely burn himself out before reaching his prime.

The consecration was held at Christ Church with the Rev. Peter Gray Sears acting as host. Mr. Sears and his pretty, young-looking, brown-eyed wife gave a reception in the rectory for Bishop and Mrs. Quin the evening before the consecration. The 87-year-old presiding bishop of the Episcopal Church, the Rt. Rev. Daniel Sylvester Tuttle, came down for the consecration and the Rev. Charles Clingman, Bishop Quin's former classmate at seminary and his successor at Trinity, took part. After the service, 40 bishops and churchmen attended a luncheon at the Rice Hotel at which Mr. Sears made the after-dinner speech. Bishop Kinsolving was unable to attend because of illness.

The next spring, Mr. Sears received a call from St. Mary's-on-the-Highlands in Birmingham, Alabama, but his vestry sent him firmly off on a fishing trip to Canada "at such time as he chose, and for such length of time as he saw fit to absent himself," with the implicit understanding that when he chose, he should come home to Christ Church.

In the summer, Christ Church sold the first mission so long known as St. John the Divine, on Leeland Avenue at Velasco Street. The vestry netted $1,478.50 on the $1,500 sale and gave the money to Bishop Quin to start a new mission the Eastwood-Harrisburg area, agreeing to contribute $50 a month toward such a mission.

In the fall, the vestry raised Mr. Sears' salary to $6,000 a year, and raised its contribution toward Mr. Windham's salary from $50 to $75 a month. That same fall, Mr. Sears began work on the plans for a War Service Memorial window to those Christ Church men who had died in World War I. A tribute to the many who had left Christ Church to enter service, it was to be a memorial to those who had died in service: Marion Collier, Herbert D. Dunlavy, Edwin T. Hathaway, Henry R. Hill, Leroy B. Hinton, and Herbert Scott Peddie.

In 1920, bowing to the General Convention ruling, Christ Church at last began a system whereby each year, one-third of the vestry would retire and

one-third come in as new members. Drawing lots, J. B. Bowles, A. R. Howard, C. L. Desel, and James L. Autry retired from the vestry. Andrew Dow, D. C. Glenn, Sam McNeill and B. B. Gilmer stayed on for two years, and E. L. Neville, K. E. Womack, A. E. Schaeffer and Sterling Myer were to stay for three years. W. S. Farish, Ennis Cargill, R. E. Williams and S. W. George were elected to fill the vacancies of the retiring members.

By 1920, the vestry allowed Mr. Horton Corbett $1,800 a year for paid singers, and the Rev. F. M. C. Bedell came down from Shamokin, Pennsylvania, to become Mr. Sears' assistant at a salary of $2,400. Mr. Sears gave him "full responsibility for the early celebration of Holy Communion, the entire work of the Sunday school, the night services, all organizations of boys and young men, girls and young women . . . We will both be together responsible for the parish visiting, looking after the sick and distressed, and relieving the poor and needy."

Meanwhile Mr. Sears was active in city affairs. He was a Rotarian, and he was intensely interested in seeing the Y.W.C.A. have its own building. The Y.W.C.A. had a cafeteria in a building back of the Christ Church property on San Jacinto and was famous for the delicious meals it could serve for 39 cents. A serving of fish cost 15 cents, two biscuits a penny, and the pies were home made.

At a vestry meeting of March 8, 1921, an incident passed without notice. The rector read a letter from A. S. Leecraft asking about a possible sale of church property and stated "that he had replied thereto that nobody in the Parish, so far as he knew, was at all interested in the matter." In 1921, they weren't.

At the meeting, the vestry raised Mr. Corbett's salary to $1,620 a year to hold him—he had received other offers. San Jacinto and Fannin Street were paved in late 1921 and early 1922. The vestry decided to give the old Sunday school organ—the beautiful organ so lovingly bought by the Rev. J. J. Clemens—to the new Eastwood Church of the Redeemer, and continued its $600 yearly contribution to the church.

1920. The Nineteenth Amendment, gives suffrage to American women.

In the early 1920's, Mrs. Sam E. Allen of Christ Church let the diocese use her summer home near LaPorte as a gathering place for young people and for church conferences. This led later to a major gift by Mrs. Allen which established Camp Allen as a permanent part of the diocesan program.

In the 1920's there were many Christ Church weddings: Rosalie Winifred Hutcheson to Laurence S. Bosworth, Roberta S. Westcott to Norwood Wilbur Beach, Mary Gibbs Jones to Jesse Holman Jones (at the residence of Mr. and Mrs. Tilford Jones) Lois Lawton Cleveland to William Alexander Kirkland (with Bishop Davis Sessums officiating) Marian E. Jenkins to Alfred Rice Elgin, Huberta Reed Nunn to Hiram M. Garwood, Winifred Bain to Samuel Henry Wheeler, Caroline Morse Shipp to Albert Morse Bowles (at the residence of C. E. Shipp) Fred Arnold Root to Virginia Lewis Knight, Lottie Baldwin Rice to Stephen Power Farish, Mary Clarke Wier to Dudley Crawford Jarvis, Adelaide Lovett to Walter Browne Baker (at the Faculty Chamber, Rice Institute) Patty Hall Lummis to Walter Bedford Sharp, Josephine Pearce Dawson to Lobel Alva Carlton, Jane Throckmorton to Presley K. Ewing, Cad Carter Wortham to Robert Cowan Davis, Mary Porter Kirkland to Arthur Stewart Vandervoort, Jr., Hildegarde Storey to George Baldwin Journeay of Liverpool, England, Helen Lewis Wicks to John Wiley Link, Jr., Martha Beatrice Henry to Clinton Harcourt

Wooten, Martha Virginia Attwell to Dr. Edward Oliphant Fitch, Ella Botts Rice to Howard R. Hughes, Jr., (at the residence of W. D. Farish, Shadyside) Clara Louise Blakely to Harry B. Gordon, Jr., Laura Fulkerson Rice to Richard Wayne Neff, Margaret Cullinan to Andrew Jackson Wray (at the Cullinan residence, Shadyside) and Nora Cunningham Cleveland to Charles Peacock Grenough Fuller of New York (with Bishop Davis Sessums officiating.) In March, 1922, the vestry talked about having the jitneys and rent cars removed from standing in front of church property. Mr. Sears spoke to the mayor, and the mayor promised immediate relief in this matter. The Sheltering Arms Association decided to become a part of the Community Chest movement, and Mrs. Tom Swope was employed as church secretary at a salary of $150 a month.

The Y.W.C.A. Board opened a drive for $800,000. Peter Gray Sears was one of the group of such Houstonians as Will and Mike Hogg, F. M. Law, Jesse H. Jones and Bishop Quin campaigning for the fund, and when at last the building was under way, Mr. Sears further campaigned to help raise the $22,000 needed for the first year's budget. The Y.W.C.A. at 1320 Rusk opened in 1922, with the Rt. Rev. Clinton Quin offering the prayers of dedication. The peripatetic Bishop Quin now had offices in the old rectory, and the Sears lived in their own home at 4613 San Jacinto.

Peter Gray Sears by 1922-23 was becoming a church leader throughout the south. He took a two-month leave of absence to go to Sewanee to raise necessary funds to complete Grace Hall. Six months later, he was working in Houston to help raise funds for the completion of Grace Hall for girls at the University of Texas in Austin, to commemorate Bishop Kinsolving's 30th year in the bishopric.

The Church of the Redeemer became independent enough in 1923 to give up its $600 annual donation from Christ Church. Christ Church was contributing to Near East Relief $1,657; Japan Reconstruction (the earthquake had killed 143,000 in Tokyo), $527; plus another $347 for Japanese children; and owed the First National Bank $5,100.

In 1923, John S. Cochran, Ennis Cargill, and L. Randolph Bryan, Jr., came on the vestry. Sheltering Arms Association had been advised by the vestry not to build anew on its property on Holman, and was offered $6,500 for its 1.8 acres. They sought permission to sell.

On June 3, 1924, the vestry received a letter from Mrs. J. R. Lee, a real estate agent. Written in long hand, it said:

"Gentlemen: We wish to put before you the most wonderful offer we are requested to submit to you, of One Million Five Hundred Thousand Dollars, for the Church property bounded by Fannin, Texas and San Jacinto Streets. . . .

"It is a fact that this property is most dear to the hearts of each and every Episcopalian in the city. Its ivy covered walls are hallowed for many who have worshipped within their consecrated boundaries for possibly half a century or more! Yet—to relinquish such an edifice is permissable when viewed from a human side. Consider the weak and the poor, the sick and the needy—the widows, the orphans and last but not least the millions of heathens who have never heard the word of God!

"Can it be right, is it just, to cling to a building and a property which if it were disposed of, would enable the work of God to be accomplished so much more gloriously, and to such a greater advantage? It is God's purpose to have the church grow and to reach out and Christianize the sinful World. How will this mission be achieved by narrow boundaries and hoarded wealth . . .

"Some of your good members may offer Sentiment as an objection to selling. Why let such an insignificant thing as sentiment ever enter into a question of such importance? What is sentiment compared to soulsaving? . . .

"Should . . . you consider this offer of One Million and a Half please give us a contract properly executed that we may have the right, the time, etc. to consumate the sale which we will do for a consideration of 2 per cent of the entire amount."

Or for $30,000 commission.

There was no discussion of Mrs. Lee's letter. The clerk was instructed to advise Mrs. Lee that the vestry would not be interested, and a committee was appointed to investigate and make recommendations on heating and ventilating the church. Rector and vestry, in other words, gave this offer as little thought as Mr. Sears had given the first one.

A year later, the vestry approved the sale of the Clemens Memorial's first chapel and property, and the purchase of a site for a new Clemens Memorial Church on Parkview Avenue, overlooking Woodland Park.

Christ Church was in this era a social pivot. When the Ladies Parish Association gave its annual style show and dance at the Scottish Rite Cathedral, it was a social event comparable to a major benefit ball given today by the Junior League or Museum of Fine Arts, and the newspapers gave it generous space.

". . . little Misses Katherine Neuhaus, Burdine Clayton, Marian Holt Neal, Effie Hunt and Winifred Safford are among the society maids and matrons who will display these costumes as 'models,' " a society editor reported. There were children in costume: flower girls, Edna Gilmer and Dorothy Taylor; cigarette girls, Nella Neville, Retta Haslip, Rosalie Sherman and Margaret Elizabeth Spotts; program distributors, Cary Baker, Billy Farish and Palmer Hutcheson, Jr.; orange crush vendors, Jane Bradley, Mary Jane Walne, Betsy Slaughter, Elinor Sherwood, Lena Carter Carroll and Henrietta Cargill; refreshment group, Mary Louise Moore, Marie Lee, Mary Tallichet, Eugenia Howard, Carolyn Bryan, Dorothy Quarles, Helen Williams, Margaret Carter, Inez Perry, Margaret Dunn and Margaret Farrar.

Misses Madge Dow, Nina Cullinan, Mary Bain, Ima Hogg, Elizabeth Hay, Adele Waggaman and Bertha Roy sold tickets. So did Mesdames E. A. Peden, E. R. Wicks, Bedford Sharp, George Rotan, W. C. Hunt, Ralph Cooley, H. G. Safford, W. T. Carter, Jr., T. A. Botts, Rufus Cage and Royston Williams. Mrs. L. A. Stevenson, Mrs. George Hill and Mrs. Louis Lobit were the committee on posters. Mrs. B. B. Gilmer was president and Mrs. E. L. Neville general chairman; Mrs. W. S. Farish sub-chairman, Mrs. Palmer Hutcheson, decorations aided by Mesdames A. D. Boice, Hugo Neuhaus, J. W. Evans, F. M. Law, T. A. Spencer, Browne Rice, Frank Clemens, Albert Bowles, N. T. Masterson, Philo Howard, P. E. Bullington . . . the list is long. And Christ Church was approaching a zenith.

1920. Houston's population reaches 138,276.

1922. King Tutankhamon's tomb is discovered and opened. John Barrymore plays Hamlet *for 101 performances and is called by many critics "the greatest actor of our time."*

1923. Adolph Hitler, arrested for his part in Munich Beer Putsch, starts to write Mein Kampf.

Chapter 35

An Offer, a Controversy and a Vote

Easter, 1925, Christ Church celebrated joyously its rector's 20th anniversary. It was a time of deep sentiment and welling admiration and affection. A whole generation had grown up knowing no other rector. Middle aged men had grown old in the service of the church under the leadership of Mr. Sears. Mr. Sears was probably the best known, best liked minister in the city, and the church on Easter morning had many visitors from other churches coming in to join in the celebration in which they felt they also had a share.

It was the highest moment Christ Church had ever known. And one month later—May 15, 1925—the letter came which was to cloud memories of the moment of joy, level the peak, and start Christ Church on a dangerous downhill path. It was not meant to do so.

Dated May 12, 1925, the letter was written on the simple letterhead "Hogg Brothers, Houston."

"My dear Doctor Sears:

"I would thank you to place before the Vestry of Christ Church the proposition I made Mr. Womack to purchase this property at a price of $750,000.00, on terms and conditions to be discussed and agreed upon at some later date after they have decided whether or not the property is for sale at this figure.

"With assurances of high regard, I am,

Faithfully yours,

W. C. Hogg."

This brief letter prompted the first serious discussion of the possibility of selling. It was not a very long discussion, and the vestry voted to decline Mr. Hogg's offer as outlined in his letter. But on the motion of K. E. Womack, seconded by S. J. Payne, the vestry voted to call a parish meeting of the contributing members at 8 PM, May 26, 1925, asking the congregation if it wished to authorize the sale of the property *"provided, . . . that in no event shall such sale be made for less than One Million Dollars gross . . ."* and that the Bishop of the Diocese approve.

The picture on the parish bulletin calling that meeting shows the property to fullest advantage—flatteringly so. Ivy covers the church, trees are tall and lush in the lawn, the rectory is charmingly screened by banana trees and shrubs, and Texas Avenue looks as broad and peaceful as the Pacific. The fact that street noises were beginning to come in through church windows open on a hot day, that the rectory made fairly cheerless office quarters which were painfully hot in July, does not show in the picture.

Bishop Kinsolving opened the special parish meeting with prayer. All outsiders and newspaper reporters were asked to leave, and did so. E. L. Neville, senior warden, was in Europe at the time, and the junior warden, P. S. Tilson, read a resolution aloud to the parish. James S. Anderson seconded. The resolution asked that action be deferred until November, 1925, and that after a reasonable period of preparatory discussion, this meeting be adjourned until November. The motion carried 165 to 11.

Views were expressed by W. S. Farish, C. L. Desel, Ennis Cargill, Presley K. Ewing, H. M. Garwood, John Charles Harris, McDonald Meachum, Chester H. Bryan, Underwood Nazro, Mrs. Charles L. Fitch, Mrs. C. K. Standish, Mrs. Walter B. Sharp and the rector. This was reasonable discussion of a reasonable offer. Every early church in Houston had faced

1924. George Gershwin composes Rhapsody in Blue, *Fred and Adele Astaire open in* Lady Be Good, *and* What Price Glory *is a Broadway hit*

similar decisions in recent years. And after the adjournment of that meeting, life went on as usual—or almost as usual—in the parish.

On the evening of June 18, Miss Alice Gray Sears married William Franklin Akin. The social pages described the ceremony, "conducted by the bride's father in historic Christ Church with which Houston has many close ties." The vestrymen served as ushers, the vested choir sang, and Horton Corbett played the wedding march. The bride entered with her brother Claude Sears of Austin.

And in June, "the Rector announced his intention, after orders of his doctor, of leaving on vacation the first of July to return about September 15th, which, upon appropriate motion, was unanimously approved by the Vestry." This suggests that Mr. Sears did not feel strongly about the outcome of the November meeting. Yet in calling a new assistant, he referred to "what the common work of the Parish will be under possibly differing and changing conditions . . ." and concluded, "I want to ask you again please to . . . come to be with me in the work already large and that promises to grow . . . to such far-reaching and splendid possibilities." The vision of what $1,000,000 could do in mission work was aglow in his mind.

Texas Avenue was being paved—the days of the wooden blocks were over— and the Houston Lighting and Power Company proposed to put three electric lamps along the property line of the church.

After proper notice, the congregational meeting of Christ Church Parish opened at 8 PM, November 24, 1925, in the parish house. Here the vestry's first resolution was read and put up for consideration: the resolution to sell the property "provided, however, that in no event shall such sale be made for less than One Million Dollars gross. . . ." Though attempts were made to have the matter settled at once by standing vote, cooler judgment prevailed and it was decided that the vote would be done by written, signed ballots deposited at the parish office within two weeks. The rector appointed five vestrymen to count those ballots: E. L. Neville, senior warden; P. S. Tilson, junior warden; A. E. Schaeffer, treasurer; L. Randolph Bryan, Jr., clerk; and Ennis Cargill. Noon, December 8, was set for the closing of the ballot boxes.

In the controversy which flared up in later months, wild, hurt statements were made by partisans of both sides, and reference was made to stuffing the ballot box. All this crept into Christ Church legend. In fact, the vote was decisive and undeniable.

December 8, 1925, the committee wrote to the rector:

"Dear Mr. Sears:

"We, the undersigned committee, appointed by you at a meeting held November 24th at Christ Church Parish beg to advise that we have canvassed the vote cast on the question of selling Christ Church property, and find the following results:

139 personal votes in favor of the proposition.
 31 favorable votes by proxy.
———
170 Total

220 personal votes against the proposition.
203 votes by proxy against the proposition.
———
423 Total

1924. Through the Hogg family, old Camp Logan becomes Memorial Park.

"The committee did not pass on the eligibility of any voter, but simply counted the total vote cast. We hand you herewith list showing names of voters, also five ballots, classification of which is doubtful.

"Respectfully submitted, E. L. Neville, P. S. Tilson, Ennis Cargill, L. R. Bryan, Jr., A. E. Schaeffer."

Of these committee men, three had voted to sell, two had voted to stay. And there in the vestry minutes, person by person alphabetically arranged—every name familiar—are the names of the members who voted to sell Christ Church and the names of the members who voted against the sale of Christ Church. Regardless of how you juggle the figures, it was an overwhelming vote to stay. Even if you cancel all the proxy votes on the side of staying, and allow all the proxy votes on the side for selling, the resolution to sell would still stand defeated. And that, everyone thought, was that.

The vestry had to deal with customary matters: W. H. Journeay, secretary of the Sunday school, reported that Miss Evelyn Spickard would come from Memphis as a church school and young people's worker.

Nieces and nephews of long-ago sexton James West sued to gain title to the cemetery property, and though nobody seemed to remember that Christ Church had bought the property fairly and squarely from Mr. West, the nieces and nephews lost their case on grounds that because Mrs. West had outlived her husband, only relatives of hers could inherit whatever community property she and her husband had held. Because of this suit, Ingham Roberts discovered that Walker Avenue had been run right across the Episcopal Cemetery to connect with Buffalo Drive—a 60-foot roadway appropriated without any permission from Christ Church. Mr. Roberts saw in this a chance to persuade the city to lease a portion of the cemetery for park, and suggested that the city could maintain the cemetery in lieu of rent on the property now being used. Neither then nor at any time during the height of the next year's controversy over selling Christ Church for money to help missions did anyone seem to think that the cemetery land had value—that it might be sold, and substantial amounts of money gained to pay off the debts of the local missions. Mr. Roberts proposed that "we could also include the Masonic portion in this agreement. In this connection you will find as many of the old members of the Church buried in the Masonic portion as in the Church portion." But the Masons made their own settlement—and got a much better price for their land than Christ Church ever did.

The Rev. James Swayne Allen accepted a call to come to Christ Church as associate, a vestry committee began to plan a new parish house, and the vestry lost its senior warden, Phineas S. Tilson. The vestry was considering bids and proposals to install a new heating and—for the first time—a cooling system in Christ Church. To outsiders, everything seemed to be going on as though nothing had occurred.

But Mr. Sears' family and the vestry knew that Mr. Sears was unhappy. He had taken the congregation's decision as a deep personal defeat—as proof that he had failed in his ministry—as proof that he had failed to teach his people the truest and most generous spirit of Christianity. He saw in their decision to stay on the old site a great selfishness, and a most un-Christian refusal to help the missions, the poor, the hungry, and the uninformed.

After the November vote, he was quite seriously ill at home for weeks. In

1925. John T. Scopes, found guilty of having taught evolution in the high school in Dayton, Tennessee, is fined $100 and costs July 24. William Jennings Bryan, counsel for the prosecution, dies July 26.

his inner suffering, he could not get away from the subject. He returned to it from time to time in private conversations and at vestry meetings. Mrs. Sears, who had always been his balance wheel, who had always managed to help this intense man relax just a little toward the inequities and hurts of life, did her best. But his preoccupation with the idea grew rather than lessened.

His successful 20-year association with Horton Corbett, the organist, ended in misunderstanding so that he asked Mr. Allen to deal with Mr. Corbett in the future, and when Mr. Corbett said sadly that he felt an antagonism to exist between Mr. Sears and himself, there seemed no alternative but for Corbett to resign. The vestry wrote appropriate regrets. At one vestry meeting the rector apologized for any remarks he might have made at the preceding meeting which might have hurt the feelings of any vestryman. The apology was warmly accepted.

In October, 1926, the Houston Athletic Club approached C. L. Desel and A. E. Schaeffer with an offer to lease for 99 years the rectory corner of the property—hoping to carve out a 100 by 150 foot lot. They would pay $36,000 a year rental. Declining this offer, the vestry moved swiftly: Frank Clemens moved, Desel seconded, and the vestry voted unanimously to ask Birdsall P. Briscoe, architect, to submit immediately the plans he had been working on for revision of the parish house so that specifications could be given to contractors and bids received.

The vestry minutes show an odd sense of haste. It was as though the vestry were rushing to head off an impending crisis by getting construction started on the parish house. Called meeting followed called meeting as the estimates were taken for the $250,000 building program, and moves were made to secure a loan and raise a subscription.

Mr. Sears tried to go along with the vestry. He met with the building and finance committee, he ordered the subscription forms printed, he suggested that the vestry might properly make the first pledges. As a result all vestrymen present made pledges ranging from $250 to $5,000. They were C. L. Desel, Ennis Cargill, Sam McNeill, A. E. Schaeffer, John S. Cochran, L. Randolph Bryan, Jr., S. J. Payne and A. E. Hartwell.

Then suddenly, Mr. Sears could go no further. In church Sunday morning, November 7, 1926, Mr. Sears again proposed selling the property "to put Christ Church all over Houston," and in his sermon said "I beg that you will not make it impossible for me to remain and work with you for the years to come by refusing to follow where I lead."

At a special meeting, he asked vestry support in calling a parish meeting to reopen the discussion of a sale, and of giving $700,000 of the proceeds to pay off the debts of all Houston Episcopal missions. The vestry refused by a vote of 8 to 2, whereupon Mr. Sears said he would call the parish meeting alone, citing canon law for his right to do so. The vestry protested by a vote of 8 to 2. And on Sunday morning, November 14, the parish bulletin called for a new meeting of the congregation to be held November 22 at 8 PM.

That morning service was the most disturbing in Christ Church history. From the pulpit, Mr. Sears resigned. It precipitated an emergency vestry meeting Sunday afternoon, and the Houston *Post-Dispatch* covered the service in full on Monday morning.

Mr. Sears' resignation was made in the name of unity. "Last Sunday, I

1925. Edna Ferber's So Big, *Hendrik Van Loon's* Story of Mankind, *F. Scott Fitzgerald's* The Beautiful and the Damned, *and Sinclair Lewis's* Babbitt *are best sellers.*

said to you that I must ask you to trust and follow my leadership and I appealed to you," he said. Quoting his own words in which a resignation seemed implicit—he continued, "Now, let me tell you that that appeal was not wholly fair to you, and I knew it when I made it. It was not considerate of you, it was not just to you, and now I wish this morning to make it fair and just and considerate, if I possibly can, by this statement to you—if you vote not to sell this property at this time, as I think you ought to do, then that vote, whether you intend it to be or not, is and must be a declination to follow my leadership. I can then no longer lead, and so I must in duty to you first and to myself next, resign the rectorship.

"Furthermore (now notice this, please) in resigning, I will hope that it may be possible to prevent any break in the unity of this congregation: that ought to be preserved at all costs. It is far more important than any consideration of any individual man's interests, whether rector or member.

"... and to eliminate me entirely from the transaction and in order to prove to myself—I need the proof more than you do—to prove . . . the reality and sincerity of my thought and purpose and aim, let me state to you that I will have to resign if it breaks my heart, and it will. I will have to resign this rectorship, if you vote to sell the property and move away, just as well as if you vote not to sell and to stay.

"So you will be done with me. And I ask you to do your duty in the presence of Almighty God, if the heavens fall."

And with that he turned and left the pulpit.

"Tears burst from the eyes of many in the great audience which almost filled the building," the Houston *Post-Dispatch* reported, "and it was evident that others were controlling their emotions with difficulty. Utter silence reigned for a moment, and then the concluding part of the service began, with the rector performing his priestly duties at the altar."

The congregation was shattered. The last thing they wanted was the resignation of their rector. Twice vestry committeemen called on him in loving conference. The next Sunday morning Mr. Sears in his more usual reasonable and calm style explained that he intended to place his future in the hands of Bishop Kinsolving and Bishop Quin in hopes they would use him in work among southern Negroes, and said comfortingly that they must not dread Monday night's meeting—all would be well. But they did dread Monday night's meeting.

The *Houston Chronicle* carried an article by Ingham Roberts on the history of the church. Mr. Roberts suggested that Christ Church might be placed as part of the envisioned civic center—facing the new Houston Public Library across Hermann Square. He echoed Mr. Sears' belief that the church could be taken down and rebuilt, brick by brick and window by window.

Ingham Roberts, who in his life had seen three bishops, five rectors and two churches, pointed out that almost every one of the early churches of Houston had moved at least once and some oftener without causing criticism, and that their congregations had continued to grow. He cited the First Baptist Church which had moved from Texas and Travis to Rusk and Fannin, to Fannin and Walker, to Main and Lamar; the First Methodist Church which had not only abandoned its historic site but changed its name in the move; the First Presbyterians who had moved from their historic site at Capitol between Main and Travis to "their present beautiful building," as well as the Lutherans, Temple Beth Israel, the First German Methodists, the German Lutherans and the St. Vincent de Paul Church.

If, on the other hand, the church decided to stay where it was, Mr. Roberts listed repairs which should be made and pointed to the fire hazard offered by Waddell's Furniture Store standing back of the church. Whatever the decision, he concluded, he would go with the majority.

Suddenly, what had been a reasonable issue for a congregation to decide on merit became a city-wide controversy. Retired Bishop Aves said that he hated to see Christ Church sold. A proper Houstonian of another denomination had a pamphlet printed urging that the historic church be kept in its original site. All those who had suffered in the heat of Houston summers the noises coming in through the open windows pronounced this sentiment selfish and unreasonable, while the idealists offered extensions and variations on Mr. Sears's belief that "it is our solemn duty that there should be a releasing for active service of the tremendous energy and power for human betterment that now lies locked up and stored away, unused largely in the ground beneath this church building and the other buildings on this property."

Editorial opinion was offered on page one of the Houston *Chronicle:* "It is not often that one church or one minister holds the interest of the major part of a great city, but there can be no doubt that the majority of Houstonians today have a feeling of fellowship for Dr. Peter Gray Sears, and a feeling of deep respect."

Citing Doctor Sears's proposal to sell the property to give money to smaller Episcopal churches and "other outstanding causes," the editorial continued: "The rector declared that the church could again give its chief efforts to serving the people of Houston and the causes of Christianity, whereas, he says, during the past 10 years it has been serving sentiment and preserving memories." But "Some will contend that the memories of many of Houston's leading citizens whose lives centered about Christ Church are worth preserving at almost any price, and others will contend that the church property occupying spacious grounds in the very heart of the congested business district will stand as a symbol of religion in the midst of the rush of commerce, and that it will thus serve in a way that no church in a residential district could serve."

But the arguments "could not obscure the ennobling example set by the Christ Church rector . . . The Church, the world, needs such leadership."

Many references were made to Trinity Church in the heart of Wall Street. Many originally opposed to the sale were less sure of their opposition now, and the public in general thought that this time, Mr. Sears might after all gain his congregation's approval of the plan.

The congregation was in a state of turmoil and distress. Mr. and Mrs. Arthur Boice, who had the year before voted against the sale, were putting on their hats to go to the Monday night meeting—dreading to go. When they discovered that Mr. Boice intended to vote with Doctor Sears, and Mrs. Boice intended to vote against, they gratefully decided they didn't have to go and stayed at home. Yet the Monday night meeting was oddly indecisive. Mr. Sears had expert reporters present, so that a complete account of that parish meeting is now bound into the permanent vestry minutes of 1926. Both senior and junior wardens made it clear that they were not in sympathy with the meeting. Both the Rev. Mr. Allen, Doctor

1926. Rudolph Valentino dies at the age of 31.

Sears' associate, and the Rev. Thomas Windham were there quietly prepared to vote with him.

Clarence Wharton offered the resolution which Doctor Sears wanted placed before the congregation. It proposed that a new committee be appointed to investigate these questions:

"1. Shall Christ Church property be sold? 2. If so, the manner, method and details of the sale. 3. If sold, recommendations as to the disposition of the proceeds of the sale. 4. If the committee recommends against the sale, then just what improvements shall be made to preserve and keep up the property and buildings at the present site and the amount of money necessary to do this and the method of raising this money."

It seemed to many in the troubled congregation that the first three of these questions had been answered in a strong negative a year before and should not be brought up year after year to unsettle them, and that the fourth had already been capably decided by the vestry in recent meetings. But the committee was appointed: H. M. Garwood, chairman; Sam McNeill, senior warden; Ennis Cargill, junior warden; L. Randolph Bryan, Jr., clerk; Frank C. Clemens, Edwin L. Neville, Andrew Dow, A. S. Cleveland, Paul B. Timpson, James Anderson, and E. R. Spotts. Mr. Sears had bent over backward to be fair. Of his committee of 11, five had originally voted for the sale. Both wardens were strongly opposed. The committee was instructed to report back to yet another congregation meeting set for January, 1927.

This meeting was never held. December 7, 1926, Doctor Sears wrote his brief letter of resignation for formal presentation to the vestry: "I think that all of you will know with what deep sorrow I have to write the word that severs my relationship with you and the congregation of dear old Christ Church. Affectionately your friend and rector."

The vestry unanimously expressed its regret over Mr. Sears' resignation and asked him to become rector emeritus. This action healed the breach. Mr. Sears replied first by letter, and then in person, expressing his affection and concluding, "I hereby accept most gladly and gratefully your call . . . with the understanding on the part of both of us that I must be free for a vacation as may be advised by my physician, and directed by my wife." Shortly after, Doctor and Mrs. Sears left for Europe.

Before the January meeting could be called, the committee appointed to study the question, and the group which had most favored sale, agreed that it would be better to let the whole subject drop and restore unity to the parish. The retiring vestry voted unanimously that the subject was closed, the new vestry turned its attention to the task of renovation, and the Rev. James Swayne Allen was called to be rector of Christ Church.

Chapter 36

James Swayne Allen

When the vestry invited Doctor Sears' young associate to take over as rector of Christ Church, the offer was made in good faith and accepted with confidence. It seemed logical to everyone. If Doctor Sears were coming back to Houston as rector emeritus, Christ Church could continue to enjoy his inspiring sermons and his counsel while Mr. Allen could take over the more taxing work of the parish. Mr. Allen was already accustomed to this role, he and Doctor Sears had worked harmoniously together, and a new rector might not fit in well.

No one could foresee that young Mr. Allen—newly turned 30—had been given for his first big church the hardest task any minister could be given, and that almost every card fate could turn would be stacked against him.

Mr. Allen was an unusually handsome man with a pleasant voice and a charming manner. Born in Fort Worth and reared in Memphis, he had been graduated from the University of the South and Virginia Theological Seminary. He was in charge of a small church in Cleveland, Tennessee, during his diaconate, and had had one year's experience as associate rector of Christ Church when he accepted the call to become rector. He had the backing of an experienced vestry, he had Mrs. Tom Swope as church secretary, and though the church property was in need of major, expensive repairs, renovations and enlargements, and the church had a $10,000 deficit, the general finances were stable.

The vestry offered Mr. Allen a starting salary of $5,000 a year, Doctor Sears $300 a month as rector emeritus, and it authorized Mr. Allen to spend $10,000 on the parish house and old rectory offices, and $5,000 on a new roof for the church. It hired J. W. Haak as business manager. Meanwhile Frank Clemens had a warm letter from Doctor Sears in Rome, saying that he and Mrs. Sears were having a delightful time. The finance committee started a fund drive for $25,000 to cover repairs and deficit. It all looked good.

But the bitter words flung about in the preceding months had done their permanent harm. Though the vestry had returned to a quite genuine harmony, many church members had lost their faith in the future of old Christ Church. Some who had long thought it easier to get to Trinity Church now drifted out to Trinity. Some who had always contributed heavily to Christ Church were still unsettled by the recent vote and unwilling to commit their funds to renovation and repairs of a site they felt might yet be up for sale. Some who had never been bothered by the gradual increase of street sounds outside were now painfully aware of them and could truthfully say that when sitting on the back pews they could not hear the sermon or the service.

Whatever the factors, contributions dropped off sharply. Christ Church had maintained a general deficit for years, and had kept a loan from the First National Bank which varied above and below $5,000—sometimes going up to $10,000 to cover emergency expenditures like those of the 1915 storm. But always this had been the kind of deficit which the vestry felt comfortably sure it could wipe out in a day if it chose.

That certainty vanished. In the first months of 1927, Christ Church began to borrow more each month simply to cover its routine expenses, so that the debt to the First National Bank was $6,700 on January 1, $7,700 on February 1, $10,700 on March 1, and $14,700 on April 1. Revenues which had totaled $13,790 in the first quarter of 1925 had dropped to $10,575 in 1927, and expenses had gone up to meet the vigorous new program of downtown parish service outlined by Mr. Allen. Neither Mr. Allen nor the vestry expected this drop-off to continue. They recognized the slump as the result of recent difficulties, and thought that given a little time, the congregation would regain its healthy stride. They asked for bids on a heating and ventilation system. Some $13,143 accumulated in the building fund. But by

1926. Ladies are bobbing their hair and getting marcel waves.

August 31, Christ Church owed $31,000 at the First National Bank.

Meanwhile, the program for students at Rice Institute had been expanding. The Rev. Harris Masterson, Jr., had moved a temporary building on to land across Main Street from Rice in 1919 as a community house for students, and in 1921, Autry House was built, as a memorial to James L. Autry—former Christ Church vestryman and member of the diocesan council. Throughout 1927, work had been under way on the handsome new Palmer Memorial Church given for the use of students at Rice Institute by Mrs. Edwin L. Neville as a memorial to her brother—the young Edward Albert Palmer who had drowned long ago in the Regatta. This church was consecrated November 27, 1927, and a minister called to take the chaplaincy work with the students.

Autry House was a diocesan program under Bishop Quin, and though some members of Christ Church—including W. A. Kirkland—worked in the Autry House association, this was within the diocesan organization. Meanwhile, Mr. Edwin L. Neville was still active on the Christ Church vestry.

In October, 1927, the vestry voted to authorize the treasurer to borrow from the bank "a sum of money sufficient to meet current expenses, not to exceed fifty thousand dollars." And the preparations were made for an every member canvass to restore finances to normal. Mr. Allen published a bulletin asking in large letters on the front: "What Kind of a Church Would My Church Be If Every Member Were Just Like Me?"

And from the pulpit he said sternly "The spirit of indifference in Christ Church Parish is not only appalling but sinful. Six hundred communicants are not pledging a single cent towards the support of Christ Church Parish. It has been this way for years and years. A small proportion of the membership of this parish furnishes the financial leadership and power for our work. We must do a downtown Church's program," Mr. Allen reminded, "and do it well, or we have no excuse for staying downtown. Our income today will not support the work which the rector has begun. After the first of the year, he will only carry on the work which you allow him to carry on through your subscriptions or pledge to the budget."

Then on November 3, 1927, lovely, gentle Mrs. Sears was killed in an automobile accident. Though Doctor Sears took this tragedy with strength, it was a loss he would feel for the rest of his life. At his request, and arranged by E. L. Neville, Mrs. Sears was buried in the Christ Church lot of Glenwood Cemetery, and the vestry asked Mr. Neville, Arthur E. Hartwell, and Fairfax Crow to draw up the resolution of sorrow. "We feel that we are expressing the thoughts of all those men who as vestrymen during the past twenty-two years have known and loved her."

In December, Doctor Sears wrote for himself, Claude, Frances, and Alice Gray, the family's appreciation. ". . . when the vestry used to hold its meetings in the library of the old rectory, nothing gave her more pleasure than getting the room in readiness and meeting and greeting the members . . . She was really a most interested and faithful working member of the vestry."

At the January meeting, Mr. Allen reported that the Rev. Peter Gray Sears had expressed himself as being very ready to preach and help with the services. The vestry welcomed his return. In February, 1928, the Rev. Mr. Allen recommended drastic curtailment of the expanded program for Christ Church parish work. Unless pledges could be increased heavily, and quickly, he recommended the discontinuance of six members of the lay staff—including Miss Evelyn Spickard and the business manager, Julius Haak; the cancelling of the church bulletin, and a number of other reductions to bring expenses within the boundaries of income. The vestry couldn't quite accept so drastic a cut. It decided on a compromise version.

Clemens Memorial began the last steps to sever its connection with Christ Church and become an independent parish. Christ Church had given the proceeds from the sale of the chapel, lot and rectory at Bingham and Sabine Streets toward the proposed new Clemens Memorial Church of the Good Shepherd. The rector of Christ Church asked James Anderson as both a member of the vestry's Clemens Memorial Committee and chairman of Bishop Quin's City-wide Missionary Expansion Work, to help Mr. Windham in the final task of transfer. And at this point, Christ Church ended its mission connection with Clemens Memorial Church, thereafter channeling its mission contributions through Bishop Quin.

Christ Church had now ended its era as Mother Church of Houston missions. When St. Stephens was founded on West Alabama in 1929, and St. John the Divine on River Oaks Boulevard (no organizational kin to the early St. John the Divine on Leeland) any help they received from Christ Church came indirectly through Bishop Quin and the Diocese.

By February, 1928, Christ Church owed $44,000 at the bank. And in June, 1928, Doctor Sears resigned as rector emeritus. He appeared before the vestry, the minutes record:

> "Since his resignation as Rector of Christ Church he had never been happy trying to work under what was an intolerable situation. He could not forget that his leadership had been repudiated as rector, and that his continuance as emeritus was impossible. He felt that he was not in accord with the program of the present rector and vestry as to the church remaining downtown. He stated that, due to the resignation of the Rev. R. N. MacCallum at Palmer Memorial at Rice Institute and Autry House, he had been extended a call to take charge of that work . . . and it was his purpose to create a parish at Palmer Memorial . . . he said that but for the cordial relations which existed between the Rector and himself, he could not have stayed as Rector Emeritus as long as he did."

The Rev. Mr. Allen and the vestry saw immediately what this would mean: that the new parish would be carved out of Christ Church congregation, taking some of the church's largest contributors in the slice. Moving to keep the church afloat, the rector asked the vestry to find 20 men who would pledge support of Allen's program to the extent of $1,000 a year.

Edwin L. Neville, Fairfax Crow, and C. M. Dow resigned from the vestry, saying they planned henceforth to support the new Palmer church. Mr. and Mrs. Robert Lee Blaffer, and several branches of the Rice family transferred. And yet work went on at Christ Church. The rector was granted leave to attend the Triennial Convention of the Episcopal Church in Washington. The vestry raised the tenor's salary $5 a month to counter the competitive offer from Palmer Memorial. And because Dr. Charles Clingman, formerly of Trinity and now of the Church of the Advent, Birmingham, had been so inspiring in Lent of 1928, the vestry invited him to return during Lent of 1929. Charles L. Desel, Chester Bryan, and R. W. Wier were elected to fill the vestry vacancies.

Early in 1929, the Rev. James Swayne Allen and Miss Madge Dow were

1928. Capt. Charles A. Lindbergh, U.S. air mail pilot, flies from Roosevelt Field, L.I., to Le Bourget air field, Paris, May 20-21 in 33 hours and 29 minutes.

married in Christ Church. The vestry leased a rectory at 2518 Prospect Avenue, and sent a silver tray as wedding gift.

Simply to clear a title on a part of the property of Jane Gray's estate, Christ Church issued a quit claim to W. P. Hobby on land off Almeda Road and Prospect Avenue. [This property was given to Rice University in 1963 by the Hobby Foundation.] C. M. Dow came back from Palmer to Christ Church and was reelected to the vestry—the vanguard of a number of families who would come back over the years.

Seeking to make Christ Church serve the downtown, Mr. Allen proposed that the fences be taken down, concrete benches be installed, and the church yard turned into a public park. This was not done, but Mrs. H. G. Safford's circle did some work in landscaping and improving the grounds. Mr. Allen, given approval by Bishop Quin, offered the use of Christ Church to the Rev. Milo Perkins for the use of his congregation—the Church of St. Raphael the Archangel (Liberal Catholic.)

In September, young William Marmion, who had spent the past year as Boys Executive at a salary of $600, went off to the Virginia Seminary. The vestry expressed its warm affection for young Mr. Marmion by giving him a check for $50 toward his seminary expenses. In his letter of goodby and appreciation, Bill Marmion wrote "The Scouts made me a present of two heavy blankets which I shall need this winter; the newsboys presented me with a framed article entitled 'The Seven Keys to Success,' and last Sunday, the Service League gave me a pair of book ends." The letter gives a quick glimpse of boys work being done in the downtown parish in 1929.

Miss Spickard resigned, and by combining her salary with that of William Marmion, the vestry felt it could afford to call the Rev. Hugh St. George Murray to be Mr. Allen's assistant and have lodgings in the old rectory.

Losses to Palmer were continuing. Robert Wier cautioned the vestry against the continued borrowing of money from the bank for operating expenses. In October, Mr. Allen asked the vestry to consider seriously three alternatives to increasing indebtedness:

1) Leasing half the property for 99 years and building a parish house next to the church. 2) leasing all the property for 99 years and building a church elsewhere. 3) closing down all parish activities, but Sunday services at 11 A.M.

The year which had begun so happily with Mr. Allen's wedding, turned up the first of the dark cards fate would stack against him. In November his doctor informed him that he had pulmonary tuberculosis and must take a leave of absence. Mr. Allen asked for three months, and was urged by the vestry to take whatever leave he needed to restore his health. On the vestry were those who remembered that young and handsome Julyan Clemens had died of TB.

At the year's end, Christ Church was informed that it could receive $100 a month from the Romney Greene legacy for mission purposes. The letter was signed by Ingham S. Roberts and Albert Bowles, trustees of the Greene Estate. The vestry asked Bishop Quin to apply this amount to the church's diocesan quota, and it was decided that $75 a month of this should go to the Rev. Charles A. Sumners, minister of the new St. Stephen's Mission on West Alabama to cover his salary, and that $25 a month go to the Rev. Alfred George Denman, of St. Mary's Mission, Houston, as one-third of his

salary. Embarrassed within its own parish, Christ Church could still—thanks to the legacy of a departed member—play its part in diocesan mission work.

Lacking money to bring Lenten speakers to Houston, the church entered into a plan with the Ministerial Alliance for Holy Week services, the Rev. A. Frank Smith, rector of First Methodist Church, preaching, and the three-hour Good Friday service to be held at Christ Church. Hugh Murray resigned as assistant to accept a call to Nacogdoches. And in August, 1930, all Christ Church gave its sorrow and sympathy to Bishop and Mrs. Quin in the loss of their son.

Bishop and Mrs. Quin had never been to a Lambeth Conference, and the diocese gave them the trip. Their son Robert, who had finished his freshman year at Rice Institute, was a young man of charm, ability, and radiant physical health. He had just come back from a house party in West Texas where he and other young people had been swimming in flood waters. The Quins sailed on a French line out of New Orleans, and on the day of sailing, Robert did not feel well. Once out to sea, he became seriously ill with symptoms not unlike those of appendicitis. The French doctor aboard did all he could, but Mrs. Quin's anxiety was not eased by the difficulties of language. After 16 days at sea, the ship landed in Le Havre, and as it docked, Robert died. The Quins learned that others of the young people on the houseparty had been sick too—with typhoid fever.

They caught the next ship back to Houston—a family heartbroken. But characteristically, both Bishop and Mrs. Quin could feel concern for Robert's friends back home. Solicitous for those in trouble throughout his ministry, Bishop Quin now had a new and deeper understanding of anyone in sorrow. "I thought I knew what they were suffering before," he said, "but now I really know."

"The wonderful thing about both Bishop and Mrs. Quin," said Mrs. J. Milton Richardson recently, "was that they took their sorrow and built upon it. Where some people turn in and are bitter, they turned their sorrow into a jewel. After that, both of them meant so much to those who lost someone they loved—and during World War II, there were quite a few people who needed that kind of understanding sympathy."

Signed by Bishop and Mrs. Quin, Derby, Dorothy and Clinton, Jr., the family letter in answer to gestures of sympathy was a moving one, and said "Through all our sorrow and loneliness, we have never been so conscious of our Heavenly Father's presence and the helpfulness of human friendship."

Mr. Allen, often assisted by Doctor Sears, read the funeral services of members old and young: Mrs. J. J. Clemens, Fred Arnold Root, Mrs. W. R. Robertson (Eva Hutchins whose father had built Hutchins House), Hiram Garwood, John A. McClellan, Miss Frances Cluett Desel, 24, and Miss Elizabeth Law, only 22, Mrs. Sam E. Allen (with Bishop Quin assisting), Mrs. J. B. Bowles, J. Robert Aston, Mrs. John L. Wortham, Henry Verhelle, Major Ingham Roberts, Henry Havelock Dickson, John Charles Harris, Mrs. Jacob Hornberg, and Andrew Dow. In the 1920s, automobile accidents first began to appear under causes of death in the Christ Church burial records. The records show a small child shot by his father who then committed suicide, a railway accident in Vera Cruz, and a number of other accidents. Each era brings its own dangers.

Given a divided church, loss of contributing members, and illness, Mr.

1930. Houston has a population of 292,352.

Allen now had to guide his congregation through the Depression of the 1930's. Despite the depression, the Rev. Lionel F. De Forest was called as assistant. Graduate of St. John's College, Greeley, Colorado, and of the Episcopal Theological Seminary of Boston, Mr. De Forest was fairly recently married and in February, 1931, came to Houston from La Junta, California.

At vestry request, Dr. Joseph Mullen spent a good bit of time that year trying to analyze the role of a church as the cathedral of a diocese. Bishop Quin sounded not too keen, though willing to be convinced, and even if Christ Church sold itself on the virtues of being a cathedral, it had no guarantee of becoming one.

Christ Church saw many lovely weddings during Mr. Allen's cure. Bishop Davis Sessums came home for the wedding of Tina Latham Cleveland to Dudley Crawford Sharp. Marie Lee and Daffan Gilmer were attendants at the wedding of Edna Daffan Gilmer to Nelson Phillips, Jr. Other weddings were those of Agnes Virginia Tallichet to Alonzo Lee Curtis, Frederica Lykes to Benjamin Franklin Thompson, Thistle York to Henry Franklin Jackson, Eleanor Wilson to Paul Wakefield, St. Clare Evans to Samuel Hudson Attwell, Mary T. Bain to James A. Haralson, Lillian Elgin Westcott to Paul Trapier Bullington, Marian Mellinger to James Lanier Britton, Lily Rice to J. R. Aston, Charlotte Nancy Robertson to Herbert Hamilton Brown, Lillian Elizabeth Horlock to Carl Illig, Jr., and Mary Marshall Ferguson to Renfrow Archer Robertson. Doctor Sears solemnized several weddings.

In this period, Faith Nixon Day was confirmed, joining in the church her husband, Stephen Delavan Day. A new Houstonian of joyous spirit, Stevo Day was related to that Episcopal family made famous in Clarence Day's *Life With Father*. That Easter confirmation class included Dr. and Mrs. Paul Ledbetter, Dudley C. Jarvis, Wallace Carnes, Frank Carter Clemens II, Henry Cornelius Cortes, Jr., Ben Francis Wilkinson, Elise Wilkinson, and Harry W. Stansbury, Jr. And in 1932, Mrs. Philip E. Fall (Lizzie) charter member of the Ladies Parish Association, died. She had attended Christ Church for 80 years.

February 4, 1931, two letters went to the standing committee of the diocese of Texas certifying that two young men were "worthy to be admitted to the Sacred Order of Deacons." They were William and Charles Gresham Marmion, Jr. Both the Marmion boys were born in Houston and graduates of Houston public schools. Gresham went to the University of Texas and William to Rice Institute, but both went to the Virginia Theological Seminary. They were ordained deacon and priest by Bishop Quin. William Marmion started his ministry in San Antonio, had a long rectorship at St. Mary's-On-the-Highlands, Birmingham, and became Bishop of Southwest Virginia in 1954. Charles Gresham Marmion held rectorships at Columbus, Eagle Lake, Washington, D.C., Port Arthur, and Dallas and became Bishop of Kentucky in 1954. Signed by James S. Allen, those two Christ Church certifications were proved valid by the years.

A letter of this period shows that E. R. Wicks, C. L. Wharton, Edmund D. McCaa, Herbert Godwin, W. E. Japhet, James P. Houstoun, L. S. Bosworth, Harry Deffebach and K. S. Dargan had left Christ Church taking their families with them—and most of these had gone to Palmer Memorial. Long time staunch supporters of Christ Church, Sam McNeill and Judge H. M. Garwood died. And though Jonas Shearn Rice was not a member at

1931. Knute Rockne, Notre Dame football coach, is killed in a plane crash in Kansas March 31.

1931. Japan invades Manchuria September 18.

the time, his death seemed an added loss to those who remembered the long ago days which from the Depressed 1930's looked so robust.

Bishop Quin was anxious that "the Church in Houston do something definite about the present unemployment situation." Mr. Allen reported to Bishop Quin that he had 20 persons in his parish who might be considered truly needy. And in reporting on his part of an every member canvass. Robert Wier wrote, "This man has been out of work a year, but I'll try him if you think I should."

Frank Clemens sent his resignation to the vestry in protest against the trend of depending upon a growing bank loan for operating expenses. In 1931, the debt at the First National Bank was $59,000. The Rev. Mr. De-Forest asked the vestry to cut his salary of $200 a month 10 per cent, but the vestry refused.

March 31, 1932, the First National Bank note was $61,000. Arthur E. Hartwell expressed deep upset that the finance committee had no plans for meeting that note. At a called meeting of April 4th, Chester H. Bryan explained that the First National Bank felt it had carried this loan long enough, and said that the Second National Bank had agreed to a three-year loan at 6½%—secured by a mortgage on Christ Church property.

Bishop Quin was asked permission for this mortgage to be made. And Bishop Quin promptly met with the vestry. The vestry minutes—for so many months resigned and apathetic in tone—are charged with the energy and conviction of the bishop. Depression or no depression, Bishop Quin said that the vestry had acquiesced to an increasing indebtedness without doing a vigorous job of canvassing and inspiring every member to contribute. He offered names of possible contributors, and said that in more than 1,000 Episcopal Churches in the United States, where Every Member Canvass was properly done, the results had been successful. On his departure, the vestry agreed to a new budget within its expected revenues, to cut the salaries of rector, assistant rector and every member of the lay staff, and to prorate any surplus between restored salaries and an operating reserve and contingent fund.

At the annual meeting in early 1933, the rector reported that though three parishes had been formed out of the membership of Christ Church, the list of communicants was larger by one than it was before these parishes were formed—a total of 1,010. Among the vestrymen who shared with Mr. Allen the worries of this period were Ennis Cargill, William Strauss, A. M. Bowles, Frank E. Hood, I. M. Griffin, Gen. J. F. Wolters, Dr. Joseph A. Mullen, E. R. Spotts, R. W. Wier, C. L. Desel, Chester H. Bryan, C. Milby Dow, H. W. Stansbury, Frank Clemens, A. E. Hartwell, McDonald Meachum, Dudley C. Jarvis, Dr. Paul V. Ledbetter, Dallas H. Moore, and C. T. Carnes. Mr. De Forest resigned as assistant to become rector of the Church of the Good Shepherd, Clemens Memorial.

And the debt at the First National Bank totaled $60,000—it had come down a notch for the first time. Better times had begun—however slightly.

In early 1934, Mr. Allen in the bulletin asked the congregation's opinion on revising the hymns and ritual of some Sunday morning services on his belief that the Christ Church congregations were made up of "one-third our own communicant list, one-third from Houston members of other churches and those who do not belong to any church, and one-third from visitors and transients." He thought it might be interesting to exchange pulpits with

1933. Adolf Hitler becomes chancellor of Germany January 30.

1933. Germany quits the League of Nations October 14, and withdraws from the disarmament conference.

ministers from other churches and of other denominations and faiths, that new words should be written to old hymns "more in line with current theological thought and the vernacular of the day." He suggested that special rituals be written to emphasize the seasons of the Christian year as well as subjects of modern thought and necessity, such as war, peace, love, neighborliness, tolerance, the Christian home, Christian parental responsibilities. The suggestion was not accepted and Mr. Allen did not insist, having no desire, as he said, to make his parishioners unhappy in their worship.

James Swayne Allen—called to two churches at once—resigned his post as rector of Christ Church April 3, 1934. "Believe me when I say the writing of this letter has not been an easy task . . . it is not necessary for me to tell how much I have enjoyed the past eight years in this dear old parish." Fond of their charming rector who had gone through such difficult years in Houston, the vestry urged him to reconsider. But weighing his decision between Church of the Good Shepherd, Corpus Christi, and historic St. David's, Austin, Mr. Allen decided to leave on May day. He went to St. David's.

Mrs. Eddie Sullivan, daughter of Captain J. J. Atkinson, gave to the church that spring a prayer desk for the acolytes' use in the sanctuary in appreciation of the work her two boys, Eddie and John, were doing, and four silver alms basins in memory of her parents, her grandmother, and her brother. The Rev. W. W. Daup of Fort Worth came to Houston for a brisk, cheerful several months in the spring and summer of 1934. But Christ Church had the task of starting from scratch to find a new rector—the first such task it had faced since 1904.

Fire, the consecration of bishops,
and the making of a cathedral. 1934-1964. 5

Chapter 37

The Fire

Christ Church—Houston's oldest church—was in 1934 at the most dangerous point in its history. Precariously balanced at the end of a waning Depression, it seemed to be at rock bottom—ready to go upward from that point, or to drift swiftly to dissolution. It must accept nothing less than a strong rector—yet it had little to offer but challenge.

Only minimum repairs had been done throughout the Depression. The church owned no rectory. The record showed that Christ Church had started its previous rector off at $5,000 a year and gradually reduced him to $3,000. The church was $60,000 in debt. Though the first sign of recovery had come in the $1,000 payment on the bank debt, it would be hard for a vestry committee to convince a potential rector that this was a vigorous, thriving, spirited congregation. But the search proved surprisingly easy.

The Rt. Rev. James Pernette DeWolfe described it with the memory of 1963 for the year 1934: "I was the most unlikely man they could have called. I was sitting in a Childs Restaurant at the General Convention in Atlantic City having lunch with my wife. Suddenly, there was Bishop Quin, and he said 'How would you like to come to Texas?'

"I said, 'I'm quite happy in Kansas City.'

"Bishop Quin said 'Come on down anyway.'

" 'I'm not really the man you want,' I protested, 'because I'm a Catholic churchman.'

" 'Just what I want,' said Bishop Quin with his usual thoroughness. 'I want those people to learn something about their church.' "

DeWolfe went home to Kansas City, and on the next Sunday morning, he saw strangers in his church. They were Albert Bowles, William Strauss and John Flanagan of Houston. "They came to the rectory after the services and issued me a call,' Bishop DeWolfe said with a delighted smile, "and I found out later that they didn't have the authority to do it!"

Albert Bowles remembers that visit too. "John Flanagan got there the day before we did," he said, "He had a complete report from the Chamber of Commerce, from other ministers, from all sorts of people, before we ever went near Doctor DeWolfe's church." They had already visited other cities and noticed that many downtown churches were rundown and poorly kept, whereas Doctor DeWolfe's church had a good choir, good congregation and a beautifully maintained property.

Mr. Bowles telephoned Frank Clemens, senior warden, who was wary. "That man is too High Church," Clemens said. "You be careful!" But Albert Bowles simply replied "Mr. and Mrs. DeWolfe are coming Thursday morning. Ask Judge Spotts to have a reception for them to meet some of the congregation."

Judge and Mrs. Spotts rose with hospitable swiftness to the call. They mailed invitations to an informal reception at their house at 3920 Yoakum Boulevard, for the evening of November 7, and readied the guest room. There was a luncheon at the Houston Club for Doctor DeWolfe to meet other leading clergymen in the city. The DeWolfes stayed with Judge and Mrs. Spotts. "The first morning I awoke to the sound of mockingbirds," said the bishop of Long Island, "and I think that changed my mind right then. But it was a wrench. Kansas City was my home town."

A Houston newspaper on November 12 announced that Doctor DeWolfe

1933. With panic sweeping the United States, newly inaugurated President Franklin D. Roosevelt closes all banks for five days to enable Congress to pass legislation to save the nation's banking system.

1933. Congress passes the National Industrial Recovery Act.

had accepted the Christ Church call. The vestry leased the house of W. A. Vinson at 1204 Lovett Boulevard as rectory.

James Pernette DeWolfe was tall, slender, with glossy black hair and dark brown eyes. He was articulate, persuasive, and had a gift both for great seriousness and for humor. Born in Kansas City in 1895, he earned his B.A. at Kenyon College, Gambier, Ohio, in 1917 and went on for his theological study at Bexley Hall, Kenyon's adjunct, and to St. John's Seminary. After four years as rector of St. Peter's in Pittsburg, Kansas, he became rector of St. Andrew's in Kansas City in 1923. In 1928 he married Elizabeth Spitler Owen, and in 1932 he received an honorary doctorate from Kenyon College. Meanwhile he did wonders at St. Andrew's. It was a mission with 80 communicants in 1923, and when he left in 1934, it was an independent parish with more than 1,200 communicants.

The Christ Church bulletin announced, "Accompanied by his wife and three children, James, Philip and Elizabeth, he will arrive in Houston about December 5." By his slimness and blackness of hair, Doctor DeWolfe looked younger than his 39 years, but he arrived at Christ Church in the full confidence and ease of a man mature in his own philosophy of the priesthood.

For the past 40 years, Christ Church had turned increasingly outward, spreading itself across the community: Beckwith and Aves through their Episcopal mission work, Sears with his inter-denominational work and civic service, Allen in the move to make Christ Church downtown the church for all who were downtown.

Doctor DeWolfe turned to the altar. In turning, he confidently expected to take the congregation with him, and to draw outsiders toward the church. "The real challenge," he said these many years later, "was a teaching ministry and the establishment of the sacramental life. I felt that my mission in Houston was to teach the people the meaning of the grace of God through the sacrament."

He spoke to the vestry of their duties—as churchmen coming to worship first, and as trustees of the church business second. To the parish, he spoke of Christ Church as "the channel for the Kingdom of God throughout this community and all the southwest," and he looked five years ahead toward a triumphant centennial celebration. This was not the talk of a man who thought of Christ Church as a building which might or might not be moved, or a congregation of sentimentalists growing tired of clinging to an untenable downtown position. "The proper attitude toward tradition," he said, "is to build upon it."

Doctor DeWolfe sensed the first upward swing of the nation from the Depression depths. "Throughout the whole country, the spirit of a new era has taken hold of the people . . . Your new rector feels that the opportunity is limitless. Christ Church is in a position to exert tremendous influence in this community. In the short time I have been here, I have learned of the respect and love even people outside of the church have for it. This is a ministry in itself . . . For 1300 years York Cathedral has stood in the midst of a large and busy metropolis, with fish markets on one side and commercial markets on the other . . . It has for all these years been the dominating influence molding the fine character of that great English city. And in meeting the needs of thousands upon thousands of individuals, Trinity Church in New York has followed a similar ministry."

1934. The Dionne quintuplets are born May 28 in Callender, Ontario.

He set a fast pace for his congregation and vestry to follow: He planned within the year to survey the community and find out what gaps might exist in community service which Christ Church could fill. He planned to have every communicant in the parish called upon that year—by himself, and by laymen and laywomen. He asked for an assistant, and he asked for a small chapel to be built off the main church building for the daily services he expected to hold. From his first Sunday morning, the congregation could see by his eucharistic vestments and ceremonial that here was—as he had said—a Catholic churchman.

Doctor DeWolfe felt strongly the unity of "one Catholic and Apostolic Church." He was vividly aware of the Episcopal Church heritage, and liked to trace it back to show the unbroken line from the early Christian missionaries in Great Britain to the beginning of the Episcopal Church in America. In his first year, he began to have daily services morning and evening assisted by lay readers. He celebrated Holy Communion at 7:30 each morning, and the lay readers read the offices. And he instituted Family Days.

"I first sent out a calling committee to each home to get all the family anniversaries—weddings, births, deaths—and asked each family to choose the day which would be theirs each year. The family was expected to be at communion at 7 AM on their day. Ten days before, I would write by hand to each family a note reminding them of their day, and before their day had ended, I would make a pastoral call. I had instituted the plan in Kansas City, and I consider it an unbeatable pastoral system," said Bishop DeWolfe.

The new rector soon began to build his own team. At his recommendation, the vestry called as assistant the Rev. George W. Barnes—an outstanding musician as well as priest. DeWolfe's choirmaster and curate from St. Andrew's, the Rev. Mr. Barnes was a graduate of the Chicago Music College and the Schumann Conservatory of Musical Art, and was a widely recognized specialist in training unchanged boys' voices. Within three weeks after his arrival, he gave an organ recital of Bach, Handel, and Mendelssohn at Christ Church. His soloist was Master James McVay, soprano soloist of St. Andrew's, who came down from Kansas City.

In exciting times as in depressing ones, daily business goes on: the Caroline Greene estate deeded the day nursery property on Capitol to the Ladies Parish Association with the provision that it must always be used for charitable purposes. On motion of Judge Spotts and Major Clemens, the vestry offered unanimously its thanks to Miss Derby Quin for her fine service at the church with the Young People's Service League. Squatters had to be ousted from the old Episcopal Cemetery property.

Doctor DeWolfe asked the vestry to thank the anonymous donor who had given the money to build his little chapel, which ran at right angles to the chancel in what had been a choir robing room. Albert Bowles and Dallas Moore were in charge of building. Mr. J. B. Bowles, after so many years as member of church and vestry, died, leaving his son Albert to carry on his tradition of service. The vestry officially approved of Homer N. Tinker, a native of Houston, as a candidate for Holy Orders. Son of Mr. and Mrs. Homer Neville Tinker of Westmoreland Place, he had been graduated from high school in Houston, from the University of the South, and Virginia Theological Seminary.

Christ Church did not pay off its $60,000 debt immediately, nor for

1934. Englebert Dollfuss, chancellor of Austria, is shot by Nazi conspirators in July.

172

several years to come, but its payment was one of Doctor DeWolfe's goals for the centennial. A start was made. Payments were made a regular part of the budget, and after so many years, the bank agreed to reduce the interest. Finances were beginning to look healthy again, with small to medium surpluses showing up after a decade of monthly deficits. The Depression had ended. Emma Shelton Robbins, for 50 years a communicant of the church, left $10,000 to Christ Church in her will, and the vestry resolution of appreciation was dated Thanksgiving Day, 1935.

Writing in purple ink, Mrs. H. T. McClung submitted her Altar Guild report at the Parish Meeting of 1936. And K. S. Mandell, Jr., announced that the new Anglican League intended to give 5% of its annual income to paying off the church deficit. Its income for the preceding year had been $20, its bank balance was none. The Ladies Parish Association reported that it had used Mr. Dow's yacht the *Mary Ellen* for a day in the spring and had had a very successful trip—socially and financially. Mrs. James Boone was chairman of the new Junior Auxiliary devoting itself to the Day Nursery.

Having had no High Church rector since the Rev. J. J. Clemens, Christ Church parishioners found DeWolfe completely different from anyone they remembered. In the diocese at the time, only Father James W. E. Airey at St. Andrew's Church, Houston, and the Rev. Stephen Moylan Bird at Brenham wore the Eucharistic vestments. Most found the change interesting, stimulating, inspiring. Many realized that the drift to Low Church had perhaps gone too far for the safety of the Book of Common Prayer service within the parish. Some were frank die-hards who did not like the more elaborate forms of ceremonialism introduced by Father DeWolfe.

He went his way not only serenely but enthusiastically. Each Sunday morning before his sermon, he gave a five minute talk on some aspect of the church or the liturgy. "We are," he would say, "one Catholic and Apostolic Church, with the Eucharist as the great central act of worship in the church and the administration of sacramental grace through the sacraments of the church from Baptism to Holy Unction." DeWolfe was a part of the movement throughout the Anglican Communion which emphasized the use of more externals, the use of vestments. "But the important thing is teaching," said DeWolfe, "with the Eucharist at the center."

Each Wednesday night he had information classes attended by prospective candidates for confirmation classes. John Epps was sexton of Christ Church when Doctor DeWolfe came. He took notes on DeWolfe's evening lectures until, in 1935, he wanted to enter the ministry. Epps was not young, but he already had his college training. Son of Rev. and Mrs. Jacob Epps of Kingstree, South Carolina, he was born in 1881 and had attended Claflin College and Allen College—both in South Carolina—before entering Howard University, Washington, where he got his LL.B. in 1914.

After proper examination, Bishop Quin made John Epps deacon in 1935, and in 1936 Bishop Quin placed the Rev. Mr. Epps in charge of Negro work in Houston. Mr. Epps was ordained priest in 1938 and for almost 20 years before his retirement, was priest in charge of St. John the Baptist Church, Tyler, Texas. Young Billy Treat of the Sunday school and acolyte guild and vestryman Arthur Hartwell were headed toward the ministry through the influences of this period.

Christ Church saw the weddings of Eleanor Derby Quin to Penrose Wiley Hirst, Frances Sara Gieseke to James Carter Boone, and Rosalie Allen Smith

1934. President von Hindenburg of Germany dies, and Adolf Hitler takes over as Fuehrer.

to Thomas S. Maffitt, Jr., all solemnized by Bishop Quin; Olive Agnes Ross to Marion Elbert Praytor, Annie Foss Myer to Clark Armstrong Polk, Beatrice Smith to Horace M. Cumming, John Haskins Hartwell to Iantha Louise Wells, Virginia Sue Green to John Morgan Fariss, Jr., Kate Ross Patton to Haylett O'Neill, Jr., Henrietta Cargill to Elbert E. Adkins, Jr., Robert Lee Melcher to Alice C. Bleker.

Christ Church recorded the deaths of Underwood Nazro, D. W. Michaux, little Marcita Link, young Thomas William House, III, Curtis B. Quarles, Judge E. R. Spotts, Mrs. Mary Calder Rice, and Adele B. Looscan, 87, whose memories had held so much of early Houston.

Doctor DeWolfe took an active interest in the training of his acolytes— Joe Drane, John Lotz, Sidney Lotz, Freeman Bokenkamp, Llewellyn Hill, Robert Reid, Philip DeWolfe, and Joe Rose among them.

Mrs. Charles Fitch and DeWolfe had become friends after an abrupt beginning. One of his first calls in the parish was to Mrs. Fitch's house on McKinney Avenue, and as she walked in to where he sat waiting, she said, "And what do you want?"

"Nothing," said Doctor DeWolfe. "I just came to see you."

"You must want something," said Mrs. Fitch. "Never knew a minister to come to see me who didn't want money."

1935. American playgoers are talking about Grand Hotel, The Barretts of Wimpole Street, Private Lives, The Petrified Forest, Victoria Regina, Idiot's Delight.

But DeWolfe soon came to know her as a person eager to give money in her own way. From time to time for the past several years, she had proposed to the vestry that she give a drinking fountain in memory of her father, Sam Ashe, to stand either in the church lawn or on Fannin Street. Always the vestry agreed, holding the right to approve the design. To DeWolfe she proposed a three-tiered fountain with the bottom tier for dogs, the second tier for birds, and the top tier for people. The proposal was referred to the committee on memorials.

Meanwhile she and Mrs. Eddie Sullivan were steadfastly keeping after a long list of parishioners in their penny-a-day and give-by-the-calendar program of contributions to the church. These efforts, added up over the years, were impressive, and more than once paid the interest on the big bank loan. The loan by December, 1936, was down to $55,000.

The Rev. Peter Gray Sears retired as rector of Palmer Memorial Church and the Rev. Stanley L. Smith was called to succeed him as rector. Father Smith was a native of Kansas City, and he and DeWolfe had been choir boys together in childhood. His coming increased the sense of partnership which had begun to grow between Palmer and Christ Church.

Doctor DeWolfe was becoming well known in the community and a pleasant addition to Bishop Aves' last days. DeWolfe was a fishing companion of Henry Aves, Jr., and once on a fishing trip, lost a particularly handsome catch. Others aboard, with knowing grins, waited to see what this priest would say to such a catastrophe, and at last someone said, "Doctor, that's what I call *profane silence.*"

Bishop Aves was still official chaplain of the Houston Yacht Club, but his best sailing days were long behind him. He could not now—as he once did with the Sears family—ride out a storm which was so terrific that the Sears and Aves were for a while reported lost and missing at sea. He was aging and much more frail—no longer the round, brisk man whom small Alice Gray Sears had called "my sausage bishop." At 83, with Dr. Paul Ledbetter on one side of his bed, Father DeWolfe and Henry Aves on the other, the old bishop died at the home of his son at 1401 Sul Ross.

Bishop Quin and Father DeWolfe conducted his funeral in Christ Church—the church built in the first year of his rectorship. His pallbearers were the Rev. Edmund H. Gibson of Galveston; the Rev. Thomas N. Carruthers, the Rev. Thomas W. Sumners, the Rev. Charles A. Sumners, the Rev. Stanley L. Smith, and the Rev. Lionel T. DeForest. The clerical escorts were the Rev. Thomas J. Windham, the Rev. Peter Gray Sears, the Rev. Gordon Reese, the Rev. Thomas Bagby, the Rev. Roscoe Hauser, and the Rev. G. W. Provost. His lay escorts were W. M. Streetman, Dr. J. M. Robinson, Milby Dow, Frank Clemens, Fred Clemens, E. W. Platzer of Kemah, Arthur Hartwell, John Dreaper, Dr. Paul Ledbetter, Dr. Abbe Ledbetter, Dr. Herbert Hayes, W. D. Cleveland, Jr., and A. S. Cleveland. Just as Henry Damerel Aves had been first bishop consecrated in Christ Church so was he first bishop buried from Christ Church. The bishop was buried at Seabrook at a site overlooking the bay he loved.

In 1936, the Rev. George Barnes led the formation of an Episcopal Choral Union with all choirs in the county invited to join, and started rehearsals for Handel's *Messiah* to be given at Christmas. But in 1937, that man of diverse talents was called to be rector of St. Thomas Church, Denver.

Doctor DeWolfe applied himself intensely to the task of finding a new organist—traveling to St. Louis and Philadelphia, writing many letters, receiving 124 applications. Aware that the church needed a new organ, he chose Edward B. Gammons, organist and choirmaster of St. Stephen's Church, Cohasset, Massachusetts. A graduate of Harvard University in music and fine arts, Mr. Gammons had done research in church music in Europe. He was one of the designers of the big organ in Memorial Church at Harvard, and had supervised the building or rebuilding of several organs in Boston. He was president of the Guild of Carillonneurs in North America.

The Rev. Francis Campbell Gray came to Christ Church as curate in 1937. Son of the Rt. Rev. Campbell Gray, he had graduated from the University of the South and General Theological Seminary, and was a general missionary in North Indiana when called to Houston. While here, he married Miss Jane Elizabeth Greenwall in a wedding ceremony with Holy Eucharist celebrated by Bishop Gray. [In 1938, Mr. Gray went as missionary to the Philippines. The Grays and their son Francis were imprisoned in Bilibid prison in Manila during World War II, and Mr. Gray ultimately became dean of St. Luke's Cathedral, Orlando, Florida.]

Because of their rector's strong conviction that church members must come to church every Sunday, parishioners were more regular in attendance, and Family Day communion services were successful. "The daily Eucharist is coming more and more to be the vital, spiritual focus of our parish life," Father DeWolfe told his people. ". . . It is not ours, it is the Church's. It is old—as old as Christianity—yet ever new, for we there find our Lord among us in the Blessed Bread and Wine . . . Just what you share in doing here is being shared in and done by other Christians of every name around the world, even to the very prayers themselves, for in the most of Christendom, the breaking of the Bread is the accepted form of worship, and the central act of worship of the whole Church. And the service used comes out of that treasury of devotion, the ancient liturgy of Holy Mother Church."

During the abdication of King Edward VIII of Great Britain to marry Wallis Warfield Simpson, Doctor DeWolfe saw that many outsiders and some

1935. Will Rogers and Wiley Post are killed in a plane crash in Alaska.

1936. King George V dies January 20, and the Prince of Wales takes the title of Edward VIII.

Episcopalians have little knowledge of church history. He was particularly bothered by those who thought that Henry VIII started the Anglican Church. Christianity was brought to the British Isles 1500 years before the birth of King Henry VIII, he said in one of his teaching missions, and possibly as early as A.D. 50. There were British bishops at the Council of Arles in 314. The Anglican Church had no contact with the Holy Roman Church until the visit of Augustine in 597. "When William the Conqueror came to England in 1066," Doctor DeWolfe said, "he found the church flourishing there and became a convert. When the Roman Pope, Gregory VII, asked William to do homage, William refused. The Magna Carta in 1215 set forth the church's true position. After Henry's death, Pope Pius ordered all his loyal followers to withdraw from the Church of England. So the Church of Rome left us and not we them, as is so often erroneously stated." Henry VIII's political severance with Rome did nothing to change the theology, the form, or apostolic succession so long established in England, DeWolfe reminded, just as the political separation of the United States from England did nothing to change the theology, the form or the apostolic succession given to the Episcopal Church of America by the Anglican Church.

Father DeWolfe's own mission at Christ Church was in the spirit of the Oxford Movement which began in 1833, when zealous young clergy at Oxford University, deploring the low state of English church life of that day, called upon the Church of England to use all the inheritance of doctrine and practice. This became the Catholic Revival which at first stressed only a stricter use of Prayer Book doctrine and devotion, but by 1860 had begun to restore old forms of ceremonial and vestments. Throughout his stay at Christ Church, DeWolfe was an active and a successful part of this movement.

Bishop Quin and Father DeWolfe together officiated at the weddings of several young ministers: Doris Anita Dissen to the Rev. Charles Gresham Marmion, Jr., and a year or so later, the double wedding of Doris E. Mings to the Rev. Thomas Woodward Sumners, and Virginia Ruth Mings to the Rev. Charles A. Sumners, with the Rev. Lawrence L. Brown and the Rev. Fordyce Eastburn as witnesses. William and Gresham Marmion came home to Houston to solemnize the marriage of their sister, Catherine Lucille Marmion, to Edward Lawrence Carroll.

In this period, there were other weddings: Sara Ella Street to Richard D. Moers, Rose P. Allen to Joe B. Drane, Meredyth Gardner to William J. Rummell, Jr., Alice Evans to Fletcher S. Pratt, Ella Campbell Myer to Edward Pearson, Dorothy Quarles to Alexander C. Dick, Mildred Wood to William Frederick Dixon, Genevieve P. Lykes to Greene Cameron Duncan, Marian Seward Neal to William Bonner Rubey, Ella Wharton to Jean Alluisi of Paris, France.

In January, 1938, A. S. and W. D. Cleveland, Jr., wrote to the vestry that as executors of the estate of their sister, Alma Cleveland Sioussat, and, acting for the surviving sisters and brothers, they wished to present the $12,000 bequeathed by their sister as an endowment fund in memory of their father, William D. Cleveland. Sterling Myer planned an instrument to assure communicants that gifts made to the endowment fund would be safe-guarded against ill-advised use. Another $1,000 was retired from the church debt by Mrs. Sullivan's penny-a-day plan. Doctor DeWolfe was invited to preach at Palmer Memorial Church, and suggested to the vestry that "in view of the friendship which exists between the rector of Palmer and the rector of

1936. Revolt begins July 17 against Spain's Republican government. General Francisco Franco proclaimed head of Nationalist (Insurgent) government October 1.

1936. Nazi Germany and Japan sign an anti-Comintern pact November 25, later joined by Italy.

Christ Church, it would do a great deal to cement the two congregations together . . . if a goodly number of Christ Church people attended."

Edward Mandell House, memorable to the nation as Woodrow Wilson's "Colonel House," died in New York City in 1938 at the age of 79. In his White House years, he had obtained from President Wilson the recommendation that Dr. Edgar Odell Lovett of Princeton be named first president of the newly proposed Rice Institute, and he became internationally known as one of the men who had helped design the League of Nations. In death, he came home to his native Houston for burial among his kinsmen in Glenwood Cemetery. The funeral service was read by the rector of Christ Church. In this general period, Christ Church lost in death Mrs. Jessamine Donnellen, Charles L. Fitch, Jules Henri Tallichet, Henry Gates Safford, aged John Henry Kirby, Mrs. Lucy Latham Boyles and Mrs. St. John Waggaman who died in the same week. Dudley Golding, at 40, was killed in an airplane crash.

A new plan was proposed for an every-member canvass to be conducted through ten teams, with a March 16 luncheon as the starting date. And in the dark hours of the morning of March 22, Christ Church caught fire.

The scrapbooks of church and parishioners are crowded with newspaper clippings about the fire—many of them more poetic than factual. Between 4:00 and 5:00 in the morning, a nightwatchman discovered that Waddell's Furniture Store was on fire. The flames spread swiftly through the six-story building and within a few hours 20 stores and buildings were destroyed or damaged. This one fire was more costly than all the fires in Houston of the year before. The first estimates were put at $536,000—but undoubtedly amounted to more. Waddell's and Christ Church suffered most. But Wilson's Stationery Store, the Y.W.C.A. Cafeteria, Foley Bros. Dry Goods Company, (then diagonally across the corner from Waddell's) and other places were damaged by flames or smoke or water.

1937. Italy announces its intention December 11 of withdrawing from the League of Nations.

"I was asleep when Mr. Strauss called to say the church was on fire," Bishop DeWolfe said, and the memory of that night was vivid in his mind after 25 years. "Mr. Will Cleveland, Mr. Sess Cleveland, and Mr. Strauss were there when I got there, and we saw flames coming up around the altar. I tried to go in to get the reserve host, but the firemen stopped me. Then I went around through the back parking lot, thinking I could go in that way, but just as I got there, the roof fell.

"I wept like a child. I had celebrated the Holy Communion so often at that altar. But Mr. Will Cleveland put his arm across my shoulder and said 'It is only a material thing. We'll rebuild.' When eventually we found the wooden tabernacle, it was scarred but not burned. It had been buried and protected from the flames by the rubble which covered it. And inside, there was a little round ring where the reserve sacrament or host had been. It had been consumed."

One fireman—a Roman Catholic—devoted himself to the rood screen, playing his hose back and forth over its carved filigree, determined to save it if he could. And fantastically, he did. Sterling Myer got there at 5:40 when the six stories of Waddell were still standing, but enveloped in flames and threatening to fall at any moment. Albert Bowles was on an early morning train coming into town, and from the train could see that the fire was certainly dangerously close to the church. He went directly there by taxi—and seeing, saw a year's hard work ahead.

1938. Hitler invades Austria March 11. Mexico nationalizes the oil industry March 18.

"It was such a quick fire," one unknown member wrote a friend. "A nightwatchman who was a friend of Mrs. Sullivan phoned her at 5 o'clock in the morning . . . and she began phoning everyone in Christ Church. She called us at 10 minutes to six and we were there on the lawn at a quarter after, and when we got there, Waddell's was burned to the ground except for one two-story corner of a gutted wall on the Fannin Street side adjoining us, which was roped and pulled down by firemen later on in the morning.

"Firemen have told us 'We have been expecting this for 40 years, for we knew if ever Waddell's caught fire, Christ Church would go.' Of course this six-story building towered over us, so when the walls fell in, we were engulfed and the entire sanctuary end of the church, from the font straight through about a third of the roof of the parish house, was crushed like an egg. Huge iron girders hurtled head-on into our sacristy, chapel, and rector's robing room, and completely demolished them.

"Our beauty spot—the sanctuary, altar—was gone, the altar buried under tons of brick with the lovely bronze crucifixion paneling of the reredos hanging to a fragment of wall.

"Our beautiful Christ Church!"

This cry—this pang—swept through the membership and was echoed by many Houstonians. The old church building, so long taken for granted, at times considered more trouble than it was worth, was suddenly and vividly precious. Old memories revived, awareness of a century of history on this one site, affection of 41 years for this one building—all combined to a fierce eagerness to restore, to rebuild, to make it as it was but with new beauty.

A 7 AM, the Christ Church bell began to ring high up in the smoke-filled air. Still burning, the church was surrounded by debris, by firemen, by fire hose and trucks.

But at 7 AM, the daily morning service of Holy Communion began at an improvised altar in the Sunday school with almost 100 Christ Church members kneeling for the opening prayers.

And at 9 AM, the vestry met in the office of the rector. With the fire still hot embers in the chancel, all present and many past vestrymen met to start anew. Fred Heyne offered the church the old Majestic Theater. Dr. Charles L. King offered use of the First Presbyterian Church for the Lenten services due to begin at noon. Robert Wier was sure that the Hermann Hospital Estate would be willing for Christ Church to use the empty First Congregational Church (now St. Matthew's Lutheran) on South Main.

Doctor DeWolfe said that daily services of Morning Prayer, Holy Communion, and Evening Prayer would be held in the Sunday school room, and a committee would see if temporary quarters would be needed by Sunday. But the worst rubble was dug out, curtains were stretched across the chancel. Five days after the fire, all three Sunday services were held in the church—each one attended by as many worshippers as the church would hold.

1938. Thomas Wolfe dies and You Can't Go Home Again *is published.*

Chapter 38

The Phoenix

The task of rebuilding was large. But by 2 PM it had begun, and support came from all directions.

At 2 o'clock, lumber was on the lawn and workmen were in the church starting reconstruction. In six days of intense effort, the destroyed chancel was partitioned off, a temporary altar set up, and because the organ had been destroyed, musicians from the Houston Symphony Orchestra under the direction of Ernest Hoffman played for that first service of morning prayer on Sunday. The nave of the church—which was the church—was filled to capacity with people standing in the back. On Monday, the work began again. A wall was built across the chancel steps, the east transept was walled off for vesting and choir rooms, an electric organ was installed, lights were repaired, the rough, dye-stained floors were sanded and polished, and the church regained a pioneer charm of an earlier day.

"We have no vestments, no linens, no hangings, no communion vessels, but the other churches are lending us enough to carry on," the unknown letter writer said on March 27. "But today, all was in temporary readiness for a service with a big confirmation class by Bishop Quin." Those confirmed that March Sunday in 1938 must carry the memory with them vividly.

"Everyone is courageous and optimistic . . . and it is hoped that now is the time to make a campaign to recondition the whole property." Christ Church was still more than $55,000 in debt—and it was coming to life with the energy of a newborn. "People feel Christ Church must be preserved for Houston, and expressions of sympathy and help are received every day. One big business man here sent Doctor DeWolfe a wire the day of the fire 'My sympathy and my pocketbook are yours.' He is a Methodist. A former member of Christ Church wrote 'I want to have my share in rebuilding Christ Church.' And one of the first contributions came from a young Jewish girl.

"So we may come out of this saving all that was lovely and desirable and get rid of all that was not. The insurance people have been very fine. Their representative flew down from New York and after going over the ruins, said to have the construction company make them an estimate and they would hand us the check."

The rood screen was saved except for the panel where a part of the organ had fallen, but was badly charred and chipped. The organ was demolished and lay out on the lawn in a few twisted and misshapen pipes—but a new one had already been promised. All the altar brasses were unearthed except for one vase. Though much of the brass was battered and one eucharistic candlestick broken in 10 pieces, craftsmen could repair, reassemble, and copy what once had been. Though the big circular window of the Resurrection was smashed, and though the memorial windows to John Scott Clemens and Mrs. Ashe were damaged, the only memorial window completely demolished was the one in memory of Lucy Cocke Beckwith. But it too could be copied.

It is a more complex job to rebuild and to replace than it is to build from a fresh start—because research must be done and endless numbers of letters must be written before decisions can be made and orders given. Albert Bowles as senior warden took over the main task of guiding this complex task. One of his first letters was to the owners of the Waddell property reminding them exactly where Christ Church property lines lay. He called attention to the deed of January 20, 1893, by which E. L. Coombs had given to the church a strip of land two feet wide and 60 feet long off the south end of Lots 6 and 7 to guarantee a perpetual easement for light and air over the north wall of Christ Church chancel.

The vestry had letters of thanks to write—the first of hundreds it would send in the next year as kindness came after kindness. Christ Church had accepted Doctor King's offer of the First Presbyterian Church for the remainder of the week's Lenten sermons by Dr. Frederic S. Fleming, rector of Trinity

1938. After the Munich conference, Prime Minister Neville Chamberlain declares "peace in our time," and Hitler occupies the Sudetenlands October 1.

Church, New York. Doctor Fleming, who was the guest of Mr. and Mrs. George Brown during his stay, preached daily and then came on to view the progress at Christ Church. Thanks went to Dr. Henry Barnston and Mr. Ike Freed for their offer of Temple Beth Israel, and to the Fire Department for the concentrated effort the firemen made to save as much of the church as could be saved.

Lenten services continued, and in the foreshortened church, DeWolfe reported, between 2,500 and 3,000 persons came to Good Friday services. During the services of Easter Day, he estimated 1,490 communions were made. This came only as further support, to a conviction he had already expressed: that the day of the downtown church had not ended. "Several years ago," he said, "there was a movement in the American church which seemed to tend toward the establishment of neighborhood parishes. The downtown church seemed to lose its hold, and this was due, primarily, to the difficulties of transportation. In this new day when transportation had been speeded up, the problem of the downtown church is no longer a great one. The renewing and strengthening of the downtown church is one of the outstanding developments of our own day."

The emergency soon took on a routine of its own. Though the vestry and former vestrymen were meeting often and with much business to attend to, the letters to them reminded—as usual—that they were expected for corporate communion at 7 AM on the morning of the day the meeting would be held. Throughout all the pressures of building, Father DeWolfe held them and the congregation to an awareness that whatever they did was in essence a service to God at the altar.

1938. Mexico nationalizes the oil industry by seizing all foreign holdings.

John Flanagan went to New York to speed the final adjustment with the insurance company, and came back with a check for $87,383.79. William Ward Watkin and Carl A. Mulvey were employed as architects to design the restoration. Albert Bowles, C. T. Carnes, and Barry York were appointed the building committee. Albert Bowles submitted plans for the new chancel, showing that the sacristy would go to the east of the chancel where the organ had been, and that the organ would be put in on the west side of the chancel in a new section of building designed for it.

John Mellinger and R. W. Horlock proposed that air-conditioning be included in the plans for the new heating system. If, Horlock pointed out, a hot air system were used instead of steam radiators, the York Ice Machinery Company could include a cooling system which would blow air over ice. Mr. Horlock offered to give five tons of ice a Sunday throughout all the summers ahead if the vestry would consent to the additional expense of installing the system.

Aware of the still large bank debt, some vestrymen expressed doubts. Doctor DeWolfe reminded the vestry that with air-conditioning, many of the street sounds—so disturbing to the congregation—could be closed out. W. D. Cleveland said promptly he'd pay his share for the air-conditioning, other voices joined his, and the decision was made.

And in this period, Sterling Myer died, and Ennis Cargill—two long time members of Christ Church and of its vestry.

Problems with the old cemetery continued. In March, 1938, the city proclaimed it a public nuisance, and the parish corporation filed suit to clear title to the land. Mrs. Emma Toole, claiming to be a grandniece of James West, filed a cross action in which she charged that the city ordinance had been "procured solicited, urged and brought" by the parish corporation. With justification, Mrs. Toole charged that far from being a nuisance, the cemetery was a "holy place of sepulchre and historical site including the graves of numerous pioneers of the City and members of said Church." With less justification, she sought reversionary rights, and the issue had to be taken through the courts for most of the coming decade.

Meanwhile, the parish corporation bought a lot at Brookside Cemetery guaranteeing perpetual care for $2,200, and went ahead with the task of moving the bodies. In this move, the late Henry W. Benchley, grandfather of Robert Benchley and one time vestryman, disappeared. Or at least, there was a stone marker on his grave in the old Episcopal Cemetery which never showed up at Brookside.

Having cleared the property, Christ Church did not quite know what to do with it. The Fat Stock Show asked permission to use it for parking ground; the vestry refused; the use was made just the same. The Rev. James W. E. Airey hoped to lease the old cemetery property for a Frontier Museum, and the vestry estimated $600 a year for rental. But nothing came of it. It was occasionally rented for parking at $75 a month. Yet already, land in the vicinity of the City Hall had sold for from $5 to $8 a square foot.

Christ Church had acquired a new curate six weeks before the fire: the Rev. Fordyce Eastburn, formerly of St. Paul's Episcopal Church, Harlan, Iowa. Son of a doctor, Mr. Eastburn had taken premedical courses at the University of Iowa before studying for the ministry. Married and the father of two children, he came to Christ Church in time to join Mr. Gammons in the emergency tasks best done by young curates in such times. Both men were commended by the vestry by their spontaneous response to the demands of the trying weeks.

Represented by Mrs. Haywood Nelms, vice president, the Maternal Health Center offered to take over the property at 1708 and 1710 Capitol Avenue, agreeing to spend $1,000 in repair and renovation, and to clear ground for additional playground space for the Caroline Greene Day Nursery. The vestry was glad to turn over this responsibility for a period to end January, 1942. Meanwhile, the Tellepsen Company was continuing construction.

The Diocesan Council Meeting of January, 1939, was approaching—and thereafter, the centennial celebration of Christ Church. The church was not yet completed, but the *Texas Churchman* told of memorials and beauties to come: The altar, being given by the small gifts of many people, was to be dedicated to the memory of Bishop Henry Damerel Aves. Eight carved figures on the altar symbolize the spread of Christianity from the Apostles to Great Britain, and from Britain to the United States to Texas. The first of the figures is Saint Joseph of Arimathea, who by tradition, carried Christianity to Britain in the apostolic age. Second is Saint Augustine, who left Rome in 597 with a mission to the then barbarous and uncultured England, and helped strengthen the Christian missions he found there. Third, is Bishop Samuel Seabury—first bishop of the North American continent. George Washington and Doctor White tried to obtain a bishop for America in 1779 at the New York Convention. When they failed, Connecticut elected Seabury bishop, and sent him to Lambeth to be consecrated. Because of the church-state link which would have required Seabury to swear loyalty to the king, he could not be consecrated there, but at the suggestion of Anglican bishops, finally went to Scotland for consecration. The fourth figure is that of the Rt.

1938. At the Munich Conference, Britain and France yield to Nazi demands that Czechoslovakia give the Sudetenlands to Germany.

Rev. Alexander Gregg, first bishop of Texas. The lower row of figures are the four evengelists: Saints Matthew, Mark, Luke and John. The altar rail is a memorial to the Rev. John Julyan Clemens.

The *Texas Churchman* listed other new memorials, among them: A classic pipe organ given by Mrs. Edwin R. Spotts in memory of her husband.

A memorial chapel—larger and infinitely more beautiful than the little chapel which had burned—given by Mrs. C. D. Golding and Fred M. Golding in memory of C. D. Golding and Dudley Golding. Altar for the chapel with tryptich, reredos and credence, given by Mrs. Sterling Myer in memory of her husband, and altar rail and sedilia including the lectern, given by Sterling Myer, Jr., and Mrs. C. W. Gwathmey, in memory of the late Sterling Myer. Window over the altar in the church given by Joseph A. Mullen, Jr., in memory of his brother, George A. Tyler, and two patens given in George A. Tyler's memory by Dr. and Mrs. Joseph A. Mullen. Paten given by Mrs. Jacob F. Wolters. Sanctuary lamp for the chapel given by Mrs. Alice Baker Jones. Lavabo given in memory of Mrs. Esther Stone and Mrs. J. W. Maas by Daughters of the King. Choir pews given by Mrs. John A. McClellan in memory of her husband. Large window in nave given by Mrs. Lulu Bryan Rambaud, Chester Bryan, and Louis Bryan, in memory of their mother, Bettie Bryan. Credence table given by Mrs. J. H. Weaver in memory of her father, Edwin R. Spotts.

Sedilia for the sanctuary given by Mrs. H. T. McClung in memory of her mother, Lizzie H. Guion, and an individual communion set from Mrs. McClung in memory of Lizzie E. Fall. Chancel prayer books and hymnal given by C. T. Carnes in memory of his parents, George T. and Lila M. Carnes. Missal for the church altar given by John S. Mellinger in memory of his mother, Maggie Sweeney Mellinger. Lectern Bible given by the church school to replace the lectern Bible given by the church school pupils of 1873.

The gifts came in more rapidly than they could be properly designated and spent, but undesignated memorials had already been given by Mrs. L. T. Noyes, Mrs. Eddie Sullivan, Mrs. C. A. Perlitz, Mr. and Mrs. Henry B. Verhelle, Mrs. W. B. O. Stevenson, Mr. and Mrs. George N. Posey, Mrs. S. A. G. Norris, A. E. Hartwell, and Haskins Hartwell, by the Montrose Chapter of the Ladies Association, and the Junior Auxiliary. Rood for the rood screen from Mrs. E. V. Hesse in memory of her daughter and son, Ethel Hesse Richards and Harry H. Richards. Set of preaching stoles from Fred M. Golding. Ciborium from Rufus Cage, in memory of his father and mother, replacing the memorial destroyed by fire. Lavabo given by Mrs. R. W. Horlock. Stone cross to surmount the outside of the chapel given by Miss Maryallen Snyder and Philip DeWolfe. Carpet and kneeling cushions for the chapel by Miss Louise M. Sommerhauser. Holy picture for the vestibule of the chapel given by Mrs. Henry J. Becker in memory of her son, Bobby.

These gifts—and others were to come—amounted to almost $65,000. The pulpit in memory of Jane Gray was restored and polished. The lectern still stood in honor of W. J. Hutchins, as did the altar cross in memory of Abbie Latham Tryon—who had died a few days after her baby so long ago.

The diocesan council in January was the prelude to the centennial celebration of Christ Church in March. At the annual parish meeting, Christ Church delegates were elected for this Ninetieth Diocesan Council: Arthur E. Hartwell, William Strauss, A. M. Bowles, W. A. Steiner, delegates, and C. T. Carnes, Dr. Paul V. Ledbetter, Dudley C. Jarvis, and H. H. Wallace,

1939. Germany and Italy announce military and political alliance May 7.

alternates.

Doctor DeWolfe appointed delegates to the Diocesan Council of Church Women: Mrs. F. M. Law, Mrs. O. S. Van De Mark, Mrs. J. H. Weaver, Mrs. John McClellan, and alternates, Mrs. H. T. McClung, Mrs. A. M. Bowles, Mrs. W. P. Craddock, and Mrs. H. L. Warren. The Diocesan Women were given a Centennial Concert by the Houston Symphony Orchestra directed by Ernest Hoffman.

But the centennial celebration topped the diocesan meeting. It began on the night of March 16 with a banquet. Mrs. T. C. Dunn, who had been a member for 76 of the church's 100 years, and Mrs. L. T. Noyes, who had been a member for 70 years ever since her parents came up from Matagorda to live in the old rectory, cut a large birthday cake with 100 candles. Major Frank Clemens, born on church property, and A. S. Cleveland, whose parents had married in Christ Church and who had followed in his father's steps as Sunday school superintendent, reminisced over the eight rectors and three bishops they had known. W. D. Cleveland, Jr., Mrs. Clinton S. Quin, William Strauss and Bishop Stephen E. Keeler of Minnesota spoke, and a medal was given to Albert Bowles in recognition of his service.

It was clear to everyone in that happy hour that the fire had done more good than harm. "There was noble activity during those months by all the vestrymen, past and present," said Bishop DeWolfe looking back to 1938. "It was a wonderful group of men—all of them. And Albert Bowles did a sacrificial work. He let his own business suffer that year, and he kept on the plans all the time. It was a real act of Christian sacrifice and service. In all my ministry, I've never known anyone who showed such devotion to the church through service."

The Spotts Memorial Organ was dedicated in that fortnight of celebration. Designed by E. B. Gammons, director of music, it was a classic organ with some of the best features of the seventeenth and eighteenth century organs included, and it lent soaring music to the celebrations of the week. Everett Titcomb of the Church of St. John the Evangelist, Boston, wrote a Christ Church Centennial offertory anthem and dedicated it to Mr. Gammons.

Centennial Sunday was an all-day celebration beginning with a corporate Communion for the Parish at 7, highlighted by baptism at noon and confirmation at night. Doctor DeWolfe invited the Rev. James Allen, former rector, to come to Houston for the celebration and with Mr. Eastburn, they read the services of the day. A choral Eucharist was celebrated at 11 AM with the Rt. Rev. Frank E. Wilson, bishop of Eau Claire, preaching, and Bishop Quin confirmed the centennial class, and preached that night.

This was the high point of Doctor DeWolfe's stay at Christ Church, the high point of many years at Christ Church. Centennials coming as the climax to a joyous and successful drive to rebuild, restore and beautify the church are rare in any decade. But there were pleasant things to come.

In 1939, Caroline Ennis Cargill McClellan—the Miss Carrie who as a young lady had been one of the most popular Sunday school teachers and who as Mrs. John A. McClellan had given always so generously to Christ Church —gave her house at 4104 Bute Street to be a rectory.

Designed by Birdsall Briscoe, the Bute Street house had been built in 1923 by Ennis Gargill and John McClellan, and in the years after, had been the home of the McClellans, Mr. Cargill and Miss Henrietta. Mr. McClellan died in 1930, Mr. Cargill in 1938, and Miss Henrietta Cargill had married—

1939. Houston becomes first port in the south and third in the nation.

leaving Mrs. McClellan the pleasure of one more generous gift to Christ Church. The house had recently been modernized and was valued at $30,000. Doctor and Mrs. DeWolfe moved into the new rectory.

The May Fete of 1939 was lovely—another triumph of centennial year. Small, red-haired Withrow Wier, daughter of Mr. and Mrs. Robert Wier, was queen of the May Fete, crowned by Paul Owen Barth, son of Mr. and Mrs. Albert H. Barth. The court included Clare Scott Attwell, daughter of the Hudson Attwells; James Davis, son of Mr. and Mrs. Morgan Davis; Virginia Anne Fitch, daughter of Dr. and Mrs. Edward O. Fitch, and Dixie Margaret Sick, daughter of Mr. and Mrs. J. E. Sick, Jr. There were visiting dukes and duchesses from other churches: Lois Jean Martin, Church of the Good Shepherd; Sally Lou Falls and James Harrington, Trinity; Almeria Thompson and William P. Hobby, Jr., Palmer; Nancy Mahon and Homer Thornhill, St. Stephens; Kathryn Wallace and Garnett Manuell, St. Paul's; Lynne Oliver and Charles Green, St. Mary's.

If the records and pictures of all the May Fetes had been kept, they would have told a story of generation-unto-generation at Christ Church. Withrow Wier's niece, Mary McNamara, became queen in the 1960's. Irma Jones (Mrs. W. C. Hunt) was queen of the May in 1896, and a generation later, her daughter, Effie Hunt (Heald) was queen. Rosalie Hutcheson (Mrs. L. S. Bosworth) was queen of the May and after her, her daughter Betty Bosworth was crowned (Mrs. Oscar N. Neuhaus). As a child Henrietta Cargill was queen in 1917; she married Elbert E. Adkins, and their daughter Antha Adkins was crowned in 1953. Marian Britton was queen, and so was her cousin, Lucile Mellinger (Mrs. John Alden Rodgers). Carolyn Cibrell Cain was queen when George Mellinger Britton held the throne as king. Both Thad and Edward Hutcheson were king in their year, with Marian Rubey and Barbara Kirkland as their ladies. And one of the fairest, rosiest, youngest queens of church history was Martha Wicks—who in the pictures looks fully three. Her king for the day was tall Howard Hughes. But she grew up to marry Malcolm Lovett.

The Houston Symphony Orchestra continued its generous partnership with Christ Church. DeWolfe was chairman of the orchestra's program committee, and once narrated *Peter and the Wolf* with the orchestra. The Ladies Parish Association sponsored the orchestra in a special series of Mozart. Mr. Hoffman planned the concert with 28 members of the orchestra, playing the Mozart G. Minor Symphony in its original orchestration. Mrs. H. M. Garwood was chairman of arrangements.

In the late 1930's, Bishop Quin asked Episcopal church women to organize their efforts at Jefferson Davis Hospital to provide systematic help in the offices and wards. Because of their uniforms, they soon became known as the Women in Yellow. Mrs. Richard Franklin, Mrs. Lamar Fleming and Mrs. Joseph W. Evans were among early members taking a lead, and Mrs. Inez Yarborough became executive secretary. Mrs. Eric Boswell remembers that as a newcomer from Atlanta, she sat next to Mrs. Evans on her first Sunday in Christ Church and the next thing she knew she was a Woman in Yellow. [The organization soon became interdenominational, and moved into its second generation after World War II when Clare Fleming (now Mrs. Sam Sprunt) began volunteer work.]

At Candlemas, Christ Church observed the Purification of the Blessed Virgin Mary commemorating the presentation of Christ in the Temple. The

1940. Winston Churchill succeeds Neville Chamberlain as prime minister of Great Britain.

service consisted of a solemn evensong, solemn procession—with incense—and the blessing of all candles to be used in Christ Church throughout the coming year.

In the matter of confession, the Anglican Communion takes the position that all may, none must, some should. But until the arrival of Father DeWolfe, few Christ Church members had ever made personal confessions. Through his teaching missions and his confirmation classes, Father DeWolfe emphasized the "all may . . . some should," until he had 30 penitants who made regular confessions.

Christ Church saw many weddings: Margaret Robards Morrison to John Spaulding John, Betty Bingham to Hillen Armour Munson, Jessica Robinson Coolidge to Robert Emmet Moroney, Dorothy Elizabeth Franklin to Erwin W. Smith, Jr., Elizabeth Barnett Stewart to John G. Wolf, Jr., Yvonne Elois Gieseke to Sidney Lee Brannon, Shirley Louise Dissen to Jeff Henry Haverlah with the Rev. C. G. Marmion officiating, Iris Frances Harper to Winzel Joseph Geiselman, Rita Elizabeth Brewster to Richard Wilkins Tidemann, Olive Duncan to Jacob Wilbur Hershey, Winifred Frances Greenwell to William Wallace Cloud, Sylvia Orline Norsworthy to Henry Kirkland Harrison, and Mary Elizabeth Morris to Paul S. Peters.

The Every Member Canvass went well in 1940. Almost 600 names were in the list of pledges published in the bulletin. The young Rev. James McKee, III, a Rice Institute graduate who had studied theology at Virginia Theological Seminary, came from St. Paul's, Waco, to be assistant at Christ Church.

But in May Doctor DeWolfe resigned to accept the call as dean of the Cathedral of St. John the Divine in New York. Episcopal laymen of Houston gave him a farewell luncheon and a scroll which said "May he take the spirit of Texas with him." Doctor DeWolfe replied "The spirit of Texas, the heart of Texas, is one of decided humanity and is not calculating and cold. With God's help and your prayers, I shall never lose it." When he became Bishop of Long Island, James Pernette DeWolfe had the steer's head of the Diocese of Texas and of Christ Church engraved on his bishop's ring.

Of Youth and World War II

Chapter 39

Many parishes, having once become either High Church or Low, stay that way. In hunting a new rector, they look first to his attitude toward externals. Christ Church throughout its history has looked primarily to the qualities of the man's mind and spirit, and as a result has swung moderately from Low Church to High and back again throughout the century. Through his missions and his confirmation classes, Father DeWolfe had developed in a great many members of Christ Church a preference for Anglo-Catholic ceremonial. But during his stay, there were always some members who were frank to say that they preferred a simpler service, and some asked that the 9 o'clock service be simplified for their comfort in worship.

When a committee was named to find a new rector to succeed Father DeWolfe, it was simply instructed to find the best possible man for the post, and it soon decided that John Elbridge Hines of St. Paul's Church, Augusta, Georgia, was that man. Son of Dr. and Mrs. Edgar A. Hines, John Hines was born in Seneca, South Carolina, and was graduated with honors and a Phi Beta Kappa key from the University of the South. He went to the

1940. In retreat from Dunkirk by British Expeditionary Forces, May 26-June 4, some 900 boats of every size and class take 338,226 troops across the English channel.

Virginia Theological Seminary for his graduate studies. He was made deacon in 1933, and ordained priest in 1934.

But this big, athletic young man with the youthful face and easy smile had had valuable experience. Before coming to Augusta, he had been curate under Dr. Karl Morgan Block of two churches in St. Louis, and rector for two years at Trinity Church at Hannibal, Missouri. In this period he married Miss Helen Louise Orwig of St. Louis. In his three years in Augusta, Mr. Hines became a civic leader. He was a member of the board of the Civic Music Association, and of the Red Cross, and worked with the juvenile court. He was also a member of the Augusta Housing Authority and of the Rotary Club. More significantly, he was for those three years rector of a church which was 190 years old and famous for its picturesque old churchyard where George Steptoe Washington, nephew of the first president, is buried.

Hines was called to the attention of the Christ Church vestry by Bishop Quin, who had first met Mr. Hines on visits to the Virginia seminary. As a student, John Hines had quarters in the midst of Texans, and the lasting friendship between these two men began then—between bishop and theologue. Mr. Will Cleveland, Albert Bowles, and August L. Selig went to Augusta to see him.

"They were quite cautious," Bishop Hines now says, "because I was so young and Christ Church so old. But they saw that St. Paul's was older than Christ Church and that helped. Their major contention to me was that Houston was a great growing city, and that the downtown church was of paramount concern to the life of that city." Mr. Bowles on his side noticed, as he was always careful to do, the excellent condition of the truly old St. Paul's, and the entire committee was tremendously impressed with the sermon they heard and with the unmistakable quality of this young man.

With his background of Virginia and Georgia, Mr. Hines was essentially a Low Churchman, and Christ Church was in for another change—though it would never again revert to the puritan simplicity it had known before the coming of the Rev. J. J. Clemens. The vested choir marching in procession behind a cross, which had seemed so High Church to the congregations of 1875, had by now become a simple essential to the Episcopal ceremony.

Though all its early rectors and a majority of all its rectors had come to the church as young men, the Rev. John E. Hines looked younger than any in the church's history. He was 30 years old—the same age at which Charles Gillett had come down from Connecticut almost a century before. Mr. Hines' youthfulness was emphasized by the arrival with him of his wife, who with her hair falling softly almost to her shoulders looked like a college girl, and their three small children—the youngest six months old and in the diaper and bottle stage.

The Hines family reached Houston in January, 1941. Ahead lay one last year of peace. The parish dinner which welcomed them to Houston was attended by 325 members of the church. The young rector found himself for a short while with two assistants—the Rev. Fordyce Eastburn, who had stayed on as priest in charge in the months after Father DeWolfe's departure, and the Rev. John McKee who, though younger than the rector, looked like a medieval friar with his chubby round face and prematurely bald head.

The church was in good repair, and it was air conditioned, which in 1941 was still fairly unusual among churches. The offices in the rectory were hot and noisy in summer, drafty and even leaky in winter, and were reached by an outside staircase. Bishop Quin's office, Bishop Hines remembers, was "a hot hole at the back of the old rectory." The vacant area just behind the rectory was used for staff parking, and both clergy and lay staff of Christ Church appreciated the good lunches so pleasantly available at the Y.W.C.A. cafeteria where the Cleveland Building now stands.

"I had come from an old church," Bishop Hines said recently, "but I was not prepared for the wide variety of membership I found at Christ Church— the variety which makes it interesting. There were not many very young people, but there was a tremendous diversity of culture—laborers, wage earners, professional men and business men, members from our poorest neighborhoods all the way across to the then new River Oaks. Eliza Wilson was our only Negro member left, as I remember, but she came every Sunday."

Tall, handsome Mr. Will Cleveland had impressed Mr. Hines from their first meeting. "He was a Christian gentleman in a rare and wonderful sense of the word," Bishop Hines remembers. "Of intense loyalty to the Episcopal Church, he was a symbol of what the Episcopal Church should be. He had a wide latitude of interests in the church, and though he was 30 years older than I, he could dissolve the difference between us by his interest and his own ability to equate us. He never declined a request made by me. He was very wise and very tolerant." Mr. Cleveland taught his young rector to fish, giving him a rod and reel which had been willed to him by Mr. John Dickson.

As senior warden, Will Strauss seemed the epitome of all a newcomer's concept of the Texan—6′ 4″ tall, weighing well over 200 pounds, with a booming, hearty voice. He wore a wide brimmed hat and sometimes boots, and was an ardent Houstonian. In contrast, R. W. Horlock, though a former track athlete, was a small man with snowy hair and a pink, fresh face which was forever young with his enthusiasm. "Heaven and the Episcopal Church were synonymous for Mr. Horlock," Bishop Hines said, looking back across the years. And to keep Christ Church at a proper celestial temperature, Mr. Horlock faithfully had delivered 10,000 pounds of ice every Sunday morning at 5—enough to cool the church for all the services of the day. Then there was Mr. Sess Cleveland, rounder of face than his brother, who never missed a service, who worked steadily at his tasks with church finances and men's organizations, and who once a week would drop by the church office to talk over what was going on with his rector. And there was Mr. Bowles.

In the interval between Father DeWolfe's going and Mr. Hines' coming, Sidney J. Mitchell died. The bachelor who had so enjoyed the Christ Church picnics of his youth left a large residuary estate to the church for charitable purposes. The first estimates of approximately $100,000 in various kinds of property and holdings proved valid. When Mr. Hines arrived, the bank debt stood at $54,750, and at the parish dinner which welcomed him, it was voted to pay $4,000 from the Fire Restoration Fund toward the debt.

Two months after Mr. Hines arrival, Mr. and Mrs. Albert P. Jones came to Christ Church on Palm Sunday. As a young married couple, they were hunting a church where they could feel most at home and rear their children. "John Hines was the greatest preacher I had ever heard," Albert Jones said looking back to that day. They were confirmed before Thanksgiving—Albert and Nettie Jones, and Mrs. Jones' mothers, Mrs. Nettie Lockart Lewis. W. J. Goldston was also confirmed in this period.

Christ Church members and members of other congregations in Houston were responding to Mr. Hines' sermons. They were often short, they always

1941. Prime Minister Churchill and President Roosevelt sign Atlantic Charter on shipboard in mid-Atlantic August 14.

seemed short, the language was simple and direct but used with unmistakable mastery.

And occasionally, the youth of the rector gave him an insight to old, old themes. He quoted St. Paul, "When I was a child, I spake as a child, I understood as a child, I thought as a child . . ." and he stripped away the sentimental interpretation so often given this passage. "Childhood," said the rector, "is very complex for it shelters an awful inconsistency. There is nothing quite so appealing as a little child . . . But did you ever stop to think how terribly selfish? . . . they cannot help it . . . but they are the most egocentric people alive, for they feel themselves to be the center of the universe . . . How primitive they often are . . . grasping with both hands, imperiously making demands that satisfy their wants, expressing their own desires, uninterested in the welfare of others . . . How much respect for your rest does your three-year-old have in the early morning? How much consideration does he have for what you want to do when he wants to eat, or play, or sleep? That is egocentricity.

"Have you ever considered what happens in a world where whole groups of men and women, where nations, are tainted with childish characteristics? They create a hell in which their fellow men are forced to live. It is one of the terrible illusions of childhood that the world belongs to them, that the universe revolves around them. Blessed is the child who wakes early from that dream. But do you know that there are millions . . . who never wake from it? Do you want to teach your children the way to happiness? If you do . . . teach them one overwhelming truth: that they live in a world with other people, that they must learn to live with those people, that it is a world which uncompromisingly demands as the price of peace the stern repudiation of childish things, the utter rejection of selfishness.

1941. Germany invades the Soviet Union June 22. North African war begins August 6.

"We want God, we Christians, but we do not want many of those who are God's children! We want God's Kingdom, with its justice and peace and good will, but we shy away from the rules that would help to establish it. God made this world and he did not make it for a childish toy. He made it for maturity, and maturity shall inherit it. It is a world in which two fundamentals are as unalterable as the law of the Medes and the Persians. For here cooperation rules, and here selfishness ruins.

"Europe did not really believe that cooperation symbolized in the League of Nations was necessary to peace and prosperity. Our own United States would have none of it. So Europe gets war and the United States gets the very pressing fear that some day she may have to fight upon both her protective seas . . . How charming . . . the mind of a child in the body of a child. How tragic is the opposite: the mind of a child in the body of a man."

Ned Gammons—to the regret of everyone—resigned to take a position at Groton, and the Rev. Fordyce Eastburn left, as he had always expected to do, to become priest in charge of Trinity Cathedral, Little Rock. John Hugh Raymond Farrell, who had received minor orders in the Roman Church, was recommended by the vestry for Holy Orders.

By Autumn, Mr. Hines found a new organist—Arthur Howes of Washington, D.C.—and the vestry had called the Rev. John R. Bentley as assistant and director of religious education. Born in Augusta, Georgia, Mr. Bentley was graduated from Hill School, Pottstown, Pennsylvania, and Yale University, but he came back to Augusta and entered the ministry from St. Paul's. He studied at Virginia Theological Seminary and was ordained in

Georgia by Bishop Middleton S. Barnwell.

Early in Mr. Hines rectorship, Christ Church lost three of its young people: James Walker Cain, Jr., died of poliomyelitis at 23; St. Clare Evans Attwell died at 33, and Robert Barron Selig at 17. The Rev. Peter Gray Sears was in late 1941 becoming very frail and often sick. At his request, his friend W. D. Cleveland, Jr., brought him to Christ Church to hear the new young rector, and Mr. Sears seemed greatly pleased. He liked John Hines' sermon, liked him, and approved the simple beauty of the service.

December 7, 1941—Pearl Harbor. With it came the expectation that both curates would soon be off to the services, that many men and boys of Christ Church already in uniform would soon be going overseas, that more would be called to duty, and that months and years of uncertainty, worry, separation, and maybe loss lay ahead for families in the congregation.

The Parish Meeting of January, 1942, was one of unusual warmth. At the suggestion of Mr. Hines, the rector, vestry, and members of Christ Church sent a telegram to Mr. Sears "in affectionate greetings and expression of appreciation of your self-sacrificing service in this parish." Writing from the John Sealy Hospital where the message had been forwarded to him by his daughter, Mrs. Frank Akin, Mr. Sears expressed his appreciation for the thought. "Some of these days, not far in the future, I hope, I shall look forward to the very great pleasure and privilege of meeting again with my old congregation, recalling with them old times, old faces and old memories which while bitter-sweet, are still very, very dear to me . . . and there are those in shining armor whom we shall recall who have passed on ahead of us into Paradise." Eleven days later, Peter Gray Sears died.

The funeral was held at Palmer Memorial Church. The pallbearers were J. H. Arnold, R. D. Farish, L. Randolph Bryan, Dudley Sharp, Dr. John Zell Jeston, and George M. Dow—among them men who had been members of both Christ Church and Palmer. And Doctor Sears was laid to rest next to his wife, in the Christ Church lot of Glenwood Cemetery.

In the first year or two of Mr. Hines' rectorship, there were a number of weddings. Among them, Margaret Warren to Dr. Henry O'Neil Weaver, Winifred Safford to McClellan Wallace with Mary Jane and Whitfield Marshall as signing witnesses, Eugenia Dabney Kendell to David B. Harris, Jerome Cartwright to Edward M. House, Rebekah Witherspoon Pannill to Lawrence Prestidge Gwin, Julia Huston Denton to Albert Hodges Wadsworth, Jr., Anne Elizabeth Hartwell to Helmuth Leroy Lamberth, Audrey Louise Jones to John Albert Boehck, Doris Elodie Monroe to James Pernette DeWolfe, Jr., Lula Jane Curtin to Benjamin Bartholemew Street, Elizabeth Vivian Carnes to Wallace Edward Brunson, Chaille Cage to John Lewis Thompson, Jr., Alma Louise Bailey to James Van Baarle, and Georgia Howard to Henry Gates Safford, Jr.

Charles Lewis Fitch and Mary Ashe Fitch gave a memorial window to their mother and father, and young Ann and Withrow Wier gave sound projector equipment. The children of Mrs. St. John Waggaman gave two lanterns in the nave to her memory. Christ Church set up an Endowment Committee to handle the S. J. Mitchell funds. Albert Bowles was named to serve for four years, W. D. Cleveland, Jr., for three years, John S. Mellinger two years, and Ralph Henderson for one year.

With a congregation made up largely of mature, or middle-aged or elderly members, and of a wide variety of backgrounds, Mr. Hines saw in Christ

1942. Dieppe Raid in the summer is the largest commando raid of World War II.

Church some of the same factors which he had dealt with in Augusta. "My feeling was," Bishop Hines says in retrospect, "that the only reason for a downtown church was for it to be involved in the life of the community." The coming of war and of gas rationing confirmed his early impressions that this was the major task.

"We had here," he says, "a most effective ministry to business women who lived in this area. We met here at the church for supper once a week, with as many as 200 in the Business Women's Club. I met with them always, and the club was open to all denominations. We had Saturday gatherings of newspaper boys who worked the downtown section. It was run by laymen, and it gave them a place to go which was off the streets. The Sea Scouts was another effective ministry, and Nelson Longnecker—whose son is now in the ministry—was in charge."

Christ Church in this period did not have a large Sunday school for two reasons. "Most of us assumed—mistakenly—that there could not be a good Sunday school in a downtown church," Bishop Hines says. "And this opinion was encouraged by gas rationing which prompted everyone to send the children to the Sunday school in their own neighborhood. We had an exceptional group of acolytes. Of perhaps a dozen, one postulant was killed during the war, and seven others went on to enter the ministry."

In May of 1942, Kinkaid School held its baccalaureate program at Christ Church as part of the 11 o'clock Sunday morning services. With the vestry's approval, Mr. Hines called together several leading Protestant clergymen of the city and suggested that they join in regular Wednesday noonday services at Christ Church. Bishop A. Frank Smith, Dr. Paul Quillian, Dr. Charles King and Dr. Donald H. Stewart agreed to take part and to help enlist speakers. But the most intensive and far reaching ministry of Christ Church during World War II was to service men and women.

The war had begun to make itself felt even before Pearl Harbor. Texas was soon dotted with air bases, and in Houston the shipyards began to build landing craft and other ships for the Navy. Camp Wallace opened at Hitchcock, and Ellington Field burgeoned. Men and women in every kind of American and allied uniform were in Houston for a few weeks, a few months or the duration, and most of them were strangers to the city. In May, 1942, Mr. Hines went to the Ladies Parish Association meeting to describe the project for throwing the entire Christ Church plant open to the service men and women. Ralph Gunn drew a plan for remodeling the Guild Hall into a service room, and Mr. Hines asked the ladies for $250 to be a part of the $1,000 to $1,300 remodeling fund which would be needed.

The Service Room opened September 27, 1942, and was quickly successful. Luncheon was served every Sunday to as many men and women in uniform as cared to come. Mrs. A. L. W. Tackaberry reported five months later that between opening day and February 28, 1943, 1,300 dinners had been served to an average of 55 men each Sunday. On Mrs. Tackaberry's resignation in the spring, Mrs. Louis Bryan took over temporarily, and then Mrs. A. Munson Goodyear took over for the duration this demanding task. The May Fete of 1942 cleared $500.79 and was the last of the war. The members were concentrating on war efforts of many kinds. They started sending 100 dozen cookies a week to Ellington Field, and then 125 dozen.

Mrs. Dudley Jarvis, vice president in charge of the Service Room, had Mrs. Ralph Gunn as chairman of Sunday waitresses, Mrs. E. T. Chew

1942. General Douglas MacArthur leaves the Philippines in March. General Jonathan Wainwright defends Bataan.

and Mrs. H. T. McClung to keep fresh flowers around the room, Mrs. Ralph Henderson as chairman of the Service Room, Mrs. Louis Bryan and Mrs. Goodyear as chairmen of the canteen, and Mrs. Jarvis expressed her appreciation to "Miss Mary Louise Fitch, Misses Daisy and Mary Alice Elgin, Misses Louise and Adele Waggaman for their helpfulness at all times."

The numbers grew larger—sometimes reaching 150 and even 200 a Sunday. The records on the whole program are surprisingly sketchy. The room was held open until 9 PM each Saturday and Sunday, and was opened week days from morning until 9 in the evening except when no hostesses could be on duty. Many of the service men came repeatedly. One was the son of a man who had come to that same room to use "the reading and writing materials" during World War I.

During the war, F. Marion Law, Jr., was operating his Houston Book Store on Main Street just south of Polk Avenue. Aware that evenings can be lonesome in a strange town, Mr. Law installed easy chairs, kept a pot of coffee hot, and left the doors of his book store open on many a long evening in an informal open house to service men. Between this Christ Church member and the well organized and equipped Christ Church Service Room, many young people in uniform found Houston a kindly place. The Sunday luncheons ended in the summer of 1945. It was estimated that 2,000 service men had been served at the church during the war. Meanwhile, the service people were coming to Christ Church on Sunday mornings. The rector asked the vestry's advice on inviting them to partake of Holy Communion, and the vestry decided that the invitation should be extended to "all those professing to be followers of our Lord, Jesus Christ."

The war began to make dents in the staff. The Rev. John McKee III, a graduate electrical engineer of Rice Institute before he became a minister, volunteered in the U. S. Signal Corps, and devoted himself to the study of British radar—then so new and wonderful. He was assistant military attache at the American Embassy in Bogota, Colombia, from 1942 to 1948. A. Balfour Patterson, Jr., son of two Christ Church members, was graduated from Seabury-Western Seminary and was made deacon by Bishop Quin. Arthur Hartwell resigned as treasurer and Sunday school superintendent, but intensified his work as layreader in churches of the area. The parish sent telegrams of greetings to its previous rectors and curates: the Rt. Rev. James P. De-Wolfe, Lt. John McKee, the Rev. Fordyce Eastburn, the Rev. James Allen, and the Rev. George Barnes. And the Bishop of Long Island, the Rt. Rev. James P. DeWolfe was invited to Houston for a week's teaching mission.

Always interested in music, Mr. Hines went to work for the Houston Symphony Orchestra, and became a member of the board and of the program committee. One day Ernest Hoffman expressed his dismay that he had no money with which to rent the music he needed for an approaching concert. He needed $50.

"I'll give you $25 of it," said Mr. Hines, "and I'll find somebody to give you the other $25." The other $25 was promptly offered by a wrestler performing in the music hall, so that the wrestler and the rector of Christ Church enabled the Houston Symphony Orchestra to put on one concert it might not otherwise have been able to play.

During the war years, Christ Church lost in death Arthur Dent Boice, Edward House Andrews, Lennie G. Latham, Sam M. Allen, and—at 88—Alice Gray Sears. In church and chapel, many weddings were solemnized

1942. Lt. Col. James H. Doolittle commands 16 B-25 bombers from the Carrier Hornet *on bombing raid of Tokyo April 18.*

1942. Women's Army Auxiliary Corps, later WAC, founded May 14 with Oveta Culp Hobby as director.

between young men in uniform and young women, both giving remote cities and states as home address. And in the last two years of the war, there were weddings of these Houstonians: Frances Ruth Lawhon to Edward Atkinson Sullivan, Mary Virginia Dancy to James Estes Baker, Jr., Barbara Wayne Kirkland to Marion Clay Chiles, Lucy Millicent Dancy to William Neilson, Jeanne Suzanne Peck to Dixon Hill Cain, Geraldine Marie Campbell to John Hess Naschke, Martha Virginia Jordan to John Lewis Goodyear, Joanne van den Berge Hill to Pieter Adriaan Cramerus of Holland; Helen Elizabeth Hutchison to Wilbur Allen Ballentine.

In 1943, Christ Church renewed its charter of incorporation under the laws of the State of Texas for another 50 years, and was host to the 94th Diocesan Council meeting. This was also the 42nd annual meeting of the Associated Women of the Diocese, and Mrs. W. E. Japhet of Christ Church was diocesan president. The council meeting was planned to end—Bishop Quin said—the moment the business was done. The Rev. John E. Hines was celebrant of the Holy Communion at 7:30 AM Tuesday, with the Rev. Aubrey C. Maxted, rector of the Church of the Redeemer, the Rev. E. Percy Bartlam of St. Stephen's, the Rev. James Thomas Bagby of St. James, and the Rev. Richard S. Watson of Trinity assisting.

This kind of massive array of clergy was a novelty during the war. Most rectors of the period found themselves attempting to celebrate Holy Communion without curates to assist them, and one Palm Sunday at Christ Church during the war, the Rev. Mr. Hines conducted the entire service without help. It was well past 2 PM before the last communicant had come to the altar rail for communion, and the recessional could begin.

While Christ Church members had started a building fund, the parish was still in debt $40,000 to the bank. The church was feeling a painful need for more room in Sunday School, guild hall, and office building, but it seemed wasteful to spend $20,000 to $30,000 on a make-shift addition.

April 13, 1943, the solution to the problem was offered. Mr. Will and Mr. Sess Cleveland proposed that a $100,000 Latham bequest be made available to Christ Church for a building of general civic use. They explained that together with the Houston Land and Trust Company (Paul Bremond Timpson president) they were executors of the estates of Lucy Latham Boyles and her sister Lennie Groesbeck Latham. Each sister had left $50,000 to be used for civic purposes as a memorial to their father, Captain Lodowick Justin Latham. The exact nature of the civic purposes was left up to the executors. The Cleveland brothers, as grandsons of Captain Latham, thought that a building on the site of the old rectory could serve community and parish needs in a way which would meet the provisions of the two wills.

Christ Church vestry and congregation were tremendously grateful. The issue was taken in a friendly suit before a benign judge. And without difficulty, the Latham funds became available to Christ Church. The Guild Hall was almost entirely given over to the use of men and women in uniform, and the old rectory was being used for so many civic purposes during the war years that the plea certainly seemed legitimate. The Sea Scouts were meeting there regularly, and looked forward each summer to an annual regatta held at the Houston Yacht Club and lasting a week. The *Christ Church Courier* reported that Troop 52 of the Boy Scouts was taking a 1,500-mile trip from Houston to Austin, to the Davis Mountains for a visit to the observatory, then down to Big Bend Country, and back through San Antonio for a look

1942. Allies land 150,000 American and 140,000 British troops in French North Africa November 8 under command of Lt. Gen. Dwight D. Eisenhower.

at the Alamo.

After 20 years and four rectors, Mrs. Tom C. Swope resigned as parish secretary. The rector wrote that he "found her patient with the idiosyncrasies with which new rectors are almost universally afflicted, accurate in her judgment, equally sympathetic with people. . . . She had had a ministry of her own." Charles T. Carnes expressed the vestry's regret. Mrs. Swope, continued as a devoted church member—leaving at her death, some years later, scrap books important to the archives.

To the dismay of the staff, the Y.W.C.A cafeteria was moved. Christ Church was offered the first chance to buy the property (upon which Cleveland Hall now stands), but the vestry declined on grounds that the parish was not interested in acquiring it at this time.

W. E. Japhet, clerk of the vestry, whose boyhood home on Prairie Avenue stood between Christ Church and Court House Square, had been named chairman of a special debt liquidation committee. He reminded the parish that the church had paid $2,027.28 in the preceding year simply in interest on the debt, and that a similar sum would be paid out each year unless the debt could be reduced or wiped out. This money, he reminded, was coming out of the budget, and if the congregation could liquidate the debt, the budget could be reduced or the money could be used for worthwhile things. The debt was brought down to $34,000 on that drive.

The rector appointed C. T. Carnes chairman, and R. W. Wier, Ralph M. Henderson, John R. Suman, John S. Mellinger, and William D. Cleveland, Jr., to the finance committee, and Albert P. Jones was elected chancellor of the parish. The Rev. Frank Ruetz, Jr., came to Christ Church for a few months as assistant to the rector. Arthur W. Howes resigned as organist. Arthur Jack Lane and his wife Pauline Lane willed their house to Christ Church. The Latham bequest of $100,000 went into escrow. And David Alkins of St. John's Episcopal Church, Roanoke, came to Houston as organist.

In the interval between the departure of Mr. Howes and the arrival of Mr. Alkins, Mrs. Albert P. Jones played the organ, and Peter A. Leach served as choirmaster of Christ Church. Mrs. Jones' son Dan was well into first grade or more, but Wishy was still very small. By custom, Albert Jones hung his hat in the nursery room and Wishy was quite content to stay so long as the hat hanging there assured him that his mother and father were still in church. But one Sunday morning as she played an anthem, the Christ Church organist heard a charming small voice saying with confidence, "I come over *here*." Wishy had joined the choir. But his career was brief.

First Charles Desel, so long a steadfast member of Christ Church and its vestry, and then big and beloved William Strauss died. War shortages made it necessary for the vestry to delay ordering bronze plaques for them until conditions should make it possible. Family Day was still being observed and Holy Communion celebrated daily at 7 AM. The Rev. Skardon D'Aubert, who had come to Houston as rector of the Church of the Good Shepherd, was asked to help Christ Church by taking the early week day services until a new curate could be obtained. And the vestry formally declared that Arthur Edward Hartwell was "sober, honest and godly, and a communicant of this church in good standing." Born in Houston and a lifelong member of Christ Church, Mr. Hartwell had gone through Gray Grammar School, had earned his B.S. degree from Massachusetts Institute of Technology in 1909, and had been a successful engineer and for years, president of the Hartwell Iron Works. An

1943. Americans are singing the R.A.F.'s Jolly Sixpence *and the Aussie's* Waltzing Matilda.

1943. President Roosevelt signs the pay-as-you-go income tax bill June 10.

1944. D-Day. Allies invade France June 6 with Gen. Dwight D. Eisenhower as supreme commander of Allied Expeditionary Forces.

194

active lay reader from 1936 on, Mr. Hartwell was now at 58 ready to start a new career in the ministry of the Episcopal Church. The vestry took a special pleasure in recommending this candidate for Holy Orders.

Miss Louise Clemens, daughter of Major and Mrs. Frank Clemens, came in as Christ Church parish secretary, but not to stay. She married Gordon Selig, and went with her husband to Baltimore. Bishop Quin officiated or assisted at several Christ Church weddings: Johnnie Lou Bace to Jack Pulliam Abbott, Rosemary Pearson to Howard William Jacobe, Harriet Ann Richey to George McNally Dow, Elizabeth Naylor to James Howard Park III, and—with Father Smith—Margaret Keith Wiess to James Anderson Elkins, Jr.

These were busy months for the vestry. Vacant lots and lots with houses belonging to the Mitchell estate were sold, one by one, at from $5,000 to $8,000 on average. Maurice Sullivan and M. L. Wirtz were employed as architects for the new Latham Memorial, and William D. Cleveland, Jr., Albert Bowles and Ralph M. Henderson were named to the building committee. The October 3 meeting of the vestry in 1944 was held at River Oaks Country Club in celebration of the birthdays of Mr. and Mrs. Hines.

The Rev. Frank S. Doremus, vicar of St. Paul's Church, Jesup, Georgia, accepted the call to come as curate to Christ Church. A native of Augusta and a graduate of Furman University, Doremus had done his theological work at Virginia Theological Seminary.

The list of telegrams of greetings to former rector and curates, was lengthening and at the parish meeting of 1945, messages went to Lt. (jg) John R. Bentley and Lt. (jg) Frank Ruetz, Jr. Albert Bowles presented plans for the new Latham Memorial. The rector told the parish that the debt had now been brought down to $21,000 and urged that the church be debt free by January 1, 1946. He hoped for an endowment of $200,000 by that date. The parish had lost by death Mrs. George T. Morse, Mrs. Louise Kirkland Haralson, Mrs. Irma Claire Self, Henry D. Aves, Jr., Walter T. Torrey, and Ida Kirkland Mullen (Mrs. Joseph A.) during the year. But a sense of continuity came from the announcement of the birth of John Moore Hines. John R. Suman resigned from the vestry to go to New York having, he said, "accepted added responsibilities in the oil business."

In March, 1945, Mr. and Mrs. Hugh Roy Cullen gave to Bishop Quin $1,000,000 for an Episcopal Hospital in the new Texas Medical Center. He formed a board of the St. Luke's Episcopal Hospital by appointing William D. Cleveland, Jr., president; Captain Edward Kelley, vice president; John H. Crooker, secretary, and R. M. Henderson, treasurer. Episcopalians began to contribute.

In April, 1945, Franklin Delano Roosevelt died suddenly—the pivot around whom the nation had swung through the Depression and all of World War II. Christ Church opened its doors, and Bishop Quin and the Rev. Mr. Hines held a memorial service to which men and women of many churches and many denominations came. "Whatever else history may record of this man," Mr. Hines said, "it can never record that he was dull or colorless, or that he lacked courage. . . . He was a fearless proponent of untried measures, and a merciless critic of traditional failures. He conceived of statecraft as an instrument in the hand of the millions of people he represented—an instrument to be used to belay the terrors of the night. He was not always right, but I believe that he was always honest. . . . He was a man of the most daring imagination, and it was salvation . . . a man who, though he possessed everything, was conscious of his relationship to all men."

Albert Jones, William D. Cleveland, Jr., and Albert Bowles were named to a committee to explore—once again—the matter of a cathedral for the Diocese of Texas. This time the exploration seemed worthwhile, because the 96th Diocesan Council had favored having a cathedral. Christ Church sent $250 to St. Peter's Mission in Pasadena for its building fund, and the young priest in charge, the Rev. Gray M. Blandy, wrote a note of thanks.

But Christ Church felt a sense of suspense. A special council had been called, to be held in Christ Church, Houston, May 22, 1945, and it was to choose a bishop coadjutor. The nominating committee was composed of six clergymen—W. Meade Browne, F. Percy Goddard, Henry F. Selcer, J. Lawrence Plumley, Charles A. Sumners, and George F. Cameron, chairman; and of six laymen—Judge J. Lee Dittert, Colonel James Anderson, Karl Sherman, K. L. Simons, Albert M. Bowles, and A. J. Dow, secretary.

They nominated Theodore Nott Barth, 46, of Memphis; William Gregg Gehri, 49, of Lynchburg, Virginia; William Robert Moody, 45, of Baltimore; Richardson Simpson Watson, 42, of Houston, and John Elbridge Hines, 34, of Houston. All were graduates of the Virginia Theological Seminary. All had distinguished records. Two were rectors of Houston churches: Hines at Christ Church, Watson at Trinity. These were the two youngest men nominated, and of them all, John Hines was the youngest with eight years to spare.

Christ Church sent its delegates: William D. Cleveland, Jr., Joseph W. Tilton, R. W. Horlock, and W. E. Japhet, with Albert Bowles, Albert P. Jones, John S. Mellinger, and C. T. Carnes alternates. The clergy of the diocese were divided between two or three candidates. The laymen were preponderantly for John Hines. Many at the meeting felt that it would take the youngest possible coadjutor to keep up with Bishop Quin who was, after all, only 57 years old himself—though nearing his 25th year as bishop.

The election took less than an hour and a half. Mr. Hines had the majority of both laymen and clergy by the third ballot, and was elected unanimously to become Bishop Coadjutor of the Diocese of Texas. Christ Church was proud and dismayed, happy and sorrowful, and in an affectionate welter of mixed feelings over the outcome. The letter of the vestry reflects this mixture. But there were things to be done.

George Hamman had the early Christ Church records of baptism, marriage and burial photostated and placed in the Houston Public Library. Mr. and Mrs. James Walker Cain sent to the bishop-elect $3,000 as the first move toward building a children's chapel in memory of their son, Walker. "For sentimental reasons, we should like very much to turn over a check to you before you resign as rector of Christ Church." The congregation gave Mr. Hines his bishop's robes, pectoral cross, and Episcopal ring, and decided to clear the church of all debt as a final tribute to this young man who had been their rector for a short four and a half years.

Finally on October 18, 1945, Christ Church saw the second consecration of one of its own rectors, the third consecration of a bishop. The Most Rev. Henry St. George Tucker, presiding bishop, was consecrator. The Rt. Rev. Clinton S. Quin of Texas and the Rt. Rev. Karl Morgan Block, of California who had known John Hines since his first years in the ministry, were co-consecrators. Bishop Everett H. Jones of West Texas, and Bishop C. C. J. Carpenter of Alabama were presenting bishops. The Rt. Rev. William Scar-

1945. U.S. joint expeditionary forces invade Iwo Jima February 19, and Okinawa April 1.

1945. Mussolini is executed by partisans near Lake Como April 28, and Hitler commits suicide with Eva Braun in Berlin April 29-30.

195

lett of Missouri—who had ordained John Hines priest—was preacher.

In his consecration sermon, Bishop Scarlett said "Society is a contract between the living, the dead and the unborn. . . . We have stepped across the threshold of a new age, which calls for a bigger concept and bigger men."

The robed procession of ministers of the consecration included the Rt. Rev. R. Bland Mitchell of Arkansas, the Rt. Rev. C. Avery Mason, co-adjutor of Dallas, the Rt. Rev. John Long Jackson of Louisiana, the Rev. Percy Goddard of St. John's Church, Marlin; the Rev. E. H. Gibson, of Trinity, Galveston; the Rt. Rev. Harry T. Moore, of Dallas; Dr. John M. Trible, secretary of the standing committee; the Rev. Robert R. Brown, St. Paul's, Waco; the Rev. C. Gresham Marmion, Church of the Incarnation, Dallas; the Rev. Thomas Sumners of St. John the Divine, Houston, and the Rev. Henry Selcer of Trinity, Marshall.

The Christ Church Choir, under David Stanley Alkins and Mrs. Orin G. Helvey, was augmented for the consecration by choir members of other Episcopal churches. Anthony E. Rahe, organist of Trinity, assisted. And Albert Bowles was chairman in charge of all the complex arrangements.

Bishop Hines' last sermon in Christ Church was his first as a bishop, and on the day after his consecration, he confirmed three persons: John Hess Naschke, and Mary Clare and David Leonard Gordon. His last service before leaving was the funeral of Robert W. Wier, who had been a steadfast and wise vestryman for so many of the difficult years.

1945. V-E Day comes May 4 when German armies begin surrendering; European war ends May 7.

On their last evening in Houston, Bishop and Mrs. Hines had dinner at Bayou Bend with Miss Ima Hogg, and the next day, the new bishop put his family on the train and turned to the task of shipping off the accumulation of years in office and rectory. He wrote in his diary: "Returned to the rectory to help the movers solve an insoluble problem—how to put too much furniture into too little space. Seized with a mad desire to hold an impromptu auction sale in the middle of Bute Street."

The war had ended with unexpected swiftness, leaving the world to grasp the meaning of the first explosion of an atom bomb and the start of the atomic age. Slowly the men and women who had gone away in uniform came back in civilian clothes to try to fit themselves into a civilian world which offered eager if sometimes awkward welcome.

Christ Church had seen 259 men and women enter the service. Twelve would never return: Charles F. Alton, Jr., Ernest M. Bailey, Jr., Melvin Barnes, Freeman H. Bokenkamp, Harvey E. Burkhalter, Wallace Mason Carnes, Donald James Carter, Gilbert C. Dickinson, Louden C. Doney, III, Robert A. Groth, Joe Berry Kendall, Charles P. Shearn, III. The vestry voted to remodel the entire vestibule of the church as a tribute to the many and a memorial to the twelve. William Ward Watkin was asked to design the memorial entranceway.

The Rev. Frank Doremus submitted his resignation to enable the new rector to select his own curate, but was asked to stay as priest-in-charge until a new rector could take over. Christ Church owned 38 shares of American Telephone and Telegraph, 265 shares of the Borden Company, 100 shares of Radio Corporation of America-common; 540 shares of the Texas Company capital stock, and 132 shares of Houston Lighting and Power Company $4 preferred, all a part of Sidney Mitchell's bequest. On grounds that the value of these stocks was considerably higher than it had been at time of purchase, the vestry decided unanimously that the conservative thing to do was to sell, and instructed Albert Bowles as president of the church corporation to do so. Mrs. Charles Desell, Miss Julia Ideson and Ralph Henderson died. The vestry learned that Mrs. Desell had left the parish $1,000, and that Sterling Myer, whose will had just been probated, had left $2,000—both sums to go to the Endowment Fund. In memory of her sister, Margaret Ideson Schwartz decided to give two alms plates and a basin.

Meanwhile, the rectory and the pulpit were empty. Committee men of the vestry went hunting for a new rector, and soon focused on Colonel Hamilton H. Kellogg, chaplain, United States Army.

Out of Uniform Again

Chapter 40

Houston at war's end was like a city let off a leash. It had raised few new buildings, built few houses during the war, and had seemed congested and crowded, as all American cities did. But V.J. Day and the end of gas rationing gave Houston a catapult start on its jet-age growth. When Bishop Hines left Houston, change had begun. Cars—which had been diagonally parked on Main Street throughout the war—now had to be parked parallel on Main Street to let the increased flow of traffic pass through.

Without being able to explain why, all America had assumed that with the war's end, life would go back immediately to the gentle, spacious ways of 1940—when every restaurant table had a linen table cloth and where there was plenty of space between tables, when houses and apartments and hotel rooms were easily come by, and when a doctor could recommend a nice two-week stay in the hospital for the mothers of new babies. Americans did not realize that the United States had been radically under-built throughout the Depression and throughout World War II, and that at the same time, the nation's population was steadily growing—swelled by newcomers from war damaged countries, burgeoning on the post-war baby boom.

1945. A-bomb is dropped on Hiroshima, Japan, by B-29 bomber August 6, on Nagasaki August 9.

Houston was suddenly inundated by former Houstonians who had been away and were now done with the life of wartime army camps and naval bases, of industrial boom towns and overseas service. And it was inundated by newcomers. Many of those newcomers were young people who had entered the war as college students or recent graduates, and who had come out of the war to enter—somewhat belatedly—the careers they had never had chance to begin. Old Houston was obscured by the newcomers brought here by the oil business, the international cotton business, the mushrooming chemical industry. With the world headquarters of the oil industry, of Anderson-Clayton Cotton Corporation, and Schlumberger Oil Well Surveying Corporation in Houston, interesting young men were brought here for a period of training and then sent out again to the far corners of the world. In that first year, the son of a prime minister of France, the son of a United States Senator, and two German princes were among the hundreds.

They saw a pleasant looking, gulf coast town with wide open skies and palm trees growing in the center of boulevards. They saw streets so full of chugholes that the city's family joke dealt with the car which disappeared into a chughole never to be found again. In 1945, many of the avenues which crossed Main Street in the business section tapered out with surprising suddenness from pavement to gravel. Or if paved, they would be pockmarked by rectangles where half the street had been left unpaved for a distance as great as the width of the front yard of the house facing the street. These

independent Texans had refused to be assessed for the paving, and until someone else bought the house, the city could not collect paving costs from the homesteader.

Houston irritated many newcomers by its shortcomings—though some of these shortcomings were war-caused, and some were because of the new sudden growth. Men who had spent five years overseas or at sea remembered their own home cities in the golden haze of prewar memory. They didn't realize that every city in the United States had suffered from war shortages, reduced staff, rationing, and overpopulation. Brought here by large corporations, moving into brand new subdivisions, many of these new Houstonians saw only each other and jumped to the conclusion Houston was a brash, new city of people who had lived here only a few years.

Those who stayed gradually began to see the old Houston which was the basis and heart of the city. Miss Ima Hogg once said that Houston was fortunate in that the first Houstonians who got rich were nice people—who gave their money to hospitals, churches, schools, art museums and symphonies. This set the pattern, this was what one did when one got rich, with the result that in this city of chug holes and crowded housing, the really important cultural efforts and public welfare causes have always been generously supported.

Christ Church—now more than a century old—stood ready as it had always stood to welcome the newcomers. The first and most important newcomers to Christ Church were the new rector and his wife. Albert Bowles, John Mellinger and Albert Jones were delegated to go to Columbia, South Carolina, to see and hear Colonel Hamilton Hyde Kellogg.

The path of such a delegation is not always smooth. It was even harder to get from Houston to Columbia in 1945 than it is now. They drove to the airport fresh on the news that an aircraft had crashed into the Empire State Building, and they took off on a milk run which landed at Shreveport, Jackson, Birmingham, Atlanta, Augusta and finally—at about midnight—in Columbia. They arrived to find that they had been allotted—a generous allotment in 1945—one single room and one double with twin beds. "John and I conceded that as dean of the delegation, Albert should have the single room," Albert P. Jones remembers with glee. "But when we got upstairs, we found that the double room was air-conditioned and the single room wasn't. We didn't think it proper to let him pull rank on us, but we did leave the other door open and gave him some of our cool air."

The rector at the church was the popular Rev. Louis Chester Melcher, and when the three Houstonians made their portentious appearance, the wary Columbia Episcopalians found it hard to welcome them properly. They were instantly warm and hospitable when they found that the visitors had come to hear the morning's preacher—Colonel Kellogg, chaplain of the First Army stationed at Fort Jackson.

Delighted with Colonel Kellogg's sermon, the delegation went to call on the chaplain and his wife, and were so impressed that Albert Bowles thought it expedient to ask General Hodges how soon they could get Colonel Kellogg out of the Army. The four star general snapped "I don't want to hear that talk." The delegation got home, and caroled so happily about not only Colonel Kellogg but his wife—charming, lovely looking, beautiful singing voice—that W. E. Japhet said "Albert, maybe we made a mistake—maybe we should have called Mrs. Kellogg."

Two weeks later Colonel Kellogg visited Houston, and heard Bishop Hines

1945. United Nations Conference of 46 nations opens in San Francisco April 25 with Senator Arthur Vandenburg representing the U.S.

preach. As they left the church, he said to Albert Bowles and Albert Jones "If you think I can preach like that, you're mistaken!" But the delegation liked its candidate, and though Colonel Kellogg had been offered churches in Philadelphia, St. Paul, San Antonio and Pittsburgh, he accepted Christ Church. He came on January 6, in time for the annual parish meeting.

The contrast between Hines and Kellogg was sharp—and immediately obvious. Kellogg's acceptance published in the Sunday bulletin reflected the war years:

SUBJECT: Acceptance of Call to the rectorship.

TO: The vestry of Christ Church, Houston, Texas.

1.) It is with a great deal of pleasure that I herewith accept the unanimous call to the rectorship of your distinguished and historic Parish which you formally and officially tendered to me in writing under date of 9 August, 1945.

2.) In view of the fact that I am still on duty as a Chaplain in the Army of the United States the date of my actual assumption obviously must be as of an indefinite date. . . .

3.) I am anticipating a *mutually* pleasant and productive relationship with the Vestry and people of Christ Church for many years to come. I regard Houston as a very thrilling and vital city with a tremendous future, and Christ Church as its great, pulsating spiritual heart—a House of God set in the midst of a great city's throbbing life to serve the people in the Blessed Master's Name.

Repectfully and sincerely yours,

HAMILTON H. KELLOGG

Chaplain (Colonel) U.S.A.

First U.S. Army Chaplain.

A native of Skaneateles, New York, Doctor Kellogg had been a gunner in the aviation corps of the United States Marine Corps during World War I, before he entered Williams College, Williamstown, Massachusetts, for his college work. He studied at the General Theological Seminary in New York and in 1924, was made deacon by Bishop Charles Fiske of the Diocese of Central New York, and ordained priest by Bishop Coley. He was priest in charge of St. Albans, Syracuse and St. Mark's, Jamesville; assistant at Christ Church, Greenwich, Connecticut from 1925 to 1929, and rector of St. James Church, Danbury, Connecticut until the start of World War II. In 1929 he married Miss Mildred Haley of Chester, Massachusetts—a graduate of the New England Conservatory of Music, Boston, and the Juillard Foundation, New York. For almost five years, Doctor Kellogg was a chaplain in the United States Army—starting as lieutenant, and ending the war as senior chaplain of the First Army in Europe with rank of colonel. He was awarded the Bronze Star, Army Commendation Ribbon, and the Belgian Croix de Guerre avec Palm. He was—in 1945—46 years old. After the army years, Colonel and Mrs. Kellogg had that ability to start quickly a new home and a new life which those years taught many Americans, and they moved into the Bute Street rectory.

Houston at that time was still a fairly self-contained city geographically. Its outlying residential sections were Garden Villas, Garden Oaks and a Memorial Drive section which ended at Post Oak Road. River Oaks was still the newest of the handsome residential sections consisting of Courtlandt Place, Broad Acres and Shadyside. Though the Hogg family houses had stood for

1945. The women of France and of Japan begin to vote in national elections, and 36 Japanese women are elected to parliament.

many years off Lazy Lane, and though the S. M. McAshan home on Inwood had begun 25 years before as the country house of Mr. and Mrs. Will Clayton, there were still many vacant lots and acres in River Oaks—property which would be quickly bought at rapidly soaring prices and built upon. Tanglewood was unborn.

The Houston Country Club had a gracious, spreading old fashioned club house on rolling ground out toward Harrisburg. River Oaks Club stood at one end of River Oaks Boulevard and Lamar High School at the other.

Rice University was a quiet campus with only a scattering of distinguished, pre-war buildings. The University of Houston had 13,000 students on a campus which as yet had only two or three permanent buildings. Texas Southern University and St. Thomas University were not yet begun.

Fannin Street ended at the Warwick Hotel, and a quiet little avenue ran from Main Street over to the Hermann Hospital. The new Navy Hospital [now the Veterans' Hospital] stood out on the corner of Almeda Road and Bellaire Boulevard, and between the two hospitals, lay a forest of park land. The Texas Medical Center was only an idea.

Between the Navy Hospital and the University of Houston lay one of Houston's most beautiful residential sections—Riverside. The bayou had cut the land to make interesting slopes and knolls upon which the wide yards stretched and the big houses stood.

Houstonians, freed of gas rationing, could go to the bay again, taking any one of several routes, each of them an oddly joined connection of streets and roads, all narrow, all fairly crowded. And they continued to play polo. Major Leslie Dufton, so long the British Consul that he had married into and become a permanent part of Houston, was one whose interest in polo was unflagging, and Robert Farish was another. The players for the most part stabled their horses at the Bayou Club, but the Post Oak area and Tall Timbers were still open land, where the few residents could keep their own horses on their own broad acreage.

Nancy Spencer, daughter of Mrs. Thomas A. Spencer, came home from her tour of the Pacific in a U.S.O. company of *Blithe Spirit,* and her wedding to Dr. James Taylor Heyl was one of the first after the war. The service was read by the Rev. John Bentley, recently returned from Navy duty. Doctor Kellogg officiated at Margaret Neal's wedding to Henry William Dodge, Jr., and at Jacqueline Anne Deering's to Joseph Sims Rose, Jr.

The Rev. Hamilton Kellogg was one of those unusual men who can ride off in all directions—and make it work. Within weeks, all Houston began to sense his presence—or feel the breeze as he passed rapidly by or through. He pushed door bells in every neighborhood of greater Houston, undoubtedly straying over the county line in his forays. He wanted to meet and to know everyone who had ever been a member of Christ Church or ever been an Episcopalian to invite them hospitably back into the parish. And if they had never been Episcopalians or Christ Church members, why weren't they?

Braving the mud of new subdivisions as well as treading the smooth front walks of dignified old ones, giving no heed to the status or the pocketbook of the family who lived behind the door, Doctor Kellogg pursued friendships with hundreds and hundreds of people with vigor, intensity and great effectiveness. He welded newcomers into the old parish with the determination and warmth of his concern, and quickly, new members and old together, began to share what became a continuing and greatly affectionate family joke about the insistent pastoral zeal of their rector.

When at Kellogg's second parish meeting, one new member was invited to say why he had chosen Christ Church for his Houston parish, he gave the shortest speech of the evening: "Because," he said, "Doctor Kellogg wouldn't let me go anywhere else." There was a shout of loving and admiring laughter from all those who had felt Doctor Kellogg's keen, personal interest—and feeling it, had come to Christ Church. For all had soon learned one thing: though his pace was fast, though he never stayed long, though this was only the third or the ninth in a dozen or more calls he would make that evening, he remembered the person, and remembering, cared whether or not they came to church, cared if something went wrong in their lives, expected to be a part of their weddings and baptisms and to prepare them for confirmation.

Having called upon a person once, he remembered the person though not necessarily everything about that person by the second meeting. Doctor Kellogg liked to see and shake hands with every member of the congregation coming out of church, and if he couldn't remember your name, he could at least remember where you lived and might say "906 Hawthorne!" by way of greeting. As the double and triple line of people went by after church, he tended to get swept out of the vestibule, down the steps, out the front gate and onto the sidewalk in his efforts to let no one get by without handshake or greeting. His parishioners began to enjoy the Sunday morning performance and were convinced that by the time he got out to the sidewalk, he was catching innocent passers-by, coming back from Annunciation or going to the railroad station. But no one doubted that if that same stranger should pass again, Doctor Kellogg would remember him and any day now might have his name on the list.

It was—with all the irritations of overcrowding and lingering shortages—a happy time for most people, and an exhilerating time to be in Houston. The sound of building was again in the air throughout this wide city as it had been in the small boomtown the year Christ Church was born in 1839. No major thoroughfare of the downtown section would be completely free of scaffolding at any time in the next 15 years.

Doctor Kellogg's energetic trips into all parts of Houston and into every Houston hospital made him aware of the size of the task he had set himself. He asked that whatever funds could be made available for staff be concentrated on curates and assistants. The Rev. William Byrd Lee Hutcheson and the Rev. Dorsey G. Smith were called and accepted. Both were native Virginians, both graduates of Virginia Theological Seminary. On his arrival, the Rev. Mr. Hutcheson solved his own housing problem by finding a house he could buy under the G.I. Bill—the first introduction of this postwar phenomenon to Christ Church financial records.

In 1945 and 1946, it was impossible for a newcomer to find an apartment or a house to rent, and most hotels still maintained a three-day limit on length of stay. Speaking to a group of young matrons of the St. Anne's Circle in the Ladies Parish Association, Mrs. Clinton Quin said that part of the Christian duty of the Houston churchwomen was to do what she could to help newcomers in these times when it was so hard for strangers to find housing. A visitor went up to Mrs. Quin after the talk, and thanked her for the thought, explaining that she had hunted an apartment intensely for four months without luck. Six months or more later, strolling across Rice Institute campus wearing a cap and gown for the inauguration of Dr. William Vermilion Houston, this same newcomer heard her name being called—it was Mrs.

1946. The League of Nations, Geneva, closes its work and gives its physical assets to the United Nations April 13.

Quin. Holding her own mortar board on to keep it from flying away as she came rapidly across the grass, Mrs. Quin called "Did you ever find an apartment?" This one new Houstonian learned then that like the bishop, Mrs. Quin could remember a face under the most differing circumstances, and hitch to that face all the important facts of name and need.

That year, Mrs. Quin had 36 clergy wives as her houseguests on Mandell. During each council which met in Houston, Mrs. Quin invited the wife of every clergyman in the diocese to come frivol in Houston while her husband pontificated. Staying at the Quins', the clergy wives were treated to country club luncheons, fashion shows, shopping trips and allowed time to see Houston friends they hadn't seen in a year.

At this time there were few air conditioned houses in Houston. Most houses were heated by floor furnaces or steam radiators, and cooled by attic fans. Houses were designed carefully to catch the prevailing breeze from the gulf, and informed shoppers bought houses facing north so that the back yard and screened porch would be breezy enough to make summer evening parties pleasant. There were few residential swimming pools. Proper Houstonians entertained in the garden in summer with the same gentle elegance of dress and service they were accustomed to indoors in winter. The postwar newcomers from out of Houston and out of Texas, with their penchant for ranch style houses, were the first to bring in the patio fashions of dress and western refreshments which prevailed in the late 1940's and early 1950's—until total air conditioning returned parties to the indoors.

By the time Doctor Kellogg's two assistants got to Houston, he already had 85 candidates ready for confirmation, and six months later Bishop Quin's diary shows: "Confirmed my largest class—106—and finally preached at Christ Church, Houston."

The Texas City blast in April, 1947, came only a few days after Doctor Houston was inaugurated as second president of Rice Institute. Houston clergy and both bishops went to see what help they could be to Mr. Doremus, formerly of Christ Church, who had, after a brief period in Kilgore, become rector of St. George's. Bishop Hines wrote, "The Rev. Frank Doremus was standing like a rock in the midst of our badly hurt people."

By spring of 1947, pledges in the diocese toward St. Luke's Hospital reached $557,000, and of this, Doctor Kellogg reported, $53,000 had come from Christ Church. And Christ Church gave to Bishop Hines $500 to go toward sites for other Episcopal churches in the Houston area. Mrs. Lulu Bryan Rambaud, Mrs. C. S. Cushing, Mrs. H. L. Thompson, and Mrs. Margaret Childress Stuart died in this period. Doctor Kellogg counted 200 confirmations in 1946 and 254 in 1947, 206 transfers in 1946 and 275 in 1947, and for total communicants, the number went up from 2,158 to 2,563. "All baptized persons in the congregation—3,926."

Christ Church saw the weddings of Neely Proctor to Joseph Eggleston Gardner, of Nancy McLean to Richard Harlan Suman, Laura Muir McClellan to John Julyan Clemens, Edith Louise Japhet to Clifton Eugene King, Anne Francis to Stephen Power Farish, Jr.

The Reverend Dorsey Smith resigned to become rector of St. Paul's Church, Houston, and the Rev. Harold O. Martin came in as assistant. A native of Maryland, Mr. Martin had gone to Washington College, and earned his bachelor of divinity at the theological school of the University of the South. As an Anglo-Catholic, Martin preferred to be called "Father Martin," and

1947. Undersecretary of State for Economic Affairs Will Clayton drafts first memorandum for general European recovery program May 23-27.

though only a few Christ Church members had ever got around to calling Bishop DeWolfe "Father DeWolfe"—or affectionately "Father Jim"—the passage of years made it easy for a great many people to call this young man Father Martin.

Doctor Kellogg had made this selection deliberately. Not content with the obvious success of his pastoral outreach, Doctor Kellogg felt that he must give the Anglo-Catholics in Christ Church an opportunity to worship in the way that suited them best. Then a deacon recently ordained in Christ Church, the Rev. Frank MacDonald Spindler observed and admired this balance, and wrote recently: "Doctor Kellogg recognized the existence of varying shades of spiritual experience and life in the parish, and he tried to provide for them, rather than to force the parish into a single mould. Hence his variety in the composition of the staff: William Byrd Lee Hutcheson as an Evangelical Canon, Martin as a High Churchman or Anglo-Catholic, and himself as the via media." Using the beautiful Golding Chapel, Father Martin celebrated the 9:30 Sunday morning services and week-day Eucharist with full ceremonial.

John Flanagan, chairman of the every member canvass in 1948, reported that pledges the year before numbered 1,073 and totaled $65,000, that in 1948, 1,119 pledges were received totaling $73,661.50. Both these totals marked achievement beyond the goals set. And Major Frank Clemens, born in the rectory, the voice of common sense and reason for so many years on the vestry, died. Bishop Quin assisted Doctor Kellogg at the funeral of this churchman he had known since his own young manhood.

Bishops in this period were getting about mostly by automobile, which were not air conditioned, trains which were, and planes which were giving up their old tendency under wartime priorities to bump passengers unceremoniously. Many of Bishop Hines' trips were made by private planes offered by Episcopalians. As another sign of the era, he was asked to bless a geiger counter. Television was still comparatively new throughout the United States, and on a trip to St. Louis, Bishop Hines experienced his first telecast. This meant, he reported in his diary, that the church service was invading bars and nightclubs because that was almost the only place TV sets were to be found.

On his return, Bishop Hines made deacon Robert Huie Reid, Jr., Bishop Hines' first ordination—and saw the Rev. Mr. Reid and his wife (Suzanne Greenwell) off to missionary work in Alaska.

Christ Church saw the weddings of Kay Hogan to Barton Wilfred Bartholomew, Mary Ellen Fields to John Dow, Jr., Jane Frances Denton to Herman Hale, Jr. (the parents of both had married in Christ Church a generation earlier), and Kathleen Blakely Gordon to William Thomas Peckinpaugh, Jr.

And in 1948, Bishop and Mrs. Quin sailed on the *Queen Mary* for the Lambeth Conference—a happy trip. Mrs. Quin had instructed her husband that he must not call any of the royalty they might meet "Sister," but at a cornerstone laying ceremony, he made the then Queen Elizabeth giggle by whispering "Sister, do you know how to handle that trowel?"

Christ Church and the Diocese were offering encouragement to the growing educational program of education on alcoholism—a new approach to an old, often fatal illness. Long a supporter of Alcoholics Anonymous, Bishop Quin went to a luncheon at which Marty Mann, president of the National Council on Alcoholism, was speaker, and a partnership of cooperation was laid between the church in Houston and this educational movement which proved to be a lasting one.

1947. The U.N. Security Council votes unanimously to place all Pacific Islands formerly controlled by Japan under U.S. trusteeship.

At last in 1948—after almost a full century of not-always-contented ownership—Christ Church moved the last remains to Brookside and sold the old Episcopal Cemetery property to the City of Houston for $52,500. The site of the historic cemetery became a parking lot.

The Diocese of Texas observed its Centennial in Christ Church by making Christ Church the pro-cathedral of the diocese. This measure did not come easily.

Chapter 41

Cathedral—Con and Pro

In January, 1946, the month of Hamilton Kellogg's arrival in Houston, Bishop Quin had asked the Diocesan Council to designate a cathedral church for the diocese. And aware that Christ Church was the mother church in the biggest city of the diocese, Doctor Kellogg appointed a vestry committee to look into all the possible problems and ramifications which cathedral status would bring.

In January, 1947, the council's cathedral committee recommended that Christ Church, Houston, be designated cathedral. It seemed a logical, sensible move. But it took another year of negotiations to form the agreement. Though Christ Church vestrymen had flirted with the idea of cathedral status for 25 years, when the chance came, a surprising number of parishioners were opposed: they feared loss of sovereignty. Albert P. Jones, with much advice from Albert Bowles, worked with J. L. C. McFadden of Beaumont in drawing up the agreement between parish and diocese.

"Actually," Mr. Jones said, "there was never any suggestion that Christ Church be a cathedral. There are only two in the nation, National Cathedral in Washington and St. John the Divine in New York. To be a cathedral would mean that Christ Church would have given up its parish, but it also would have meant that the diocese would have to support us. It was therefore only thought that Christ Church would be a pro-cathedral."

The agreement was drawn up with many debates on fine points—fine points which have never since risen up to bother anyone. And when it became known throughout the diocese that both Trinity Church, Houston, and St. John the Divine, Houston, were willing to take the responsibility of cathedral status if Christ Church were in the least reluctant, the opposition suddenly lessened.

At last in January, 1948, the rector took the cathedral question to the parish in a clear statement in the *Christ Church Bulletin*. Christ Church would, he explained, retain all parish identity, remaining self-governing, self-supporting, and in full control of its investments, and would continue its regular parish activities and services under leadership of rector and vestry. The Cathedral Church would be available for diocesan functions when not in conflict with stated services of the parish. The rector would become dean of the pro-cathedral but continue as rector of the parish. Christ Church would provide property for a diocesan building for offices, and upkeep of that building would be a diocesan expense.

"If the existence of a Cathedral Church will further the work of Our Lord in this diocese, a cathedral should be designated," Doctor Kellogg wrote. "Christ Church, as the Mother Parish . . . and with its strategic location and strength is the logical choice." At the parish meeting which came the next

1948. Mohandas K. Gandhi, lifelong champion of freedom for India, is shot and killed by a Hindu fanatic January 30.

Tuesday, Albert Bowles presented the committee agreement, and John H. Crooker of the vestry moved its acceptance. The parish voted 204 to 13 to accept cathedral status. And at the Centennial Meeting of the Council in 1949, Christ Church was consecrated as the cathedral, and Hamilton Hyde Kellogg was installed first dean.

Bishop Quin put the whole business in scale when he wrote, "This grand old Parish started us on our way, and continues to blaze the trail. You are, as of today, proclaimed the Cathedral Parish of the Diocese of Texas. The word cathedral means seat. The bishops in this diocese have always had a seat, but until this occasion, we were never asked to come in and sit down. So this is the seat of the Bishop of Texas, and I count myself honored also in this new partnership. May God bless each one of you."

It was a gay and ceremonial council. Bishop and Mrs. Quin had open house in the bishop's house on Mandell, and 750 came.

In the same month, Ann Wier—daughter of Mrs. Robert Wier and the late Mr. Wier—married Dr. Dan McNamara, a young man just at the start of a career as a pediatric heart specialist—and Nancy McFarlane married William Bonner. Bishop Quin, Father Smith, and Dean Kellogg together read the funeral service for Torrey James Bettes, and there were other deaths: Frank Preston Harrison, Samuel Farrow Styles, William Michael Elkins among them.

Lt. Lamar Fleming III, who had been shot down over Germany during the Battle of the Bulge and buried in a military cemetery in France, was brought home to Houston, and Bishop Quin read the burial service for him in the Christ Church Chapel before the casket was taken to Glenwood Cemetery. And word came from Alaska that young Robert Huie Reid, who had gone off so hopefully to serve the church in Alaska, had drowned.

Nancy White married Robert Farrington Flagg, and at the reception after at the old Houston Country Club, the receiving line stretched for a block through the balmy night.

The Rev. Arthur Hartwell solemnized the wedding of Marjorie Brown to Edward Mussey Hartwell, his son who was also entering the ministry. Dean Kellogg, sometimes with Bishop Quin or Bishop Hines, officiated at the weddings of Margaret Bondurant Jarvis to Durward Richard Anderson, Fanny Wortham Davis to Arthur Chester Diehl, Jr., of New York, Mary Louise Fitch to Harold Marion Soule, Marian Joan Potter to Joseph Stephen Cullinan, Bette Anne Bettes to Frank Jefferson King, Beverly Anita Frambach to Clifton Reedy Caldwell, Jr., Maud Michaux Powell to Dr. Russell J. Leonard, Elizabeth Avon Smith to Craddock K. Duson, Patricia Ann Shepherd to David T. Wells. And when Mary Olivia Fuller of 5319 Cherokee married Horace Maxwell Orfield, she was the second bride from the second Christ Church family marrying from that address—the first was Betty Brewster.

With 3,699 church members, and 433 children in the Sunday school, with Bishop Quin and Dean Kellogg and the cathedral staff clambering in hot weather and cold, rain and hail, up the outside staircase to the second floor offices in the old rectory, Christ Church Cathedral needed the long envisioned Latham Memorial Building with increasing urgency.

Up to this midpoint in his rectorship, Dean Kellogg had had as a quiet source of "generous, gentle, kind and loving wisdom," Mr. Will Cleveland. He had had as successive senior wardens Albert Bowles and Charles T. Carnes, and as successive junior wardens, Albert Jones, A. Munson Goodyear and W. E. Japhet. These men with John Crooker, August L. Selig, Arthur Terrell, James Walker Cain, W. J. Goldston, John Flanagan, John S. Mellinger, David L. Gordon, Joe W. Tilton, James Elkins, Jr., and General Roy Heflebower were among the many who supported Dean Kellogg in his vigorous pastorship. And with the cathedral issue settled, the big task ahead was building the Latham Building.

The Latham memorial bequest had grown now to $110,000. Mr. and Mrs. James Walker Cain had so far given $5,000 toward the children's chapel, but building costs were rising each year and at last count were $10.50 a square foot. Malcolm McCorquodale, speaking for the Diocese, reported that funds were not yet available for the diocesan section of the building to be built. But in July, 1950, the vestry decided to go ahead. July 28, 1950, the massive rectory which had stood since 1902 was razed to make way for a $400,000 brick building designed by Maurice Sullivan, to be named the Captain Lodowick Justin Latham Building. This would be the major part of a $500,000 expansion program which would include the diocesan office building to go up on the parking lot back of the old rectory. In September, 1950, the trustees of the Bishop Quin Foundation authorized to the diocese a grant of $50,000 and a loan not to exceed $45,000 for the purpose of building permanent offices.

Albert Bowles was chairman of the building committee, and once again began the task of innumerable letters, innumerable telephone calls, a thousand details and decisions, which he had carried at the time of the rebuilding after the fire, and which W. V. R. Watson had so often carried a generation earlier.

Meanwhile the Y.W.C.A. had sold their property to the Taylor Jewelry Company, which meant that Christ Church could no longer use parts of that building for Sunday school rooms. Sunday school space had been cramped for decades. Office space had been cramped forever. Now suddenly, Sunday school and offices had to be dumped out of the old rectory, out of the Y.W.C.A. building, into the Guild Hall, and for almost two years, it's a wonder that either Sunday school teachers or clerical staff ever got anything done at all. Christ Church and diocesan records got mixed up at this time, and it is likely that many records important to the archives of both were lost.

There were many weddings in chapel and cathedral church in the early 1950s: Carroll Sterling Cowan to Harris Masterson, III, with the Rev. Arthur Knapp officiating; Mary Catherine Farrington to William James Miller, Jr., with the Rev. Thomas Sumners officiating; Virginia Randolph Baugher to Francis Parke Smith, Jr., with the Rev. Gray M. Blandy officiating; Eva Wilson to Kenneth Stuart Mandell, Jr., Virginia Ann Fitch to Ralph Gordon Berkeley, Jr., Jerauld May Lollar to Raymond Monroe Hill, Sue Evelyn Ledbetter to Paul Gervais Bell, Jr., Virginia Cleveland Kirkland to Warren Batjer Pond, Jr., Eliza Lovett to Edward Randall, III, of Galveston; Clare Elizabeth Masterson to Jesse Lee Worsham, Jr., Martha Mathilde McGarrity to Boyd H. Watkins, and with Dean Kellogg officiating, Mary Withrow Wier married John Caldwell Meeker at St. John the Divine.

The Rev. J. Milton Richardson of St. Luke's Church, Atlanta, Georgia, was speaker at the 112th annual parish meeting which marked Dean Kellogg's fifth anniversary at Christ Church. Christ Church parishioners had not before seen Mr. Richardson, but he had seen Christ Church three or four years earlier. During a stopover in Houston on his way to Dallas, Mr. Richardson had made a point of going to see the old church whose three previous rectors he knew, and he decided then that it had one of the most beautiful chancels he had ever seen. This undoubtedly added to his conviction when he spoke to the parish dinner on the importance of a strong downtown church to the life of the Episcopal Church in a big city. "Mr. Richardson, speaking most eloquently with his pleasant southern accent, left a most profound impression with every member present . . . ." This visit added to the growing respect and liking which Dean Kellogg and Mr. Richardson had begun to hold for each other since meeting at the General Convention in San Francisco in 1949.

By March, even the Guild Hall had to be given over the the builders, but it was all going to be worthwhile. Behind the high fences which enclosed the excavations, concrete was being poured and structural steel placed. The plans called for a first floor with an entry, 10 classrooms, kitchen, and rest rooms, and on the second floor, an auditorium seating 350 with stage, six classrooms, and seven parish offices. A separate section of the second floor would also hold four diocesan offices, chapel, and chapter room, and another nine diocesan offices would go on a third floor covering part of the total floor plan. Equipment room, laundry, Boy Scout room, would be in the basement.

In this period—with the Korean War on—Episcopalians throughout the diocese were maintaining a prayer vigil at the request of Bishop Quin. Somewhere at every minute of the day and night in some church in the diocese, some churchman or churchwoman was in front of an Episcopal altar, praying for peace. Each time Christ Church's turn rolled around, volunteers were assigned their hour, and many a Christ Church member learned a new feeling of oneness with the old church—a new sense of the strength of prayer—in going alone at 5 AM or 9 PM to kneel for an hour asking God as earnestly as he knew how to give human kind one more chance at building world peace.

By April, the vestry was beginning to tote up costs: Total cost, $434,000, including air conditioning, architect fees, and kitchen equipment. Of this the Diocese of Texas would bear $93,000, the Latham Bequest was now worth $107,000, leaving $234,000 to Christ Church—plus some $19,600 for renovation of the Guild Hall for a total of $254,000. Pledges from the 1949 building fund campaign, unpaid and collectable, amounted to $58,-400, bringing assets up $150,000 in round numbers. In April, the vestry started a building fund campaign to raise an additional $94,000. Joseph W. Tilton was chairman.

With the lawn a mass of construction materials, equipment, and dug-up earth, the Ladies Parish Association held the May fete at Montrose School with Mrs. Norman Sick chairman. Among men of the church who were ushers in this period were Ross Bennett, David Quentin Bates, Roy Cox, Kelley M. Fogg, Daffan Gilmer, Gentry Kidd, James P. Rembert, General Roy Heflebower, Marion Law, Merrick Phelps, Ralph Gunn, Dr. Edward T. Clarke, William S. Clarke, K. A. Frambach, H. Grant Thomas—a different group every Sunday. Among the active acolytes were Allen Brady, Tommy Terry, Bill Sick, Jimmy McGlothlin, Don Ray, Jimmy Ray, Dan Jones, David Schepp, Donald Derby, Thomas Walker, Frank Ennis, David Bratton, Bill Dobbs, Russell Wofford, Jim Davis, Reggie Ennis, Jim Williford, Jim Neff, Bill Mount, Jerry Schnepp, Jerry Logan, David Sellars, Bill Williamson, Ronnie Laughter, Andy Estes, Alvis McConnell, Kenneth Mandell and Marston Watson.

1950. Two Puerto Rican fanatics attempt to shoot their way into Blair House to kill President Truman.

Holly Hall was begun with Bishop Quin breaking the ground. St. Stephen's School, Austin, observed its first anniversary. And the summer program was announced for Camp Allen—the camp made possible to so many diocesan activities through the generosity of Mrs. Rosa Allen.

Through all the extracurricular demands of that year, Dean Kellogg continued his pastoral outreach to newcomers. He went unasked and came when needed to his parishioners. His sermons, which in the immediate months after V.J. Day had so often struck a military note, had become increasingly universal in their approach and their appeal. Once a shy boy, he spoke of the hard road he had walked through his introverted college years to learn that all human beings welcome—and perhaps need desperately—to be spoken to and met half way. No adolescent, and no one with a memory of adolescence, went away that Sunday without a warmer understanding of the walls of shyness which so often separate every individual from every other.

He spoke with clarity and conviction on "The Immaculate Conception and the Virgin Birth," clearing the confusion which exists in many minds between the two. He spoke on "The Unchristian Tongue," and no one has greater right. As his successor, Dean Richardson, recently said, "Dean Kellogg more than any one I have ever known would find it impossible to hold a grudge against anyone or to speak or think unkindly of him."

One parish bulletin spoke out clearly on "The Christian Burial" and the rector recommended: 1) let the service be held in church. Most homes are too small and poorly designed for the purpose, and even a beautiful funeral home cannot create the atmosphere that a church can for the Episcopal service. 2) If music is desired, let it be the great Easter hymns . . . the use of favorite hymns and sentimental music usually increase the sufferings of those who mourn. 3) Reduce floral offerings to a minimum—for the casket only and from relatives. Let others contribute to a church need or to a charitable institution. 4) Do not be extravagant in casket, cemetery plot, or headstone. Our loved ones do not live in the ground, they reside in the spacious fields of eternity.

And seemingly all year, he gathered the jokes which he would tell in a barrage at the annual parish dinner, making that evening as gay as the red flower in his wife's blonde hair as she and other members of the Ladies Parish Association served dinner.

When the Petroleum Club was first organized and planning its new quarters on top of the Rice Hotel, Dean Kellogg grew interested. The Christ Church rector always has a membership in River Oaks Country Club, but Dean Kellogg thought how pleasant it would be for visiting ministers and bishops, so often lodged at the Rice during a week of missions, to be able to use the club for any scant moments of relaxation they might find. He asked one of his friends about a membership.

"It's only for the oil industry," his friend said regretfully.

"Well," said Dean Kellogg with conviction, "ministers spread oil on troubled waters." On this unchallengeable logic, the friend presented the matter to the admissions board, and special memberships were made available to the clergy of the city.

June 3, 1951, Bishop Quin and Dean Kellogg laid the cornerstone for the combined Latham Memorial and Diocesan buildings. More than 35 parishes of the diocese were represented at the ceremony. Gradually the Guild Hall came back into use. Major H. A. Schumacher was Sunday school superin-

1951. UN General Assembly names Communist China the aggressor in Korea February 1, and votes arms embargo against China May 18.

tendent, and Wayne D. Close assistant, setting up first temporary and then permanent arrangements as additional space was completed and opened. In October, Christ Church celebrated with a series of four fellowship suppers in the new Guild Hall. Dividing the congregation up into four groups alphabetically, Dean Kellogg and his staff and members of the vestry played host each night for four nights.

On Loyalty Sunday a new cypress cross was dedicated and put atop the tower. The Fifth Annual Epiphany Feast of Lights Festival was held and the 113th parish dinner, and 91 were confirmed. And after five years of close association, the Rev. Mr. Hutcheson, who had been made a canon of the cathedral, resigned to accept the Church of the Good Shepherd in Richmond, Virginia.

A plaque was dedicated showing the names of those honored by the gifts of memorial lights in the Nave and Transept. Several of these memorials have been mentioned earlier, but in addition, there was the gift in memory of her son and daughter, Harry and Ethel, by Mrs. Emma V. Hesse; of John J. Sweeney by John S. Mellinger; of Ella B. Q. Perlitz by C. A. Perlitz, C. B. Quarles and Dorothy Quarles Dick; of her son Henry B. Verhelle, Jr., by Mrs. Henry Verhelle; of Mary Ann Sweeney by Mrs. James L. Britton; of their sister "Little Minnie" by Mrs. Lula Bryan Rambaud, Chester L. Bryan, and Mr. and Mrs. Louis A. Bryan; of John F. Sullivan II and Edward A. Sullivan by Mrs. Sullivan, and "in thanksgiving for Eliza G. Wilson" by Mrs. Eddie A. Sullivan.

The Rev. Keith Bardin, chaplain of Episcopal students at the University of Texas, accepted the call to succeed Canon Hutcheson. A native of Kentucky, Mr. Bardin had been graduated from the University of the South and studied at General and at Union Theological seminaries in New York before his ordination by the Rt. Rev. Charles Clingman, bishop of Kentucky—and former rector of Trinity Church, Houston. Lane Denson, a theological student at the newly-established Seminary of the Southwest, Austin, spoke at Christ Church. Bishop Quin told a story and conducted the annual Easter afternoon children's service where all the Sunday school children bring their mite boxes and flowers to build a cross of living flowers. And Dean Kellogg— elected bishop coadjutor of the Diocese of Minnesota—resigned.

This was not the first call which had come to him, but this was the call he felt he must take. And he wrote to Christ Church members, "It will not be easy for me to leave you whom I know so well and love so truly." While vestry committees flew off in several trips to hunt a new dean, Dean Kellogg offered a last class of 93 for confirmation, welcomed the Kinkaid School's baccalaureate service to Christ Church, finished his tasks as chairman of Armed Forces Day, and on Sunday afternoon, June 8, assisted Bishop Quin and Bishop Hines in the dedication of the Latham Memorial, Cathedral Parish House and Diocesan Building. Albert P. Jones, for the cathedral and vestry, presented Albert M. Bowles with a testimonial scroll of appreciation for his work as chairman of the building program.

The farewell parties—official and personal ones—were loving, proud, and regretful. The parish gave to their dean the Episcopal ring, the pectoral cross and the robes he must have as bishop. He invited his first junior warden, Albert P. Jones, to come with him to Minnesota as the layman who would read the certificate of his ordination at the consecration service. And finally, Dean Kellogg made one last charge to his congregation—a charge aimed at re-

1951. Gertrude Lawrence and Yul Brynner open on Broadway in The King and I *March 29.*

1951. President Truman relieves General Douglas MacArthur of his command in the Far East April 11.

minding the congregation that the church was theirs historically—theirs to maintain, theirs to preserve for future generations, not a container to be picked up and discarded when the rector inside was gone.

"Frequently there is a curious feeling in the hearts of some church folks that the best and strongest way to fulfill their loyalty to the priest who has just left them is through withholding it from his successor, for a while anyhow. Please remember that my successor, whoever he may be, did not apply for the deanship here, nor did he dismiss me. He will be invited by the vote of the vestry who are your elected representatives . . . He will not do everything as I have done it any more than I have done things as Bishop DeWolfe or Bishop Hines did them . . . . I urge you not to look back for the purpose of observing the contrast and difference between us . . . . Whatever looking back is done will be, I hope, only for the purpose of fond and pleasant remembrance of the days when we were privileged to work together for the glory of God in and through the life of this wonderful parish . . . . It is not the individual who counts; it is the cause . . . . Carry on so the next chapter in the life of our beloved cathedral will be one of even greater and more joyful service."

Chapter 42

1951. "Peaceful liberation" of Tibet announced by Communist China May 27.

The Exodus

In the spring of 1952, Christ Church Cathedral had much to offer a new dean. The vestry committee looked into two or three possibilities, but Dean Kellogg, busy with preparations to go to Minnesota for his consecration, obviously favored J. Milton Richardson of Atlanta as his successor.

One Sunday morning, Judge John H. Crooker turned up at both services at St. Luke's Church, Atlanta, and though he said he was there for a Masonic meeting, St. Luke's senior warden was upset—he knew all the signs when he saw them. In a long afternoon conference with Mr. Richardson, Judge Crooker said he was chairman of the committee hunting a successor to Dean Kellogg. "I was greatly impressed by Judge Crooker," Dean Richardson recalls, "and felt attracted to any church which had even one member of this calibre." Mr. and Mrs. W. A. Kirkland, on their way back from a bank meeting in New York, dropped by St. Luke's. Noticing the handsome couple, Mr. Richardson made a point of meeting them in the hope of getting them for St. Luke's, but they said they were just passing through. These were the preliminaries.

Not long after, when Mr. Richardson was in New York for a two week course at Union Theological Seminary, Judge Crooker telephoned to ask if a committee from Christ Church could come to see him. "I was staying at the Abbey Hotel," Dean Richardson said, "because it was one of the few air conditioned hotels in New York at the time. My fellow ministers at the seminary thought I was high hatting the dormitory, and I'm sure that Albert Jones and August Selig thought I was slumming. But when they came, I was struck by the fact that Christ Church should have such a young senior warden and vestryman as August and Albert."

The three went to St. Bartholemew's that Sunday, with Mr. Richardson feeling in a quandary. "I was gloriously happy at St. Luke's" he says, "but I felt that if they asked me, maybe I should go. Certainly, a call from any church—however small or little known—must be given serious consideration. And I remember thinking 'If I can hold off 20 minutes without their calling me, that means I'm home free!' " But Selig and Jones issued the call.

Feeling he would get little out of the remaining lectures, Mr. Richardson flew to Chicago to see Dr. Joseph G. Moore, who taught parish administration at Seabury-Western Theological Seminary and had recently made a study of Christ Church. He then stopped in Richmond to ask the Rev. William B. L. Hutcheson about the situation in Houston. Then with his wife, he flew to Houston where they were met by A. L. Selig and Albert P. Jones.

"Judge Crooker joined us, Mr. Mellinger had us to River Oaks Country Club for dinner, I went to all three services Sunday and someone looked after me at each one—changing the guard at 7:30, 9:30, and 11. The Seligs had us and the Quins to dinner at the old Houston Country Club. It was all charming." Always thorough, Mr. Richardson studied the Sunday school, met Harold Martin and Keith Bardin, talked with the staff, went to see other Episcopal churches, visited James Clements whom he'd known in seminary. It was July. The rectory which had stood closed since June was searingly hot when they walked in. "But when I got back home," the dean remembers, "Atlanta had never been hotter. And this made Houston seem not so hot."

Born in Sylvester, Georgia, James Milton Richardson earned his B.A. at the University of Georgia and membership in Phi Beta Kappa and Omicron Delta Kappa. He received his master's at Emory University, and studied at the Virginia Theological Seminary. After his ordination by the Rt. Rev. Henry Judah Mikell, he became priest-in-charge of the tiny St. Timothy's Church in suburban Atlanta. Two years later he accepted the call as assistant at St. Luke's Church, and married Eugenia Brooks, daughter of Dr. Preston Brooks, dean of the University of Georgia.

For three years, Mr. Richardson continued as assistant in St. Luke's Church to John Moore Walker (later Bishop of Atlanta), and his successor, George P. Gunn (now bishop of South Virginia) and in 1943, at the age of 30, became rector of the big metropolitan Atlanta church, the largest parish in the state of Georgia.

When Mr. Richardson came to Houston, he was 39 years old, and national president of the Alpha Tau Omega fraternity. St. Luke's, Atlanta, had now sent two rectors to Christ Church in 66 years. Mr. Beckwith came alone in 1886. But in September, 1952, the new dean brought with him his merry dark-haired wife, three children (Jim, 10, Genie, 8, and Joan, 6). With them came his tall, soft-voiced mother, Mrs. J. M. Richardson, Sr., who with gentle but queenly dignity is known by every one as "Pal."

Christ Church had never looked so good. The Latham Building had been finished during the summer, and was ready for the new dean. The Diocesan Building stood adjoining on San Jacinto, and the Guild Hall was freshly remodeled. But between Dean Kellogg's departure in June and Dean Richardson's arrival in September, members had drained out of Christ Church Cathedral in a startling exodus.

The communicant strength plummeted.

There were perhaps two major reasons: First, in the immediate postwar years, a tremendous number of Christ Church members—old Houstonians and new—had moved out to the new sections stretching farther and farther out from town. Many, who had looked with interest at the new and more convenient neighborhood churches, chose the summer between deans as

1952. President Truman orders U.S. seizure of the steel mills to avert a strike by 600,000 CIO United Steelworkers.

the best time to go. Second, the almost two years of disrupted Sunday School had prompted many young married couples to take their children to other Sunday schools nearer home. When Dean Kellogg left, it seemed simpler to join the children in the neighborhood than to transfer them back to Christ Church which had a brave new building, but a still unknown academic future.

Christ Church Cathedral lost 448 members that year—the largest single loss in its history, the largest loss in the diocese that year, and it accounted for more than half of all the losses reported in the diocese that year.

Throughout Houston, neighborhood churches gained: Palmer Memorial, 8; the Good Shepherd, 13; St. Francis, 106; St. James, 66; St. John the Divine, 159; St. Mark's, 68; St. Martin's, 203; and St. Michael's, 191. Not all these gains came from Christ Church. And of the cathedral's losses, some were among people transferred out of Houston by the companies or military service which had first brought them here, and some were from death.

"I had had my natural qualms about coming to Christ Church Cathedral," Dean Richardson says candidly. "I had heard Bishop Quin say that in DeWolfe, Hines, and Kellogg, Christ Church had had a great priest, a great preacher and a great pastor. Naturally I had wondered what was left for me to contribute. When this exodus happened, all I knew was not to panic, to let those who wished winnow out without reproaches, and then to build with what we had left. I hoped to maintain as much as possible the preaching of Hines and the pastoral out reach of Kellogg, but felt that we must add a strong educational program for the Church school.

"I believe that Christian education is the keystone to any parish. It is essential to have a high quality of Sunday school to attract children and bring in young couples. The downtown church must," Dean Richardson said with conviction, "have its share of youth."

Fortunately, Dean Richardson had with him a strong vestry, composed of A. L. Selig, senior warden; R. E. Robertson, junior warden; John S. Mellinger, treasurer; John Crooker, chancellor; Floyd Temple, clerk; James A. Elkins, Jr., comptroller; James Bradbury, James L. Britton, Edwin Rice Brown, John C. Flanagan, Erwin R. Heinen, Albert P. Jones, W. A. Kirkland, Dr. F. O. McGehee, Jasper A. Neath, and J. E. Sick.

Fortunately too, the dean had a deep conviction in the importance of the downtown church—first expressed in his speech to the parish dinner in 1951. "A communion cannot have a dominating influence upon a city unless in addition to residential churches it also has a virile and vital downtown church," he said. "The responsibilities of Christ Church Cathedral are unique because of its location in the central business district of a metropolitan area, its numerical size, and its financial strength. Such a downtown center of city-wide influence should strengthen the entire Episcopal life of Houston. If we do our work well in the Cathedral, every Episcopal Church in this whole area will be stronger. It is my hope that Christ Church will increasingly become the effective ally of every church in Houston and the Diocese."

Dean Richardson began by trying to meet everyone in the parish through a series of cottage meetings in the various neighborhoods. In his first month, the meetings were held in the homes of Mr. and Mrs. William C. Perry, 2708 Nottingham; Mr. and Mrs. Leonard W. Cannon, 1360 Chippendale; Mr. and Mrs. E. T. Chew, 424 Hathaway; Mrs. J. Russell Mount, 2107 Goldsmith; Misses Alma and Fannie and Mr. Charles Culmore, 2212 Hamilton; Mr. and Mrs. Lawrence Cowart, 8038 Grafton; Mr. and Mrs. Arthur P. Terrell, 3709 Over-

1952. First jetliner passenger service opens May 2 between London and Johannesburg.

brook Lane; Mr. and Mrs. Robert Tyler, 928 Highland; Dr. and Mrs. Roy Heflebower, 1325 Banks; Mr. and Mrs. Albert P. Jones, 2126 Sunset Boulevard, and Mr. and Mrs. Walton Nuzum, 5103 Evergreen, Bellaire.

The congregation began to discover that this dean, who had so impressed them as a speaker when he had come as a visitor the year before, was the kind of minister who Sunday after Sunday delivers clear, thoughtful, satisfying sermons which help the person to face the coming week with fresh inspiration and a fresh resolution to do better, and to be a better person. He was, they soon saw with contentment, the kind of dean a congregation could enjoy over the long haul of years—willing to bring to them the brilliant and the famous of the Anglican Communion when possible, pleased to bring back former rectors and curates for a renewal of old ties. And in the cottage meetings they sensed that with his Georgia accent, the new dean had a droll humor which could lighten hard tasks, and that his wife had the liveliest wit yet to lift the spirits of Christ Church parishioners.

Houston at large—unaware that the sudden loss of membership threatened the stability of the parish—had seen only the orderly change from one dean to the next, and was welcoming the new dean as an interesting speaker and an intelligent addition to civic leadership.

Dean and vestry together counted their losses and assessed their prospects. Though the balance on the Latham Building debt had yet to be paid, and though the outcome of the first Every Member Canvass was yet unknown, the church had some reserves through various gifts to a variety of endowment funds. Not all of the endowment properties could be used to meet parish emergencies. For instance, the Mitchell funds were to be spent for charitable purposes only. The income from Sidney Mitchell's property has been a joy to every rector and dean, often enabling him to give desperately needed help when no other funds were available. But this money could not be used to pay off the debt, advance the parish, or cover current expenses.

There had been a number of other bequests in recent years, some for specific useful purposes, many still kept in separate accounts. Dean Richardson saw that Christ Church must take what unlabeled funds it had and use them as a nucleus for a permanent incorporated endowment, and when the late Dr. Walter H. Scherer left $10,000 to the parish, this sum was promptly added to that nucleus.

W. A. Kirkland was chairman of the Every Member Canvass, and the loyalty dinner was held in the big new Temple Emanu-El on Sunset Boulevard. It was evident that those who had remained as parishioners of the cathedral were men and women who firmly intended to support the cathedral and its new dean. The first 55 pledges to come in totaled $20,748.50—more than $6,000 more than the same 55 persons had pledged the year before. The total pledged by the 54 men working in the canvass was twice that of the year before. And as the cards come in, this encouraging trend continued. A. M. Bowles, W. J. Goldston, Ralph E. Gunn, Howard S. Hoover, and Gen. Roy C. Heflebower came on the vestry. Albert P. Jones succeeded August L. Selig as senior warden.

There were weddings: Beverly Jean Taylor to Robert Weldon Maurice and Jane Gwathmey to Walter Scott Frost with Dean Richardson officiating, and Iris Lytle to William Virgil Ballew, Jr., with Father Martin officiating.

And by spring, as is customary, staff members who had remained to span the gap between one rector and another, began to move on to other calls. Arthur E. Hall, organist since 1946, resigned effective in September. Keith M. Bardin, associate rector, accepted a call to St. Paul's Church, Orange, and Canon Harold

1952. Puerto Rico becomes first commonwealth of the United States July 25.

1952. First hydrogen device exploded by U.S. at Eniwetok proving grounds.

Martin accepted a call to St. James' Church, Greenville, Mississippi. Meanwhile there were pleasant signs of continuing faith in the cathedral. Mr. and Mrs. S. P. Martel gave a window in memory of Mrs. Lena Gohlman Fox, and the window which Webb Mading had planned as a memorial to his wife, Cora Good Mading, was—after his death—dedicated to them both. By autumn of 1953, Dean Richardson was beginning to gather staff for the program he thought essential.

Where Doctor Kellogg, newly turned civilian, had scanned a city filled with newcomers and seen the need of assistant pastors to help him reach as many of this tide of thousands as possible, Dean Richardson sensed that the first post-war influx had now leveled to a steady climb. "If the cathedral is to mean something to this entire city," he told the vestry, "then the cathedral must have the best Sunday school in the city and the best music in the city." He asked that funds be concentrated on the best qualified man available in the field of Christian education and the best qualified man available in the field of church music. He would shoulder the task of pastoral care until such time as the cathedral's income might allow a curate or assistant.

The Rev. Joseph A. Johnson of New Haven was called as associate rector in charge of Christian education. Born in Stratford, Connecticut, Mr. Johnson had graduated from Trinity College, Hartford, and Berkeley Divinity School, New Haven. He was rector of St. Paul's, Huntington, Connecticut, before becoming instructor at Berkeley, and he had just completed his own studies toward a Ph.D. at Yale University. Mr. Johnson arrived in August. In September, Jack Ossewaarde came to Christ Church to be organist and choirmaster. After earning his bachelor's and master's degrees at the University of Michigan, Jack Ossewaarde had continued graduate study with Dr. David McK. Williams, former organist and choirmaster of St. Bartholemew's, New York, and at the Union Theological Seminary School of Sacred Music. An associate of the American Guild of Organists, he was one of 12 outstanding Episcopal Church musicians invited to Washington Cathedral to discuss the formation of a College of Church Musicians. The arrival of these two young men and their attractive young families, gave to the autumn a sense of new and interesting beginning.   . .

The rebuilding of the church school would take a little time, and as Dean Richardson said recently, "By the time people started noticing Christ Church Sunday school, we had a *good* one." But after Ossewaarde's first Sunday, the dean wrote delightedly in the bulletin, "In the 15 years of my ministry, I have never seen such an enthusiastic response as was given by our congregation to the glorious music that we enjoyed in the first Sunday that Jack Ossewaarde served as our organist."

The oldest member of the lay staff in point of service then—and now—was Eldridge Carrier, sexton. Long an employe of Mrs. James Walker Cain, Eldridge gradually began to spend more and more time at Christ Church on missions for her many activities as chairman of the Altar Guild, and in 1946, Carrier was transferred to the church payroll. Of French Catholic background from Louisiana, Eldridge seldom gets a chance to go to his own parish church, but most Sundays stops by the Church of the Annunciation for an early mass before coming on to the cathedral to open up for early service Sunday mornings. Louise Carrier, his wife, soon became well known at the church for her expert help when called upon for suppers and other events. And when Lionel Bellard was added to the staff, his wife, Lee Anna, was another pleasant aide who could be counted upon when needed.

The lovely little Chapel of the Christ Child, designed by Staub, Rather and

1952. King Farouk of Egypt abdicates July 26 after Maj. Gen. Mohammed Naguib seizes power.

1952. Defeated at 63 in his third bid for presidential nomination, Senator Robert Taft becomes new President Eisenhower's chief senate supporter.

Howze, was completed after so many years of generous planning by Mr. and Mrs. Cain. Dedicated to the memory of James Walker Cain, Jr., by Bishop Quin, Bishop Hines and Dean Richardson, it was opened the Sunday after Christmas, 1953, to all the generations of cathedral children who worship there and consider it their own.

The dean organized the Chancellors' Club of younger men in the cathedral, had a series of Wednesday night dinners, established coffee hour after church each Sunday in the Guild Hall, promoted picnics on the bay, all aimed at getting old cathedral members better acquainted with new ones.

In 1954, Mr. Alexander Sessums Cleveland died at the age of 82. Like his father, he had given devotedly and with high heart to Christ Church throughout his life, bequeathing to it his children, grandchildren, and great grandchildren.

Christ Church Cathedral saw several weddings: Randa Lee Kerr to Morgan Lee Davis, Jr.; Alice Michaux York to John Delabarre Staub; Mary Bain Haralson to Gary Pinkney Pearson, Jr.; Martha Matilda Moore to Emile Marc Cuenod; Jane Michaux York to John Raymond Black, Jr.; Patricia Ann Peckinpaugh to Ford Hubbard, Jr.; Jean Elizabeth Forsyth to Wilmer St. John Garwood, Jr.; and Patricia Ann Carter to James Spencer Dickerson. Though confirmation classes were smaller than those peak days under Dean Kellogg, baptisms were growing in number and Dean Richardson seemed to enjoy them.

Cathedral to the Diocese

Christ Church parish had come through its danger period, and was entering into the era which should establish it forever as the pivotal church for Houston and the diocese—no longer mother church to missions, but cathedral church to all Episcopalians.

By early 1954, Christ Church Cathedral resounded to exciting organ and choral music with increasing frequency. On the first Sunday in Lent, Jack Ossewaarde began a series of choral evensongs, and two Sundays later, the choir sang Debussy's rarely heard cantata—"Prodigal Son"—after evensong.

The Sunday school had begun to grow rapidly. The Rev. Mr. Johnson had found at the cathedral several teachers around whom he could build—Miss Dorothy Swope, Mrs. Margarette Russell, Miss Elise Wilkinson among them. Adding staff wherever well trained people could be found and recruited, Mr. Johnson developed the most interesting program of Christian education for children and adults in the city, and several neighborhood churches used the cathedral program as a pattern for their own revisions and improvements. This was exactly the kind of stimulus which Dean Richardson thought the cathedral should be able to provide.

The bulletin announced that a nursery was opened "patterned after a hospital nursery in terms of sanitation and sterileness. Germicide lamps are hung from the ceiling . . . each crib and table is separate and functions as a private unit . . . A registered nurse is in charge. We suggest each parent bring to the nursery a filled bottle and a diaper change." The announcement was so impressive that the next Sunday, the bulletin had to add hastily that the new nursery was free of charge. Many young parents had assumed that all this *must* cost something. The Rev. Mr. Johnson had the courage to start a Sunday evening youth

program when he had only three youngsters—but soon he had a dozen, and then he had to start dividing his youth groups up by ages.

Dean and Mrs. Richardson had come through a danger period of their own. Their oldest son Jim was born with a heart defect, and in Atlanta, the best specialists of the period could only pronounce it inoperable. In Houston at the Texas Medical Center, where one of the greatest centers of heart surgery in the world had already sprung into being, specialists advised surgery. Jim Richardson's operation was a success, and he could begin to enjoy a bicycle and swimming with his school mates.

Bishop Kellogg was welcomed back for Lenten noonday services, and the Very Rev. James Pike, dean of the Cathedral of St. John the Divine in New York, came next.

When the church became a cathedral, the rectors of the five other oldest and charter member churches of the diocese were made honorary canons. Dean Richardson invited them one a week, to celebrate Holy Communion at 10 AM Thursday and speak on the history and work of those charter churches. The first to come was the Rev. Aubrey Maxted, of Christ Church, Matagorda, the only church older than the cathedral in the diocese, and the second was the Rev. Edmund H. Gibson of Trinity Church, Galveston.

In October, the Rt. Rev. Michael Coleman, bishop of Qu'Appelle in Canada, came for a teaching mission. Though new to Houston, Bishop Coleman was well known in the eastern United States. He had been acting vicar of All Hallows' Church, near the Tower of London. Older than London itself, Druid before it was Christian, All Hallows' had many links with Colonial America. When it was bombed, Vicar Coleman came to this country to raise funds for the rebuilding, and later became a missionary in British Columbia. In 1950, he was consecrated Bishop of the Diocese of Qu'Appelle. Americans had always found him an inspiring missioner, and Dean Richardson prepared the way for the October mission with care. Bishops Quin, Hines, and Kellogg wrote in the church bulletin their pleasure that Houston was to hear Bishop Coleman. Lloyd Fadrique was chairman of a large committee on arrangements.

The mission was a deeply rewarding one for all who went, and marked the beginning of Bishop Coleman's now annual visits to Houston.

By December, 1954—two years and three months after the exodus of 448 members—Christ Church Cathedral had outgrown its plant.

After all those years when wartime gas rationing, repeated polio epidemics, and postwar construction had discouraged Sunday school attendance, the cathedral was now embarrassed for lack of Sunday school rooms.

When it reached the point that the dean had to give up his study to a Sunday school class, the vestry thought it time to see what could be done. The first proposal was to bisect the Guild Hall horizontally, gaining 1800 additional square feet of space for choir and Sunday school rooms. This was not immediately done, because it was apparent that in the long view, the cathedral needed more buildings than it had, more land adjacent, and a permanent guarantee of parking space.

Throughout the vast and prolonged program of expansion, Dean Richardson had the backing of Judge John H. Crooker, W. J. Goldston, and R. W. Holtz, and the vestry was quick to see that expansion was essential if the cathedral was to survive in its downtown close. Since his arrival, the dean—with vestry approval—had plumped in talks and bulletins for the Christ Church Cathedral Endowment Fund, not so necessary now as it will be in 1970, the year 2000 and beyond.

This fund had gone from $40,000 in 1952 to $102,00 in 1954.

But now an immediate project came to the fore. The property across San Jacinto from the Latham Building, once the site of the big old Central Fire Station, was up for sale, and a bus company thought of buying it as site for a bus terminal. This would have closed the parking lot nearest to the cathedral. It would have thrown the entire burden of peak traffic for funerals, Advent and Lenten noonday services, luncheons and weddings on the parking garage immediately north of the church. And it would have destroyed that sense of easy access on Sunday morning which the lot across the street creates.

"Unless," Dean Richardson said, "our parishioners can easily find parking space close to the church, they will understandably stop at the neighborhood church with the parking lot on all sides." Durell Carothers, head of Allright Auto Park, had for many years—as he still does—cooperated generously with Christ Church, making available on Sunday morning all lots and garages in his chain. But as the pending sale proved, it was only by buying the Texas Avenue-San Jacinto property that the church could be sure of permanent access to parking.

The vestry—after many discussions of finance—announced at the parish dinner of 1955 that Christ Church Cathedral would buy the parking lot. To be leased at a rate which would make the lot ultimately pay for itself, it would still be free to Christ Church members each Sunday and for special evening events. And the vestry announced a Capital Fund Campaign to carry out the full expansion program needed. "This campaign is the beckoning of an even greater future," said W. A. Kirkland at the dinner. "Every church in the city and diocese has been strengthened on Christ Church." said Albert P. Jones, "and will be further strengthened by the success of this Cathedral Fund Campaign." "Providing additional space for our growing Sunday School, the liquidation of our indebtedness, and the down payment on parking facilities will help insure the future of the parish," said Judge Crooker. "This Loyalty Dinner has been one of the most inspiring occasions I have ever known in Christ Church," said J. A. Elkins, Jr. And "This is the greatest opportunity Christ Church has had in its history," said Albert Bowles. "It was a God-given opportunity."

The congregation felt the excitement and responded to it. And family by family, they responded to the spirit of the letter written by the dean: "If you believe in having a downtown church in Houston; if you think the religious education of little children important in our parish; if you see that parking facilities are indispensable to our future here; then, this campaign should challenge your maximum gift." Within a week, the first $97,630 had been pledged or paid toward the goal of $225,000.

In the spring, 1955, the Rev. F. Percy Goddard, for 27 years rector of St. John's Church, Marlin, was elected suffragan bishop. His consecration in August was the fourth in the history of Christ Church Cathedral. Bishop Quin was consecrator; Bishop Hines and the Rt. Rev. Everett Holland Jones of West Texas co-consecrators. The Rt. Rev. John Joseph Meakin Harte, suffragan of Dallas, and Bishop Kellogg, coadjutor of Minnesota, were presenting bishops. Dean Richardson and the Rev. Thomas W. Sumners were attending presbyters. The cathedral's committee of arrangements consisted of Mrs. Louis Bryan, Lloyd Fadrique, William J. Goldston, Harry Grubert, Mrs. Ralph E. Gunn, Canon Johnson, Mr. Ossewaarde, Edward Schulenburg, and Mrs. Eugene Williams.

The procession of 10 bishops, one dean, four priests and two laymen was

1954. Racial segregation of the public schools is ruled unconstitutional by the U.S. Supreme Court May 17.

1955. Winston Churchill, 80, retires as prime minister and is knighted by Queen Elizabeth.

telecast as it walked from cloister to the church door.

At the University of the South in Sewanee, a new Cleveland Hall was begun in memory of Alexander Sessums Cleveland of Houston. And in June, Mrs. L. Gus Mueller, lifelong member of Christ Church, who remembered a time when people milked cows on North Main Street, celebrated her 90th birthday. She was born, reared, and married and then reared her own children in the same block in what is now Houston Heights.

In Christ Church, Bishop Quin ordained Claude William Behn, Edward C. Rutland, Harland MacMillan Irvin, Jr., Joe Cavileer Treadwell, John Gordon Swope, Jr., deacons and Harold Gene Norman priest. And he announced that Harold Edwin Bates, James Aubrey Hudson, John Lane Denson III, Herbert Alexander Willke, John Augustine Desel, Francis Park Smith, and George Carlisle Lawson would soon become priests.

By September, the vestry with W. J. Goldston as senior warden had decided to spend the next $40,000 available on liquidating the Latham Building debt, and to bank the subsequent funds, as they came in on pledges for the work of creating new Sunday school space in the old Guild Hall. By the time this announcement reached the bulletin, $7,500 had already been paid, and the Latham Building debt brought down to $32,500. Lloyd Fadrique was chairman of the approaching Every Member Canvass.

Christ Church Cathedral gave a reception in the Latham Building one September evening in honor of Bishop and Mrs. Clinton Quin—a family party to which an enormous church family came. Bishop Quin was planning to retire and to move to Richmond, Texas. When brisk young Clinton Quin became bishop coadjutor in 1918, the Diocese of Texas had 45 clergymen, one postulant, 6,855 communicants, 2,916 Sunday school children, and 34 parishes. At Bishop Quin's retirement 37 years later, the diocese had 123 clergymen, 59 postulants, and candidates for holy orders (the largest number of any diocese in the country), 36,374 communicants, 15,214 Sunday school children, and 63 parishes. In December 1955, Bishop Hines was installed in the cathedral as fourth bishop of Texas. While 1200 looked on, Bishop Quin handed him the pastoral staff used by Texas bishops since 1859. After Bishop Quin's retirement, he and Mrs. Quin moved to their charming new house in Richmond, leaving the bishop's house in which so many potential Episcopalians and confirmed Episcopalians had visited and in which 17 annual house parties of clergy wives had been held—each one larger than the last.

Bishop and Mrs. Hines and their children moved back to Houston and to Mandell. Both Bishop and Mrs. Hines are antique collectors, and they filled the house with the soft gleam of polished pewter and lovely old wood. Ralph Gunn redesigned the garden. Quickly famous for her iced coffee and coffee ice cream in a punch bowl, Mrs. Hines gradually became known for her knack with new babies, as first one young Hines and then a second married and brought grandchildren home. And looking not in the least grandparental, Bishop and Mrs. Hines sometimes drove a low-swung Mercedes coupe, and sometimes rode bicycles. "If you see somebody in the neighborhood on a bicycle," commented Sika Dantone, "it's somebody from Poe School or Rice University, or it's Bishop or Mrs. Hines."

Whenever someone gives a memorial, large or small, to the Endowment Fund, the names of those so remembered are recorded in the Book of Remembrance. Dean Richardson writes these inscriptions in the big red leather book himself, and each year on All Saints Day, these memorials are printed in the

1955. The anti-polio vaccine developed by Dr. Jonas Salk is pronounced a success April 12.

1955. Leopold Stokowski becomes director of the Houston Symphony Orchestra.

Christ Church Bulletin. In 1955, on All Saints Day, Beatrice Schroeder, harpist, and David Wuliger, timpanist, joined the cathedral choir under Jack Ossewaarde to present the Brahms German Requiem (to differentiate it from the Roman Mass) with Jo Ann Merrell, soprano, and William Cunningham, baritone, as soloists. At Christmas, Congregation Beth Israel sent Christ Church Cathedral a beautiful poinsettia in good wishes for the cathedral's Holy Season. The Latham debt come down to $15,000 from the year before's $50,000. John Suman was chairman of the Every Member Canvass. with Hirst Suffield as his campaign chairman; and as chairman of the Cathedral Endowment Fund, Judge Crooker reported that the principal had grown from $40,000 in September, 1952, to $120,000 in January, 1956. But $2 million is needed for this endowment to be effective in the future toward which it is aimed.

Canon Joe Johnson resigned in 1956 to become rector of the Church of the Good Shepherd in Hartford, Connecticut, much to the regret of the dean, the church school, and vestry. By this time, it was apparent that many young parents moving to Houston were attracted to the cathedral because of its Sunday school.

James Parker Clements, rector of St. Mark's Church, Houston, was elected suffragan, and in August, 1956, became the fifth bishop consecrated in Christ Church Cathedral. The Most Rev. Henry Knox Sherrill, presiding bishop, was consecrator, Bishop Hines and Bishop Quin co-consecrators, and again ten bishops marched in procession under the cloisters, along the east wall, and into the front door of Christ Church Cathedral.

The cathedral committee on arrangements consisted of Edward Adolphe, Harry Grubert, Mrs. Ralph Ellis Gunn, Frank O. McGehee III, Mrs. John S. Neilson, J. H. Ossewaarde, the Very Rev. J. Milton Richardson, August L. Selig, and Jean Shepherd (Mrs. Tascal P.).

The Rev. Howard C. Rutenbar accepted the Christ Church call as associate rector for Christian education. A graduate of Albion College, Albion, Michigan, and of Berkeley Divinity School in New Haven, Mr. Rutenbar had done graduate study in Christian education at Yale Divinity School and Union Theological Seminary in New York. He had held parishes in Connecticut and Michigan before coming to Houston, and was able to carry on the church school program with happy understanding. Mr. Rutenbar, who was later elected canon by the diocese, brought with him his wife and three children. A week later, the Rev. Mark E. Waldo arrived to become associate rector—the first in Dean Richardson's tenure called to assist in pastoral work. A native of Savannah, Georgia, Mr. Waldo was graduated from the College of William and Mary and Virginia Theological Seminary. For the preceding six years, he had been rector of St. Andrew's Church, Douglas, Georgia, and he brought to Houston his wife and three children.

In this period, former curates and assistants were coming back one each week to conduct Thursday morning services: the Rev. Lionel T. DeForest, of Grace Church, Galveston; the Rev. John McKee, the Rev. John Bentley and the Rev. Keith M. Bardin.

Continuing the Thursday series, the services were conducted by seven Texas clergymen who entered the ministry from Christ Church Cathedral: the Rev. C. Osborne Moyer, the Rev. J. Gordon Swope, Jr., the Rev. Nelson C. Longnecker, the Rev. E. C. Rutland, the Rev. Francis Parke Smith, Jr., the Rev. W. R. Woods and the Rev. Arthur E. Hartwell.

1956. Egypt seizes the Suez Canal July 26. and Hungarians revolt October 23 against Soviet-dominated regime, but Soviet armed forces crush revolt by November 4.

And on Texas Thanksgiving Day, in St. Luke's Episcopal Hospital built through his enthusiasm and determination, Bishop Quin died. Few men in death receive so many tributes from so many people of so many different faiths. The funeral was conducted by the Bishop of Texas, the suffragans of Texas, the dean of the cathedral, and by the Rev. Scott Copeland, his parish priest in Richmond, and the Rev. Penrose Hirst, his son-in-law. The choir sang a Brahms anthem, an orison by Jack Ossewaarde, and a recessional ending in a triumphant "Alleluia!"

Houstonians stood still on the sidewalks as the four-block-long funeral procession passed by, and Bishop Quin was laid to rest beside his young son, Robert, in Forest Park Cemetery.

In 1956, Eliza Wilson died, and her funeral was conducted in the Christ Church chapel. Though she had continued to receive the parish bulletin and Ladies Parish Association yearbooks, she had been too old in her last years to come to church. With her death, Christ Church lost its last Negro member— and one of its most devout.

In Advent, the Rt. Rev. Hamilton H. Kellogg came to the cathedral for the first of the annual Advent series of noonday services. All Episcopal churches in Houston take part, and each year, the Advent services give prep·aration for Christmas, as the Lenten services prepare for Easter.

From time to time at the 11 o'clock service, the cathedral observed the ancient custom of singing the litany in procession—a custom dating back as far as 1400 and put in final form in the Book of Common Prayer by Archbishop Cramner in 1544. And in the spring, the first of the Diocesan Choral Festivals was held with Dr. David McK. Williams, formerly of St. Bartholemew's, New York, in Houston to conduct the massed choirs.

For a choral Solemnization of Matrimony for Gloria Ann Goldston and Allan Carlisle King—with the dean as officiant—the choir under Mr. Ossewaarde sang Handel, Bach, and Vaughan Williams and, after the bishop's blessing, an orison by Jack Ossewaarde. The reception after was the first held in the new Houston Country Club. There were other lovely weddings in the period: Gwendoline Averell to Michel J. Mellinger; Geraldyne Ann Whitfield to James Angus Saye; Lucile Meachum Mellinger to John Alden Rodgers; Betty Anna Sears to James Ernest Riffe, with Father D'Aubert officiating; Jacquelyn Drane Bartell, granddaughter of Mrs. Joe B. Drane who was long president of the Altar Guild, to Jay Cowan Tapp, who was a young kinsman of the Rev. T.R.B. Trader and Henry F. Gillette; Dixie Margaret Sick to Lloyd Waldo Leggett, and Mary Ann Sexton to Thomas Calvin Mathis.

Francis Marion Law, a long time good friend to Christ Church and Frances Mann Law, a devout communicant, quietly celebrated their 60th wedding anniversary. With Episcopal Churches of the nation, Christ Church Cathedral celebrated Jamestown Sunday in commemoration of the first Holy Communion celebrated on Jamestown Island, Virginia, on June 14, 1607, and a week later, William J. Treat, once an acolyte under Father DeWolfe, was made deacon by Bishop Hines.

Dean and Mrs. Richardson celebrated their fifth anniversary at Christ Church in September, 1957. Floyd E. Bates, senior warden, and Ralph W. Holtz, junior warden, issued the vestry invitation to a reception in their honor, and listed the achievements: "A new program of Christian education, improved program of church music, the founding of a Chancellors' Club, the creation of five new chapters of the Ladies Parish Association and the Advent noon day services, adequate parking facilities by the purchase of the Texas Avenue parking lot which will soon be self-liquidating, the Parish House and Guild Hall have been completely modernized and additional facilities provided for the Sunday school, the Sunday School staff has been reorganized and enlarged to meet the growing needs of the increased attendance."

The count could have been amended to give Mrs. Richardson part credit for stimulating new chapters in the Ladies Parish Association, and to report that the endowment fund had been more than tripled in those five years. Another unmentioned achievement was the birth of Preston Richardson in 1954. The cathedral library opened in 1958, beginning with 200 books, to lend books of religious emphasis as well as of more general nature.

The new Southwest Freeway threatened the rectory on Bute Street, and with a final resolution of gratitude to Mrs. John McClellan for the years the church had enjoyed her home, the vestry sold the property and bought the new rectory at 14 Shadowlawn Circle—a house ideally suited in size and location not only for the Richardson family but for parish meetings which might need to be held there. The Richardsons have always taken the attitude that a great many parish and civic meetings should be held there, and the dean's wife and his mother, with their gift for good coffee and delicious refreshments beautifully served, have transformed many a routine, business session into a warm, attractive gathering of friends meeting to do business. Characteristically, the Richardsons opened the new rectory with a reception for the whole congregation on the Saturday afternoon after Easter—two days before the 119th anniversary of Christ Church's founding.

Christ Church vestry postponed for a year its own long-planned secondary cathedral fund drive to make way for the Episcopal Diocesan Development Fund Drive. Leslie Coleman was cathedral chairman for the drive, and William D. C. Lucy, chairman of advance gifts.

The cathedral quiet was shattered one Saturday afternoon in April as Mrs. W. A. Kirkland arranged flowers on the altar, and Eldridge Carrier vacuumed the carpet. A young woman in despair had shot herself. Thirty-six hours later, a burglar shot and lightly wounded in the knee, Paul Waite, uniformed patrolman for the Burns Detective Agency guarding the cathedral, who fired two shots into the dark. The cathedral made headlines—unwonted and unwanted.

The American Guild of Organists held its national convention at Christ Church that year. With this as a climax to his years in Houston, Jack Ossewaarde resigned to become organist and choirmaster of St. Bartholemew's Church, New York, where he had so often been invited to play.

It was easier for the cathedral to put pride in his achievement over sharp regrets at his going when Dean Richardson found that William Barnard could come to Christ Church. A native of North Carolina, Mr. Barnard earned his bachelor's and master's degrees at the University of Michigan where he first met Jack Ossewaarde and where he studied under the same teachers. After three and a half years in the army, Mr. Barnard became organist and choirmaster at the First Congregational Church in Toledo, Ohio. He later studied at the School of Sacred Music at Union Theological Seminary, and became organist and choirmaster of Christ Church, Short Hills, New Jersey.

Mr. Barnard continued easily the musical program Ossewaarde had begun, offering special musical services with each season of the church year,

1957. The U. S. S. R. launches Sputnik October 4, the first man-made satellite to go into orbit around the planet earth.

directing the growth of the choir until it has become one of the outstanding choirs in the Southwest. He offered the first Houston church performances of many contemporary choral works by such composers as Benjamin Britten, Zoltan Kodaly, and Francis Poulenc. And he continued to bring the Diocesan Choral Festival each year to Christ Church, with as few as seven churches and as many as 22 taking part.

Under Canon Rutenbar, the Sunday school continued to grow until the seven new classrooms gained by halving the Guild Hall were crowded and the Sunday school plant outgrown again. There were a number of clergy children on the rolls—children of the Rutenbars, the Waldos, the Richardsons, and the Hines, and when the Rev. Lane Denson come to Rice Institute as chaplain of Episcopal students, his family came to the cathedral.

Hattie Ingram, coped with the babies and toddlers in the nursery, and several refused to be graduated for months after their birthdays. Mrs. Margarette Russell, with red-gold hair and slim chic, was in charge of the three year olds and handled them so serenely that the shyest newcomer felt instantly better at the sight of her. Mrs. A. F. Campbell had the four year olds and it was only her kind, deft way which made it bearable for them to leave Mrs. Russell, and made it so hard to leave Mrs. Campbell when the time came. Growing up is made both easier and harder by such fierce affections. Miss Elise Wilkinson, Miss Dorothy Swope, Mrs. Elden Fogler, and Mrs. Cabot Stein continued to be pillars of the church school.

The cathedral reputation for the high quality of training of its school staff grew to such proportions that one Sunday morning in mid-summer, when a mother walked in and found Mrs. Russell on vacation, she promptly asked the young substitute, "Do you have your degree in elementary education?" When the young girl admitted she did not, the mother was obviously tempted to take her child back home again.

In this decade across the nation, the concept of religious education changed from emphasis on content to emphasis on teaching built to the individual needs and grasp of the child at each age level. "The content or heritage or lore of the church in the Bible and the historical traditions have much more meaning and reality to a child when they are put in their proper place," Canon Rutenbar said. "At the first grade level, a child cannot understand fully what 'discipleship' means, but he can understand that Jesus needs helpers, just as Mr. Weingarten needs helpers at the shopping centers to carry on his business. At sixth grade level, when this same child is confronted with the Life of Christ, he can understand at greater depth what discipleship means, what it demands as part of his own life. Christianity basically is living—living a life which strives to consider the example of our Lord."

Canon Rutenbar recruited several couples who—together each Sunday—took classes of older children. Mr. and Mrs. Paul Bode—until Mr. Bode went to Austin as assistant headmaster to St. Stephen's School—Mr. and Mrs. Craig Ludlow, Mr. and Mrs. Hirst Suffield, and Dr. and Mrs. John McFarland were among them. And Big Sam Wheeler became an institution of both Sunday school and youth program, recruiting substitute Sunday school teachers from the congregation on a flood morning when a regular teacher couldn't get through, making cannon balls out of modeling clay for a three-year-old who thought his parents had abandoned him, playing a quiet game of chess, lending a 10-year-old girl a lovable boa constrictor for a week, taking

1958. General Charles deGaulle becomes French premier, and 23-year-old pianist Van Cliburn of Kilgore becomes the sensation of the concert stage.

1958-59. Alaska and Hawaii are admitted as 49th and 50th states.

the young people's groups on hayrides to his place near Sugarland, and sending them home from a Sunday evening youth program in full Indian warpaint. "I am glad," said one ninth grader, "that he's on *my* side."

Each All Saints Day, the list of names of those inscribed on the Book of Remembrance was growing longer. Bishop Clinton Simon Quin . . . L. Gus Mueller . . . Miss Gussie Howard . . . Mrs. Calvin Garwood . . . Arthur S. L. Toombes . . . Elbert E. Adkins . . . Eliza Wilson . . . Mrs. J. M. Geiselman . . . Jasper Arthur Neath . . . Miss Mec Mellinger Botts . . . Harry Joseph Crooker . . . Mrs. Caroline Ennis Cargill McCellan, . . . Mrs. John H. Freeman, Jr. . . . William D. Cleveland, Jr. . . . Kirkland Vandervoort . . . Mrs. E. H. Chapin . . . Ben Rice . . .

Mr. William D. Cleveland, Jr., died at 85, and the newspaper story on his death said he had been a charter member of the Houston Country Club, of the Eagle Lake Rod and Gun Club, and told of his business achievements and many civic contributions, of his long membership in the Masonic order. Remembering the many hours he had given in the many years to Christ Church, older members of the congregation marveled that he had time to accomplish all these other things.

There were beautiful weddings in Christ Church Cathedral in 1959, and in 1960: Allie Autry Kelley to Joseph Elmer Dittmar; Mary Patricia Cravens to Achille Arcidiacono; Barbara Jane Fry to Vincent Abel Moncrief, Anne Best Winterbotham to Peter Evans Pratt; Nancy Sabrina Hines to Taylor King Smith; Bess Kirby Tooke to Milton England Black. Sara Davis and John A. Croom were married in the chapel.

In May, 1960, the vestry started the Cathedral Advancement Fund Drive for $191,000 to build additional classrooms and commons where young people could meet, and to straighten the leaning tower of the church. Chairmen of the drive were James A. Elkins, Jr., George C. Morris, and John M. Winterbotham, with William J. Goldston chairman of advance gifts.

Mr. Goldston throughout these years of constant expansion, as the dean once said, was "a quiet force for every good in the Cathedral." Twice senior warden, he had taken the leadership in the vestry's move to buy three rectories needed for dean and two canons, and he saw from the beginning the importance of expanding the program so that young families would be attracted and the future of the cathedral assured. Having once envisioned a worthwhile goal, he had the will and the ability to press toward it.

Wednesday after Rogation Sunday, the entire parish dined in the Emerald Room of the Shamrock Hilton. Porter Parris of the congregation was manager of the Shamrock, and through his arrangements, and the generosity of a Christ Church member who insisted on being an anonymous host, the dinner was one of the most elaborate and one of the most gay in cathedral history— so handsome in fact, that when the hotel waiters in uniform marched in military formation across the dining room with flaming swords and baked Alaska, the congregation had the sense of humor to laugh as well as applaud: how far the parish dinner had come since its gentle beginning as a church supper a century or more ago.

In September, the arrival of 310 children on the opening day of enrollment proved the need of the Cathedral Advancement Fund Drive. R. W. Holtz as senior warden was quietly going through prolonged, tedious negotiations which require almost superhuman patience, in the effort to buy for the church the Taylor Jewelry Company building north of the Sunday school on

1960. Camelot *opens in New York starring Julie Andrews and Richard Burton.*

San Jacinto. The property was for sale, but Mr. Holtz had to try to bring the price and terms within the reach of the cathedral. In Lent—as he had and as he does each year—the dean went off on the preaching missions to New York, Washington, Minneapolis, and a variety of cities, the kind of trip which brings other outstanding preachers of the Anglican Communion to the Cathedral at Lent and Advent.

In the 1960s, Mr. Barnard continued the high quality of music at the cathedral, highlighting his weekly program with brilliant special events. Among the choir singers were Jody Elliott, Anne Waldo, Mary Neuhaus, Annette Donaldson, Elsie Kadera, Mary Sieber and Kenneth Mandell. Each year, Mr. Barnard trained a new children's choir, and the traditional partnership between the cathedral and Houston Symphony Orchestra was close. The congregation was charmed by his use of Easter carols from many lands during the long quiet of the Easter communion service, but Houston music lovers remembered such programs as the Eastertide Evensong of 1960 which had 18 instruments and a harpsichord from the orchestra to supplement organ and choir. Soloists were Elsie Kadera, Mary Ann Gifford, Phyliss Hand, Thomas Clark and Joseph Naron, for Bach's cantata *Christ Lay in Death's Dark Prison,* and his canticle *Magnificat in D.*

Under Canon Waldo, the Young Peoples' Fellowship met every Sunday evening, often at the home of such members as Jennifer John, Joan Richardson, Caroline Shaver, David Elliott, or the sponsors, Mr. and Mrs. Charles McCurley. After one meeting, they went to see *The Diary of Anne Frank.*

On Good Friday, 1961, Mr. Barnard inaugurated the annual presentation of the Passion of Our Lord in one of many musical settings. For the first year, he chose Bach's *St. John Passion* sung with accompaniment by twenty musicians from the Houston Symphony Orchestra. On other Good Friday evenings, settings by Heinrich Schuetz have been used, one with St. Mathew's text, and one with St. John's.

Canon Mark Waldo accepted a call to become rector of Church of the Ascension in Montgomery, and the Rev. H. Douglas Fontaine became associate rector. A native of Charleston, West Virginia, Mr. Fontaine was a graduate of the West Virginia University and Virginia Theological Seminary. He had first come to Houston to visit his mother, a communicant of Christ Church, and in coming to stay, he brought his wife, the former Jeanne Ellis of Charleston, and their three children.

In April, 1961, the vestry announced the purchase of the adjacent property formerly occupied by the Taylor Jewelry Company. "The cost of the land and remodeling," the announcement said, "will be provided by the Cathedral Advancement Fund. The building itself is the gift of Mrs. A. S. Cleveland and Mrs. William D. Cleveland, Jr., and is given in memory of their late husbands, who were brothers and devoted communicants of the Cathedral." John H. Freeman, Jr., vestryman and architect, designed the new building, consulting often with Mr. Fontaine and allowing for teen-age tastes as reflected by his daughter Connie and her friends. Through his work as project architect, Charles Hubbard and his wife became interested, entered a confirmation class, and are now members of Christ Church.

Christ Church lost two of its great ladies—great in beauty and in the spirit of spontaneous Christian service to all in need. Mrs. Lamar Fleming, Jr., born in England, had given unnumbered hours to Jefferson Davis and M. D. Anderson Hospitals, her great courtesy always at its gentlest when

1961. The United States breaks off diplomatic relations with Cuba.

1961. At 43, John Fitzgerald Kennedy becomes youngest president in the history of the United States.

helping the forlorn and the penniless. No human record shows the extent of her quiet bounty. Mrs. F. M. Law, from her first years in Houston as a young matron, had helped with the Sunday school and helped the city with early park and recreational efforts. In 1922, she became Houston's first Girl Scout commissioner, and she was a member of the first Houston Parks and Recreation Board. She had been a member of Christ Church for 46 years. Men and women of many walks of life and many civic interests came to those two funerals—both at Christ Church Cathedral.

Their names went in the Book of Remembrance, joining the lengthening list . . . Stephen Delavan Day . . . Mrs. Susan Vaughn Clayton . . . Edward Adolphe . . . Clifford Drane . . . E. R. Wicks . . . Mr. and Mrs. Kenneth Franzheim . . . Dr. W. S. Red, Jr. . . . Mrs. George J. Mellinger . . . George J. Mellinger . . . David Gordon, Jr. . . . William States Jacobs, Jr. . . . L. A. Stevenson . . . Bettie Ford Elgin . . . Mrs. Pearl Guion McClung . . . the Rev. Peter Gray Sears . . . Charles Milby Dow . . . Mrs. Lloyd Gregory . . . Wharton Weems . . . Henry H. Bokenkamp. . . .

There were weddings in cathedral and chapel: Kyra Anne Kerr to Dan Pearson Jones, Kristi Shipnes Buchanan to William Bourke Cassin, Mary Carter Bradford to Allen Harn Caldwell, Jr.; Maria Lucas Burke to Duncan Tellef Butler with Bishop Hines, Dean Richardson and the Rev. Tom Bagby conducting the service, Margaret Merle Steven to Francois Louis Jean Benicy, Maria Meade Winterbotham to John Dale Maclay, Winifred June Rayzor to Donald Allison Elliott, Emily VanZandt Attwell to Oscar Holcombe Croswell, Gladys Jane Sick to Herschel McCarver Vaughan, Jr., Elizabeth Rice Winston to John Wilson Kelsey, Elizabeth Drane Bartell to Stuart Getz Haynesworth, Justa Joiner Helm to Richard Gordon Rorschech. And Mr. and Mrs. W. Ernst Japhet celebrated their 50th wedding anniversary.

Douglas Fontaine was elected canon pastor of the cathedral, and the Rev. Scott Field Bailey, former Houstonian now back in Houston as executive assistant to the bishop, was made canon to the ordinary. His family became members of the cathedral parish.

And on the second Sunday after Easter, Bishop Hines dedicated Cleveland Hall in memory of Alexander Sessums Cleveland and William D. Cleveland, Jr. Adult members of the parish toured the gleaming new rooms —downstairs a pleasant club house for long, probing conversations, for listening to music, for playing billiards or chess or checkers, for reading, and upstairs well planned classrooms. But the young people of the church soon found there at last a place that was truly theirs. Cleveland Hall seemed a lovely and smiling memorial to a story begun early one spring morning just after the Civil War when the Rt. Rev. Alexander Gregg solemnized in Christ Church Cathedral the marriage of young William D. Cleveland and Miss Justina Latham—without the consent of the bride's parents.

Canon Fontaine, young enough himself to understand his teen age charges but strong enough of mind and personality to hold his leadership, has used Cleveland Hall to develop a constantly growing Young People's Fellowship and Young People's Service League. And any junior high or high school member of Christ Church is likely to insist on taking any family visitors from out of town to see Cleveland Hall—if he likes the family's visitors well enough to want them not to miss anything.

The wardens and vestry of Christ Church Cathedral invited the congre-

1961. Commander Alan B. Shepard, Jr., is rocketed from Cape Canaveral 116.5 miles above the earth May 5 in the first U.S. manned suborbital space flight.

gation to a reception in the Guild Hall to honor Dean and Mrs. Richardson on his tenth anniversary as dean and rector. The Guild Hall was crowded with guests when John Winterbotham rose to present an anniversary present—something, he said, which the vestry thought would be lasting. The words conjured up teapots or trays in silver, but to the pleasure of everyone there, Mr. Winterbotham continued, "And so we are sending them on a trip to Europe." Blonde Genie and dark haired Joan Richardson were serving punch at the refreshment table, and their joy in their parents' gift heightened the delight of all there.

Busy with cathedral affairs, the dean wisely left the planning of that trip to his wife Gene, and those two expert travelers ranged across Egypt, Lebanon, Jordan, Israel, Greece, Italy, Spain, Portugal, and France, sailing across the Nile and among the Greek Islands, seeing Pyramids, Jerusalem, Lourdes and the Eiffel Tower with understanding and frequent humor. The dean's mother—who must inevitably go down in any history of Christ Church as Pal—and her grandson, Preston, held the deanery fort at home, and though it was unfortunate that Preston should have broken his leg, the cast did have the virtue of anchoring him and saving him from perhaps more serious accident until his parents could return.

The Rev. Canon Howard C. Rutenbar ended his seven year ministry at the cathedral to become vicar of St. Barnabas' Church, Florissant, outside St. Louis. Canon Rutenbar had served widely in Houston—in Little League, in Cub Scouts, as a member of the clergy advisory committee of Planned Parenthood, and on the youth advisory committee of the Houston Council of Churches. The cathedral regretted his leaving. After his resignation, the vestry was happy to discover that the Rev. Joseph A. Johnson, who had first shaped the new Church school in 1954 and 1955, could return to the cathedral. Dean Richardson was particularly gratified, as he had always enjoyed working with Mr. Johnson.

Mrs. Ralph Gunn, who had been active in the Ladies Parish Association since her girlhood when she told stories to the Caroline Greene Nursery children, who had written and narrated many May Fetes and many Festivals of Light, could no longer give to the cathedral the time it had always demanded of her. She had become president of the Episcopal Church Women of the Diocese.

In 1963, Hilda Bouchan Lozano married Erik laCour Olsen, and in one of the most beautiful weddings of many years, Sandra Keith Smith married Robert Livingston Gerry III. The bride wore the same white lace wedding dress her grandmother, her mother and her aunt had worn in their weddings, and the reception afterward was held on Longfellow Lane at the home of her parents, Mr. and Mrs. Lloyd Hilton Smith. Great pink pavillions were set up on the lawn, for the refreshments, the orchestra and dancing. And a few months later, carrying on the tradition of the Christ Church choir, Annette Donaldson of the choir married William Norcom Barnard, organist and choirmaster.

Christ Church Cathedral seemed to have settled into a comfortable present, filled each Sunday by old Houstonians and new, by third generation members and first, by people who lived downtown and people who lived on the county's edge, by visitors, and by those who—like the telephone linesman or the waitress—found it a pleasant place to worship on their way to or from work. Lawrence Arnim at the front vestibule and Henry Hollis at the

1962. Soviet offensive build-up in Cuba is revealed to the American people October 22 by President Kennedy, and crisis eases October 28 with Soviet agreement to dismantle bases.

1963. Pope John XXIII issues historic encyclical April 10 calling for the establishment of a supernation to which all countries would belong to insure world peace.

driveway to the parking lot were among those giving cathedral welcome to all comers. Scattered through the Sunday school were Barney and Andy Baldwin whose parents were new Houstonians from New York, Andy, Rusty, Peter and Doug Johnston, whose parents came to Houston after World War II; Laura, Paul and Andrew Hobby, whose great-grandparents were married a century ago by the rector of Christ Church; Stephen and Barbara Pond, whose father, grandfather, great-grandfather and great-great-grandfather were Christ Church vestrymen, and Robert Koelsch whose maternal grandmother—Rosa Allen—was the second girl to marry in the new church of 1893, whose great-grandmother gave Camp Allen to the diocese, and whose great-great-great-grandmother was a member of Christ Church. At a recent communion service, four generations knelt together at the communion rail: Mrs. Edith Ann Axell, her daughter Victoria Maude (Mrs. J. Orville Davis) her granddaughter Dorothy (Mrs. Robert Baldwin) and her great-granddaughter Linda Ann Baldwin. All are descendants of an earlier Christ Church member, Mrs. W. F. Biggs, Mrs. Axell's mother.

The Every Member Canvass brought in $195,000. The Endowment Fund as the year neared its end had $475,000—almost one-fourth of the total goal of $2,000,000 set by Dean Richardson as the minimum necessary to the cathedral's future. And names written by the dean in the big Book of Remembrance now filled a volume and a half. Under Canon Fontaine, the Young People's Fellowship and the Young People's Service League were meeting each Sunday evening in Cleveland Hall. In 1962 and 1963, they had for advisors Mr. and Mrs. Edward Gaylord, Mr. and Mrs. G. Sidney Buchanan, Mr. and Mrs. C. P. Ufer, Mr. and Mrs. Peter Grandjeans, Mr. and Mrs. Ralph Harper, Mr. and Mrs. Sam Wheeler, Mr. and Mrs. James Richardson, Jr., Mr. and Mrs. David Collins, and Mr. and Mrs. Burt Young.

Just after noon on a Friday in November, the news swept Houston that President Kennedy was dead—shot in Dallas. Only the day before, he had been in Houston, his young face alive with laughter, his hair chestnut red in the sunshine. Bishop Hines went into the cathedral and began a quiet service for those who began to gather, an instinctive turning to God in time of shock. Sunday morning, Dean Richardson faced a congregation deeply subdued. And at noon Monday, Christ Church Cathedral was filled as it had never been filled, with men, women and children standing in the aisles and doorways, and overflowing into chapels, for the memorial service to the nation's youngest and most vivid president. Bishop Hines, Dean Richardson, Canon Fontaine, and the Rev. Joseph A. Johnson conducted the service.

This was not the first memorial service in this old building for a dead president. People of Houston had gathered in this church when President McKinley was shot, and when President Roosevelt died, but this all seemed more peculiarly personal—because a president had been killed in Texas, and a Texan had become president. And there was true anguish for the pain of his wife and children.

"To the presidency," Bishop Hines said, "John Fitzgerald Kennedy brought the gifts of high intellect, youthful verve, a saving sense of humor, and undiscourageable single mindedness. He was possessed of a dignity beyond his years, set amid personal family relationships of modesty and love which endeared him to parents, and to husbands, everywhere. He was a symbol of dynamism which has been and still is an important dimension of the American dream. His unmistakable, though never pretentious, religious faith marked

1963. More than 200,000 persons march in Washington in support of Negro demands for full civil rights, the largest demonstration in capital history.

1963. West Germany reports August 7 that more than 16,000 East Germans have escaped through, over or under the Berlin wall.

227

him as a man who understood clearly both his origin and his destiny."

Bishop Hines concluded with a quotation from Maxwell Anderson: "There are some who lift the age they inhabit until all men walk on higher ground in that lifetime."

Thanksgiving Day services, coming so soon after, were somber, and throughout the Advent season, the congregation reflected the quiet which seemed to lie over the United States through Christmas.

In late December and early January, Christ Church Cathedral offices were intensely busy in preparation for the Diocesan Council coming back—as it should—to the cathedral in this year of special anniversary. Dean Richardson had looked forward to 1964 from as early as 1962. Many months in advance, he invited all past rectors and deans of Christ Church to plan to come to Houston in April for the annual dinner. And William Barnard, looking ahead, gained consent from Sir John Barbirolli to conduct the Cathedral Choir and Houston Symphony Orchestra members in a sacred work in the cathedral at some time during 1964.

For on March 16, 1964, Christ Church Cathedral observed its 125th anniversary—an anniversary which marked a new beginning.

Each day the cathedral, each day the men and women and children of the cathedral, are making history. No one book could tell the whole story of what has gone before, and this one has only told scattered highlights—by no means all of them—of the first 125 years.

Christ Church Cathedral has lived through changes of government, depression, yellow fever epidemics, cholera, wars, and the dislocations of war, fires, changes of city patterns of living, human whim and human error, floods, hurricanes, offers to buy and sell, polio epidemics, burglaries, gun fire, two major exoduses of members, and times of grave financial danger. But in its moments of greatest need it has managed always to call and to secure the rector or the dean best suited to save it, and in its moments of greatest opportunity, it has had the leadership to profit by that opportunity.

It stands today on land that money could not buy. And it seems by destiny to have been elected to live. All Houston needs it, all Episcopalians turn to it. Yet its future lies in the dedication of those who use it most, of those who kneel at its chancel rail and worship at its altar.

1963. NASA's Manned Spacecraft Center is built on 1,600 acres southeast of Houston.

Acknowledgements

Just as there is no such thing as a self-made man, so—I believe—nobody ever writes a book alone. Certainly I did not write this one without tremendous amounts of help—generously, spontaneously and thoughtfully given. Without it, the book would be of meagre fabric, because the Christ Church archives had suffered through the years from hurricane, removals from old buildings to new, the dynamiting of safes by thieves, and simple casualness.

Throughout the Christ Church records from 1839 to the present, diverse spellings of proper names appear. Whenever a person's signature was available, that spelling was used. When there was no record to show how the person preferred for his name to be spelled, the Houston City Directory version was accepted. Now obsolete spellings of such words as Gulph and Corea were retained in quoting old diaries and letters, as was the original punctuation of those highly personal writings.

Many of the gaps have not yet been filled for lack of accurate material with which to fill them. But there would have been more were it not for the kindness of many men and women—non-members as well as members of the cathedral.

I am grateful to:

Mrs. W. P. Hobby, president and editor of *The Houston Post* for tangible help of many kinds.

Dr. Andrew Forest Muir of Rice University, associate editor of the *Journal of Southern History,* for his generous loan of the diary of Charles Gillett, the diary of Caleb Ives, and the list of marriages done by Episcopal clergymen in Harris County between 1839 and 1874; for his permission to quote from his articles; for his generous gift of additional data, his counsel and his time in reading this book in typescript.

The Rev. Frank MacDonald Spindler of Washington, D.C., not only for his permission to quote from his thesis on St. Bartholemew's Church, Hempstead, but for his great kindness in copying and sending to me other information about Dr. W. T. D. Dalzell which would have been hard for me to obtain.

John D. Dreaper, who though he left Christ Church 50 years ago, drew on his unique memory of the Beckwith and Aves period, and gave us the use of photographs and gold Sunday school medals.

Mrs. Frank Akin, who not only gave the use of important material from the family papers of the Rev. Peter Gray Sears and the Gray family, but helped with research as well.

Mrs. Albert P. Jones for making the research trips to Austin a pleasure.

Dr. Lawrence L. Brown, diocesan archivist, for his permission to quote from his newly published *The Episcopal Church in Texas, 1838-1874,* and for suggestions on sources.

Dr. Virginia Nelle Bellamy, archivist of the National Archives of the Protestant Episcopal Church, Austin, and her staff; Chester Kielman, archivist of the Archives of the University of Texas Library, Austin; Mrs. David Knepper, director of the San Jacinto Monument Museum of History Association; Mrs. Raymond Ulmer, historical room librarian, Houston Public Library, and Mrs. D. L. Simpson, Houston Post library—for guidance through their archives and the loan of material.

To present and former rectors and members of Christ Church who gave time-consuming interviews and the use of pictures, scrapbooks, historical sketches: the Rt. Rev. James Pernette DeWolfe, the Rt. Rev. John Elbridge Hines, the Rt. Rev. Hamilton Hyde Kellogg, the Rev. Joseph Johnson, Mr. William Barnard, the Rev. Howard Rutenbar, Albert Bowles, Mrs. Frank Clemens, Mr. and Mrs. W. A. Kirkland, Albert P. Jones, Miss Willie Ada Pettit, Miss Daisy Elgin, Mrs. J. Milton Richardson, Miss Adele Waggaman, Miss Louise Waggaman, the late Mrs. Ernest Humphrys, Charles T. Carnes, Mr. and Mrs. W. Ernst Japhet, Mrs. Ralph Gunn, Mrs. Nell Lee VanValkenburgh, Mrs. James T. Heyl, Mrs. James A. Elkins, Jr., Mrs. Joseph W. Evans, Mrs. Richard Neff, Dr. and Mrs. A. Philo Howard, and many others.

Charles Thobae for his willingness to let us draft him as a member of the publishing team and for the use of pictures and information from his files.

To members of the cathedral staff: Mrs. Esther Chaplin, Mrs. Mildred Lytle, Mrs. Jo Culberson, Eldridge Carrier, Lionel Bellard, and in the diocesan office Mrs. Prim Specht.

To Mrs. A. Jean Shepherd, keeper of Christ Church deeds and documents and stimulating companion from the early months of the research task.

To James V. Culberson, not only for the beautiful design of this book, but for his wisdom and patience in guiding me through the maze of preparing a book for publication. To Fred DuBose for his perceptive drawings, and to Gulf Printing Company for the interest given to the printing of this book.

To Patricia Barnes, Susan Barnes and Polly Barnes for help in charting vestry lists, and Steven Barnes for lending an extra hand. To Mr. and Mrs. Robert C. Johnston for frequent stimulating encouragement. To Mrs. James V. Smith for making it possible for me to get away for research trips and writing stints. To my husband and children for making the two year task an enjoyable family project.

And I thank heartily and warmly the Very Rev. J. Milton Richardson, dean of Christ Church Cathedral, for seeing that a history of the church should be written now before time could rob the historian of further major sources, for steadfast encouragement of a journalist new to the task of historiographer, and for generous and spirit-lifting support throughout the two years required for the completion of this book.

Marguerite Johnston
April 15, 1964

Rectors of Christ Church

The Rev. Robert Martin Chapman, missionary. *November, 1838 - June 9, 1839.*

The Rev. Henry B. Goodwin, rector pro tempore. *Christmas, 1839-Easter, 1840.*

The Rev. Benjamin Eaton, missionary. *January through May, 1841.*

The Rev. Charles Gillett, missionary and first rector.

February, 1843 - January, 1852.

The Rev. Henry Sansom. *January - December 31, 1852.*

The Rev. J. J. Nicholson. *January, 1854 - May, 1855.*

The Rev. W. T. D. Dalzell. *Early 1857 - May, 1861.*

The Rev. Edwin A. Wagner. *January 1, 1862 - Spring, 1864.*

The Rev. J. M. Goshorn. *Summer of 1864.*

The Rev. J. M. Curtis. *Fall, 1864 - September, 1866.*

The Rev. Joseph Cross. *Late 1866 - early 1869.*

The Rev. T. R. B. Trader. *Christmas, 1870 - 1873.*

The Rev. John Julyan Clemens. *November 15, 1874 - early 1885.*

The Rev. William C. Dawson. *Spring, 1885 - Easter, 1886.*

The Rev. Charles Minnegerode Beckwith. *October, 1886 - July 31, 1892.*

The Rev. Benjamin Andrew Rogers, rector pro tempore.

August - December, 1892.

The Rev. Henry Demarel Aves. *December, 1892 - November, 1904.*

The Rev. Peter Gray Sears, Rector. *March, 1905 - December 7, 1926.*

Rector emeritus. *January, 1927 - June, 1928.*

The Rev. James Swayne Allen. *January, 1927 - April 3, 1934.*

The Rev. James Pernette DeWolfe. *December 5, 1934 - May, 1940.*

The Rev. John Elbridge Hines. *January, 1941 - October 18, 1945.*

The Rev. Hamilton Hyde Kellogg. *January 6, 1946 - June, 1952.*

The Rev. J. Milton Richardson. *September, 1952 - ——*

Wardens of Christ Church

William Fairfax Gray........1839, 1840, 1841..........Erastus S. Perkins
Erastus S. Perkins.............. 1842 ....Archibald S. Ruthven
No record .... 1843-1844 .... No record
Erastus S. Perkins.............. 1845 ....Henry F. Gillett

May 12, 1845, a new constitution and by-laws provided that henceforth, the rector would appoint a senior warden, and the vestry would elect a junior warden.

Senior Wardens		Junior Wardens
Erastus S. Perkins..............	1846	.............Abner Cooke, Jr.
Erastus S. Perkins..............	1847	.................Peter W. Gray
Erastus S. Perkins..............	1848	.............John D. Andrews
Archibald S. Ruthven..........	1849, 1850	..............Peter W. Gray
Archibald S. Ruthven..........	1851	..........Dr. Francis Moore, Jr.
Archibald S. Ruthven..........	1852	..................W. W. Stiles
John D. Andrews..........	1853, 1854	................W. W. Stiles
John D. Andrews..............	1855	.............Leonard S. Perkins
John D. Andrews..........1856, 1857, 1858............		Dr. W. H. Eliot
Peter W. Gray..........1859, 1860, 1861, 1862.........		Dr. W. H. Eliot
Dr. W. H. Eliot............1863, 1864, 1865...........		A. S. Richardson
William J. Hutchins...........	1866, 1867	..............A. S. Richardson
A. S. Richardson..............	1868, 1869	.................C. A. Darling
A. S. Richardson..............	1870	.....R. M. Elgin
A. S. Richardson..............	1871, 1872	............George B. Mitchell
William J. Hutchins............	1873	.............George B. Mitchell
A. S. Richardson................	1874	................W. D. Cleveland

Records are missing or imperfect from 1875 to 1893.

A. S. Richardson..............	1880	...........William D. Cleveland
William J. Hutchins..............	1881	...........William D. Cleveland
R. M. Elgin..................	1882-1912	.........William D. Cleveland
R. M. Elgin..................	1913	.....Rufus Cage
Rufus Cage..................	1914-1917	.................Sam McNeill
Sam McNeill..............	1918, 1919	.............Charles L. Desel
Sam McNeill..................	1920	....................Andrew Dow
Edwin L. Neville..............	1921	.....Ennis Cargill
Sam McNeill..................	1922	.................Ennis Cargill
Sam McNeill.................	1923, 1924	.............Edwin L. Neville
Edwin L. Neville..............	1925	...................P. S. Tilson
P. S. Tilson..................	1926	...............Sam McNeill
Sam McNeill..................	1926	.................Ennis Cargill
Sam McNeill.................	1927, 1928	............Edwin L. Neville

William Strauss	1929, 1930	Albert M. Bowles
Frank Clemens	1931	Henry W. Stansbury
None	1932	Albert M. Bowles
Frank Clemens	1933, 1934	Albert M. Bowles
Frank Clemens	1935	Dallas H. Moore
William Strauss	1936, 1937	Albert M. Bowles
Albert M. Bowles	1938	Charles T. Carnes
William Strauss	1939	Charles T. Carnes
William Strauss	1940, 1941	Albert M. Bowles
William D. Cleveland, Jr.	1942	Albert M. Bowles
Charles T. Carnes	1943	August L. Selig
Charles T. Carnes	1944	Albert M. Bowles
Albert M. Bowles	1945	W. Ernst Japhet
Albert M. Bowles	1946	Albert P. Jones
Charles T. Carnes	1947	A. Balfour Patterson
Charles T. Carnes	1947	A. M. Goodyear
Charles T. Carnes	1948	W. Ernst Japhet
John C. Flanagan	1949	A. M. Goodyear
W. Ernst Japhet	1950	A. M. Goodyear
August L. Selig	1951	A. M. Goodyear
August L. Selig	1952	R. E. Robertson
Albert P. Jones	1953	R. E. Robertson
John H. Crooker	1954	August L. Selig
William J. Goldston	1955	Albert M. Bowles
George C. Morris	1956	Charles E. Shaver
Floyd E. Bates	1957, 1958	John H. Freeman, Jr.
William J. Goldston	1959	Ross P. Bennett
George C. Morris	1960	Ralph W. Holtz
Ralph W. Holtz	1961	Porter P. Parris
James A. Elkins, Jr.	1962	Henry T. Hollis
John F. Lynch	1963	Richard W. French
Charles E. Shaver	1964	Arthur P. Terrell

20th century Treasurers of Christ Church

Rufus Cage	1893 - 1899. 1905 - 1913
P. M. Timpson	1900 - 1903
O. M. Pudor	1904
Frank Clemens	1913 - 1917
A. E. Schaeffer	1917 - 1927
A. E. Hartwell	1927 - 1943
John Mellinger	1943 - ——

Vestrymen of Christ Church 1839—1964

William Fairfax Gray...................1839-1842
John Birdsall 1839-1840
Memucan Hunt 1839-1841
A. F. Woodward......................1839-1840
James Webb 1839-1840
William Pierpont 1839-1840
Tod Robinson 1839-1840
Erastus S. Perkins..1839-1842. 1844-1848. 1862-1867.
  1870
D. W. C. Harris............1839-1841. 1848-1849
John D. Andrews..1839-1842. 1844-1848. 1853-1858.
  1862
Charles Kesler........................1839-1840
George Allen 1839-1841
James Reily........1839-1842. 1844-1846. 1848-1855
A. A. M. Jackson.....................1839-1840
William Douglas Lee.....................1839
William R. Baker.....................1840-1841
John W. Pitkin.......................1840-1841
Charles T. Hedenburg.................1840-1841
John B. Houghtaling....................1841
Archibald S. Ruthven...........1842. 1844-1854
E. J. Felder.............................1842
William W. Swain..............1842. 1844-1847
Cornelius Ennis........1842. 1844-1847. 1852-1856
Jacob Cruger..............1842. 1844-1849
H. Evans 1842
John F. Torrey........................1842
Peter W. Gray........1842. 1844-1864. 1866-1867.
  1869-1874
Leonard S. Perkins...........1842. 1844. 1854-1855
Henry F. Gillett......................1844-1846
Thomas M. League....................1844-1846
E. B. Nichols.........................1845-1850
William Marsh Rice..........1845-1847. 1852-1856
William A. Van Alstyne..........1845. 1849. 1854
Abner Cooke, Jr. 1846. 1848-1849
William M. Taylor.......................1847
William J. Hutchins....1847. 1849-1851. 1853-1867.
  1869-1884
J. D. Groesbeeck........................1847
John P. Conger.......................1848-1849
Thomas W. Clark.......................1848
Dr. Francis Moore, Jr. 1849-1853
F. Scranton 1849
Robert Brewster 1849-1851. 1858-1861
George Fisher 1849
B. F. Tankersley.....................1849-1852
J. H. T. Stanley......................1850-1852
Paul Bremond 1850

Dr. W. H. Eliot....................1850-1865. 1867
Major J. Dupree......................1851-1852
W. W. Stiles.........................1851-1854
E. W. Taylor.........................1848-1854
H. Sampson 1853
A. N. Jordan.........................1855-1858
Henry Perkins ....1855-1856. 1865. 1868-1869.
  1871-1875
Louis A. Bryan.......................1855-1856
James F. Cruger......................1855-1856
Alex Keech, Jr. 1856-1859
Owen L. Cochran......1856-1861. 1863-1869. 1871
A. S. Richardson.....................1858-1899
Joseph H. Evans...............1858. 1860-1861
Benjamin A. Botts.......1859-1862. 1864-1867. 1875.
  1878-1880
Edward M. Taylor.....................1859-1861
Allan C. Gray........................1862. 1865
H. W. Benchley..........................1862
W. D. Robinson..........................1863
C. M. Congreve.......................1863-1864
C. A. Darling.............1863. 1867-1871
Albert Somerville 1865-1866
E. R. Wells...............1866. 1873-1876
Captain Hugh T. Scott.................1866-1867
Major J. P. Harrison....................1867
Roland Allen.........................1867-1868
William D. Cleveland........1868-1869. 1871-1912
George Goldthwaite 1868-1869. 1877
Robert M. Elgin......................1868-1913
Samuel Williams 1868. 1870-1872. 1879-1885
George B. Mitchell..........1870-1876. 1881-1882
L. F. de Lesdernier......................1870
A. Ewing 1872
Thomas Conklin 1873-1876
Walter B. Botts......................1873-1874
T. R. Franklin.......................1874-1876
W. V. R. Watson......................1878-1907
L. S. Rayfield..........................1879
Rufus Cage 1886-1899. 1904-1918
W. M. Mitchell.......................1888-1892
Frederick Allyn Rice.................1876-1880
R. Greene 1880
S. K. McIlhenny..........1881-1887. 1890-1897
H. R. Roberts........................1881-1892
J. Waldo 1883-1889
B. F. Weems...........1883-1889. 1908-1909
Henry Scherffius 1885-1889
R. L. Pollard........................1890-1894

Presley K. Ewing.........................1890-1909
William Hines Kirkland.................1895-1897
Sam McNeill 1898-1924. 1926-1928
Simon Priester 1899
P. B. Timpson...........................1900-1903
Frank Cargill 1896-1904
Joseph B. Bowles.............1899-1907. 1910-1919
Dr. R. T. Morris.................1903. 1908-1911
John Charles Harris.....................1908-1909
Alexander Sessums Cleveland...1908-1916. 1936-1938
D. D. Cooley.............................1908-1909
Sterling Myer 1908-1921. 1924. 1935-1937
James L. Autry.........................1909-1919
R. Fairfax Crow....1910-1911. 1922-1924. 1927-1928
William Stamps Farish........1910-1911. 1920-1922
Major Frank Clemens........1910-1917. 1926-1928.
                                       1931-1935
Alex Peddie 1912-1917
Charles L. Desel....1912-1919. 1922-1923. 1925-1932
Dr. Joseph A. Mullen..............1912. 1929-1931
Herbert Godwin 1912-1914
William D. Cleveland, Jr......1913-1917. 1940-1942.
                                       1944-1946
M. A. Westcott.............................1914
A. R. Howard.........................1915-1919
Edwin L. Neville.......1915. 1918-1921. 1923-1925.
                                       1927-1928
D. C. Glenn...........................1916-1920
Andrew Dow 1917-1920
A. E. Schaeffer..............1917-1921. 1924-1926
K. E. Womack..............1918-1921. 1923. 1925
B. B. Gilmer................1919-1920. 1922-1924
Ennis Cargill......1920-1922. 1924-1926. 1928-1930.
                                       1933-1934
R. E. Williams........................1920-1922
S. W. George.........................1920-1922
P. S. Tilson.................1921-1923. 1925-1926
A. E. Hartwell.....1921-1923. 1926-1934. 1936-1939
C. Milby Dow.....1921-1923. 1927-1932. 1935-1937.
                                       1940-1943
J. S. Pyeatt.........................1922-1924
Underwood Nazro 1923-1925
James Anderson, Jr. 1923-1925. 1927-1928
Lewis Randolph Bryan, Jr. 1924-1926
John S. Cochran......................1924-1926
C. R. Wharton........................1925-1927
S. J. Payne..........................1925-1927
Robert Stuart 1926-1928
William Strauss ...1927-1930. 1935-1937. 1939-1941.
                                       1944.

Albert M. Bowles..1928-1930. 1932-1934. 1936-1938.
                 1940-1942. 1946-1948. 1953-1955
F. E. Hood.................1928-1930. 1932-1934
Chester Bryan 1928-1932. 1934-1936. 1938-1940
Robert W. Wier....1928-1932. 1934-1936. 1942-1944
Jacob F. Wolters.......................1929-1931
Edwin R. Spotts.............1929-1931. 1933-1935
I. M. Griffin.............................1929
Henry W. Stansbury.....................1930-1931
H. L. Warren.........................1931-1933
McDonald Meachum 1931-1932
Dudley Jarvis 1932-1933. 1945-1947
Dr. Paul Ledbetter..1932-1937. 1939-1941. 1945-1947
Dallas H. Moore.......................1932-1940
Charles T. Carnes..1933-1935. 1938-1939. 1941-1944.
                                       1946-1948
John C. Flanagan..1934-1936. 1938-1939. 1947-1949.
                                       1951-1953
Barry York 1935-1937. 1939-1941. 1947-1949
R. W. Horlock....1936-1938. 1940-1942. 1944-1946
James Walker Cain..........1937-1938. 1947-1949
A. Balfour Patterson..........1937-1939. 1946-1948
Dr. J. H. Weaver......................1937-1939
John S. Mellinger..1938-1940. 1943-1946. 1954-1956
Arthur L. Young.......................1939-1941
August L. Selig....1940-1943. 1945-1947. 1950-1952.
                                       1954-1955.
Dr. J. Harold Turner.....................1940
Otis Van de Mark.....................1940-1942
Dr. W. H. Scherer....................1941-1943
I. M. Wilford........................1941-1943
Thomas L. Walker.....................1942-1943
Ralph Henderson 1942-1944
Jack Grantham 1943-1944
W. Ernst Japhet.............1943-1945. 1948-1950
John R. Suman.............1943-1944. 1956-1958
K. A. Frambach.......................1943-1945
W. J. T. Ford............................1944
George N. Posey.................1944-1945. 1958
Albert P. Jones.........1944-1946. 1949. 1951-1953
Dr. Thomas Burke...........1945-1947. 1955-1956
A. M. Goodyear.............1945-1947. 1949-1951
Bernard Luscher 1945
W. Norman Sick......................1945-1946
J. Leroy Jeffers............1946-1948. 1950-1951
Jasper Neath 1946-1948. 1950-1952. 1955-1956
Joseph W. Tilton.....................1946-1948
William J. Goldston.........1947-1949. 1953-1955.
                 1957-1959. 1960-1963
T. J. Bettes.........................1948-1949
John H. Crooker...1948-1950. 1952-1954. 1959-1961

William F. Rice..........................1948
Arthur P. Terrell...........1948-1950. 1962-1964
J. Raymond Black......................1949-1950
David L. Gordon......................1949-1951
W. D. C. Lucy........................1949-1951
Clarence Roberts 1949-1951
Williard B. Wagner...................1949-1950
Raymond E. Baarts....................1950-1951
James A. Elkins, Jr..........1950-1952. 1956-1958.
1960-1962. 1964
George C. Morris...1949-1951. 1954-1956. 1958-1960
James Lanier Britton...................1951-1953
Edwin Rice Brown.....................1951-1953
Webb Mading 1951
James Bradbury 1952
Erwin R. Heinen.......................1952
William A. Kirkland...................1952-1954
Dr. F. O. McGehee....................1952-1954
R. E. Robertson.......................1952-1953
J. E. Sick............................1952-1954
Floyd Temple 1952-1954
Ralph Gunn 1953-1955
General Roy C. Heflebower.............1953-1955
Howard S. Hoover.....................1953-1955
L. Daffan Gilmer......................1954-1956
Charles L. Shaver...........1954-1956. 1962-1964
Lloyd Fadrique 1955-1957
Ralph W. Holtz.............1955-1957. 1959-1961
Edward Schulenburg 1955-1957
C. Harcourt Wooten...................1955-1957
Floyd E. Bates........................1956-1958
John S. Dunn.........................1956-1958

Tom P. Walker....................1956-1958. 1961
John H. Freeman, Jr..............1956-1958. 1962
Ross P. Bennett.............1957-1959. 1963-1964
David F. Sanderson.....................1957-1959
Hirst B. Suffield.....................1957-1959
Quentin Bates 1958-1960
Dr. Dan G. McNamara..................1958-1960
Harris Masterson 1958-1960
H. Grant Thomas.....................1958-1960
Robert P. Bushman, Jr. 1959-1961
Dr. John McFarland........................1959
Porter P. Parris.......................1959-1961
H. L. Simpson........................1959-1961
T. A. Claiborne......................1960-1961
Leslie Coleman 1960-1962
Stuart Helman 1960-1962. 1964
Henry T. Hollis.......................1960-1962
Richard W. French.....................1961-1963
John F. Lynch........................1961-1963
Harry C. Webb, Jr. 1961-1963
John M. Winterbotham.................1961-1963
C. D. Cantrell, Jr. 1962-1964
Warren B. Pond, Jr. 1962-1964
Paul A. Smith........................1962
Bruce Jones 1963-1964
Dr. George C. Morris, Jr...............1963-1964
James R. Roos........................1963-1964
Jerry P. Turner......................1963-1964
Henry Weaver 1963-1964
Phelan Hunter 1964
Hugo V. Neuhaus, Jr. 1964
Dr. G. Forrest Wortham, Jr. 1964

OFFICERS OF THE LADIES PARISH ASSOCIATION OF CHRIST CHURCH

1871 - 1873
President...................Mrs. Cornelius Ennis
Vice President...............Mrs. Rufus K. Cage
Secretary and Treasurer......Mrs. Sarah M. Perkins

1873 - 1874
President...................Mrs. Cornelius Ennis
Vice President............Mrs. Thomas H. Conklin
Secretary and Treasurer........Mrs. Kate W. Groce

1875 - 1876
President..................Mrs. Cornelius Ennis

1877 - 1878
President...................Mrs. (Dr.) E. Palmer
Vice President...........Mrs. Thomas H. Conklin
Secretary and Treasurer.........Mrs. Ella Connell

1879
President........................Mrs. J. G. Tracy
Secretary and Treasurer.........Mrs. Ella Connell

1880
President........................Mrs. J. G. Tracy

1881 - 1882
President.....................Mrs. J. G. Tracy
Vice President...............Mrs. James H. Blake
Secretary and Treasurer.......Mrs. Thad A. Smith

1883
President....................Mrs. Peter W. Gray

1884
President....................Mrs. Peter W. Gray
Vice President...............Mrs. Henry Blake
Secretary and Treasurer.......Mrs. Thad A. Smith

1885 - 1887
President....................Mrs. Peter W. Gray
Secretary and Treasurer..........Mrs. L. T. Noyes

1888 - 1890
President...................Mrs. Peter W. Gray
Vice President...........Mrs. Thomas R. Franklin
Treasurer....................Mrs. Mary F. Gentry
Secretary....................Mrs. W. C. Crane

1891
President...................Mrs. Peter W. Gray
Vice President....................Mrs. Sam Ashe
Secretary....................Mrs. Sam McNeill
Treasurer....................Mrs. Mary F. Gentry

1892
President...................Mrs. Peter W. Gray
First Vice President...............Mrs. Sam Ashe
Second Vice President.........Mrs. B. C. Cushman
Secretary....................Mrs. Sam McNeill
Treasurer..................Mrs. Mary F. Gentry

1893
President...................Mrs. Peter W. Gray
First Vice President............Mrs. W. C. Crane
Second Vice President...........Mrs. M. G. House
Secretary....................Mrs. Sam McNeill
Treasurer..................Mrs. Mary F. Gentry

1894
President.........Mrs. Peter W. Gray succeeded by
Mrs. J. A. Huston
First Vice President............Mrs. J. A. Huston
Second Vice President......Mrs. George Goldthwaite
Secretary....................Miss Jennie Moore
Treasurer..................Mrs. Mary F. Gentry

1895 - 1896
President..............Mrs. George Goldthwaite
Vice President...................Mrs. E. S. Tracy
Secretary....................Mrs. Sam McNeill
Treasurer....................Mrs. Mary F. Gentry

1897
President....................Mrs. Mary F. Gentry
Vice President..................Mrs. J. A. Huston
Secretary....................Mrs. Jesse Bryan
Treasurer....................Mrs. Rufus K. Cage

1898 - 1900
President....................Mrs. Mary F. Gentry
Vice President.................Mrs. J. A. Huston
Treasurer....................Mrs. M. E. Bryan
Secretary....................Mrs. B. A. Randolph

1901
President....................Mrs. Mary F. Gentry
First Vice President.............Mrs. B. F. Weems
Second Vice President.........Mrs. B. A. Randolph
Secretary....................Mrs. John B. Ashe
Treasurer....................Mrs. M. E. Bryan

1902
President....................Mrs. Mary F. Gentry
First Vice President.............Mrs. B. F. Weems
Second Vice President.........Mrs. B. A. Randolph
Secretary....................Mrs. Mamie Tinsley
Treasurer....................Mrs. M. E. Bryan

1903
President....................Mrs. Mary F. Gentry
First Vice President.............Mrs. B. F. Weems
Second Vice President.........Mrs. Mamie Tinsley
Secretary....................Mrs. E. S. Tracey
Treasurer....................Mrs. Mary E. Bryan

1904
President....................Mrs. Mary F. Gentry
Secretary.................Mrs. Florence N. Dancy

1905
President....................Mrs. Mary F. Gentry
First Vice President..................Mrs. Dancy
Secretary....................Mrs. Florence Dancy

1906 - 1908
President....................Mrs. Mary F. Gentry
First Vice President...........Mrs. Mamie Tinsley
Second Vice President.........Mrs. Wharton Bates
Secretary.................Mrs. Thomas McGonigle
Treasurer....................Mrs. Mary E. Bryan

1909 - 1910
President ....Mrs. Mary F. Gentry

1910 - 1911
President....................Mrs. Mary F. Gentry
First Vice President............Mrs. Philip H. Fall
Second Vice President...........Mrs. Sam McNeill

Secretary..........................Mrs. E. A. Cooke
Treasurer..................Mrs. Mary E. Bryan

1912 - 1913
President...................Mrs. Mary F. Gentry
First Vice President............Mrs. Philip H. Fall
Second Vice President...........Mrs. Sam McNeill
Secretary.........................Mrs. J. S. Akin
Treasurer......................Mrs. M. E. Bryan

1913 - 1914
President...................Mrs. Mary F. Gentry
First Vice President............Mrs. Philip H. Fall
Second Vice President..........Mrs. E. S. Heffernan
Secretary.........................Mrs. J. S. Akin
Treasurer......................Mrs. M. E. Bryan

1914 - 1915
President...................Mrs. Mary F. Gentry
Vice President..............Mrs. A. S. Cleveland

1915 - 1916
President..................Mrs. Alexander Peddie

1916 - 1917
President..................Mrs. Alexander Peddie
Vice President..................Mrs. D. C. Glenn
Secretary...........Mrs. George Bruce Fuller
Treasurer...............Mrs. Kenneth E. Womack

1917 - 1920
President.....................Mrs. D. C. Glenn
Vice President...........Mrs. John A. McClellan
Secretary......................Mrs. E. L. Neville
Treasurer.....................Mrs. K. E. Womack

1920 - 1921
President......................Mrs. A. D. Boice
Vice President..................Mrs. E. L. Neville
Secretary.....................Mrs. W. H. Noble
Treasurer.....................Mrs. K. E. Womack

1921 - 1922
President.....................Mrs. E. L. Neville
Vice President..................Mrs. W. S. Farish
Secretary......................Mrs. J. W. Evans
Treasurer.....................Mrs. K. E. Womack

1923 - 1924
President....................Mrs. B. B. Gilmer
Vice President...................Mrs. W. S. Farish
Secretary......................Mrs. John P. Johns
Treasurer.....................Mrs. K. E. Womack

1925
President................Mrs. Palmer Hutcheson

1926
President......................Mrs. W. H. Noble

1927
President......................Mrs. E. L. Neville
Vice President...................Mrs. J. W. Evans
Secretary......................Miss Madge Dow
Treasurer....................Mrs. K. E. Womack
Charter members. Mrs. Lizzie E. Fall, Mrs. J. R. Morris

1928
President...............Mrs. McDonald Meachum

1929
President......................Mrs. E. R. Spotts

1930
President......................Mrs. E. R. Spotts
Secretary....................Mrs. John F. Scott

1931
President......................Mrs. A. M. Bowles
Vice President....................Mrs. J. W. Cain
Treasurer....................Mrs. Frank Clemens
Secretary.....................Mrs. John F. Scott

1932
President.....................Mrs. H. L. Warren
Vice President................Mrs. Dudley Jarvis
Treasurer..................Mrs. Quinlan Daffan
Secretary.....................Mrs. John F. Scott

1933
President.....................Mrs. H. L. Warren
Vice President........................No record
Treasurer..................Mrs. Quinlan Daffan
Secretary.....................Mrs. John F. Scott

1934
President.....................Mrs. E. T. Chew
Vice President..................Mrs. Fred Dixon
Treasurer..................Mrs. Quinlan Daffan
Corresponding Secretary........Mrs. A. E. Hartwell
Recording Secretary............Mrs. John F. Scott

1935
President....................Mrs. Fred Clemens
Vice President..................Mrs. Fred Dixon
Secretary....................Mrs. J. A. Haralson
Corresponding Secretary........Mrs. A. E. Hartwell
Treasurer..................Mrs. Quinlan Daffan

1936 - 1937

President..............Mrs. Leeland D. Fletcher
Vice President..................Mrs. S. F. Dixon
Treasurer......................Mrs. Robert Lester
Secretary...............Mrs. George P. Townsend
Corresponding Secretary........Mrs. A. E. Hartwell

1938

President................Mrs. John A. McClellan
Vice President..................Mrs. E. R. Spotts
Second Vice President............Mrs. E. T. Chew
Secretary.......................Mrs. Louis Bryan
Corresponding Secretary........Mrs. A. E. Hartwell
Treasurer......................Mrs. Robert Lester

1939

President................Mrs. John A. McClellan
First Vice President.............Mrs. E. R. Spotts
Second Vice President............Mrs. E. T. Chew
Treasurer......................Mrs. Robert Lester
Secretary........................Mrs. A. L. Selig
Corresponding Secretary.........Mrs. A. E. Hartwell

1940

President.................Mrs. John A. McClellan
First Vice President...........Mrs. A. B. Patterson
Second Vice President............Mrs. E. T. Chew
Secretary........................Mrs. A. L. Selig
Corresponding Secretary........Mrs. A. E. Hartwell
Treasurer......................Mrs. Robert Lester

1941

President....................Mrs. A. B. Patterson
First Vice President..........Mrs. Arthur L. Young
Second Vice President..........Mrs. H. L. Warren
Secretary......................Mrs. S. H. Wheeler
Corresponding Secretary........Mrs. A. E. Hartwell
Treasurer......................Mrs. Robert Lester

1942

President....................Mrs. A. B. Patterson
First Vice President.............Mrs. A. L. Young
Second Vice President..........Mrs. H. L. Warren
Third Vice President...........Mrs. Dudley Jarvis
Secretary......................Mrs. S. H. Wheeler
Corresponding Secretary........Mrs. A. E. Hartwell
Treasurer......................Mrs. Robert Lester

1943

President.......................Mrs. A. L. Selig
First Vice President...........Mrs. Dudley Jarvis
Second Vice President..........Mrs. E. E. Adkins
Third Vice President...........Mrs. W. A. Toland
Secretary......................Mrs. S. H. Wheeler

Corresponding Secretary.......Mrs. George N. Posey
Treasurer......................Mrs. Robert Lester
Historian.....................Mrs. A. E. Hartwell

1944

President........................Mrs. A. L. Selig

1945

President.....................Mrs. W. E. Japhet
First Vice President..........Mrs. Dudley C. Jarvis
Second Vice President........Mrs. Morgan J. Davis
Third Vice President..............Mrs. J. W. Cain
Recording Secretary............Mrs. A. M. Bowles
Corresponding Secretary.........Mrs. A. L. Young
Treasurer...................Mrs. George N. Posey
Parliamentarian............Mrs. Bud A. Randolph
Historian.....................Mrs. Arthur Hartwell

1946

President.....................Mrs. W. E. Japhet
First Vice President...........Mrs. W. A. Toland
Second Vice President........Mrs. Morgan J. Davis
Third Vice President..............Mrs. J. W. Cain
Recording Secretary.............Mrs. J. E. Gough
Corresponding Secretary.........Mrs. A. L. Young
Treasurer...................Mrs. Jack Grantham
Parliamentarian................Mrs. H. H. Ueckert
Historian.....................Mrs. Arthur Hartwell

1947 - 1948

President.....................Mrs. W. A. Toland

1949 - 1950

President.....................Mrs. J. A. Haralson

1951 - 1952

President ....Mrs. Leroy Bell

1953

President...............Mrs. C. Harcourt Wooten
First Vice President...........Mrs. J. Orville Davis
Second Vice President.........Mrs. Frank Clemens
Third Vice President........Miss Louise Waggaman
Recording Secretary.............Mrs. Robert Tyler
Treasurer...................Mrs. J. A. Roberdeau
Parliamentarian ....Mrs. Ralph Gunn

1954

President...............Mrs. C. Harcourt Wooten
First Vice President........Mrs. Renfrow Robertson
Second Vice President.........Mrs. Frank Clemens
Third Vice President...........Mrs. Herbert Hake
Recording Secretary.............Mrs. Ross Bennett
Corresponding Secretary.........Mrs. Robert Tyler
Treasurer............Mrs. A. J. Kincannon Smith
Parliamentarian ....Mrs. Ralph Gunn

1955 - 1956

President.................Mrs. Ralph Ellis Gunn
Vice President............Mrs. Renfrow Robertson
Recording Secretary.............Mrs. Ross Bennett
Corresponding Secretary......Mrs. George C. Morris
Treasurer and
   Finance Chairman........Mrs. Charles E. Shaver
Parliamentarian..............Mrs. Carroll Church

1957

President..................Mrs. Charles A. Hillier
Vice President...............Mrs. J. A. Roberdeau
Recording Secretary.........Mrs. G. Bruce Staples
Corresponding Secretary.....Mrs. Aphra K. Bradford
Treasurer.................Mrs. Charles E. Shaver
Parliamentarian................Mrs. L. T. Barrow

1958

President..................Mrs. Charles A. Hillier
Vice President...............Mrs. J. A. Roberdeau
Recording Secretary.........Mrs. G. Bruce Staples
Corresponding Secretary.....Mrs. Aphra K. Bradford
Treasurer............Mrs. S. Russel Pat Casey, Jr.
Parliamentarian................Mrs. L. T. Barrow

1959

President.................Mrs. Arthur P. Terrell
Vice President..............Mrs. Arthur L. Young

Recording Secretary.........Mrs. Charles Headrick
Corresponding Secretary......Mrs. E. R. Oberwetter
Treasurer..................Mrs. John H. Naschke
Parliamentarian.................Mrs. Robert Tyler

1960-1961

President....................Mrs. Gary Pearson
Vice President................Mrs. J. W. Bartram
Recording Secretary............Mrs. Julia P. Taylor
Corresponding Secretary....Mrs. E. Stanley Crawford
Treasurer..................Mrs. John H. Naschke
Parliamentarian...........Mrs. H. Alvis McConnell

1961-1962

President.....................Mrs. Gary Pearson
Vice President................Mrs. J. W. Bartram
Recording Secretary............Mrs. Julia P. Taylor
Corresponding Secretary....Mrs. E. Stanley Crawford
Treasurer.....................Mrs. E. W. Fogler
Parliamentarian...........Mrs. H. Alvis McConnell

1962-1963

President.................Mrs. Dan G. McNamara
Vice President.........Mrs. Richard W. French, Jr.
Recording Secretary...........Mrs. Harrie Swinford
Corresponding Secretary........Mrs. H. J. Brogdon
Treasurer.....................Mrs. E. W. Fogler
Parliamentarian..............Mrs. Sidney H. Pack

Bibliography

Brown, Lawrence L. *The Episcopal Church in Texas, 1838-1874.* Austin: Church Historical Society. 1963.

Carroll, B. H. *Standard History of Houston.* Nashville: 1912.

Chorley, E. Clowes, *Men and Movements in the American Episcopal Church.* New York: Charles Scribner's Sons. 1946.

Doyle, Gerry. *Camels in Texas?* San Jacinto Museum of History Association. 1956.

Hines, John Elbridge. *Christ Church Sermons.* Houston: Christ Church Cathedral. 1946.

Houston, A History and Guide. WPA. Houston: The Anson Jones Press. 1942.

Lindsley, James Elliott. *A History of Saint James' Church in the City of New York.* 1960.

Morgan, William Manning. *Trinity Church, Galveston, 1841-1953.* Houston: The Anson Jones Press. 1954.

Murphy, DuBose. *A Short History of the Protestant Episcopal Church in Texas.* Dallas: Turner Company. 1935.

Spindler, Frank MacDonald. *A History of St. Bartholemew's Episcopal Church, Hempstead, Waller County, Texas.* Unpublished thesis for Master's degree, University of Houston. 1955. Copies in Waller County Library and University of Houston Library.

Texas in 1837. Edited by Andrew Forest Muir. Austin: University of Texas Press. 1958.

Yoakum, H. *History of Texas.* New York: Redfield. 1855.

Album of Photographs of the City of Houston by W. Fritz. Circa 1890. Courtesy of W. Ernst Japhet.

The Clerical Directory of the Protestant Episcopal Church. New York: Church Hymnal Corporation. 1962.

Houston Blue Book. Houston: Published by J. R. Wheat, Cummings & Sons Printers. 1896.

Houston City Directories of 1866, 1877-78, 1880-81, 1884-85, 1887-88, 1889-90, 1894-95, 1897-98, 1899, 1903-04, 1907, 1910-11, 1915, 1917, 1919, 1922, 1923-24, 1925, 1926, 1927, 1928, 1929-30, 1932-33, 1934, 1936, 1937-38, 1939, 1941-42, 1946-47.

Social Directory of Houston. Houston: 1955.

Christ Church Bulletin. Houston: 1952-1963.

Historical Magazine of the Protestant Episcopal Church. Vol. XXVIII, No. 4, December, 1959. Vol. XXXI, No. 3, September, 1962.

Journals, Diocese of Texas. 1849-1963.

Spirit of Missions. October, 1838-August, 1849.

The Texas Churchman.
Waco: Special Edition. December, 1933.
Bryan: Vol. XLII, No. 3. April, 1939.
Houston: Vol. 59, No. 12-Vol. 60, No. 1. 1956-57 and Vol. 58, No. 12, 1955.

The Flyleaf. Vol. XI. No. 1. Fondren Library. Rice University. October, 1960.

Diary of Charles Gillet. January 31, 1843-September, 1849. Courtesy Dr. Andrew Forest Muir.

Private Journal of Caleb Ives. January 1, 1842-May 28, 1848. Typescript courtesy Dr. Andrew Forest Muir. Original in the Diocesan Archives, Austin.

Diary of Milly R. Gray. Typescript in Archives of the University of Texas Library. Austin.

History of the Ladies Parish Association by Lizzie Fall (Mrs. Philip E.). Typescript courtesy of the Ladies Parish Association. 1921.

History of the Ladies Parish Association 1871-1946 by Clare Hartwell (Mrs. Arthur). Typescript courtesy of the Ladies Parish Association.

Minutes of the Vestry of Christ Church, Houston:
Manuscript volume 1839-1875.
Manuscript volume 1893-1908.
Typed bound volumes 1908-14; 1914-22; 1923-27; 1928-30; 1931-33; 1934-36.
Typed loose leaf volumes, incomplete: 1938-39; 1938-40; 1941-42; 1943; 1944; 1946-47; 1950; 1951-54; 1955.
Typed bound volumes 1956, 1957, 1958, 1959, 1960, 1961, 1962.

The undersigned agree to unite together as a Christian Congregation in the City of Houston; — to observe the forms of worship, and be governed by the Constitution of the Protestant Episcopal Church in the United States of North America. — Houston March 16th 1839. —

6 History in pictures

Moseley Baker – One Hundred Dollars

C H Yales   One Hundred Dollars

Geo. C. Childress – One hundred

Tho L Rusk   fifty dollars

A. Sidney Johnston   Fifty dollars

[illegible]   Fifty Dollars

Memucan Hunt   Two hundred Dollars

J D Andrews   Fifty dollars

Tod Robinson $50

W D Lee 1800 feet Lumber

C C Woodward   one hundred and
fifty dollars – – – $150 –

I B Ransom   Fifty   50 – 0

Henry Thompson   Fifty Dollars

Ashbel Smith   Fifty dollars

H H Allen   Fifty dollars

J M Allen one hundred dollars ($100)

W Richardson $100 in Lumber or brick

G Wm Adams   fifty dollars

John Boldin   One hundred Dollars

C F Copeland   Thirty Dollars

The first subscription list of March, 1839, was signed by men who became famous in the Republic, in Houston, and in the Confederacy. The signatures of Secretary of War Albert Sidney Johnston (later General), Thomas L. Rusk (for whom Rusk Avenue was named) Ashbel Smith, J. D. Andrews (later mayor of Houston) Captain Moseley Baker and others are visible here.

A. C. Allen pledged "Four hundred dollars in lumber. Also half of Block 55 for church and school" on the subscription list of 1839.

Mrs. William Fairfax Gray
(Mildred Richards Stone)
1800-1851
Diarist and churchwoman
Painting in San Jacinto Museum
of History

William Fairfax Gray
1787-1841
Founder and First Warden
Painting in San Jacinto Museum
of History

The Rev. Robert M. Chapman, First Missionary
—1838-1839 (Photograph made later in life)

The Rev. Charles Gillett, First Rector—1843-1852

Shaded by pine, oak, ash and magnolia trees, Buffalo Bayou was cluttered
with logs and snags when the Allen brothers first brought Francis Lubbock
upstream to see the new capital of the Republic of Texas in 1837. It
looked then much as it did in 1890 when this picture was made.

The Rev. W. T. D. Dalzell, Fourth Rector—1857-1861 (Photograph made later in life)

The Rev. Edwin A. Wagner
Fifth Rector—1862-1864

The Rev. J. M. Curtis
Seventh Rector—1864-1866

The Rev. T. R. B. Trader
Ninth Rector—1870-1873

The Rev. John Julyan Clemens
Tenth Rector—1874-1885

The Rev. Charles Minnegerode
Beckwith
Twelfth Rector—1886-1892
(Photograph made later in life)

The Rev. Henry Demarel Aves
Thirteenth Rector—1893-1904
(Shown as Missionary Bishop
of Mexico)

The Rev. James Swayne Allen, Fifteenth Rector—1927-1934

The Rev. Peter Gray Sears, Fourteenth Rector—1905-1926

The Rev. James Pernette DeWolfe, Sixteenth Rector—1934-1940
(Later Bishop of Long Island)

William Marsh Rice
Vestryman and Benefactor

The Rev. John Elbridge Hines
Seventeenth Rector—1941-1945
(Later Bishop of Texas)

The Very Rev. Hamilton Hyde Kellogg
Eighteenth Rector—1947-1952
(First dean, later Bishop of Minnesota)

The Very Rev. J. Milton Richardson, Nineteenth Rector—1952-——— (Second dean)

Mrs. Peter W. Gray
Co-founder of the Ladies
Parish Association

Judge Peter W. Gray
For whom Gray Avenue
was named

The Rt. Rev. Alexander Gregg, First Bishop of Texas—1859-1893

The Rt. Rev. George Herbert Kinsolving, Second Bishop of Texas—1893-1928

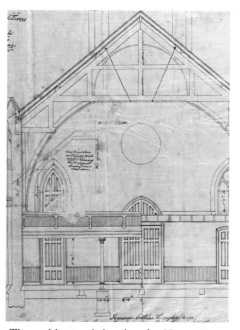

The first rectory was built on Texas Avenue in 1857, was added to in the 1870s, acquired electricity in the 1890s, and housed rectors and their families until 1902. This picture was taken in about 1894.

The architectural drawings by Henry Congdon show expansions made in 1876 on the 1859 church. The present church, built in 1893, was the first without an upstairs gallery across the back.

In the remodeling of 1876, "King of Glory" was lettered over the altar, and "Who For Us Men and Our Salvation Came Down from Heaven" over the center arch leading to the chancel.

Christ Church of 1876— showing the Westminster Abbey ivy, the rose garden laid out by the Rev. J. J. Clemens, and Friday Carr, sexton.

Court House Square seen from the north in about 1890, with Sweeney and Coombs Opera House (formerly Gray's Opera House) at the right, and the square tower of Christ Church in the distance. Grass grew in the streets, and early church Easter egg rolls were held on this lawn.

The old Capitol Hotel was built on the site of the capitol of the republic where Christ Church members held their services in 1839 and where the Rice Hotel now stands. In this picture made in about 1890, the Y.M.C.A. faces the hotel across Texas Avenue, and telephone wires are beginning to accumulate.

Christ Church in about 1890—showing the house of E. E. Coombs behind it, the streetcar avenue on unpaved Texas Avenue, and small boys with their velocipede.

Sunday school teachers' picnic in the 1880s. Front row, left to right: Mrs. W. V. R. Watson, Mr. Watson, Mrs. Henry Fall, W. D. Cleveland, Mrs. Tracey, Mrs. Williams, three unnamed. Second row, Mrs. L. T. Noyes, Miss Swindell, Miss Lou Kirkland (Mrs. Haralson), Miss Lillie Adey, Mrs. Dunn, Miss Hattie Adey, Miss Louise King, Miss Blanche Gray (Mrs. Nelson Munger) Miss Dot Richardson (Mrs. Gus Street) Mrs. Joseph Mullen, Miss Lizzie Hay, an unknown, Mrs. J. J. Clemens, Mrs. Margaret Hadley Foster. Third row, Will Cocke, Dr. Tom Robinson, Dick Cocke, unknown, Mr. Frank Cargill, and L. T. Noyes. The Rev. J. J. Clemens is at top center.

The 1876 church was completely razed in 1893. This scene looking from Prairie toward Texas Avenue shows the Light Guard Armory diagonally across from the Fannin Street corner. Gambler Bill Perry lived out of camera range on the right, where the Windham Hotel later stood. Mrs. F. Hite lived across Texas from the church, and the D. F. Stuarts across from the rectory.

The Rev. Charles M. Beckwith's famous male choir in about 1890. Left to right, front row, Lindsay Dunn, Johnnie Dreaper, DeWitt Dunn, St. John Waggaman, George Cleveland, Tom Botts, Robert Ring, unidentified boy. Second row, Alvin Hitchcock, three unidentified, George Gibbons, Edgar Gentry, Robert Schneider. Third row, Norman Dumble, Johnny White, Will Tinsley, Jake Garvey, a boy named Green, Will Priester, Charlie Peyton, Cecil Angell, Walker White. Fourth row, Willie Robertson (later Father Robertson), Charlie Fitch, Mr. Emmett, an unknown, E. M. Haralson. Fifth row, Albert Hail, Mr. Green, Robert Elgin, Ingham S. Roberts, perhaps another Mr. Green. Sixth row, Tom Humason, Willie Humason, Massie Dolan, two unknowns without instruments, J. Arthur Tempest. Back row, Mr. Norsworthy, Ernest Hail, Alf Elgin, Fred Root, and an unknown. The choir's cottas were at the laundry.

Some Christ Church parishioners never got over the shock of women in the choir. The choir of 1893, posed against the newly completed cloisters, left to right: Front row, Gus Street, Jr., George Hart, Edgar Gentry, Will Priester, Arthur Scudamore, Roy Street, Douglas Bright, Miss Susan Rogers (soon Mrs. J. Arthur Tempest). Second row, probably Miss May Hart, Johnnie Dreaper, Fred Clemens, Robert Wood, Robert Schneider, Miss Carrie Fraser, boys choir director; Albert Bailey, Jake Garvey, Lawrence Gilfrey, Bubba Tinsley. Third row, a Miss Brown, Mrs. M. Sterling (later Mrs. Ingham S. Roberts), Miss Georgia Davis, Miss Katie Dreaper (Mrs. Tom McGonigal), an unknown, Miss May Scudamore, J. B. Angell (Mrs. Dearborn Byrd), an unknown, Miss Cardwell and Miss E. Cardwell with mandolins, Miss Algie Angell. Third row, Earnest Hail, Alf Elgin, Massie Beavens, A. J. Alban, Ingham Roberts, F. Sawyer, an unknown, Oscar Longnecker, J. Arthur Tempest, Harvey Dumble, and the Rev. Henry D. Aves.

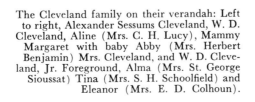

The Cleveland family on their verandah: Left to right, Alexander Sessums Cleveland, W. D. Cleveland, Aline (Mrs. C. H. Lucy), Mammy Margaret with baby Abby (Mrs. Herbert Benjamin) Mrs. Cleveland, and W. D. Cleveland, Jr. Foreground, Alma (Mrs. St. George Sioussat) Tina (Mrs. S. H. Schoolfield) and Eleanor (Mrs. E. D. Colhoun).

This picture of the Gray Grammer School, taken about the turn of the century, was given to Albert M. Bowles by Mark Westcott. Not all the boys can be identified, but from left to right on the first row are Louis Lewyn, Marcus Westcott, Clarkson, Harry Prince, and Latham Vann. Albert Bowles is the middle boy on the second row with Leonard Aves at the right end. The Rev. Henry D. Aves is on the left of the third row, and next in line are Stanley Beard, Harold Hahl, Arthur Hartwell, William Prince, Delano Aves and another boy.

Five Cadets of St. Andrew were going to drill at Christ Church in 1902 when a lady asked to take their picture. Left to right: Beale Smith, Howard Burns, Ed Hoenke, Fletcher Asbury (great-grandson of Mrs. Obedience Smith) and Captain John Dreaper, with a medal for competitive drilling.

Eichler University was attended by a remarkable group of children before World War I. Left to right, first row, Howard Hughes (aviator, motion picture producer, aircraft manufacturer) Marian Spencer, Helen Wicks (Mrs. J. W. Link, Jr.) Elizabeth Dillingham (playwright Elizabeth Hart whose play was a hit of London's 1963-64 season) Minnie Gates, and Tommie Rice. Second row, Louise MacClain (Mrs. Edwin D. Adams) Lila Gates (Mrs. W. L. Redd) Miss Jennie Eichler, Alice Gray Sears (Mrs. W. Frank Akin) Ella Rice (later Mrs. Howard Hughes, now Mrs. J. O. Winston). Third row, Dudley Colhoun, Thomas William House, and Dudley Sharp (Secretary of Air in Eisenhower's administration.)

The Christ Chuch close as it looked from 1902 until the early 1920s, when the wooded bois d' arc street blocks gave way to paving on Texas Avenue. The Aves and Sears families lived in this rectory before it became offices. It was this property for which Will Hogg offered $750,000 and which the congregation voted not to sell—even for $1,500,000.

Dr. and Mrs. James DeWolfe were living in a rented house when Mrs. John McClellan gave her house at 4104 Bute Street to be the Christ Church rectory. Four successive rectors lived here until the freeway threatened the property in 1957.

Five days after the fire of March, 1938, Sunday morning services were held in Christ Church. A curtain concealed this scene of destruction. The roodscreen and pulpit were still in use in 1964.

The Rev. James Pernette DeWolfe begins celebration of the Holy Eucharist with the Rt. Rev. Clinton Quin (left) assisting. This picture was made after the fire but before completion of repairs.

Christ Church celebrates its centennial with a banquet at the Rice Hotel. Dr. James P DeWolfe is master of ceremonies

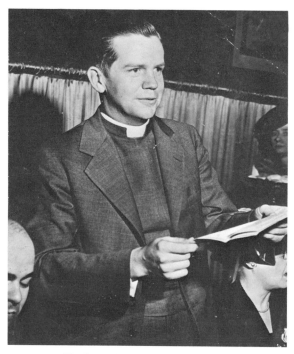

Newly arrived from one of America's oldest churches in Augusta, Ga., the Rev. John E. Hines speaks to his first parish dinner at Christ Church in January, 1941. Mrs. Clinton Quin is at the right, and the Rev. John McKee at the left.

In 1951, the Rt. Rev. Clinton S. Quin (left) and the Rev. W. L. B. Hutcheson (right) with a gathering of communicants watch the Very Rev. Hamilton Kellogg store treasures in the cornerstone of the new Latham Memorial Building.

The Rt. Rev. Clinton S. Quin, the Rt. Rev. John E. Hines, coadjutor, and the Very Rev. Hamilton H. Kellogg, dean and bishop-elect, dedicate the new Latham Memorial Building in June, 1952. They are shown with James Bradbury (left) and Bill Mount, acolyte.

The Rt. Rev. Clinton S. Quin and Albert P. Jones, vestryman, present a vestry resolution of appreciation to Albert M. Bowles (left) for "giving generously of his time, his talents and his substance" to Christ Church Cathedral in the building of the Latham Memorial and cathedral parish house.

Dean Richardson meets a favorite Sunday school teacher Miss Elsie Wilkinson.

W. D. Cleveland, Jr., welcomes Dean Richardson to Christ Church.

On his first Sunday in 1952, everyone wanted to greet the new dean. He met Charles Shaver (left) Mr. and Mrs. John Flanagan (right) and August Selig (extreme right) three of his future senior wardens. There were no iron railings at the time, and the Windham Hotel across Fannin was past its prime. When one parishioner asked the dean's mother "How do you like the new dean?" Mrs. J. M. Richardson, Sr., replied " Just fine."

Morning Prayer at the cathedral in 1960. Dean Richardson in the pulpit.

Chapel of the Christ Child
In memory of James Walker Cain, Jr.

Canon Howard Rutenbar officiates at a wedding in the Golding Chapel.

Mrs. Margarette Russell, who in the 1950s and 1960s charms every three-year-old, also attracts numbers of teen-age volunteer assistants.

Mr and Mrs. Paul Bode were popular church teachers in the early 1960s. Mr. Bode is shown with a sixth grade class.

The Christ Church Cathedral nursery in the 1950s and early 1960s, with Hattie Ingram as supervisor.

Mrs. Robert Tyler with a church school class in the 1950s.

At the cathedral communion rail in 1960. The Rev. Canon
Mark Waldo (left), and the Rev. Canon Howard Rutenbar (right).

Cleveland Hall, given by
Mrs. A. S. Cleveland and
Mrs. W. D. Cleveland Jr.,
in memory of their hus-
bands, opened in May, 1962.
The two Mrs. Clevelands
are shown at the dedication
with Dean Richardson.

At the Cleveland Hall
opening, May, 1962: John
H. Freeman, Jr., vestryman
and architect of the hall;
the Very Rev. J. Milton
Richardson, Henry Hollis,
Arthur Terrell and John
Winterbotham of the vestry.

Dean Richardson in 1964 with Judge John H. Crooker who was chairman of the committee which called the dean to Houston in 1952, and was senior warden in 1954.

Dean Richardson in 1964 with William J. Goldston, senior warden in 1955 and in 1959, and "a quiet force for every good in the cathedral."

The Christ Cathedral rectory at 14 Shadow Lawn Circle was purchased in 1957. Shown on the terrace in the spring of 1964 are Joan Richardson, Mrs. J. Milton Richardson, Preston, and the dean's mother, Mrs. J. M. Richardson, Sr.

The Rt. Rev. Michael Coleman, retired bishop of Qu'Appelle returned to the cathedral for Lenten services in 1964. He is shown with James Elkins, Jr., Jimmy Elkins, Mrs. James Elkins, Jr., Elise and Dean Richardson.

William Barnard in 1963
Organist and Choir Director

The Rev. Canon Joseph Johnson, who in 1953 laid foundations for the mid-century development of the cathedral's department of Christian education, and returned to the cathedral in 1963.

Discussions may be serious or may be amusing or both under leadership of the Rev. Canon Douglas Fontaine, shown in Cleveland Hall with members of the Y.P.S.L.

John Mellinger, frequent vestryman and treasurer of Christ Church Cathedral from 1943 to the present.

Tom Travis, Jr., speaks to Dean Richardson after morning service in 1964, followed by Quentin Bates, vestryman 1958-60.

Dean Richardson with Vestryman Phelan Hunter in 1964.

The Very Rev. J. Milton Richardson, dean of Christ Church Cathedral, speaking during Lent, 1964.

Senior wardens gathered for the 125th anniversary dinner. Left to right and in order of service: First row, Albert M. Bowles, John C. Flanagan, August L. Selig, Albert P. Jones, John H. Crooker. Second row, William J. Goldston, George C. Morris, Ralph W. Holtz, James A. Elkins, Jr., John F. Lynch, and Charles E. Shaver. W. Ernst Japhet, Charles T. Carnes and Floyd E. Bates were unable to be present.

In April, 1964, the members of Christ Church Cathedral celebrated the 125th anniversary of the church with a ban

The three most recent rectors of Christ Church Cathedral met at the 125th anniversary banquet. From right to left and in order of service: the Rt. Rev. John E. Hines rector 1941-1945; the Rt. Rev. Hamilton H. Kellogg, rector and first dean, 1946-1952, and the Very Rev. J. Milton Richardson, second dean, 1952_____.

e Rice Hotel, which stands on the site of the capitol of the republic where the first Episcopal services were held 125 years before.

When Howard Hughes was king of the Christ Church May fete, his queen was small Martha Wicks (Mrs. Malcolm Lovett). Starting at the front, Alice Gray Sears (Mrs. Frank Akin) at left, with Dudley Sharp behind her; Mary Louise Fitch (Mrs. Harold Soule) center; Jane Myer (Mrs. Brown Gwathmey) at right with Thomas William House beside her. Second row, Dorothy Ethel Seaman, Lilly Rice, Patty Benjamin, Tina Cleveland, Laura Kirkland Bruce. Elizabeth Law is behind Lilly Rice and St. Clair Evans on the row above. Libbie Masterson, Helen Wicks and Mary Stricker are in the next row, and to the right are Ella Winston and Allie May Autry.

Lilly Rice (Mrs. J. R. Aston) was queen of the May and Elizabeth Masterson maid of honor in a May fete before World War I. Reading down: Martha Louise Maynard, Bessie Parker Dunn, Lila Godwin, St. Clair Evans, Laura Shepherd Kirkland, and on the front row with serious expression, Tina Cleveland (Mrs. Dudley Sharp.)

Edward Hutcheson and Barbara Kirkland reigned in the late 1920s, with Morton King and Aubrey Randolph in the court at the right. A generation earlier, this queen's father, Bill Kirkland, was one of six horses who drew Queen Lois Cleveland to the throne in a little wicker wagon. And when Queen Barbara's sister Virginia was queen, Roy Moore, son of the Dallas Moores, was king.

By the 1940s, the May pole dancers encircled a May pole in the shadow of skyscrapers.

Thad Hutcheson as king and Marian Seward (Mrs William Bonner Rubey) as queen, of a Christ Church May fete in the 1920s.

King Dan Harrison, Jr., and Queen Lorna Terrell, daughter of Mr. and Mrs. Arthur Terrell, were enthroned at the 56th annual Christ Church May Fete in 1960.

In 1961, James Walker Cain, II, son of Mr. and Mrs. Dixon Hill Cain, reigned with Elise Elkins, daughter of Mr. and Mrs. James A. Elkins, Jr., as queen, at the 57th annual Christ Church May Fete.

Mrs. Ralph Gunn (Esme Patterson) narrating the 1964 Christ Church May fete. In 1963 she was president of the Women of the Diocese.

In 1964, David Bates, son of Mr. and Mrs. Quentin Bates, was king, and Penny Morris, daughter of Dr. and Mrs. George Morris, was queen.

This cliff-hanger's view shows the entire Christ Church Cathedral property of 1964: church, Guild Hall, Latham Building and Diocesan Headquarters in the original half block claimed in 1839; Cleveland Hall north of the Latham and diocesan buildings on San Jacinto, and the church parking lot across San Jacinto on Texas Avenue.